To Noah,
whose prese[nce]
has been woven in[to]
the writing of these
pages in more ways tha[n]
can be acknowledged.

Debrati
april 6, 2007

The Violence of Modernity

PARALLAX  RE-VISIONS OF CULTURE
AND SOCIETY

Stephen G. Nichols, Gerald Prince, and Wendy Steiner
SERIES EDITORS

The Violence of Modernity

Baudelaire, Irony, and the Politics of Form

Debarati Sanyal

The Johns Hopkins University Press
Baltimore

The Johns Hopkins University Press
2715 North Charles Street
Baltimore, Maryland 21218-4363
www.press.jhu.edu

Library of Congress Cataloging-in-Publication Data

Sanyal, Debarati, 1969–
    The violence of modernity : Baudelaire, irony, and the
politics of form / Debarati Sanyal.
        p. cm. — (Parallax, re-visions of culture and society)
    Includes bibliographical references and index.
    ISBN 0-8018-8308-3 (hardcover : alk. paper)
    1. Baudelaire, Charles, 1821–1867—Criticism and
interpretation. 2. Violence in literature.   I. Title. II. Series:
Parallax (Baltimore, Md.)
PQ2191.Z5S28 2006
841'8—dc22   2005021649

A catalog record for this book is available from the British
Library.

Contents

Acknowledgments

This book was several years in the making and I have incurred more intellectual and personal debts than is possible to adequately acknowledge in these few lines. My first thanks go to Suzanne Nash, who shaped my initial encounter with Baudelaire, and to Thomas Trezise, who encouraged me to think about the stakes of critique. Yale provided a stimulating environment for the elaboration of this project. I am particularly grateful to the intellectual community of the *Yale Journal of Criticism,* to the graduate students in my poetry seminars, and to Vilashini Cooppan, John Mackay, and Susan Weiner for the warmth of their friendship and the generosity of their engagement with early versions of this work. My thinking was also enriched by conversations with Susan Blood, Peter Brooks, Denis Hollier, and Christopher Miller.

At Berkeley I found a vibrant community of colleagues and students that sustained me through this book's completion. Suzanne Guerlac, Ann Smock, and Soraya Tlatli made invaluable suggestions on the manuscript itself, David Hult offered friendship and guidance, and I benefited from conversations with Karl Britto, Tim Hampton, Tom Kavanagh, Michael Lucey, Susan Maslan, and Nicholas Paige. I am also grateful to my students, and particularly to the participants of a Baudelaire seminar in Spring 2000 who will no doubt recognize reverberations of our conversations in what follows. A Humanities Research Fellowship in 2000–2001 gave me the time to orient this project toward questions of trauma and violence.

Many inspiring exchanges in formal and informal settings have also found their way into these pages. My thanks go to Ross Chambers, Margaret Cohen, James Helgeson, Elisabeth Ladenson, Christophe Lagier, Brigitte Mahuzier, Kevin Newmark, Geoff Nunberg, Richard Sieburth, Kevin Smith, Sonya Stephens, Dick Terdiman, and Gordon Teskey. David Peritz provided intellectual guidance early on and remains a cherished interlocutor; Ellen Wayland-Smith patiently perused these chapters' roughest drafts and helped to coax them into shape; Christina Sanders edited an early version of the manuscript; Noah Guynn and Julie Trager were anchors of friendship throughout; Shayan

Acknowledgments

and Manon arrived in time to celebrate. I am also grateful to Larry Kritzman and Gerry Prince for their support as I sought to place the book. It was a pleasure to work with my editors at the Johns Hopkins University Press. A special thanks to Peter Dreyer, whose editorial expertise saved me from many errors. The ones that remain are my own.

Portions of this work first appeared in earlier versions as articles in several scholarly venues that I would like to acknowledge here: "Baudelaire and the Trauma of Modernity," *Bulletin Baudelairien* 39 (2004); "The Tie That Binds: Violent Commerce in Baudelaire's 'La Corde,'" *Yale French Studies* 101 (2002); "The Object of Poetry: Commodity and Critique in Baudelaire," *Confrontations: Politics and Aesthetics in Nineteenth-Century France,* Rodopi (2001); "Broken Engagements: Sartre, Camus, and the Question of Commitment," *Yale French Studies* 98 (2000); "Conspiratorial Poetics: Baudelaire's 'Une Mort héroïque,'" *Nineteenth-Century French Studies,* 27/4 (1999). I am grateful to the editors for permission to reprint this material.

It is hard to find words of thanks for those who have virtually co-existed with an endeavor. Suffice it to say that this book would not have been completed without the extraordinary support of Lynne Huffer. I am deeply grateful to my parents whose wisdom and irony as they navigated multiple worlds made so many things possible, and to Michael Iarocci with whom I closed one book and opened another.

Abbreviations

A	Rachilde, *L'Animale* (1893; Paris: Mercure de France, 1993)
BM	Virginie Despentes, *Baise-moi* (Paris: J'ai lu, 1994)
Corr.	Charles Baudelaire, *Correspondance*, ed. Claude Pichois (Paris: Gallimard, 1973)
E	Albert Camus, *Essais*, ed. Roger Quillot and Louis Faucon (Paris: Gallimard, 1965)
OC	Charles Baudelaire, *Oeuvres complètes*, ed. Claude Pichois (Paris: Gallimard, 1975–76)
Sit.	Jean-Paul Sartre, *Situations*, vols. 3–5 (Paris: Gallimard, 1945–64).
T	Albert Camus, *Théâtre, récits, nouvelles*, ed. Roger Quillot (Paris: Gallimard, 1962)
TM	Jean-Paul Sartre, "Réponse à Albert Camus," *Les Temps modernes*, no. 82 (August 1952): 334–53

The Violence of Modernity

Introduction

We live in an era of trauma and terror, when experience is increasingly viewed through the categories of shock, wounding, and victimization. As global information networks virtually bring home the course of history, we find ourselves in disturbing proximity to distant eruptions of violence and are alerted to its menace in our daily lives. In what critics call our contemporary "wound culture," the affective registers of trauma, melancholy, and mourning provide tempting alternatives to more active engagements with history.[1] We are beckoned to submit to historical processes as spectators, witnesses, or even victims, rather than as agents with implicit ties to the violence that is represented. The rhetoric of trauma and terror fosters a sense of vulnerability and crisis that often obscures the complexity of our own historical embedding.

This turn to historical experience through affective and therapeutic models is reflected in contemporary critical discourse. In the aftermath of poststructuralism's dismantling of stable values, "trauma," "testimony," and "crisis" have emerged as dominant terms in the humanities for examining the relations between literature and history. Yet this focus on trauma is by no means a new phenomenon. Following Walter Benjamin, among others, shock and modernity have come to be seen as interlocking categories. Trauma itself emerges as a "structure of feeling" under the material conditions of nineteenth-century urban modernity, and Charles Baudelaire is often cited as its exemplary bard.[2] Baudelaire's poetry serves as an essential point of reference in theories that define modernity as a trauma inaugurating a "crisis of representation." The poet's notoriously vexed relationship to reference, his disarticulation of self, meaning, and history, captures our sense of the "modern" as a breach with all preceding frameworks for interpreting consciousness and experience, as a moment when "all that is solid melts into air." Baudelaire's position in the modern literary and theoretical canon has shaped and continues to inflect our understanding of historical experience and its literary representations through models of shock, crisis, indeterminacy, and trauma.

This book argues for Baudelaire's value in thinking about the contestatory possibilities of literary experience at this particular historical juncture, when the very concept of critique is muted by the dominance of trauma and terror, terms that reinforce our status as victims rather than as agents of resistance and change. In a cultural climate that privileges crisis over critique, affect over analysis, it seems all the more urgent to attend to the critical and contestatory powers of literary representation and to return to basic questions such as: What does literature have to teach us about the violence of history? How does the representation of violence differ from its exercise in real life? Can literature offer a space for a critique of violence? And what is the place of violence in critique? These are some of the broader questions addressed here through the example of Baudelaire in the hope of opening up alternative readings of modernism and modernity that acknowledge the role of irony, contestation, and critique in challenging the imbricated violences of modern experience.

As one of the first poets to represent the aesthetic and political characteristics of urban modernity, Baudelaire grasped the central place of representation in the practice and legitimation of power. By exploiting the complicity between poetry and other discursive régimes, his work probes the overlapping symbolic relations that create and sustain aesthetic production and social formations. Baudelaire envisioned violence, not as a monolithic force wielded by identifiable perpetrators, but as a complex and dynamic operation that takes place at multiple sites and through diverse media, including poetry itself. This complex and differential view of violence is particularly timely today, when trauma and terror are packaged by the media for consumption by citizens interpellated as passive spectators of history's course. Although recent theory has led to sophisticated accounts of the decentralized and ungraspable quality of power, its dissemination in academic circles and in general public culture has tended to foster melancholy resignation or even cynicism rather than a sense of possibility, resistance, or agency.[3] For Baudelaire, the individual's abdication before the forces of history was one of the most terrifying faces of capitalist modernity. His ironic denunciations of power's deployment—through new postrevolutionary political and economic configurations—retain their critical relevance today.

As any overview of this century's theory and criticism reveals, Baudelaire has always been an exemplary figure for thinking about the various articulations between history and literature. Since his canonization as representative of *l'art pour l'art* (by Paul Valéry among others), his poetry has been successively claimed by the most eminent theoretical schools: structuralist poetics, Freudian and Lacanian psychoanalysis, phenomenology, deconstruction, new historicism, cultural studies, and postmodern theories of trauma.[4] But if Baudelaire is fertile ground for the production of theory, theory rarely contains the contradictory force of his poetry. This is hardly surprising, given the poet's vociferous objections to the closure of systems, described by him as "a sort of damnation that pushes us into perpetual abjurations."[5] Perpetual abjurations seem the norm when approaching Baudelaire's corpus. There is an explosive vitality to his poetry—conveyed by Benjamin's image of the poet as conspirator and terrorist—that exceeds theoretical frames and forces readers to redefine their critical horizons.

This book seeks to bring this volatile force to bear on the cultural preoccupations of Baudelaire's historical moment—the formation in the aftermath of 1848 of a postrevolutionary bourgeois majority, and its ideologies of consumerism, progress, and conquest. But it also aims to recover the critical power of Baudelaire's legacy for our current theoretical and political concerns. Reading Baudelaire as an engaged ironist whose poetry actively challenges the violence of modernity foregrounds the ethical and political force of irony for crucial historical junctures, including our own.

The opening chapters argue that Baudelaire's central status for a conception of modernity (as a historical rupture or trauma) and a view of modernism (as literature's drift away from history and commitment) need to be rethought simultaneously to recover the relevance of his oeuvre today.[6] To this end, the book offers three (re)contextualizations of Baudelaire. The first is theoretical, and traces the definition of modernity *through* the models of rupture, shock, and trauma, a definition that owes much to a particular reading of Walter Benjamin by deconstruction and psychoanalysis. One of the most important theoretical paradigms to emerge in recent decades, "trauma" is by now a deeply entrenched but rarely interrogated category for reading history and literature. In literary studies, the turn to trauma often relies on a reading of Baudelaire's "poetics of shock" and belongs to a broader meditation on the Holocaust as modernity's defining "crisis of representation." Yet trauma is a paradigm that operates both inside and outside the academy, informing broader readings of cultural production *and* of historical events (as the surge of "trauma literature" around 9/11 attests).[7]

What are some of the consequences of this canonization of Baudelaire—and of the modernity he represents—as a witness to the trauma of history? As a theoretical formulation, what are the ideological limits of approaching literature as a "testimony" to historical crisis? What kinds of mediation between literature, history, and ethical-political agency does such a model occlude?[8] One of the many problems that arise in the overwhelming focus on literature as the testimony of a "crisis of representation" is that it privileges a highly textual view of modernity in which the particularity of history as an empirical force experienced by bodies and subjects evaporates into abstraction. As I argue in Chapter 1, the treatment of modernity itself as a structure of trauma also tends to conflate very different historical crises by way of structural analogies, such that the shocks of the nineteenth-century metropolis are incorporated into a narrative of historical trauma culminating in the collective violences of the twentieth century. The accepted view of modernity as a "crisis of representation" runs the risk of treating history as a "contentless form" voided of its particular violences, both symbolic and real. Further, as a way of reading the conjunction between history and literature, models of shock and trauma overlook how texts—and people—actively contest the particular violences of a given historical moment (rather than simply "bearing witness" to them). Given how deeply Baudelaire has shaped our sense of historical experience, steering the course of his scholarship away from models of trauma and toward questions of agency, contestation, and commitment has implications that reach beyond the limits of literary analysis into the realm of contemporary cultural politics.

If Baudelaire's legacy retains its critical energy, it is because his poetry teaches us how to *read* and *resist* historical violence, particularly in periods of crisis that aim to co-opt or short-circuit more direct forms of dissent. Irony—one of modernity's dominant modes of self-understanding—is thus examined here as a powerful tool for critique in Baudelaire's poetry and, more generally, in the modernist project he has come to represent. Irony is traditionally defined as a rhetorical figure that creates two or more disparate meanings in a text. This ambiguity has a contestatory purpose in a context of shared values. Its postmodern identifications with contingency, indeterminacy, and relativism, however, have dulled irony's oppositional edge. This book is an effort to invigorate irony's contestatory impetus by recovering the ideological valences of modernism's retreat into form, in the hopes of reenergizing literature's spirit of critique vis-à-vis historical violence.

The question of "modernism" also brings me to a second (re)contextualization of Baudelaire, this time in terms of the literary tradition. My readings return to the established canonization of Baudelaire—and of the European tradition of high modernism he represents—in terms of *l'art pour l'art,* seeking to bridge the traditional rift between literary form and ethical-political commitment. From Théophile Gautier's defense of "art for art's sake" to Jean-Paul Sartre's dismissal of poetry for the purposes of *engagement* a century later, formal experimentation has repeatedly been divorced from ethical and political commitment. In a sense, our current turn to trauma and testimony as lenses for reading Baudelaire rehearses the more familiar story of modernism as inaugurating literature's retreat from history, materiality, and praxis. Indeed, it may be worth considering what recent formulations of the trauma and unrepresentability of history owe to normative views of modernism as an anti-representational aesthetic. The theorizations of modernity as a trauma and of modernism as a "crisis of representation" need to be reconsidered together for the emergence of a more nuanced picture of what the literary interrogation of reference can *do* at particular historical junctures.[9]

This study charts a reading of the modernist turn that attends to the contestatory power of literary form. I address the literary phenomenon of modernism—its interrogation of reference and withdrawal into form—as an active critique of historical modernity. Baudelaire incorporates ethical and political preoccupations into the self-consciousness and formalism that define the modernist experiment. My readings examine how the hallmarks of modernism (irony, self-reflexivity, intertextuality, and the bid for aesthetic autonomy) illuminate and challenge the violence of history. Formal reflexivity, textual opacity, intertextuality, and irony—devices traditionally thought to remove literature from ethical and political concerns—are precisely what spark a critical encounter between the literary and historical domains.

Baudelaire's use of aesthetic form as the site of cultural critique is taken up and revitalized by later writers whose diversity defies the straightforward periodization associated with the poet (late romanticism, symbolism, decadence, modernism, and even postmodernism). My third (re)contextualization turns to a number of post-Baudelairean authors whose reflections on form and commitment open up a critical engagement with historical violence. These readings bring into relief a number of Baudelairean "committed ironists" from the center and the margins of the canon, including such figures as Rachilde (the nom de plume of Marguerite Vallette-Eymery), Albert Camus and, most recently, contemporary women authors such as Virginie Despentes. My selection of these particular authors has been motivated by their explicit or implicit dialogues with Baudelaire, but also because their attention to the dynamics of textual production, to the links between representation and violence, and to the fate of the body in literature and history, affiliate them to the nineteenth-century poet's legacy of irony as counterviolence. In their works, irony, self-reflexivity, and textual violence become tools for a critical testimony that mirrors the violence of history from a spectrum of positions. Violence is subjected to analysis, critique, and denunciation not from above but from within the symbolic operations of a given historical moment. My hope is that such discussions will begin to map an account of modernism that attends to one of its neglected currents. A current charged with irony, it engages in a self-conscious critique that resists assimilation into scripted ideological positions while refusing the melancholy abdications of postmodern approaches to history.

This contestatory legacy takes its cue from Baudelaire himself, who challenges the notion of the modern writing subject as a victim of history's course when he declares: "Non seulement, je serais heureux d'être victime, mais je ne haïrais pas d'être bourreau—pour sentir la Révolution de deux manières !" (*OC,* 2: 961). The poet's willingness to be at once victim *and* executioner, in order to have the revolution "both ways," beckons us to consider how poetry responds to historical processes through active forms of resistance and critique. Baudelaire's attunement to the *violence* of modernity—and to his own contradictory position within this violence—exposes the often hidden structural relations of force that govern art, history, and everyday life. His poetry maps out the underlying conditions that enable a subject's emergence or destruction in literature and history, offering a differentiated genealogy of how persons are produced, diminished, or extinguished on the textual stage *and* on the historical scene.

Following Baudelaire's own claim that he wished to be at once victim and executioner of history's revolutionary course, then, this book reads his poetry, not as a witness to the trauma of modernity, but as a self-conscious critique of its violence. A focus on critique rather than crisis, on irony rather than trauma, affords a more complex understanding of a person and a text's positioning in history by underscoring the intimate links between the trauma of modernity and the enactment of its violence. By recovering a range of positions occupied by persons, texts, and readers, irony opens up a more nuanced theoretical passage into the historical scene of modernity.

The relations between literary form, historical violence, and commitment are thus a central preoccupation of this book. My discussions of Baudelaire—and of later works in dialogue with his legacy—pay attention to the ideological valences of literary operations. They integrate the practice of close reading into historical concerns generally addressed under the rubric of "cultural studies." The methodological value of close reading is particularly vital today, when the specificity of literary discourse is imperiled by approaches that view the literary text as yet another cultural artifact "reflecting" its historical context. This "referential" approach to reading flattens out the texture, distinction, and energy of literary expression. Of course, close readings continue to be practiced in the classroom and in specific strands of literary and cultural criticism. In the aftermath of New Criticism and its focus on a work's textuality, deconstructive and psychoanalytic approaches popular in the 1980s and 1990s continue to foreground the rhetorical features of literary works. The current convergence of deconstruction and psychoanalysis in trauma theory uses close reading to identify the blind spots, contradictions, or "aporias" in a text's rhetorical system as signs of the force of history.[10] This strand of literary criticism thus differs from the cultural studies model by working outward to historical concerns from within the text itself.

Yet despite their methodological differences, both the historicist impetus of cultural studies and the rhetorical focus of trauma studies tend to turn the literary text into a *symptom* rather than an active critique of its historical moment. While my book builds upon both historicist and textualist approaches to Baudelaire, it seeks to develop a theory of reading *out* of specific literary texts in order to account for the agency of a text's engagement with its context.[11] The close readings of Baudelaire, Balzac, Mallarmé, Rachilde, Camus, and Despentes attempt to reenergize the relations between literary form and ideological critique. They attend to the dialectical relations—the mutual reinforcement, but also the gaps and differences—between Baudelaire, his surrounding ideological terrain, and his successive readerships. It is through the deployment of poetic form and specific rhetorical strategies that Baudelaire and his readers expose and challenge the representational systems of a given historical moment. Close readings that attend to specific literary operations such as allegory, irony, and intertextuality are thus central to recovering the reciprocal and critical relations among a text, its historical horizon, and the modalities of its reception.

To better elucidate the stakes of defending poetic form as a vehicle for critique, I now turn to an influential formulation of the split between form and commitment: the famous divorce between poetry and prose found in the opening pages of Sartre's *Qu'est-ce que la littérature ?* and challenged by Adorno in his essay "Commitment." Sartre envisioned prose as a collective signifying practice in which reading and writing constitute a dialectical exchange of mutually enforcing freedom between writer and reader. Freedom is ideally at once represented in the committed work of art and enacted in its reading. By contrast, poetry's cultivation of linguistic ambiguity necessarily bars the genre from commitment, since the very process of figuration fetishizes words and alienates them from a collective semiotic economy.[12] Sartre's first step toward developing a model of writing as communicative praxis, then, was to establish a division between genres that ascribed to poetry those literary features that obscure linguistic transparency. Prose emerged purified from "literary" language and its viscous accretions of meaning to become a transparent designative instrument for political actions.[13]

Given Sartre's analysis, what might the figural operations of poetry offer to theories of *engagement*?[14] How can poetry's reflection on its forms, and indeed, upon the very concept *of* form, in turn open up alternate forms of commitment? This, of course, is not a new question. Indeed, one of the most famous challenges to the Sartrean divorce between aesthetic form and *engagement* is found in Theodor Adorno's considerations of form itself as a privileged site for political critique and ethical reflection. For Adorno, poetic thought articulates a subjective resistance to the reification and social antagonisms of the modern world. Lyric poetry constitutes "a sphere of expression whose very essence lies in defying the power of social organization—either by refusing to see it, or in overcoming it through the pathos of distance, as in Baudelaire or Nietzsche" (*Adorno Reader,* 213). The later experimentations of the aesthetic avant garde, for Adorno, continued to challenge the violence of a bourgeois, technocratic, and bureaucratic society through the shock of aesthetic form. Their dissonant negativity unveiled the aporias of modern society in a performative transmission of alienation far more powerful than any direct, thematic denunciation. By "zeroing in on the dregs of the administered world," authors such as Kafka "laid bare the inhumanity of a repressive social totality" (ibid., 247). Their experimentation with form was precisely what enabled them simultaneously to witness and to denounce the violence of history.[15] For Adorno, then, the Sartrean view of commitment as transparent action upon the world failed to recognize "the effects produced by works whose own formal laws pay no heed to coherent effects," and therefore missed "what the shock of the unintelligible can communicate" (Adorno, "Commitment," 303). Literary form is a privileged vehicle for the transmission of human fear, alienation, or suffering under the inhuman conditions of the modern bureaucratic world of instrumental reason.

In order to assess the ongoing influence of this opposition in current critical debates, it is useful to map the divergence between Sartre and Adorno as one between, on the one hand, commitment or a vision of language as action upon the world, and, on the other, testimony or an approach to language as witness to the world's resistance to signification. Whereas the Sartrean view of commitment preserves a certain "aboutness" and specificity in the representation of experience, Adorno suggests that literature's testimonial value resides in a performative enactment of its shock. Mapping these binaries—between content and form, commitment and testimony, or "writing history" and "writing trauma"—helps us see more clearly what is at stake in the recent turn to literature as a site of trauma and testimony.[16]

The escalating violence of modern historical experience has led to theories of representation that address powerful questions. How do we understand, represent, and transmit events that, because of their unthinkable atrocity, were not fully assimilated and understood even by those who experienced them? Can literature bear witness to the irreducible singularity of these events by putting pressure on established frameworks and fostering a recognition of the violence of their explanatory frames? How do we attest to the victims of history and the ongoing, untheorizable fact of suffering without falling into the treacherous consolations of aesthetic—and ideological—redemption?

Adorno's famous dictum that "to write poetry after Auschwitz is barbaric" (*Prisms,* 34) is a classic articulation of art's dilemma before the tangible fact of violence. While figural representations convey something of the lived particularity of historical violence, their figurality is bound to betray the singularity of a victim's experience. Adorno's declaration is often misread as a ban on representations of the Holocaust, as an indictment of literary figuration itself for betraying the victims' suffering, and as an exhortation to silence.[17] Yet its paradoxical formulation captures a living tension that exists in all art responding to unthinkable and unjustifiable forms of violence. For while the artistic rendering of suffering risks diminishing and betraying the singularity of a victim's experience, it is nevertheless in art alone that "suffering can still find its own voice, consolation, without immediately being betrayed by it" ("Commitment," 312). Art's power lies in its performative transmission of another's suffering, through the disruptive power of form. The recent dominance of testimony and trauma as modes of literary access to history thus serve to heal the breach opened up by Sartrean accounts between the figural processes of literature and the historical demands of commitment.[18] Approaching a literary text as testimony of a "crisis of representation" allows readers to forge connections between form, content, and context, seeing ambiguity and resistance as signs of what Cathy Caruth has termed "unclaimed experience," forms of historicity that simultaneously demand and defy our witness. The literary text's aporias thus "bear witness" to the unthinkable and unjustifiable terror of history.

Yet subsequent accounts of literature as testimony tend to eclipse Adorno's own highly dialectical understanding of literary form as the site for an enactment and critique of historical violence, as well as Sartre's view of the writing subject's agency, situatedness, and responsibility in history. Indeed, in recent formulations of literature's testimonial function, the critical and denunciatory dimensions so central to Adorno are muted, if not displaced, by affective registers of melancholy and mourning that convey the disempowered trauma of a subject crushed by historical forces. This can only give us an incomplete reading of historical violence that makes absolute the experience of the "victim," thereby foreclosing further inquiry into the complexity of a historical moment and a subject's place in its ethico-political weave.[19] Violence is, after all, an operation that takes place in all aspects of lived experience. We can alternately—and sometimes even simultaneously—take on the roles of victim, executioner, witness, proxy witness, accomplice or collaborator, or unsuspecting enforcer of violence we perceive as external to us. Our current focus on "victim" and "witness" as subject positions occupied by texts views literature as a primarily reactive testimony to the violence of historical processes. This dulls the critical and oppositional edge of literature's relationship to power by turning the text into a symptomatic inscription of historical crises. It fails to address how literature might engage with specific forms of power through dynamic relations of complicity or resistance, or give its readers a genealogy of the production of violence from a range of contestatory and complicit—as well as testimonial—positions. The ambiguities and ironies of literary experience enable us to hold thought and counterthought, violence and counterviolence, in the same dialectical hand and against a differentiated history. A variegated approach to the representation of violence captures the complexity of a subject's (and a text's) relations to power in different histories and sites, while retaining categories of agency, responsibility, and critique.

The following discussion of Baudelaire's contestatory legacy seeks to mediate between the content of Sartre's commitment and the form of Adorno's testimony.[20] Albert Camus, the subject of my closing chapter, plays an important historical and conceptual role in this attempt to navigate the rift between commitment and testimony through irony and counterviolence. In his acceptance speech for the Nobel Prize, Camus made a powerful call for literature's allegiance to the *victims* of history: "Par définition, il [l'écrivain] ne peut se mettre aujourd'hui au service de ceux qui font l'histoire: il est au service de ceux qui la subissent" (*E,* 1072). This conception of history as an external force that unfolds outside the sphere of human agency was derided by Sartre as proof of Camus's naïve disregard for the writer's inevitable situatedness in history. In the aftermath of World War II, the break between these two intellectuals and fellow *résistants* was but another example of the accepted rift between literary form and ethico-political commitment. Sartre had already condemned Baudelaire, and the trajectory of French literature associated with him, for withdrawing from history, and Camus was now also relegated to Sartre's *capharnaüm* of Baudelairean *littérateurs* who shun the demands of praxis.

Yet Camus, like Baudelaire, is an exemplary ironist whose dialectical understanding of the relations between aesthetics and ideology is manifest throughout his works. From *Caligula* to *La Chute,* Camus's oeuvre bears witness to forms of terror shared by the literary and aesthetic imaginations. Like Baudelaire and the other authors considered here, Camus suggests that there are many ways of "bearing witness" to the violence of history. Irony emerges in his works as one of the most committed forms of testimony. In contrast to Sartre's view of commitment, which as Denis Hollier has argued, is a "politics of prose," the authors examined in this book fashion what I call a "poetics of violence," an ironic mode of critique that performs the links between literary representation and historical terror.

My reading of Baudelaire's poetics of irony, counterviolence, and critique thus hopes to make visible a strand of committed ironists that remains active today. Theirs is a self-reflexive literary practice attuned to the ethical implications of their representational procedures. They accept the betrayal endemic to representation itself, and yet refuse the melancholy defeat of a purely testimonial relationship to history. Rather than exploiting affective relations with the reader (who would be urged to take the place of the victim of textual and historical violence), they interrupt such intimate modes of identification, beckoning instead to what I call a proximate yet implicated relation to the histories that they represent. The gaps opened up by their ironic registers enable a more differentiated reading of textual and historical violence. Their irony navigates between the interventionist claims of commitment and the commemorative function of testimony, producing a disenchanted but corrosive critique that contests the structural violences of historical experience from within.

The Organization of the Book

This book is divided into two parts. Part I, "Violence and Representation in Baudelaire," pursues the inquiry detailed above specifically in terms of Baudelaire's poetry and prose. Part 2, "Unlikely Contestations: Baudelaire's Legacy Revisited," examines a number of later writings in dialogue with his legacy of irony as counterviolence.

Chapter 1, "Baudelaire's Victims and Executioners: From Symptoms of Trauma to a Critique of Violence," provides an overview of Baudelaire's canonization as the poet of trauma to argue that violence offers a more powerful hermeneutic for a historical inquiry into Baudelaire's modernity. I begin by examining how deconstruction and trauma theory have used a de Manian reading of irony and a partial reading of Benjamin's shock to theorize modernity itself as a "crisis of representation." The chapter sets up an alternative paradigm for considering the relationship between poetry, history, and ethics through violence, counterviolence, and irony. I read two key Baudelairean texts on irony, the poem "L'Héautontimorouménos" and the essay "De l'essence du rire," which open up a different view of irony, not as an epistemological crisis or trauma, but as an exemplary mode of contestation.

While the first chapter addresses theorizations of modernity through Baudelaire, Chapter 2, Passages from Form to Politics: Baudelaire's *Le Spleen de Paris,* repositions Baudelaire in established accounts of modernism as a retreat from content into form. By putting the models of irony, counterviolence, and critique to work in detailed analyses of *Le Spleen de Paris,* I show that Baudelaire's "modernism" establishes a direct connection between poetic forms and postrevolutionary social formations. I examine several poems that develop "counterviolences" to existing violences in the Second Empire's body politic: the repressive regime of Napoleon III, the bankruptcy of republican idealism, the collapse of an oppositional political culture, and the violence of commerce, consumerism, and the media. My readings focus on one particular site for the exercise of violence: the human body. Baudelaire's representation of the body as the ground and vehicle for aesthetic *and* ideological representation opens a passage between poetry and history that challenges accounts of modernism as a retreat from reference, materiality, and history. The following chapters thus focus on the body and its aesthetic, sexual, and cultural determinations through Baudelaire and his legacy.

Chapter 3, "Bodies in Motion, Texts on Stage: Baudelaire's Women and the Forms of Modernity," pursues this inquiry into the poetic and social fashioning of bodies by opening Baudelaire's poetry up to questions of gender. The chapter is framed by readings of Balzac and Mallarmé and traces the articulation of nineteenth-century conceptions of "modernity" through competing representations of the female body (as regressive materiality, as commodity, as art, and as racialized "other"). For Baudelaire, "woman" is a site of contested meaning at the crossroads of aesthetic modernism and the material conditions of capitalist, urban modernity. His representations of women map the violence of a body's inscription into form within an increasingly market-oriented imperial and colonial culture. This preoccupation with the body's "production" through forms of sexual, economic, and racial violence is tied into a critique of poetry's performative force, that is to say, of poetry's explicit and often violent production of the bodies it designates. In presenting women's bodies as exhibition pieces, Baudelaire calls into question the nature and ground of these bodies, pointing out instead the ideological investments that produce and make them signify. This demystification of the body's "nature" is conducted *through* the self-reflexivity and formalism that we generally associate with modernism. Modernism's often-observed crisis of representation might be reconsidered as putting bodies in motion and texts on stage, thus exposing the conditions of a subject's emergence in the broader cultural field.

Part II, "Unlikely Contestations: Baudelaire's Legacy Revisited," traces the legacy of Baudelairean irony and counterviolence in a number of unlikely French authors from decadence to postmodernism. While the writers I consider lack obvious or canonical relationships to Baudelaire, their intertextual dialogue with the poet's legacy illustrates the claims established in the book's first three chapters. Rachilde, Camus, and Despentes address modern experience through a critique of violence rather than a testimony to trauma, their use of *form* as a passage between literature and history revises accepted accounts of modernism, and their self-reflexive operations explore the human body's status as a vulnerable materiality shaped by aesthetic and historical violence.

Chapter 4, "Matter's Revenge on Form: Bad Girls Talk Back," addresses two women writers in dialogue with Baudelaire's poetry: the decadent author Rachilde (playfully dubbed "Mlle Baudelaire" by her contemporaries) and the contemporary "punk" writer Virginie Despentes, both of whom faced censorship for their transgressive representations of sex and violence. Their work acknowledges and contests the cultural legacy of modernism and high literature generally associated with Baudelaire: the victory of form over matter, the violence of allegorical inscription, and the gendering of poet and muse. From their very different historical vantage points, Rachilde and Despentes resignify central Baudelairean motifs such as the dandy, the flâneur, and the woman as prostitute, beast, or vehicle for literary transports, enacting what I call a "revenge of matter over form." As such, they prove to be exemplary readers of Baudelaire, for their combative engagements with his aesthetic legacy perform the act of reading itself as a "counterviolence." Their use of violence, the negativity of their critique, and their rejection of political agendas challenge straightforward feminist recuperations of their works. But I contend that this negativity opens up important insights into the sexual politics of "high literature" and into shame and abjection as modes of resistance to the body's aesthetic and social inscription. Their writings stage the proximity of violence in everyday life, and invoke the body's fragility and resistance before it.

Chapter 5 is entitled "Broken Engagements: Albert Camus and the Poetics of Terror." In the aftermath of World War II, as intellectuals confronted emergent as well as ongoing forms of terror, Camus's critique of ideology, or what he termed "les religions horizontales de notre temps," offers a compelling, albeit neglected, alternative to Sartrean models of engagement. I begin with an overview of Camus's *L'Homme révolté* and its meditation on the links between aesthetics, ideology, and terror. Camus's analysis of the overlapping violence of art, politics and everyday life develops a "poetics of terror" that is distinct from Sartre's "politics of prose." It is also attuned to the intellectual's capacity to collaborate with historical violence. I situate Camus's "poetics of terror" within the legacy of committed ironists issuing from Baudelaire. Camus's vexed relationship to *engagement* belongs to a long-standing preoccupation with literature's complicity with other regimes of power, a preoccupation I have traced in works by Baudelaire, Mallarmé, Rachilde, and Despentes. Camus puts this "poetics of terror" into practice in *La Chute,* a novel whose important Baudelairean intertext also illustrates the links between art, rebellion, and violence theorized in *L'Homme révolté.* Using Baudelaire as an intertextual thread, my reading seeks to draw out the resonances between Camus's "poetics of terror," the strategies of irony and counterviolence explored thus far, and our contemporary historical horizon. As an engaged intellectual wrestling with the dilemmas of postwar French politics, Camus provides a powerful elucidation of irony's value in an ethical and political critique of violence.

This book highlights an inquiry into violence that is embedded in French modernism and yet exceeds any one periodization. My reading of Baudelaire's poetry and its intertextual reworkings map one vector of this inquiry through a hermeneutic of irony and counterviolence, in the hope of contributing to a more nuanced reading of violence and its representations. The ironists considered in this study offer a bracing corrective to our contemporary "wound culture." In an age of escalating terror, their strategies of counterviolence disclose the relations of force that structure a given historical moment from a range of identifications, reminding us that violence is not an immutable condition, or a weapon wielded by readily identified perpetrators, but a dynamic and differential operation. History situates us in contradictory relations to the causes, deployments and effects of violence—as witnesses and victims, to be sure, but also as accomplices, bystanders, and executioners. The mobility of these ironists' identifications nevertheless attune us to the differences between experiences of violence in distinct histories and places, differences often eclipsed by established systems of representation, including those of literature and criticism.

PART ONE

Violence and Representation in Baudelaire

1 Baudelaire's Victims and Executioners

From the Symptoms of Trauma to a Critique of Violence

J'oserai pousser plus loin ; j'affirme que l'inspiration a quelque rapport avec la congestion, et que toute pensée sublime est accompagnée d'une secousse nerveuse, plus ou moins forte, qui retentit jusque dans le cervelet.

> Baudelaire, "Le Peintre de la vie moderne"

Que faites-vous ? Vous marchez. Vous allez en avant. Vous dotez le ciel de l'art d'on ne sait quel rayon macabre. Vous créez un frisson nouveau.

> Victor Hugo, letter to Baudelaire, October 6, 1859

It has become something of a commonplace to canonize Baudelaire as the quintessential poet of the modern experience and to envision this modernity as inaugurating a "crisis of representation." What Victor Hugo called a "frisson nouveau" invented by the younger poet is increasingly described as a shock that dissolves language's ability to refer, and in doing so, captures the essentially traumatic nature of modern experience. The myriad theoretical articulations of modernity through the example of Baudelaire, however distinct in their approach and methodology, all converge on one point: the abiding sense that his poetry is unique, indeed, unprecedented, for capturing a psychological, historical, and ethical condition that exceeds all previous frames of reference.[1]

Readings of Baudelaire as the inaugural poet of the modern experience, particularly since Walter Benjamin, often describe "modernity" itself in terms of rupture, crisis, and trauma. But what exactly makes modernity traumatic? And is it possible to historicize modernity and modernism through a paradigm such as trauma? Trauma designates an experience that, due to its shattering nature, is unavailable to conscious recollection and understanding. The traumatic event is often described as a "missed experience," since its occurrence was so explosive that its victim was unable to assign it a place and a meaning in his or her consciousness. Instead, its impact is belatedly recorded and rehearsed by the psyche—and the literary text—in complex and displaced form, such that the origins or causes of a trauma elude representation.

Given the precariousness of its location in time and space, how do we establish whether the trauma associated with "modernity" is a historical phenomenon, a transhistorical condition of language, or even a structural feature of the psyche itself? Baudelaire scholarship since Benjamin and Paul de Man has wrestled with this question when addressing the referential and contextual instabilities of poetic discourse. Some readers of Baudelaire locate "trauma" temporally, as a rupture with traditional patterns characteristic of the postrevolutionary modern metropolis. For Benjamin, Baudelaire's poetry bodies forth the shocks and contradictions of urban life under the alienating conditions of high capitalism. With the advent of industrial modernity, Benjamin argues, the human subject undergoes a radical alteration of experience in which precapitalist modes of receiving and transmitting experience (through story and ritual) no longer obtain. Baudelaire's poetry is truly "modern" in its witness to this fundamental alteration of experience, to the emergence of consciousness out of the alienating jostle of the city. Benjamin's reading locates the trauma of modernity in a set of historical conditions particular to the postrevolutionary industrial metropolis—although, as we shall see, his account opens up an ambiguous relationship between the psychic and material origins of this trauma.

Benjamin's canonization of Baudelaire as the bard of modernity's trauma has made a lasting imprint. Yet subsequent readers inspired by this portrait of the poet as "traumatophile," particularly those working within a deconstructive and psychoanalytic framework, argue that the shift in experience and consciousness conveyed by Baudelaire's poetry resists straightforward historical location. It is a trauma inherent in the human psyche or endemic to the iterable nature of language itself. Paul de Man's by now canonical readings set the stage for such accounts by suggesting that Baudelaire's poetry enacts the trauma of a self emerging differentially in language and time.[2] Similarly, Barbara Johnson's readings of *Le Spleen de Paris* demonstrate how the prose poems deconstruct poetic codes to interrogate the very functioning of language and representation. In the aftermath of deconstruction, several influential critics have returned to Benjamin's theory of shock through a de Manian reflection on language and temporality, but also by way of Freudian and Lacanian psychoanalysis.[3] Their readings have mobilized Baudelaire's poetry to define modernity *as* a trauma. Yet, in keeping with deconstruction's focus on rhetoric, these readers have tended to introject the historical dimension of Benjamin's analysis into the psychic and linguistic registers of Baudelaire's poetry. Trauma is redefined as a structural condition of the psyche, as an internal wound that unravels the very workings of consciousness and memory, and thus fundamentally eludes historical determination.

Approaches to Baudelaire's modernity through the notion of a "crisis of representation" tend to either locate this crisis in historical terms, invoking political and material conditions such as the revolution of 1848, Louis-Napoléon's coup d'état, and the shock of industrial urban modernity.[4] Or they conceptualize it in psychic and linguistic terms, suggesting that the structural traumas to which Baudelaire bears witness resist historical embedding. Baudelaire's emblematic modernity, then, is alternately located in (1) the shocks of the modern metropolis and the postrevolutionary body politic; (2) the eddies of a self emerging differentially in language and time; and (3) a psychic shattering constitutive of identity itself. Whether the crisis is addressed in historical, textual, or psychic terms—or in the complex interplay between them—trauma has been a central category for some of the most influential readings of Baudelaire and of the modernity he is said to inaugurate.

The Introduction addressed some of the broader consequences of trauma's deployment as a model for reading history. As a model for reading literature, three further problems beset its current use: an overwhelming focus on the impossibility of representation; a view of literature as a symptomatic "acting out" or rehearsal of shock; and a positioning of the text as a witness and victim to historical and psychic forces. I propose in this chapter that violence, rather than trauma, provides a more fruitful point of entry into Baudelaire's poetry and the dynamism of its modernity. For whereas trauma designates an internal dislocation of which the psyche is victim, violence is an operation that involves agents and recipients, executioners as well as victims. A consideration of "modernity" in light of its imbricated violences allows an ethical inquiry into the relationship between poetry and history, rather than a purely epistemological reflection on the possibility of knowledge and representation. Shifting the paradigm from trauma to violence also opens up a range of positional options within the text, between the text and its contexts, and between the text and its readership.

My aim is not to substitute violence for trauma as the master trope of modernity, but rather to tease out alternative approaches to the question of reference and ethics in discussions of modernity as a crisis of representation. A related aim is to soften the implicit dichotomies—in trauma theory and more generally in poststructuralist thought—between a shattered self emerging from an originary trauma, on the one hand, and, on the other, a fully constituted self that may contemplate trauma from an external vantage point. This dichotomy engenders further theoretical dualities: between the violent mastery of full representation and the unrepresentability of experiences that fall outside the frame of conceivable thought, between perceptions of history as a fully owned event that can be plotted in a linear fashion or as a shadowy memory that contains the remnants of other histories.[5] To soften these polarities also entails prying loose some of the links established by recent criticism between referentiality, violence, closure, and totality. For only then can we account for the ways in which literature deploys irony and self-irony as forms of critique, and representational violence as a form of counterviolence to history. But before turning to the possible relationships between poetry, violence, and critique, let us return to Benjamin's portrait of Baudelaire as "traumatophile" to assess the consequences of this canonization for established accounts of modernism.

Representation in Crisis: Baudelaire as "Traumatophile"

For Walter Benjamin, Baudelaire's modernity lay in his paradoxical predicament as a lyric poet writing in the era of high capitalism, an era in which the very experience of the lyric—the self-contained fullness of lyric subjectivity, the authority of bardic speech, and the aura of cultic art—is on the brink of obsolescence. Depicting the social space of the Second Empire as a force field of conflicting energies, Benjamin shows how the overwhelming jostle of the urban metropolis, the jarring rhythms of industrial production, the increasingly commodified quality of experience, and the alienation felt in a world ruled by the marketplace all made their mark upon Baudelaire's poetry.[6] As "Le Soleil" famously describes it, poetic creation is a "fantasque escrime," a wayward duel in which the poet hurtles though the city, parrying its shocks, and stumbles upon images and rhymes. It is within the crucible of modernity's disruptive forces, within the sense of radical rupture with the patterns of the past, that Baudelaire forms his poetry. In Benjamin's memorable formulation, Baudelaire attests to "the disintegration of aura in the lived experience of shock."[7]

Despite the apparent historical grounding of modernity's trauma, Benjamin's account opens up a fundamental instability in its referential frame, an instability endemic to the psychoanalytic definition of trauma. When discussing Baudelaire's representation of the shock experience in the city, Benjamin turns to Freud's *Beyond the Pleasure Principle* and its separation of consciousness from memory. For Freud, consciousness and memory belong to separate systems of experience: excitatory processes leave behind traces that found the basis of memory without necessarily having entered into consciousness.[8] Consciousness protects the organism from the overwhelming stimuli or "shocks" of external reality by "parrying" or defending itself against them. Once parried, the shock is given the weight and temporal position of a lived experience and thus incorporated—in "sterilized" and mastered form—as a conscious "souvenir."[9] The subjectivity that emerges out of the shocks of urban modernity, then, is peculiarly fractured, since its very memory is constituted by shocks that may not have been consciously lived out as such. Modernity thus marks the traumatic dispossession of the individual, in terms not only of the past (in the form of collective traditions, rites, and patterns) but of memory itself.[10] As Kevin Newmark elucidates, for Benjamin, "modernity names the moment when the thinking subject can no longer be said to be completely in control or conscious of the actual events that necessarily comprise 'his' own past" ("Traumatic Poetry," 238).

Benjamin is faithful to Freud's own view of trauma as a borderline experience between event and psyche. Trauma cannot be located since the experience was missed in its occurrence and only emerges through its delayed, symptomatic replay in the psyche. The *Nachträglichkeit* quality—or afterwardness—of the trauma's manifestation thus foils attempts at locating its origins.[11] As Margaret Cohen remarks, for Benjamin, modern subjectivity is "constituted by a traumatic shock that is both psychic and material in origin" (*Profane Illumination,* 214). This oscillation between psychic and material conditions may be discerned in Benjamin's famous reading of "À une passante," where the shattering nature of the poet's experience as he gazes upon a passing woman is produced by the intersection of a general psychic trauma—"the kind of sexual shock that can beset a lonely man"—and the external, material conditions shaping the modern urban experience of love—"the stigmata that life in the metropolis inflicts upon love" ("On Some Motifs in Baudelaire," 169). Historical trauma and structural trauma converge in Benjamin's reading to point out the precarious location of such an experience in space and time.

A further consequence of Benjamin's poetics of shock—one central to later formulations of trauma—is its valorization of what is absent from the text itself. Indeed, in his reading of "À une passante," Benjamin argues that the urban masses at the heart of the shock experience are so profoundly internalized by the poetic consciousness that they are not represented in his poetry: "The masses had become so much a part of Baudelaire that it is rare to find a description of them in his works. His most important subjects are hardly ever encountered in descriptive form."[12] By suggesting that crowds were so central to Baudelaire's experience as to be incorporated into the poetic psyche, Benjamin echoes Baudelaire's own reflection on the intoxicating pantheism of urban subjectivity: "Ivresse religieuse des grandes villes. — Panthéisme. Moi, c'est tous ; Tous, c'est moi. Tourbillon" [*OC,* 1: 651]). But his translation of Baudelaire's ontological rapture into a practice of representation also suggests that the most crucial elements of subjectivity's encounter with history elide description. The privilege granted to what is erased or absent from the text's frame of reference will culminate in recent claims that the historical insights of Baudelaire's poems emerge through their resistance to reference. Benjamin's portrait thus opens up a number of instabilities that inform later approaches to the poet as "traumatophile": the precarious location of the traumatic experience and the evaporation of the descriptive, representational axis of his poetry. Such instabilities allow Benjamin to position Baudelaire both as a witness to the contemporary sociopolitical forms of industrial modernity and as a visionary who offers a prophetic glimpse into the unparalleled violence of the twentieth century, witnessed by Benjamin less than a hundred years later.[13]

Benjamin's consecration of Baudelaire as a witness to the trauma of modernity has made a lasting imprint. Yet critical readings informed by—and in dialogue with—Baudelaire's "traumatophilic" dimension have privileged the psychoanalytic aspect of Benjamin's interpretation (by referring primarily to "On Some Motifs in Baudelaire") at the expense of the historical, cultural and material contextualizations proposed in, for example, *The Arcades Project.*[14] These psychoanalytic readings displace the historical resonances of Benjamin's analysis into textual processes, such that "history" itself is viewed as a series of blind spots that resist representation. As we have seen, this view of history as a point of resistance in the literary text is endemic to the very definition of trauma—a *missed* encounter with the reality of an event and its symptomatic replay in the text or psyche. According to some readers, it is precisely this rupture with "history" that—paradoxically—assigns Baudelaire's historical place as our first modern poet.

The displacement of poetry's historical elements onto psychic and linguistic registers of poems has contributed to the emergence of a "textual history" that attempts to rupture established views of history as a developmental narrative and to illuminate its inescapably figural basis. As de Man famously expressed it, "the bases for historical knowledge are not empirical facts but written texts, even if these texts masquerade in the guise of wars or revolutions" ("Literary History and Literary Modernity," 165). If an ethico-political insight is to be gleaned from textual undecidability, for de Man this insight cannot be applied to the world of bodies, things, and relations, in history. In readings influenced by Benjamin's notion of shock and de Man's analysis of undecidability, the literary work is perceived as rehearsing the trauma of history in an endless repetition that always misses its mark. Readers must renounce the illusion—and violence—of recovering stable historical knowledge from its undecidabilities.[15]

The theorization of history as trauma seeks to disclose the *force* of historical representation, the violence of ideologies' inscription of events along narrative and tropological models. Deconstructive approaches to the literary work thus tend to read the modalities of the text's resistance to representation as signs of its historicity. Baudelaire's rupture with the grand narratives of "History" is precisely what accounts for his historical status as our first "modern" poet. Indeed, the notion that Baudelaire's exceptionality lies in his poetry's stubborn refusal to integrate itself into a larger pattern of duration has been central to de Man's representation of the poet as the "emblem of tragic isolation of postromantic literature" ("Allegory and Irony," 119), cut adrift from his predecessors, and of Benjamin's vision of his poetry as shining "in the sky of the Second Empire as a 'star without an atmosphere.'"[16]

This view of Baudelaire—as a poet who undoes the narrativity of history—remains entrenched in current criticism. It has been revitalized in the past decade by the dominance of "trauma" and "testimony" in Holocaust studies. For example, in a recent study, Ulrich Baer has argued that Baudelaire and Celan "indisputably bookend the modern tradition" (*Remnants of Song*, 7). Celan's confrontation with the unprecedented event of the Holocaust returns him to Baudelaire's articulation of an experience that challenges all preceding frameworks, "Yet it is a return to 'a dark zone,' to an impenetrable obscurity and blindness bearing the name of 'Baudelaire' in which the tradition originates. Such a return means to write poems in a language that derives its authority and historical thrust from experience that is unassimilated and, as we will see, properly ahistorical rather than fully integrated into consciousness" (ibid., 6). Baer thus reads the oeuvre of Baudelaire and Celan as records of "missed experience," forms of knowledge that lie outside memory or history but are nevertheless "constitutive of the self" (ibid.). Such traumatic knowledge is "ahistorical," in that it cannot find incorporation in historical narratives. But this is precisely what assigns Baudelaire his historical place at the origins of a modern tradition culminating in Celan's testimony to the Shoah.

Implicit in this argument is an important—if problematic—claim for a post-Shoah literary ethics founded on the impossibility of representing historical trauma. This traumatic split between poetry and history, articulated as a rupture between the psyche and the world affords a glimpse for Baer into uncharted forms of knowledge that both demand and defy our witness. A poem's blind spots, aporias, flare-ups, and indeterminacies function like a flash "which is reflected in the puddles that gather where history's *grands récits* are cracked" (Baer, *Remnants of Song,* 151). Presenting "L'Étranger" as one of three exemplary and inaugural poems, for instance, Baer argues that it is only when the text relinquishes all claims to readable, applicable, and intersubjective notions of morality, and when it demonstrates the impossibility of pinning down the functioning of its rhetorical mode, that it becomes "ultra ethical." Like the clouds that float above the stranger's head, experience that is unclaimed, unremembered, and free of organizing schemes gives a flash of understanding into "unclaimed experience."[17]

I have traced a critical arc that starts with Benjamin's theory of the shock experience, runs through de Man's formulations on history as a tropological structure, and continues to dominate in reflections on the relationship between literature and history today. In these accounts, the force of history splinters into indeterminacies in the poetic text. Complications in the poem's rhetorical mode are symptomatic of an encounter with what Georges Perec described as "l'Histoire avec sa grande hache" (Perec, *W,* 13). They are blind spots sparking insight into a trauma both constitutive of the psyche and produced by the force of an unrepresentable history. The literary text emerges as a witness that, insofar as it may gesture to what lies outside its margins, does so as a victim bodying forth the shocks and contradictions of history. The ethical moment in poetry, then, emerges through the association of unrepresentability, witnessing, trauma, and victimization.

As I argued earlier, the view of history as a tropological structure privileges figure over content, representation over events, and perilously overlooks the particularity of "history" as empirical forces experienced by bodies and subjects in a particular social content. This can lead to a conflation of historically distinct traumas by way of structural analogies, such that the shocks of life in the modern city are seen as analogous to the trauma of the Holocaust, insofar as both events induce a "crisis of representation." It also encourages reading the literary canon of modernity backwards from its "limit event," such that the Holocaust and its defining crisis of representation become the measures by which other historical crises and their literary representations are reread. This has the paradoxical effect of inscribing the irreducible singularity of historical events along a narrative teleology in a retroactive periodization. Modernism's interrogation of reference is seen to prefigure the epistemological and ethical impossibility of representing the Holocaust.[18] In the name of its radical singularity, the Holocaust itself is reduced to a transhistorical figure; it serves as an allegory for history's resistance to figuration, a resistance that both founds and frames modernity as a "crisis of representation."[19]

What sorts of mediations between history and literature does this model of trauma and testimony occlude? As a mode of reading literature, such a symptomatic view short-circuits any sustained consideration of how the Baudelairean text actively engages with historical forces through irony, violence, counterviolence, and critique. Instead, the recent displacement of historicity into a text's symptomatic gaps, silences, and aporias positions literature as victimized witness to a history whose force exceeds representation. Poetry becomes a purely reactive stage for "acting out" trauma, for the compulsive rehearsal of the shocks and contradictions of its historical moment. It is approached as a pathological system scarred by unreadable lesions that attest to the violence of an unrepresentable history.

Yet "history" is not a monolithic force that works through passive texts and psyches. History locates violence in specific sites; it positions subjects in specific ways, not only as victims, but also as agents, subjects, objects, witnesses, executioners, readers, and writers. Literature is a privileged terrain for the inscription of history's multidirectional force. Baudelaire's poems are a case in point, for their own complex deployment of violence rehearses and locates the violence of history itself in multiple sites, operations, and positionalities. This rehearsal of violence, its multidirectional deployment, is what gives the relationship between poetry and history in Baudelaire's work its ongoing critical energy.

Baudelaire himself vigorously objects to such a positioning of the writer as a passive witness to the violence of history. Indeed, toward the end of his life, during his self-imposed exile in Belgium, Baudelaire declares: "Non seulement, je serais heureux d'être victime, mais je ne haïrais pas d'être bourreau, — pour sentir la Révolution de deux manières !" (*OC*, 2: 961). In a statement that can be read as a key to the poet's entire corpus and its manifold contradictions, Baudelaire opens his work out to historical processes, not—as one might expect—from the standpoint of traumatized victim or witness, but as executioner and agent in history. How might this arresting declaration help us to recover the dialectical force of Baudelaire's engagement with the violence of modernity?

The Representation of Violence and the Violence of Representation

Violence is an ever-expanding category in our contemporary critical climate. "Stretched beyond its former clearly demarcated boundaries, meaning 'the use of physical force' (a characterization still to be found in standard English dictionary definitions), violence now includes such phenomenologically elusive categories as psychological, symbolic, structural, epistemic, hermeneutical and aesthetic violence," Beatrice Hanssen writes.[20] Rather than attempt to provide an exhaustive definition, I shall for now maneuver around one important distinction between trauma and violence: whereas the psychoanalytic, literary view of trauma posits the subject as the site and victim of an epistemological violence, the term "violence" generally designates a relation *between* subjects, indicating a more encompassing, energetic and relational structure involving intersubjective relations and multiple positionalities. As a category for literary analysis, violence enables a consideration of the relationship between poetry, history, and critique by exploring how a text both occupies and opens up for the reader a range of positions toward the violence that is represented, including those of executioner, accomplice, and bystander.[21]

To be sure, one can argue that trauma theory also locates violence as a circulating force endemic to the very project of representation. Representation betrays its object by arresting an infinitely particularizing discourse that might do justice to the singularity of an experience or a person. Yet a sweeping account of representation *as* violence flattens out the specificity of different historical experience and erases necessary distinctions between victims, executioners, accomplices, witnesses, and spectators. The category of violence captures the circulation of power in particular historical events, while maintaining the distinctions between these subject positions. When describing *Le Spleen de Paris,* Baudelaire suggestively remarks that this literary corpus has "ni queue ni tête, puisque tout, au contraire, y est à la fois tête et queue, alternativement et réciproquement" (*OC,* 1: 275). It is this sense of simultaneity, multidirectionality and mobile particularity that I hope to convey in the following readings of violence and representation.

A discussion of the role of violence in Baudelaire's poetics necessarily entails examining what the representation of violence has to say about real violence, and how "real" violence is itself enmeshed in representational violence. To argue for a connection between violence and representation assumes what Teresa de Lauretis has called the "semiotic relation of the social to the discursive" ("The Violence of Rhetoric," 240). Yet to what extent can we talk about violence as a symbolic operation while still doing justice to the *reality* of a violent act, encounter or practice? And how might the connection between the representation of violence and the violence of representation be used to serve critical, and even ethical, ends by literature and its criticism? Can the deployment of violence in poetry illuminate or even contest the violences—in representation and practice—of a particular historical moment?

While it has traditionally designated eruptions of force or breakdowns in the social fabric, violence, as recent theory teaches us, can characterize a certain pattern of dominance just as easily as it does breakdowns in this pattern. Violence in the sphere of the law, for example, as shown by the work of Foucault, Derrida, and Butler, among others, operates at structural, linguistic levels that performatively shape the daily reality of our social practices.[22] Following such poststructuralist dismantlings of normative ethico-political positions, "counterviolence" has become an important figure for a critique of the underlying structural violences of the social sphere. As Hanssen suggests, "the use of a symbolic, figurative, discursive force, wielded as a counterprinciple" has been theorized as a strategy for illuminating—as well as contesting—the hidden relations of force in a given sociopolitical structure:

> Indeed, one "figure" of violence whose persistence and recurrent circulation in contemporary post-structuralist thought the book pursues is that of a counterforce or counterviolence (*Gegengewalt*) that takes the form of what Foucault and Derrida respectively have called "antidogmatic" or "antimetaphysical" violence. Thus, the use of a symbolic, figurative, discursive force, wielded as a counterprinciple, is meant to undo metaphysical, institutional sedimentations of force, especially the violence exercised by instrumental reason, with its logic *and* practices of exclusion. (Hanssen, 14)

The concepts of "violence" and "counterviolence" are useful for unraveling the contestatory potential of poetic discourse. Indeed, one of the central claims in this book is that the literary representation of violence illuminates the violence of historical representation by imbricating aesthetic self-consciousness within ideological critique. In the texts I examine, irony functions as a textual violence and a historical counterviolence. Baudelairean irony—the hallmark of his "modernity"—conducts an ethico-political critique at the level of poetic form and of language itself. Poetic strategies of representation are embedded in the larger tropological systems of his historical moment. By explicitly staging the violence of poetic representation (rather than symptomatically parrying the trauma of history), Baudelaire offers a genealogy of violence and thereby opens up a critical relationship between a text and its contexts.[23] The force of irony in Baudelaire's oeuvre functions as a counterviolence that teases out imbricated social, economic, and representational violences embedded in the postrevolutionary social body. The recurrent linking of violence and representation throughout his work exploits literature's performative force and uncovers zones of complicity between poetic discourse and other regimes of power. This rehearsal of violence opens up a space for the critique and resignification of accepted cultural practices through irony, performativity, intertexuality, and citationality.[24]

Let us for a moment imagine Baudelaire's poems as a kind of "theater of cruelty" in which existing violences are staged and contested, in turn, through textual violence. This rehearsal gives a genealogy of the production of violence both on the textual stage and on the historical scene. By violence, then, I refer to the empirical violence "out there" in the world, the violence exercised through words upon things in the world, and the imbrication of these violences in Lauretis's "semiotic relation of the social to the discursive." In other words, I consider violence in its material, social, psychic, epistemological, aesthetic, and ethical contexts. In its most inclusive definition, "violence" will designate a particular mode of conceptualizing a represented object that diminishes, reifies, or violates that object in a way that resonates against underlying sets of cultural assumptions. For Baudelaire, violence is a vehicle that inscribes competing fields (aesthetic, economic, ideological, and so forth) within the poem itself. It serves as a figure for representational tensions existing both within and between these fields. The myriad structures of "victime" and of "bourreau" in his scenes of violence trace complex correspondences within and between the poetic and social text, thus offering a powerful yet nuanced critique of the violence of modernity.[25]

This next section turns to Baudelaire's "L'Héautontimorouménos," a poem that will serve as a leitmotif throughout this book, to illustrate how Baudelaire's notorious self-reflexivity operates a shift from the epistemological realm—in which the poet and ironist is both subject and object of reflection—into a historicized realm of victims and executioners. From a rehearsal of irony's trauma, the poetic text is redefined, through irony and citationality, as an encounter between text and intertext and between self and other.

The Poet as Ironist and as Héautontimorouménos

"L'Héautontimorouménos" is a key poem and figure for Baudelaire's poetics. Initially conceived as a "projet d'épilogue" for *Les Fleurs du Mal,* its portrait of consciousness as both "plaie et couteau," "victime et bourreau," has made it emblematic of Baudelairean—and modernist—self-reflexivity. Sartre, for instance, viewed the *héautontimorouménos* (in Greek, "self-punisher" or "self-tormentor") as a figure exemplary of the poet's bad faith, that is to say, his desire to simultaneously become reflexive and reflected consciousness, the eye that perceives and the "I" perceived. Yet the poem itself stages the failure of this attempted self-coincidence. Instead, by showing the emergence of consciousness *as* a wound, it gives us what first appears to be a case study of trauma:

> Je te frapperai sans colère
> Et sans haine, comme un boucher,
> Comme Moïse le rocher !
> Et je ferai de ta paupière,
>
> Pour abreuver mon Sahara,
> Jaillir les eaux de la souffrance.
> Mon désir gonflé d'espérance
> Sur tes pleurs salés nagera
>
> Comme un vaisseau qui prend le large,
> Et dans mon coeur qu'ils soûleront
> Tes chers sanglots retentiront
> Comme un tambour qui bat la charge !
>
> Ne suis-je pas un faux accord
> Dans la divine symphonie,
> Grâce à la vorace Ironie
> Qui me secoue et qui me mord ?
>
> Elle est dans ma voix, la criarde !
> C'est tout mon sang, ce poison noir !
> Je suis le sinistre miroir
> Où la mégère se regarde !
>
> Je suis la plaie et le couteau !
> Je suis le soufflet et la joue !
> Je suis les membres et la roue,
> Et la victime et le bourreau !

> Je suis de mon coeur le vampire
> — Un de ces grands abandonnés
> Au rire éternel condamnés,
> Et qui ne peuvent plus sourire ! (*OC,* 1: 78–79)

In this parodic rewriting of the lyric address, the I-thou relationship mutates into a relentless, rhythmical beating that is virtually enacted by the regularity of the octosyllabic lines, the caesuras and exclamations. The poem projects into the future a ritual punishment voided of cause, motivation, or affect. The executioner, figured as a Sahara, a desertic place of nothingness, turns to the victim to sate its ontological hunger. As we may surmise from the repetition "sans colère et sans haine" and the homonymy of *sans* and *sang,* the very substance of this "Je," is nothing more than its projected act of violence. The poetic subject will wound the surface of the other to create an ontological location and depth. The delicate plane of the beloved's eyelid releases a fountain of tears on whose watery surface the poet's desire will glide ("Mon désir gonflé d'espérance / Sur tes pleurs salés nagera"); her sobs will ring out like the taut skin of a drum that is struck ("Tes chers sanglots retentiront / Comme un tambour qui bat la charge !").

The poem thus stages a sacrificial scenario in which a singular yet vacuous "je" ("mon Sahara"; "mon désir") turns to the diffuse liquefaction of a "tu" (figured as "eaux de la souffrance" and "pleurs salés"), who in a literalization of metaphor itself (as *metaphorein*), promises to transport this "je" into a promised *ailleurs* ("Comme un vaisseau qui prend le large").[26] Yet the metaphors themselves dissolve the precarious distinction between self and other, or victim-executioner, for the victim's sobs—produced by the executioner's blows—themselves ring out like the blows of a military drum.

Thus, in the central stanza, the victim-thou position has washed away and Irony reveals itself as constituting the very identity of the lyric "I":

> Ne suis-je pas un faux accord
> Dans la divine symphonie
> Grâce à la vorace Ironie
> Qui me secoue et qui me mord ?

Irony, personified as an aberrant and external feminine principle, a muse turned shrew ("la criarde"; "la mégère"), appropriates the "je" and usurps its poetic voice. Yet the otherness of irony proves to be part and parcel of the poet's substance: "C'est tout mon sang, ce poison noir." The interiorization of both victim and irony reveals an otherness constitutive of the self, which appears to seal the poetic subjectivity—and the poem itself—into the infinite regress of ironic reflexivity: "Je suis le sinistre miroir / Où la mégère se regarde."

Let us for a moment consider this interiorization of an external figure as an "other within the self" through the optic of trauma.[27] The *héautontimorouménos* initially attempts to relocate its selfhood through the fragmentation and the reappropriation of its victim. Yet its sadistic ritual shades into self-mutilation with the realization that the dialectic between subject and object, self and other, executioner and victim, takes place entirely within a self fractured by irony's trauma. The subject, agent and executioner is revealed as constituted by its object, other and victim (figured here as irony):

> Je suis la plaie et le couteau !
> Je suis le soufflet et la joue !
> Je suis les membres et la roue,
> Et la victime et le bourreau !

If we read the poem as a case study of trauma, the poem "acts out" a process of interiorization, wherein an incompatibility between self and world reveals incompatible registers within the self. Executioner and victim, striker and struck, are forces at war within a self-different subjectivity ("C'est tout mon sang, ce poison noir").

When read in this perspective, "L'Héautontimorouménos" bears striking resemblances to Cathy Caruth's analysis of Torquado Tasso's *Gerusalemme Liberata*, a text she views as the paradigmatic literary study of trauma. Tasso recounts how Tancred unwittingly slays his beloved Clorinda on the battlefield. After her burial, he enters a magic forest and slashes a tree, only to realize, belatedly, that the tree contains his beloved's soul. Caruth presents Tancred as a parable for the "unarticulated implications of the theory of trauma," for his double killing is an unwitting and unwilled reenactment typical of the repetition compulsion of traumatic neurosis (*Unclaimed Experience,* 3). More significant for our analysis of Baudelaire, however, is Caruth's point that Tasso's traumatic scenario turns both Clorinda and Tancred into victims of trauma (defined here as the fatality of an injury twice inflicted and received), as figures for a divided self. Tancred is the dissociated subject of a traumatic neurosis, and Clorinda—his victim—is his "other within the self," an internal witness to Tancred's own injury, for she remembers what Tancred can never fully know. Similarly, Baudelaire's "L'Héautontimorouménos" begins with a sacrificial scenario (with an obvious difference: Baudelaire's poetic subject inflicts pain with ritualistic deliberation) yet the victimized "tu," like Clorinda, is revealed as an "other within the self."

The comparison between Baudelaire and Tasso is illuminating, for Tancred's example (as read by Caruth) reveals a problem endemic to theorizing subjectivity through trauma. Indeed, when approached through trauma, the infliction of violence becomes but another instance of self-shattering. The relations of force that actually exist between victim and executioner (Tancred has, after all, killed Clorinda twice) are overlooked in favor of an analysis that takes place exclusively within a subject victimized by trauma. Further, such a reading would assume that the literary text serves as a mirror for the compulsive repetition of trauma. In this light, Baudelaire's poem would mirror the poetic subjectivity's rehearsal or "acting out" of a split subject. Yet we should note that in "L'Héautontimorouménos," the self is not merely constituted by an alterity it once perceived as external, for the poetic subject does not directly identify with the victim turned executioner or the muse turned shrew. Rather, the poetic subject becomes the mirror in which irony contemplates *itself.*

> Je suis le sinistre miroir
> Où la mégère se regarde !

The "I" is a location, a place in the structure of reflexivity, one that mirrors back difference and irony.[28] This shift in the representation of the self from substance (blood, poison) to location and form ("le . . . miroir / Où") suggests that the "Je" becomes the site of reflexivity rather than the subject-object of trauma. What is at stake in this distinction between text as mirror and text as site or stage for trauma, is a view of the poetic text not as pathological symptom—or reflection—of traumatic neurosis, but instead, as a mise-en-scène for an oscillation that is both within the self and between selves and others. The restaging of trauma as a form of ironic reflexivity introduces an analytical distance from the experience. It also situates this trauma within a dialogical and intersubjective context. For even in this most relentlessly solipsistic of poems, the final verse opens out in a gesture of address, signaled by the caesura:

> —— Un de ces grands abandonnés
> Au rire éternel condamnés,
> Et qui ne peuvent pas sourire.

The caesura introducing "un de ces grands abandonnés," and the break out of the singular form into the plural, initiate a recognition of commonality with other victims of irony's lucid madness. It gestures toward a community of displaced, spectral souls akin to the wandering exiles commemorated in "Le Cygne," with whom the fragments of authorial subjectivity identify ("Je pense aux matelots oubliés dans une île / Aux captifs, aux vaincus ! . . . à bien d'autres encor !"). In "L'Héautontimorouménos," the authorial subject does not exclusively attest to the specularity of trauma, to the recurrent yet missed encounter with an "other within the self." Instead, it stages a collective existential fall into irony. The break out of pure solipsism also occurs intertextually, across linguistic and cultural difference. Indeed, the concluding allusion to the Melmothian figure who laughs but cries no more is a translated fragment straight out of Poe's "Fall of the House of Usher." Baudelaire's poem is thus in dialogue with Poe's poem "The Haunted Palace," embedded in the short story:

> While, like a rapid ghastly river
> Through the pale door
> A hideous throng rush out forever
> And laugh—but smile no more.[29]

The ghostly traces of Poe's "Haunted Palace" in turn haunt Baudelaire's poem, rewriting irony in the context of a shared *mal du siècle* that, significantly, is transmitted through literature.[30] Baudelaire's text thus fulfils the promise of the inaugural poem, "Au lecteur." The reader, as "Hypocrite lecteur, — mon semblable, — mon frère," becomes the contaminated accomplice to a fall into irony. Ironic lucidity is transmitted by a contagious text. The critical energies unleashed by irony circulate within and between these texts, coercing the reader into relations of recognition, identification and complicity.[31] This is not to say that Baudelaire's poem beckons an immediate identification (or transference) in which the reader submits to a pathological state of textual trauma. On the contrary, the text's escalating ironies keep such identifications at bay by introducing a critical distance from the trauma it depicts. The Poe intertext reframes the solipsism of the individual trauma into a collective *ethical* predicament: the recognition of evil, or *la conscience dans le mal.*

"L'Heáutontimorouménos" appears to record a crisis of representation (of the self, the text, and the collective), and as such could be read as an illustration of the trauma of modern consciousness as it emerges without any normative point of reference beyond itself. Yet it offers an embryonic response to this predicament. For it maps a trauma that is constitutive of the poetic subjectivity first as an epistemological state—expressed through irony—*and* as an ethical condition shared by "ces grands abandonnés." And this is where I turn to a second reason for resisting the temptation to read poetic violence through trauma. Indeed, the paradigm of the "other within the self" (or of Cathy Caruth's reading of Clorinda as a figure for Tancred's "self-difference") at the basis of trauma obliterates the distinction between victim and executioner by making both the agent and the recipient of violence avatars for a divided self. Such a slippage, as Ruth Leys has observed, is ethically fraught, since it erases the necessary distinctions between the subject and object of violence.[32] Baudelaire, however, maintains this tension between subject and object, victim and executioner, even as his poems stage these as ambiguous, circulating positions. This tension is sustained by the distance the poem displays toward its own rhetorical mode—through strategies such as intertextuality, irony, and interpellation.

At stake in the distinction I make between the self-referentiality of trauma and the self-reflexivity of irony is the possibility that a self-reflexive poem (one that complicates its mode of representation) retains its demystifying, critical force. Baudelairean irony conducts its critique from within the pathology it denounces. In the context of "L'Héautontimorouménos," the violence of irony is rehearsed with an acute attunement to how differences in power, for instance, between a masculine subject/executioner and a feminine object/victim, constantly shape even the most "autonomous" acts of creation. Irony—a rhetorical figure for disparate meanings—is continually reframed in a context disclosing the underlying violence of acts of knowing the self and the other.

Irony as Counterviolence

How does Baudelairean irony retain its critical powers despite its notoriously self-undermining structure? And how might the deconstruction of a rhetorical mode open up—rather than foreclose—the passage between text and world? A brief history of irony's vexed relationship to critique will be useful here in order to elucidate how the deconstructive impetus of Baudelairean irony engages ethical and political concerns.

Traditionally defined as a rhetorical figure that intentionally creates two or more disparate meanings in a text, a dissemblance having a critical function in a context of shared beliefs, irony's more recent identification with contingency, undecidability, and aporia has made it one of modernity's most pervasive modes of self-understanding.[33] Paradoxically, the expansion of irony's relevance to political and philosophical thought on identity is met with skepticism about the viability of its insights for experiences existing outside the literary text. Particularly in the wake of deconstruction and its radicalization of irony as a constitutive indeterminacy of meaning, the contestatory function of irony (as satire) is threatened with irrelevance. Not only does the ironist fail to offer alternatives to the conceptions that are demystified; the ironist's vigilance toward the authority of his or her own claims seems to enclose the ironic position into the infinite downward spiral staged in Baudelaire's "L'Héautontimorouménos." Contemporary definitions of irony thus tend to relegate it to the private realm of individual self-reflection or to the aesthetic realm of formal self-consciousness, and as fundamentally irrelevant to the articulation and analysis of shared values.

The gap between irony's insights and a historically defined reality reaches back to the romantics and their redefinition of irony as a mode of apprehending the self and world. German romantics such as Friedrich Schlegel viewed irony as a property of the creative consciousness itself and saw the literary text as emerging out of a dialectic of authorial self-creation and self-destruction, or parabasis. Irony is proof of the imagination's unfettered sovereignty, for the poet may create and revoke the fictional world at will, soaring "on the wings of poetic reflection, and can raise that reflection again and again to a higher power, can multiply it in an endless succession of mirrors."[34] Romantic irony thus celebrated the supremacy of the creative spirit over the constraints of empirical phenomena. As Vladimir Jankélevitch observed, romantic irony responds to the Fichtean promise of "Comment être *causa sui*—ce sujet qui est l'objet, cet agent qui est son propre patient, ce rieur qui est le risible ?" (Jankélevitch, *Ironie*, 25). Such a predicament, as we saw, forms the paradoxical core of Baudelaire's *héautontimoroumenos* and its exalted despair at being both subject and object, cause and effect, victim and executioner of its own laughter and reflection.

By celebrating the irrealizing powers of the imagination, romantic irony played off the gap between literary reflection and the empirical constraints of history. Such a hypostatized view of aesthetic autonomy is precisely what drew criticism: for Søren Kierkegaard, the ironic position was one in which "the subject is continually retreating, talking every phenomenon out of its reality in order to save itself—that is, in order to preserve itself in negative independence of everything"; it suspended the work of art "outside and above morality and ethics."[35] Similarly, Hegel denounced romantic irony as a form of absolute and infinite negativity. Irony invested the ego with the capricious freedom to create and revoke "everything genuinely independent and real" at will; in doing so, it voided the artistic work of content or of connection to historical actuality.[36] The reception of romantic irony thus viewed self-reflexivity—that is to say, literature's reflection upon its procedures of presentation—as a rejection of the real for the autonomy and moral indifference of private self-creation.

Romantic irony invests the creative imagination with absolute power, since it posits a subjectivity that has become its origin and effect, both a free, creating consciousness and the object it creates. Yet, as the example of "L'Héauton-timorouménos" shows us, it also inaugurates a fractured subjectivity that is evacuated of content and emerging only *through* parabasis, or discontinuous reflections. Baudelaire's most powerfully self-reflexive poems capture this oscillation between Fichtean absolutism and anxious self-division. We are now in a position to assess what a poststructuralist theory of irony such as de Man's (as a structure of radical discontinuity) and of trauma (as repetition and negativity) owe to these romantic articulations. If for Schlegel, irony's parabasis mirrors the infinite play of the universe, the poststructuralist view of irony as trauma situates this parabasis in language and identity itself. For de Man, whose theory of irony builds on Schlegel's Athenaüm fragments, irony alerts us to our linguistic nature, to our emergence through the iterability of the sign and its temporality. In this account, irony signals an epistemological crisis that unravels the identity of the self and the text; a crisis that has no communicative content beyond the repetition of its blindness: "Irony is no longer a trope but the undoing of the deconstructive allegory of all tropological cognition, the systematic undoing, in other words, of understanding. As such, far from closing off the tropological system, irony enforces the repetition of its aberration."[37]

De Man uses Baudelaire as a central figure for this articulation of irony *as* trauma, as a crisis of representation undoing the identity of the self and the text. His influential essay "The Rhetoric of Temporality" turns to Baudelaire's "De l'essence du rire" to theorize irony as a "lucid madness" and as the trauma of a repetitive blindness. Several readers have since approached Baudelaire's essay on laughter as a map for the fault lines of a subject emerging discontinuously in language and in time. Laughter's aporetic quality is addressed as a trauma enclosing the text in a series of divided reflections. Yet the terms of this constellation—laughter, irony, and trauma—need to be separated out to allow for a more particularized reading of Baudelaire's irony. Otherwise, we risk remaining locked in an interpretive cycle in which laughter, irony, and trauma slide into each other and are ultimately subsumed under a horizon of undecidability. My reading of "De l'essence du rire" is indebted to accounts of laughter's aporetic quality in Baudelaire, but it argues that laughter does more than signal incommensurable registers within the self or in language itself. In Baudelaire's "De l'essence du rire," as in "L'Héautontimorouménos," the trauma of irony expressed by laughter is a shared epistemological condition that activates relations of power within and between a text and its contexts.[38] Rather than approaching the essay as the symptomatic enactment of a pathology without cure, I shall examine how its deconstruction of healthy, normative, or pure states existing "beyond" or "outside" the disruptive force of laughter is essential to developing a theory of irony as a form of critical counterviolence.[39]

Trauma, Irony, and Critique in "De l'essence du rire"

"De l'essence du rire" is more than a defense of caricature as a viable artistic genre; it articulates conceptual oppositions that are central to Baudelaire's writing as a whole: grace and fall, metaphysics and history, the pure and the impure, the metatextual and the intertextual, symbol and allegory, art for art's sake and art for progress. The alleged purpose of the essay, the author confides, is the release of a quasi-physiological obsession, which will be exorcised once presented in an orderly fashion and digested by the reader: "Ces réflexions étaient devenues pour moi une espèce d'obsession ; j'ai voulu me soulager. J'ai fait, du reste, tous mes efforts pour y mettre un certain ordre et en rendre ainsi la digestion plus facile" (*OC,* 2: 525). The phenomenon of laughter is examined through several lenses: theology, physiology, psychology, metaphysics, popular culture, and finally, comic traditions at home and abroad. Yet, the experience of laughter in these meticulously expository sections remains irreducible to conceptual digestion. The structure of laughter is double, its effect is an unrepresentable convulsion; it is a symptom or a hieroglyph, yet its roots, its referent, its very "essence" remain unspoken, if not unspeakable: "Le rire n'est qu'une expression, un symptôme, un diagnostic. Symptôme de quoi ? Voilà la question" (*OC,* 2: 534).

To elucidate this question, Baudelaire sets up a series of antitheses between a primordial, metaphysical state of purity and a fallen, historical condition defined by laughter: "le rire humain est intimement lié à l'accident d'une chute ancienne, d'une dégradation physique et morale" (*OC,* 2: 527–28). Laughter, then, denotes a fall into reflexivity, historical time, and irony. The theological manifestations of a state of grace prior to and beyond laughter are prelapsarian innocence or divine omnipotence; its literary manifestation is *poésie pure;* its historical incarnations are primitive societies in which skepticism has not taken root or projected socialist utopias. Yet, the essay very deliberately sabotages all references to such ideal states of purity, showing each to be "always already" fractured by laughter, difference, and fallenness. Laughter thus contaminates every heuristic ideal—literary, political, or metaphysical—evoked in opposition to it. For instance, Baudelaire's opening maxim, "Le sage ne rit qu'en tremblant" (*OC,* 2: 526)—the crux of his distinction between the sacred and the fallen—invokes the transgression of laughter as temporally prior to a state of purity. The dichotomy between purity and laughter is only constructed in hindsight, for the sage does indeed laugh first, even if it is in fear and trembling. The source of this enigmatic maxim (Ecclesiasticus, quoted by Bossuet) is also erased, and the author-analyst wonders aloud as to whether he read it in a text by Joseph de Maistre or Bourdaloue.[40] Further, the entire description of a "paradis terrestre" prior to mankind's fall into laughter is plagiarized from the unpublished *Contes normands* by Jean de la Falaise, alias Philippe de Chennevières.[41] These citations, caught in a dense relay of sources, unmistakably convey that the primordial, edenic state is but a derivative construct.

The realm of art itself is similarly polluted by laughter. While Baudelaire invokes *poésie pure* initially as a redemptive way out of the fallenness and decrepitude of the human condition and into a suitably "poetic" state of elevation, his formulation presents us with a conceptual conundrum. "[S]i dans ces mêmes nations ultracivilisées, une intelligence poussée par une ambition supérieure, veut franchir les limites de l'orgueil humain et s'élancer hardiment vers la poésie pure, dans cette poésie, limpide et profonde comme la nature, le rire fera défaut comme dans l'âme du Sage," our analyst declares (*OC,* 2: 532–33). Yet the roots of this spirit, or "intelligence," lie in the proud desire to transcend the realm of pride. The state of *poésie pure* is itself created out of those very conditions (the conviction of superiority, which is both the cause and the consequence of laughter) that *define* the fall into laughter and historical time. The essay thus repeatedly gestures toward a lost condition of grace yet voids these redemptions of credibility with masterful deconstructive strokes. Although described as an aberration, laughter ultimately becomes the norm that arises from the breakdown of every ideal that would exclude it.

The figure of Bernardin de Saint-Pierre's Virginie haunts this essay and encapsulates its paradoxes. Baudelaire imagines the fall of this paragon of innocence upon encountering a caricature on the streets of Paris:

Essayons, puisque le comique est un élément damnable et d'origine dia-
bolique, de mettre en face une âme absolument primitive et sortant, pour
ainsi dire, des mains de la nature. Prenons pour exemple la grande et
typique figure de Virginie, qui symbolise parfaitement la pureté et la naïveté
absolues. Virginie arrive à Paris encore toute trempée des brumes de la mer
et dorée par le soleil des tropiques, les yeux pleins des grandes images primi-
tives des vagues, des montagnes et des forêts. Elle tombe ici en pleine
civilisation turbulente et méphitique, elle, toute imprégnée des pures et
riches senteurs de l'Inde. . . . Or, un jour, Virginie rencontre par hasard,
innocemment, au Palais-Royal, aux carreaux d'un vitrier, sur une table, dans
un lieu public, une caricature ! une caricature bien appétissante pour nous,
grosse de fiel et de rancune, comme sait les faire une civilisation perspicace
et ennuyée" (*OC,* 2: 528–29).

Emblematic of a lost correspondence between the natural world and the
human spirit, seamlessly connected to her land and family, Virginie embodies
a metaphoricity that forms the core of romantic theories of imagination and
of Baudelaire's own conception of *correspondances.* She is a symbol of the very
process of symbolization: a *typique figure,* brimming with images, or symbols,
of her native tropical landscape. Virginie's fictional encounter with the Parisian
caricature constitutes a fall into self-reflexivity, one illustrating a shift from
primitive grace to modern fallenness, and in terms of literary history, a shift
from the unifying properties of the symbol to the division of allegory and
irony. Yet we may wonder why—in attempting to illustrate the shocking en-
counter between absolute innocence and civilized corruption—our analyst
would resort to a preexisting fictional character such as Virginie. For while she
convincingly embodies the immediacy and purity of a natural state preceding
laughter, we are nevertheless reminded of her mediated origins. Virginie's
emergence out of nature's very hands is itself caricatured by the emphasis on
the metaphoricity of her natural origins ("sortant, *pour ainsi dire,* des mains de
la nature"; emphasis added). After all, the "nature" from which she emerges is
not some primordial Eden: Virginie is a Creole from the île Bourbon
(Réunion) and carries upon her unsuspecting shoulders the burden of colonial
history. Even more amusing is the allusion to stock figures Virginie might en-
counter in these hypothetical caricatures, such as Marie-Antoinette, desig-
nated as "la proverbiale Autrichienne" (ibid.). Virginie may have emerged
from nature's hands in Saint-Pierre's novel (published in 1787), but by Baude-
laire's time, like Marie-Antoinette, she too is a stock figure represented, circu-
lated, and quite literally "handled" in countless miniatures, illustrations, and
no doubt caricatures.

Virginie's virginal status is thus compromisingly handled and manipulated by the essay. Her *flânerie* through the metropolis leads her to stumble upon the scandal of caricature. The fall from her original unity into a self-differentiating reflexivity is triggered by the duplicity of caricature: "La caricature est double : le dessin et l'idée : le dessin violent, l'idée mordante et voilée ; complications d'éléments pénibles pour un esprit naïf" (*OC*, 2: 529). Virginie's speculated encounter with caricature will mark her awakening into the collective dissonance of the age, into the contingency and ambiguity of historical existence. The subversion of laughter, its contamination as it ripples from text to context, desacralizes even this paragon of innocence: from her incarnation as the symbolic, she falls into the doubleness of allegory, and plays out, *en abyme,* the reader's own position in the text. Indeed, her stance before the complexity of caricature at the Palais-Royal prefigures the reader's own position before textual undecidability. Her laughter is the point of entry into a shared predicament, a solidarity with the "nous" repeatedly addressed in the essay.

Virginie may stand in for the reader's encounter with—and violation by—the scandal of textual duplicity. But the collective "nous" sharing the cosmopolitan artifacts of a particular historical moment are also positioned as voyeuristic accomplices to Virginie's fall. Breathlessly anticipating her corruption, the analyst titillates the reader with the scandalous possibilities of the image in question: "une caricature bien appétissante pour nous, grosse de fiel et de rancune, comme sait les faire une civilisation perspicace et ennuyée" (*OC*, 2: 529). The reader, as a fellow "analyste et critique," is incited to witness the defilement of Virginie's immaculate innocence and her birth into the worldly realm of knowledge and laughter. The essay's initial project of exorcising the trauma of laughter becomes a coercion into complicity prefigured by Virginie's own defilement. Laughter inscribes the reader into the text, just as Virginie's fall rewrites her into an alternative literary history, inaugurated, as it were, by the promise of her own laughter and survival: "Sans doute, que Virginie reste à Paris et que la science lui vienne, le rire lui viendra" (*OC*, 2: 529).

If laughter signals the breakdown of selfhood and its symbolic representations, the fall from transcendence into an existence composed of discontinuous historical moments, why would the author seek to exonerate works of art that arise from this painful self-division? What value may lie in the spectacle of human disfigurement and mystification beyond the masochistic repetition of the fall rehearsed by the *héautontimorouménos*? The primal scene of Virginie's encounter with caricature suggests a possible response. At a critical moment of her fall into self-reflection, Baudelaire notes: "Virginie a vu ; maintenant, elle regarde. Pourquoi ? Elle regarde l'inconnu" (529). Virginie's encounter with duplicity not only marks her birth into shared historical experience. It also signals her awakening into agency. Laughter catalyzes the shift from the passivity of seeing to the activity and analysis of "looking."

Laughter emerges in this essay as an escalating mode of experiencing both the self and the world in a fallen context, and paradoxically, as a valuable instrument of knowledge and agency. Laughter induces both trauma and lucidity; it is at once the pathology and its analysis. As Baudelaire notes, the experience of laughter banishes customary boundaries between analyst and analyzed. In an ironic gesture toward the essay's claim to disclose the essence of laughter, he wonders if physiologists of laughter are not themselves engulfed by the phenomenon they claim to study: " Je ne serais pas étonné que devant cette découverte le physiologiste se fût mis à rire en pensant à sa propre supériorité" (*OC*, 2: 530). Knowledge can only perpetuate the fall into mystified superiority, and the author is all too aware of the fragile position of the analyst and critic claiming to stand securely at the edge of the abyss. Laughter persistently eludes the classification promised by this essay, mutating into a perverse textual *fou rire* that contaminates the very method by which the author would exorcise its madness. Yet it serves mankind's "puissance intellectuelle," for laughter bears within it the seeds of an empowering agency.[42] In *De l'essence du rire*, we are immersed in a historical and reflexive moment that is fractured at its very core, Laughter signals a lucidity purchased at the cost of faith in all representations of absolute authority—theological, political, and textual. The comic, by virtue of transgressing and exceeding conventional horizons, opens a space for the critique and rearticulation of norms established and sustained by these horizons.[43]

"Ce n'est point l'homme qui tombe qui rit de sa propre chute, à moins qu'il ne soit un philosophe, un homme qui ait acquis, par habitude, la force de se dédoubler rapidement et d'assister comme spectateur désintéressé aux phénomènes de son *moi*" (*OC*, 2: 532), asserts the author when elucidating the catalysts for laughter in everyday life: the (mystified) sense of superiority that one harbors vis-à-vis another's mystification. Here, mystification is figured as the illusion of bodily control, the moment of lucidity as tripping over cobblestones and falling. However, the superiority of the laughing subject over the person who falls, or the empirical predicament that triggers the laughter, is a mystification that is always susceptible to reversal. One who claims, as does Baudelaire's snide spectator, that "*moi* je ne tombe pas, *moi* je marche droit" (531) is blind to his or her fragility, be it physical, or, as is ultimately the point, epistemological, and will indeed fall. The essence of the comic, Baudelaire suggests, lies precisely in this continuous reversal of power relations.

The comic artist's task is to reenact the scenario of laughter from the standpoint of subject (the one who laughs) and object (the one who falls) so that the reader in turn may experience the delights of superiority, but also recognize the mystification upon which this superiority rests. In this portrait of the artist as an *esprit-philosophe,* Baudelaire proposes that the aesthetic work *stages* the division of the subject into self and other so that readers and spectators undergo a similar division. Artists, then, are professionals who "ont fait métier de développer en eux le sentiment du comique et de le tirer d'eux-mêmes pour le divertissement de leurs semblables, lequel phénomène rentre dans la classe de tous les phénomènes artistiques qui dénotent dans l'être humain l'existence d'une dualité permanente, *la puissance d'être à la fois soi et un autre*" (*OC,* 2: 543; emphasis added). A written text functioning according to these principles incorporates the other, inciting a virtual reenactment of the author's reflexive process, for the ability to be self and other, as Baudelaire repeats throughout his essay, is a shared, human predicament, as well as the founding principle of art.[44] The artist-philosopher's task is thus identical to that of the poetic subject in "L'Héautontimorouménos": both figures rehearse a duality that lies at the core both of the artistic phenomenon and the readerly condition to which it appeals.

The self-division of Baudelaire's laughing philosopher has particular resonance for theories of irony formed in the crucible of romanticism. The comic as a "textual practice" recreates a dynamic of self-creation and self-destruction (figured as the fall and acknowledgement of frailty), which Friedrich Schlegel attributed to irony.[45] Yet, while Schlegel's conception of irony tended toward an ultimate synthesis of contradictions, Baudelaire describes laughter as an infinite and unrecuperable disruption. The dialectic between autocreation and autodestruction is thus structurally identical to ironic parabasis, but in a theologically fallen context that forecloses an ultimate reconciliation.[46] The comic-ironic text, then, performatively transmits the trauma of laughter, for it induces the reader to fall into reflexivity and complicity.

Given the apparent aporias of Baudelairean laughter, its kinship with disruptive forms of knowledge, it is not surprising that Paul de Man should turn to "De l'essence du rire" in his formulation of irony as a traumatic structure of repetitive blindness. In his seminal essay "The Rhetoric of Temporality," de Man envisions irony as a species of trauma, as a lucid madness that interrupts all connection between the literary text and its context of production or reception. If Baudelairean laughter expresses the awareness of a division that exists within the self as it takes itself as an object of reflection, it further encloses consciousness within its reflexive eddies. For de Man, irony illuminates a relationship between the subject and the object of perception, only this relationship is between a self that emerges *in* language and an empirical self out there in the world. The figure of the artist as writer is a case in point: "The ironic, twofold self that the writer or philosopher constitutes by his language seems able to come into being only at the expense of his empirical self, falling (or rising) from a state of mystified adjustment into the knowledge of his mystification. The ironic language splits the subject into an empirical self that exists in a state of inauthenticity and a self that exists only in the form of a language that asserts the knowledge of this inauthenticity. This does not, however, make it into an authentic language, for to know inauthenticity is not the same as to be authentic."[47]

The splitting, or *dédoublement,* is triggered by a fall from a mystified sense of superiority over nature and by the attitude of detached laughter adopted by the new self-aware subject toward the prior self. The ironic subject therefore only comes to know itself through an increasing differentiation from what it is not but thought that it was. For de Man, then, ironic demystification can only occur at the expense of the empirical self. The temptation to use irony's insight in an intersubjective relationship that would assist the empirical self in the "actual world" is to be resisted, since the authentic experience of temporality that irony reveals is only apparent from the fictional perspective of a difference constituted *in* language: "Irony divides the flow of temporal experience into a past that is pure mystification and a future that remains harassed forever by a relapse within the inauthentic. It can know this inauthenticity but can never overcome it. It can only restate and repeat it on an increasingly conscious level, but it remains endlessly caught in the impossibility of making this knowledge applicable to the empirical world" ("Rhetoric of Temporality," 222). The temptation to lapse into renewed blindness can only be resisted by at once ironizing this very predicament, that is, by constantly renewing the rupture between the empirical and the ironic selves in a process of infinite specularity: "Far from being a return to the world, the irony to the second power, or 'irony of irony' that all true irony at once has to engender asserts and maintains its fictional character by stating the continued impossibility of reconciling the world of fiction with the actual world" (ibid., 218). De Man's account of irony thus postulates a radical split between self and self, self and text, self and other, self and world. Absolute irony is a traumatic unraveling of self, text, and meaning: "absolute irony is a consciousness of madness, itself the end of all consciousness; it is a consciousness of a non-consciousness, a reflection on madness from the inside of madness itself" (ibid., 216).

Yet de Man's theory of irony as a vertiginous madness is derived from an incomplete reading of Baudelaire's own essay. It relies exclusively on the category of the "absolute comic" in "De l'essence du rire" to develop a model of irony as a purely self-reflexive, pathological vertigo that can only retain its authenticity in its perpetuation. Baudelaire, however, clearly sets out two forms of laughter induced by comic art, one owing to the magic of the *comique absolu,* the other, to the more analytical trigger of the *comique significatif. Le comique absolu* (also termed "grotesque") represents a realm of absolute otherness, "les créations fabuleuses, les êtres dont la raison, la légitimation ne peut pas être tirée du code du sens commun" (*OC,* 2: 535). The absolute comic is an irreducibly singular artistic expression that is apprehended in its totality and sensuous immediacy. It induces a rapturous vertigo in the spectator and must be grasped intuitively, from within its own economy. Baudelaire's celebration of the *comique absolu* echoes that of *poésie pure* and its magical fusion of subject and object through the alchemy of the sovereign imagination, "la reine des facultés." *Le comique significatif,* however, is an altogether different species. It is analytical, requiring reflection and judgment in its reception, and because of its ultimate legibility, it is readily grasped by the unschooled. Focusing on intersubjective relations of power, *le comique significatif* is contextual and relates to ordinary life situations. Baudelaire mentions Molière's "comique des moeurs" as an example of this comic form. Whereas the *comique absolu* recreates man's superiority over nature, the *comique significatif* pivots upon man's superiority over man. Baudelaire opposes the latter's derivative, imitative status to the former's autonomous, visionary nature. This distinction links up to a broader tension between art for art's sake and utilitarian or committed art, an opposition privileging the purity of autonomous art over the contamination of a contextually bound production: "Il y a, entre ces deux rires, abstraction faite sur la question d'utilité, la même différence qu'entre l'école littéraire intéressée et l'école de l'art pour l'art. Ainsi le grotesque domine le comique d'une hauteur proportionelle" (*OC,* 2: 535).

In spite of these distinctions, however, Baudelaire's opposition between absolute and signifying forms of comic art swiftly unravels. Having established that the grotesque is a creation, whereas the comic is but an imitation, the author proceeds to define the comic as "une imitation mêlée d'une certaine faculté créatrice, c'est à dire d'une idéalité artistique" and the grotesque as "une création mêlée d'une certaine faculté imitatrice d'élements préexistants dans la nature" (*OC,* 2: 535). The stark opposition between these categories is softened into a subtle ratio between creation and imitation. Since the opposition between these art forms cannot be grounded in terms of intrinsic properties, the author turns to the responses they provoke in the viewer, underscoring thus the importance of the *reader* in his theory of laughter. The absolute comic is grasped intuitively and as a whole (like the symbol in romantic aesthetic theory), the other is characterized by doubleness ("l'art et l'idée morale") and deferral ("le rire après coup"), and hence shares the same structure as allegory or caricature. Yet, the author concludes, the difference between them is not of essence but in their reception ("c'est une question de rapidité d'analyse"). The hierarchical opposition between these comic forms is anything but stable in Baudelaire's essay. The entanglement of absolute and signifying forms of the comic and their final determination by the reader describe an open-ended aesthetic practice informed by its context of production *and* of reception.[48]

De Man's translation of the *comique absolu* into a paradigm for irony as epistemological trauma—at the expense of the *comique significatif*—is questionable. For it is the *comique significatif* and its structure of discontinuity and deferral, its horizontal axis of intersubjective relations, that functions according to the doubleness and play of difference de Man attributes to absolute comic and irony.[49] At stake in de Man's privileging of the *comique absolu* and its basis in a relationship between nonidentical entities is his investment in the necessary self-difference or discontinuity of a subject emerging in language, or "the *distance* constitutive of all acts of reflection," and the "discontinuity and a plurality of levels within a subject that comes to know itself by an increasing differentiation from what it is not" ("Rhetoric of Temporality," 213). For de Man, Baudelaire's essay establishes a clear hierarchy between the absolute comic (its reliance on a relationship to a nonself, or to an "other within the self") and the *comique significatif.* The absolute comic is true, "absolute" irony. The signifying comic is merely humor. It is an intersubjective practice, "and thus exists on the necessarily empirical level of interpersonal relationships," and stages the "superiority of one subject over another, with all the implications of will to power, of violence, and possession which come into play when a person is laughing at someone else—including the will to educate and to improve" (ibid., 212). It is, therefore, a representational practice that fails to perpetuate the gap between fiction and actuality that de Man sees as the only "authentic" experience of irony.

De Man's exclusive reliance on the absolute comic as a relation to the nonself eclipses the communicative axis of Baudelairean irony, as well as the intersubjective, contextual, and demystifying elements that situate the *comique significatif* in an empirical realm of material realities and interpersonal relations. Yet Baudelaire's essay repeatedly gestures toward the comic work's relationship to reception, analysis, and critique. It also incites a vigilant reading of its own categories, first by emphasizing that the *comique absolu*, like edenic nature itself (or pure art, for that matter), is a heuristic concept, since the comic can only be absolute relative to our fallen condition. Thus, both theologically and aesthetically, Baudelaire situates his reflections in an impure, fallen, and relative context. His refusal to delineate clearly between the absolute and the significant incarnations of the comic is obvious in the two concrete examples of the comic he gives: E. T. A Hoffmann's *Daucus Carotta* and *La Princesse Brambilla*. These tales combine the *comique absolu* and its creation of alien horizons, with the *comique significatif* and its reliance on the discontinuity between utterance and meaning, as well as its demystification of intersubjective social structures. Hoffmann interweaves elements of *comique profond* and *raillerie significative*, unrepresentable vertigo, and the crafting of a science and ethics that stretch common frames of understanding and, in so doing, exemplify the fluidity of Baudelaire's categories.[50] This combination of textual address with creative *ivresse*, of science with poetics, of aesthetics with morality and ethics, forms the core of Baudelaire's own practice in the essay. Both an analysis and an implied performance of laughter, both inside and outside its madness, the author's voice skillfully weaves the reflections of the "médecin-moraliste" into the pathological experience itself.

We are now in a better position to assess the consequences of de Man's exclusive reliance on the *comique absolu* for theorizing irony as abyssal reflexivity. This theory of irony establishes rigid dichotomies between fiction and actuality, authenticity and inauthenticity, disjunction and conciliation, aesthetics and praxis, irony and critique. In declaring that there is no cure for the madness of irony, de Man sets the stage for later readings of textual undecidability through trauma. Both trauma and absolute irony postulate a radical separation of spheres between the real and the fictional, the empirical and the linguistic.[51] Irony, in de Man's account, locks the text into an infinitely reiterated trauma with no exit.

Kevin Newmark addresses this issue in his essay "Traumatic Poetry: Charles Baudelaire and the Shock of Laughter," a critique of de Man's split between consciousness and reality as one that would suggest that the ironic consciousness, "however 'mad', could nonetheless remain wholly enclosed within itself and therefore devoid of any substantial contact with material, historical reality" (249). Newmark notes that this self-enclosure is not evidenced in Baudelaire's own text, which looks at laughter from a historical vantage point.[52] He suggests, rather, that Baudelaire's essay represents a trauma whose destructive effects are to be mastered through philosophical analysis. Baudelaire attempts to provide a cure for the traumatic disjunction of laughter by dividing its experience into a phase of falling and a phase of reflection, such that the pathology of trauma opens up the possibility of a cure through analysis. Yet Newmark observes that there is no remedial "outside" from which a therapeutic intervention can be conducted. This is not only because of the conspicuous absence of an extrahistorical realm untainted by the shock of laughter, but because trauma is located at a level that is deeper than history. It inheres in the iterability of language itself, its inability fully to signify or ever to attain the plenitude of pure thought and being: "Laughter occurs as shock because it occurs semiotically as language, and as language, laughter is traumatic because it always refers to its inability to occur as anything other than a compulsively repeated reference that is never allowed to come to rest in the fullness of final meaning" (251).

For Newmark, then, Baudelaire's essay transmits the shock of laughter, it "laughs traumatically whenever it is read" and confronts the transparency of philosophical analysis with the opacity of language, its iterability and evasion of the determinations of source and fixed meaning—figured here as the obsessive maxim "le sage ne rit qu'en tremblant," whose author and origin remain unknown. The two levels of Baudelaire's text, then, as a "blindly compulsive" enactment of a trauma that is a condition of language itself and as a detached attempt to fix and understand the phenomenon of laughter, constitute the essay's central, unresolvable aporia.[53]

Yet the displacement of trauma into language itself opens up the same kinds of slippages I discussed in the more general context of trauma theory. The assimilation of trauma as a condition of language itself makes distinct historical traumas lose their specificity. In the case of Baudelaire's essay, this historical specificity, although never a stable ground, is nevertheless suggested, since laughter erupts only in fallen civilizations whose mystifications are intimately linked to urban modernity's symbolic and material upheavals. The comic experience (both in its absolute and signifying forms) always emerges within a shared representational context or *habitus*. When Baudelaire rewrites Virginie's fall, survival, and laughter in the modern metropolis, he underlines that the caricatures she could encounter are familiar to the reader and belong to a common reservoir of representations. Indeed, caricature is based upon a social reality as well as a shared representational economy. Baudelaire's interpellations of the reader are constant reminders of this shared, fallen currency.[54]

Even more significant is Baudelaire's resistance to a binary opposition between "acting out" and "working through," between writing as reenacting trauma and writing as healing the traumatic breach through the closure and transparency of analysis. Baudelaire's deconstructions of such binaries suggest the aesthetic work to be a complex interplay of shock and analysis, of blindness and insight.[55] Rehearsing both the trauma and the analysis elicited by laughter, Baudelaire suggests that the truly philosophical text serves as a stage for reflexivity, for the capacity to be *soi et autrui*. As we saw earlier, this vision of the text is illustrated in "L'Héautontimorouménos," which posits the subject as a *site* for the self-reflexive operations of irony: "Je suis le sinistre miroir / *Où* la mégère [l'ironie] se regarde." It is also crucial to bear in mind the *ternary* structure of laughter (rather than remain at the level of self-duplication). Indeed, Baudelaire's inclusion of the reader as a spectator of another's fall (such as Virginie's) inscribes this reader as the third position in a textual scenario dramatizing the fall into reflexivity and lucidity. The many figurations of the reading process foreground a text-reader-context relationship at odds with the autonomous demystification that de Man views as essential to the authenticity of irony's insight. Rather, it is the very separation of spheres that is demystified in Baudelaire's references to a shared context of reflection and contamination.[56]

This shared condition is not only a site of epistemological trauma, as de Man would have it. It is woven out of intersubjective relations of power, pedagogy, and critique, elements that Baudelaire attributes to the social register of the *comique significatif.* As the deployment of cultural frames in the essay suggests, then, irony's reflexivity does not merely posit the self *as* other. It rehearses the opposition between self and other as one between superiority and inferiority, between *bourreau* and *victime,* and thus wrestles with the relations of force that laughter both causes and reveals. The comic reveals the violence of representation, its ability to reshape the reading subject by inducing a fall into reflexivity and laughter, from the passivity of "voir" to the agency of "regarder." This violence is not only represented but also performed: the essay does violence to literary history, to its sources and its intertexts, and most important of all, to the reader, who is coerced into occupying the fallen position of an "Hypocrite lecteur, — mon semblable, — mon frère."

One figure vividly encapsulates the poetics of Baudelairean laughter: the

Pierrot of English pantomime. Baudelaire's portrait of Pierrot's sublime and self-conscious violence resonates with his own writing practice as an epistemological doubling into subject and object, one that also becomes an ethical doubling into executioner and victim. The English Pierrot is noted for the violence of his comic mode, or irony: "je fus excessivement frappé de cette manière de comprendre le comique" (*OC,* 2: 538). He incarnates the *ivresse terrible et irrésistible* of the absolute comic and yet solicits the analytical distance of the signifying comic. While the spectator is swept up by the "vertige de l'hyperbole" incarnated by Pierrot, the latter is also a spectacularly artificial figure. His mask is grafted upon his face "sans gradation, sans transition"; and his painted grimace practically splits his face into two, as if to remind the viewer of his hyperbolic theatricality. Baudelaire describes a scene in which Pierrot's compulsive kleptomania leads him to the guillotine. Once decapitated, his head rolls on stage, "montrant le disque saignant du cou, la vertebre scindée, et tous les détails d'une viande de boucherie récemment taillée pour l'étalage" (*OC,* 2: 539). The monstrous is transformed into a "réalité singulièrement saisissante," hurling the beholder into a visionary—or traumatic—experience of otherness in which common hermeneutic codes have no relevance. Yet, as the display of the butchered head suggests, Pierrot's dismemberment is a dramatic *mise en spectacle* of his persona. The layers constituting his staged body are exposed as constructed pieces for display, as potentially infinite levels of artifice. The visceral impact of the scene, which requires the intuitive grasp of the *comique absolu,* is thus mediated by the exposure of the artificial layers that compose this figure on stage. Pierrot survives the guillotine, and in the madness of pantomime, he even keeps his head, if not on his shoulders, at least stuffed into his pocket: "Mais voilà que, subitement, le torse raccourci, mû par la monomanie irrésistible du vol, se dressait, escamotait victorieusement sa propre tête et . . . la fourrait dans sa poche" (*OC,* 2: 539). Pierrot's refusal to relinquish his head transmits the shock of otherness as well as its demystification, trauma and its analysis, and that sparks points of contact between the fantastic and the real.[57]

"Pourquoi la guillotine au lieu de pendaison en pays anglais ?" Baudelaire conspicuously asks in his report of this scene. The nationalization of Pierrot's death—through the guillotine rather than the gallows—not unlike Virginie's imagined encounter with caricatures of the monarchy's dissolute mores, are ludic gestures toward a revolutionary history that, even after 1851, Baudelaire will continue to evoke in negative, ironical terms.[58] It is also a gesture of complicity with the audience that recasts the atemporal *féerie* of pantomime into a shared historical postrevolutionary context. The frenetic, mute Pierrot, guillotined and resurrected, brandishing his own head, can be read as a figure for the symbolic mutilation of a poetry that renounces its power to transfigure the world through language and instead ironically recollects the symbolic vestiges of past revolutions, from the standpoint of "victime et bourreau."

Like the vertiginous capers of the English pantomime, the text of laughter transmits the trauma of the *comique absolu* yet filters and contextualizes it through the strategies of the *comique significatif,* that is to say, through irony, parabasis, intertextuality and interpellation. The trauma of otherness is thus put into dialogue with familiar frames of reference that spur the recognition of a collective predicament. The reader is incited to occupy both the traumatized position of one who has cognitively "missed" the textual experience and yet been contaminated by its shock, and that of the accomplice to the imposer of textual meaning, to the corruptive violence of the authorial persona (as shown in the example of Virginie's defilement). This alternation between victim and executioner dislodges any stable notion of the subject, to be sure. But the shock of Baudelaire's irony does far more than dispossess this subject of its plenitude. It discloses language's power to shape a reality that is both semiotic and singularly material. For the "réalite singulierement saisissante" of the performance before which the narrator's pen "trembles," like the laughter that erupts from the philosopher's unsteady lips, or Virginie's shock before the offending caricature, alert us to the power of language as a praxis, to the force of signification. Such moments awaken the reader from the passivity of seeing to the agency of looking and point one's gaze to the often violent relations that constitute—and represent—a historical moment.

2 Passages from Form to Politics
Baudelaire's *Le Spleen de Paris*

*Qu'est-ce que l'art pur selon la conception moderne ? C'est créer
une magie suggestive contenant à la fois l'objet et le sujet, le
monde extérieur à l'artiste et l'artiste lui-même.*

Baudelaire, "L'Art philosophique"

In what is celebrated as the defining gesture of literary modernism, Baudelaire declares in his essay "Théophile Gautier [I]" "La poésie ne peut pas, sous peine de mort ou de déchéance, s'assimiler à la science ou à la morale ; elle n'a pas la Vérité pour objet, elle n'a qu'Elle-même" (*OC*, 2: 113). This withdrawal of poetry from the public domain of communication, social utility, and truth claims, its redefinition as constituting its own object of reflection ("elle n'a qu'Elle-même"), seems to defend a formalist program of aesthetic autonomy that originates in Gautier's emancipation of art from moral and sociopolitical exigencies in his preface to *Mlle de Maupin* (1836) and culminates in the symbolist poetics of Mallarmé and Valéry. In this canonical narrative of modernism, Baudelaire ushers in the moment of poetry's virtual "disembodiment," its drift away from the claims of reference, materiality, and history. One need only to open the various textbooks that introduce his poetry in classrooms from the *lycée* to the university to confirm his consecration as the exemplary practitioner of *poésie pure* and of the self-reflexive aesthetic of *l'art pour l'art* that we associate with modernism. Key terms in this canonization of Baudelaire are *correspondances*, imagination as *la reine des facultés*, and *sorcellerie évocatoire* as the alchemical miracle of pure poetry. These principles form the core of his aesthetics and define his legacy for high modernism.[1]

Whereas the previous chapter addressed Baudelaire's recent incarnation as poet of modernity's trauma, this more traditional account of the poet as precursor to high modernism will be my point of entry into a discussion of aesthetic form and its ideological investments in *Le Spleen de Paris*. Baudelaire's aesthetics of *poésie pure* not only places him at the origins of a particular narrative of modernism, but also at the heart of theories of aesthetic modernity's self-reflexive attitude. According to Jürgen Habermas, the term "modernity" names a historical moment characterized by its attempt to define itself from within and to produce sui generis its normative principles. It is also when the aesthetic avant-garde abdicates before the demands of praxis and fails in the public sphere: "Modernity can and will no longer borrow the criteria by which it takes its orientation from the models supplied by another epoch; it has to create its normativity out of itself. Modernity sees itself cast back upon itself without any possibility of escape" (Habermas, *Philosophical Discourse,* 7). For Habermas, postromantic art's retreat from politics in the late nineteenth century is the inevitable consequence of attempting to ground subjectivity from within, and thus to conceive of aesthetic and cultural production ex nihilo. From Baudelaire to the surrealists, the rebellious, transgressive, and hypersensitive "spirit" of modernity neutralized standards of morality and utility, thus radically alienating art from other domains of the life-world. The Baudelairean dandy's perpetual self-fashioning, his loyalty to edicts that are entirely generated from within, and that find no echo in public consensus, is an exemplary recapitulation of modernity's failed attempt to ground normativity from itself.

This critique of modernity as a project whose incompletion is figured in the sterile self-fashioning of the dandy is strikingly similar to Jean-Paul Sartre's indictment of the nineteenth-century literary avant-garde's withdrawal into private self-creation. Sartre's psychobiography of Baudelaire, for instance, takes the *héautontimorouménos* as its guiding motif, illustrating again and again the "puerile" strategies by which Baudelaire will attempt both to seize himself and to create himself through textual production and through the gaze of the other. This self-reflexive predicament, as we observed, is virtually enacted in the *héautontimorouménos,* an "executioner" of the self who puts to death—as it executes—its subjectivity. For Habermas and Sartre, then, the avant-garde's bid for autonomy from the public sphere was primarily reactive. Its exclusive focus on aestheticism and self-fashioning as modes of critical reflection on— and opposition to—the dominant culture merely deepened the rift between the aesthetic, moral, political, and legal spheres. Like the critique of irony's uses for the public sphere discussed in Chapter 1, the avant-garde's retreat into form is often read as leaving us with the dubious legacy of an aesthetic practice at once reified and alienated from the public domain.

In these narratives of modernity through the exemplary modernism of Baudelaire, "art for art's sake" is a compensatory retreat rather than a contestatory intervention. Its formalism carves out an aesthetic realm of absolute sovereignty from within the political and economic pressures of a rapidly evolving urban context. As I suggested earlier, this view of modernism—as a crisis of representation that withdraws poetry from the realm of praxis and historicity—has been unexpectedly revitalized by trauma theory. Of course, the terms theorizing this crisis differ greatly, since one account views this withdrawal as an oppositional gesture displacing the utopian moment, while the other envisions it as a response to traumatic psychic and historical conditions. But these approaches mirror each other, insofar as the referential, communicative, and contextual dimensions of Baudelaire's poetry are diminished, if not dissolved, whether by the deployment of a sovereign imagination or by a textual unconscious. Indeed, I would suggest that a continuous narrative binds the myth of aesthetic autonomy to the more current view of art as testimony to unrepresentable history. This chapter and the next interrogate both narratives by attending to the political valences of Baudelaire's textualization of violence. I argue that modernism's interrogation of reference constitutes a productive critique that resists its later conversion into testimony to ongoing trauma.

Chapter 1 invoked the critical possibilities opened up by Baudelairean irony, possibilities that emerge when texts are approached, not as symptomatic inscriptions of traumatic experience, but as forms of counterviolence that position poetry in relation to the production of historical violence. In this chapter, I examine more specifically the counterviolence harbored in categories of genre, especially when genre itself is ironically deployed as an aesthetic category with particular ideological valences. This first section attends to Baudelaire's concept of *poésie pure,* then goes on to observe how prose poetry turns genre itself into a vehicle for extratextual critique.

If the principle of purity is upheld in Baudelaire's theoretical writings, it is almost always compromised—if not deconstructed—in his poetic practice. As *De l'essence du rire* suggests, while the promise of *poésie pure* may haunt Baudelaire's corpus, it nevertheless almost always emerges out of an impure, fallen, and historical discursive crucible. The most thought-provoking readers of Baudelaire have illuminated how poetry's will to autonomous and self-reflexive formalism is repeatedly foiled by the return of the historical repressed. "Pure poetry" is inevitably contaminated by traces of the material and even economic conditions that it strives to banish from its midst. Yet are Baudelaire's vertiginous deconstructions of aesthetic autonomy simply a *constat d'echec* of poetry's power to co-opt and redeem history? Or can we imagine the deployment and sabotaging of "pure art" as a gesture invested with critical value?

What if the bridge between poetry and the historical were constructed *through* the self-reflexive autonomy that ostensibly evacuates such concerns from poetry? In order to explore this possibility, let us turn to Baudelaire's own articulation of the relationship between pure poetry, irony and history.

Surnaturalisme et ironie

"Deux qualités littéraires fondamentales : surnaturalisme et ironie" (*OC*, 1: 658). In this cryptic definition of literature's fundamental properties, Baudelaire articulates a central tension in his literary practice that may help us to unravel the relationship between *art pur,* irony, and critique. The tension in this declaration is sparked by the ambiguous status of the conjunction *et:* is *surnaturalisme* sustained or unraveled by *ironie?* Are these terms distinct, supplementary, or interchangeable? By *surnaturalisme,* the poet designates a visionary refiguration of the world by the creative imagination, a transformation of things into sensory intensities freed from their representational function: "Le surnaturel comprend la couleur générale et l'accent, c'est-à-dire intensité, sonorité, limpidité, vibrativité, profondeur et retentissement dans l'espace et dans le temps" (ibid.). The vibratory deployment of sound and color across time and space vaporizes reference, creating a dense sensory and analogical network, such as the symbolic forest in "Correspondances." Hugo Friedrich's canonical study of the transition from romanticism to modernism presents *surnaturalisme* as a key principle in Baudelaire's protosymbolist aesthetic precisely because it dissolves phenomenal reality into resonance, asserting thus the primacy of the creative imagination: "Baudelaire désigne du nom de 'surnaturalisme' cet art, né d'une imagination créatrice qui enlève aux choses leur 'choséité,' qui les réduit à des lignes, à des couleurs, à des mouvements désormais indépendants, un art qui jette sur les choses une lumière qui dissout leur réalité dans le mystère."[2]

Baudelaire's *surnaturalisme* celebrates the artist's consciousness as the origin and end of the creative process, as an idealizing force that evacuates the world of its materiality, refiguring it through the metaphoric orchestration of *correspondances.* As such, *surnaturalisme* appears to harmoniously cohabit with *ironie,* understood here in its romantic sense as creativity's conquest of reality. Yet, as "L'Héautontimorouménos" suggests, there is an inevitable tension between the will to creative transcendence and the inscription of critical reflection in the artistic work. Critical reflection mutates into a *vorace ironie* that gnaws into the illusion of imagination's sovereignty over its material conditions. Irony as parabasis, as the inscription of the process through which the poetic vision is constructed, unveils the gap between ideal and actuality. It keeps the poetic subjectivity in a constant oscillation or "double postulation" between *spleen et idéal.*

The tension between *surnaturalisme* and *ironie* raises questions about the nature of self-reflexivity and the status of *art pur* in Baudelaire's poetic practice. As we saw earlier, Baudelairean irony does not empower speculative thought but, instead, topples the creative subject off its hieratic throne in a beheading whose violence is captured in the headless Pierrot of "De l'essence du rire." The oscillation between the creative will to transcendence and the demystifying operations of irony lends Baudelaire's oeuvre its characteristic duality (between spleen and ideal, elevation and fall), a duality traditionally mapped upon a vertical, theological axis. Yet, as we shall see, this oscillation also opens horizontal passages between poetic, political, and cultural preoccupations.

Baudelaire's very formulation of poetry as an exclusion of all things beyond its own self-representation, "La poésie . . . n'a pas la Vérité pour objet, elle n'a qu'Elle-même," purifies the aesthetic by evacuating the very notion of content. As Barbara Johnson has noted, this declaration syntactically enacts the exclusions that it proposes: "Que cet acte d'exclusion et de coupure . . . est en fait *constitutif* de la poésie, la syntaxe des formules baudelairiennes à ce sujet le démontre assez, par la répétition insistante du 'ne . . . que'" (158). Its very articulation strives to carve out a space free from the material as well as moral and political pressures on literary production. The constraining, if not mutilating, tastes of a primarily bourgeois readership and a censorious régime that dragged both Flaubert and Baudelaire into court on charges of *outrage aux bonnes moeurs;* the co-optation of art as just another cultural commodity to be put into the service of utilitarianism, consumption, and pedagogical imperatives (*l'hérésie de l'enseignement*); and the obligation to sell one's texts by the line are some of the more obvious conditions against which pure poetry defined itself.

Baudelaire's declaration of aesthetic autonomy is directed at the postrevolutionary historical scene, the rising tide of democracy under the Second Empire's apparent leveling out of class differences, the bourgeoisie's unparalleled ascendancy, the acceleration of technology, urbanization, industrialism, and consumerism, and the overwhelming jostle of crowds, of *bodies,* in the streets of Haussmannized Paris. Sartre, Benjamin, Bourdieu, and Terdiman, among others, have traced how the transformation of the social field in late nineteenth-century Paris informs the literary avant-garde's retreat from its surrounding culture, an uneasy withdrawal that, for contributors to Gautier's *Le Parnasse contemporain,* such as Baudelaire, but also Leconte de l'Isle, Mallarmé, Banville, and Verlaine, expresses itself as an evacuation of social content from art. Pure poetry's detachment from this social context is a detachment from social content itself, from its degraded materialism and materiality. Baudelaire's gesture has thus quite rightly been read as a withdrawal of poetry from the domain of utility, circulation, and consumption, as an evacuation of content itself and a retreat into a compensatory aestheticism that safeguards artistic integrity and sovereignty. The emancipation of art from political and historical relevance is thus, paradoxically, deeply embedded in the ideological pressures of postrevolutionary society.

In light of this retreat into form, the significance of Baudelaire's participation in the 1848 revolution remains a contested terrain in criticism.[3] For the moment, I shall recall some facts and leave speculation about his intentions and commitments aside. On February 22, Baudelaire had witnessed an unarmed insurgent being bayonneted by municipal soldiers as he attempted to escape; the next evening the poet was in the streets when the shooting on the boulevard des Capucines occurred. He was armed at the barricades on February 24. In Jules Buisson's account, Baudelaire fired his rifle, not for the sake of the republic, but to defy his stepfather, General Aupick, then head of the École polytechnique and representative of the conservative order that the poet sought to demolish.[4] Under the provisional government, Baudelaire founded the *Salut public* with Champfleury, a republican journal that survived for only two issues; he adhered to Blanqui's Société républicaine, and after the April elections, was involved with a democratic, reformist journal, *La Tribune nationale.* During the bloody June days, Baudelaire fought with the insurgents on the barricades, and, an admirer of Pierre-Joseph Proudhon, sought to alert the republican democratic socialist of a plot against his life.[5] After the coup d'état of December 2, 1851, and the elections that legitimated Napoléon III's Second Empire, however, Baudelaire withdrew from the sphere of politics. Claude Pichois points out that those dates correspond to the composition of the famous lines from "Le Reniement de saint Pierre":

> — Certes, je sortirai, quant à moi, satisfait
> D'un monde où l'action n'est pas la soeur du rêve ; (*OC,* 1: 122)

"Le 2 décembre m'a physiquement dépolitiqué," Baudelaire told Narcisse Ancelle in the aftermath of Louis-Napoléon's coup (*Corr.,* 1: 188), indicating how deeply his retreat from politics responded to historical factors. The evacuation of politics from the poet's body is caused by a legitimation crisis in the body politic. Yet Baudelaire later revokes this declaration of immunity when he describes the republican spirit of 1848 as a force circulating in the collective body with the tenacity of a venereal affliction: "Nous avons tous l'esprit républicain dans les veines comme la vérole dans les os. Nous sommes Démocratisés et Syphilisés" (*OC,* 2: 961). This portrait of the republican legacy as an incurable disease suffered by the poet and the body politic alike signals an ongoing tension between pure poetry and historical contamination, between the extraction of politics from the poet's body, *physiquement dépolitiqué* by history in the shape of *le 2 décembre,* and the inescapable contagion of this history's legacy. Such contradictory representations of purification and contamination obviously raise the question of the relationship between the political body and the poetic corpus. It suggests that the familiar story of Baudelaire's exorcism of politics from poetry, and his subsequent retreat into the austere conservatism of Joseph de Maistre and the logic of Edgar Allan Poe, could be told differently.

Despite the gesture of immunity inscribed in the very expression *art pur,* Baudelaire's poetry remains caught in the irresistible contagion of politics. For even after the rupture with politics declared in 1852, signs of the political continue to haunt Baudelaire's later poetic corpus with the enigmatic persistence of scars that refuse erasure. The question, then, is whether these are merely symptoms of poetry's inevitable contamination by the political, or if we can read a more intentional and contestatory relationship between poetry and politics. Let us return to the relationship between purity and impurity in Baudelaire's poetics, this time from the standpoint of genre, to see how the formal reflection on properties of genre might help us answer this question.

Contaminations: Prose Poetry

> *What I propose is to show how Baudelaire lies embedded in the 19th century* [Baudelaire zu zeigen, wie er ins neunzehnte Jahrhundert eingebettet liegt]. *The imprint he has left behind there must stand out clear and intact, like that of a stone which, having lain in the ground for decades, is one day rolled from its place.*
> Walter Benjamin, *The Arcades Project* (April 16, 1938)

> *Profondeur immense de pensée dans les locutions vulgaires, trous creusés par des générations de fourmis.* Baudelaire, "Fusées," I

It is ironic that Benjamin's portrait of Baudelaire's embedding in the nineteenth century's ground should echo the poet's own vision of *lieux communs* as deep holes of collective wisdom dug by generations of ants. Benjamin's metaphor of embedding raises questions about the relationship between literature and its "ground": how is Baudelaire's poetry embedded in its historical terrain, and how do successive, historically embedded readerships in turn recover "the imprint he has left behind there"?[6] Is the poem grounded in its cultural setting like other literary genres and cultural productions? The image of embedding, after all, characterizes a spectrum of cultural objects that Benjamin catalogues as material replica or imprints of bourgeois consciousness in the nineteenth century—the Parisian arcades, fashion, photography, journalism, and dioramas—cultural artifacts that, under scrutiny, reveal the mystifications of high capitalism, the phantasmagoria through which the bourgeoisie concealed the relations of production that sustained it as a class. Is Baudelaire's poetry to be approached as another such artifact, one that unconsciously records and bodies forth the shocks and contradictions of urban modernity?

Baudelaire's fascination with the *locution vulgaire,* the *lieu commun,* the verbal expression that has acquired wisdom, or even, historical memory in its circulation and sedimentation within the social body, betrays an awareness of what his own voice owed to such commonplaces.[7] For if, as Benjamin proposes, his poetry made such an indelible imprint in the nineteenth century's ground, Baudelaire acutely sensed his own indelible shaping by what he purports to exclude. Nowhere is poetry's willful embrace of its surrounding terrain better illustrated than in Baudelaire's prose poetry, described in the preface to *Le Spleen de Paris* as an impure discursive space, the site of a "croisement de rapports" not only between the lyric and prosaic but also between the self and the city, the subjective and the intersubjective: "Quel est celui de nous qui n'a pas, dans ses jours d'ambition, rêvé le miracle d'une prose poétique, musicale sans rythme et sans rime, assez souple et assez heurtée pour s'adapter aux mouvements lyriques de l'âme, aux ondulations de la rêverie, aux soubresauts de la conscience ? C'est surtout de la fréquentation des villes énormes, *c'est du croisement de leurs innombrables rapports* que naît cet idéal obsédant" (*OC,* 2: 275–76; emphasis added). Prose poetry emerges from the crossroads of urban experience, from the multiplicity of bodies and discourses that jostle together in the public sphere. Pure poetry's descent into the commonplace is strikingly conveyed in the prose poem "Perte d'Auréole," where the consecrated poet loses his halo and quite literally *falls* into the *mauvais lieu* of the *lieu commun.*[8]

Since Suzanne Bernard's classic work on the prose poem in France, several compelling studies have suggested that prose poetry critically engages with the tradition and purposes of lyric poetry and simultaneously interrogates the power relations that constitute the social field. Barbara Johnson's *Défigurations du langage poétique* considers the prose poem as a deconstruction of the lyric's claim to unity, autonomy, and totality and implicitly proposes an isomorphic relation between poetry and capital, between rhetoric and praxis that might open up an ideological interrogation through rhetorical analysis. Sonya Stephens's study of Baudelaire examines how irony and other duplicitous discursive strategies in *Le Spleen de Paris* destructure established systems of value and meaning.[9] Richard Terdiman's readings of Baudelaire most explicitly argue that the genre of prose poetry constitutes a counterdiscourse to the hegemonic, dominant bourgeois discourse of the Second Empire: "The prose poem needs examination *from the side of prose:* as a strategy for intervention in the dominant discursive apparatus of the nineteenth century. . . . From this perspective, the reflection on the discursive which the prose poem constituted by problematizing the entire realm of discourse appears as a sophisticated— and deeply subversive—scrutiny of its mechanisms of control, and of their points of potential fracture" (Terdiman, *Discourse/Counter-discourse,* 261).

Terdiman examines how the relatively novel genre of the prose poem harbored a particularly acute consciousness of its historicity, a consciousness that enhanced its capacity for illuminating the naturalization of cultural formations and social realities under the Second Empire. Prose poetry not only calls into question an established rhetoric of genres that defines the field of literature but also conjures up the contestatory possibilities of poetry itself, here endowed with the capacity to produce a critical genealogy of the bourgeoisie's life-world. Terdiman identifies two major strategies for such contestation: absolute counterdiscourse (such as the assertion of *poésie pure*) and recitation (such as Flaubert's *Dictionnaire des idées reçues,* a derisive catalogue of bourgeois platitudes). Yet, he notes that such a counterdiscursive endeavor was continually compromised and contaminated by the very discursive structures it sought to contest.[10] But what if this contamination was a heuristic ploy rather than a symptomatic expression of the semiological disquiet generated by the symbolic crisis of imperial modernity? What if, rather than claiming a distinction between discourse and counterdiscourse, Baudelaire's *Le Spleen de Paris* explored the critical possibilities opened up by the *lack* of distinction between them?

Prosaic Scraps and Urban Debris: The Poet as Ragpicker

In order to probe further into the ideological resonances of such a conception of prose poetry, let us for a moment consider Baudelaire's portrait of the poet as a *chiffonnier,* or ragpicker. In sharp contrast to the Hugolian topos of the poem as ruin, Baudelaire's modern poet is cast as a *chiffonnier* who gathers up the debris disgorged by the modern industrial city. His verbal booty often takes the form of phantasmagorical rememberings sparked by haphazard encounters:

> Je vais m'exercer seul à ma fantasque escrime,
> Flairant dans tous les coins les hasards de la rime,
> Trébuchant sur les mots comme sur les pavés
> Heurtant parfois des vers depuis longtemps rêvés. ("Le Soleil," 1857)

This portrait of the poet-*chiffonnier* interweaves the production of poetry and the collection of refuse. Like the ragpicker, the poet is the keeper of an urban junkyard, an alternative historian who composes the archives of urban waste:

> Tout ce que la grande cité a *rejeté,* tout ce qu'elle a *perdu,* tout ce qu'elle a *dédaigné,* tout ce qu'elle a *brisé,* il le catalogue, il le collectionne. Il compulse les archives de la débauche, le capharnaüm des rebuts. Il fait un triage, un choix intelligent ; il ramasse, comme un avare un trésor, les ordures qui, remâchées par la divinité de l'Industrie, deviendront des objets d'utilité ou de jouissance. . . . Il arrive hochant la tête et butant sur les pavés, comme les jeunes poètes qui passent toutes leurs journées à errer et à chercher des rimes. ("Du vin et du haschisch," in *OC,* 1: 381; emphasis added)

By now, the topoi of the poet as a wandering *chiffonnier* or a drunken vagrant whose poetic inspiration intersects with fragments of urban reality are as familiar as those of the poet as a flâneur or a prostitute. One has to return to contemporary typologies such as the *physiologies* to appreciate the provocation of Baudelaire's analogy.[11] In *Les Français peints par eux-mêmes* (1861), *chiffonniers* are abject figures wholly identified with the refuse that they collect: "Voici des types monstrueux, d'ignobles figures, d'abominables moeurs : la forme, le fond, le dessus, le dessous, tout est pourri chez les chiffonniers."[12] Even in this disgusting portrait (which ends with a defense of the ragpickers' humanity and a plea for their social integration), the analogy between poet and ragpicker is readily discernable: just as the former sifts through the dirt of the city dreaming of "poétiques chenilles," that is to say, rubbish that can be turned into gold, the poet too will go in search of opportunities for the alchemical transformation of mud into gold: "Tu m'as donné ta boue et j'en ai fait de l'or" (*OC,* 1: 192).

Walter Benjamin fully grasped the importance of the *chiffonnier* as an analogue for the poet, and envisioned the ragpicker's activity as a metaphor for Baudelaire's poetic composition, as well as for his own historical mosaic of nineteenth-century Paris:

> This description is one extended metaphor for the procedure of the poet in Baudelaire's spirit. Ragpicker or poet—the refuse concerns both, and both go about their business in solitude at times when the citizens indulge in sleeping; even the gesture is the same in both. Nadar speaks of Baudelaire's "jerky gait" ("*pas saccadé*"). This is the gait of the poet who roams the city in search of rhyme-booty; it must also be the gait of the ragpicker who stops on his path every few moments to pick up the refuse he encounters. (Benjamin, *Charles Baudelaire,* trans. Zohn, 79–80)

But Benjamin's focus on Baudelaire as the last *lyric* poet of modernity leads him to privilege *Les Fleurs du mal* at the expense of the more obvious literary analogue for the poet-as-ragpicker, that is, the prose poems of *Le Spleen de Paris.* Baudelaire's series of prospective titles for this collection underscore the homology between ragpicker and prose poet: "Le Promeneur solitaire," "Le Rodeur parisien," "Poëmes nocturnes," "La Lueur et la fumée," and "Petits poëmes lycanthropiques" were some of the alternate titles entertained by the poet. They convey the image of a figure cast out of Rousseau's edenic nature and wandering through an urban world of light and fog. The poet's incarnations as werewolf, vagrant, and solitary urban wanderer, powerfully conjure up the *chiffonnier*'s abjection, his nocturnal peregrinations in search of salvageable waste. Far from the rhetorical blossoms of *poésie pure,* both ragpicker and prose poet harvest debris from the field of urban modernity itself.

In contrast to the sovereign, subjective realm of pure poetry, then, the prose poem is offered up as a common intersubjective space, the site of a "croisement de rapports" that acknowledges figures of sympathetic or alien identification from the social content. For if the hurtling rhythm of prose poetry grasps the private experience of urban life, it also translates the thickness and motion of voices and of things that lie outside of the self. Just as the *chiffonnier* salvages what the great city as discarded, disdained and smashed ("tout ce que la grande cité a *rejeté*), the prose poem as a genre collects the prosaic minutiae of daily life banished from the citadel of poetry ("tout ce qui se trouve exclu de l'oeuvre rythmée et rimée"). Catalogues of *choses vues,* the prose poems record what would otherwise fall outside of the city's representation and into oblivion. The abject figures haunting the imperial splendor of Haussmann's Paris, those who inhabit "plis sinueux des grandes capitales,"— the beggar, the widow, the *saltimbanque,* the urchin, the prostitute, the *négresse,* and others cast off by capitalist modernity's ideology of progress—are uneasily hosted, if not held hostage, by these texts. The human debris of the industrial empire echo the poet's own condition as an anachronistic figure in exile.

Yet even this portrait of the poet as a melancholy witness to those exiled by modernity does not do justice to the dialectical energy of the prose poet's identifications in *Le Spleen de Paris.* To be sure, a poem such as "Le Cygne" is a powerful example of how allegory rescues "les éclopés de la vie," as Baudelaire calls them in "Les Veuves" (*OC,* 1: 292), and places them in a *musée imaginaire.*[13] But the ironic texture of the prose poems defies a purely melancholy or nostalgic reading. The parallel between poet and ragpicker affords insight into one last but crucial aspect of the politics of Baudelaire's prose poems. Both the poet and the *chiffonnier* collect the precious debris of the modern industrial city, but the *chiffonnier* does so in order to feed this debris back into the urban machinery and its production of commodities: "il ramasse, comme un avare un trésor, les ordures qui, *remâchées par la divinité de l'Industrie, deviendront des objets d'utilité ou de jouissance*" (emphasis added). If the poet is indeed something of a symbolic *chiffonnier,* avidly gathering up the vestiges of modernity's symbolic production, Baudelaire also suggests that he fully participates in the smashing and reassimilation of this urban refuse, in the interwoven violences that make up the social fabric that the poet elsewhere claims to cut out of his poetry. As we shall see in *Le Spleen de Paris,* the poet, like the *chiffonnier,* is complicit with the social violence that names his abjection and is incorporated in the city's daily rhythm of production and consumption. Baudelaire suggests that the poet, whose victimization in terms of social legitimacy and economic survival finds its analogue in the *chiffonnier,* is also a *bourreau,* incorporated into the structural violences of the city itself.

The prose poem as Baudelaire envisioned it is a particularly apt genre for exploring *croisements de rapports,* not only between lyric expansion and urban convulsion, or the cadence of verse and the jolts of prose, but also between the poetic and the political terrains. These *tronçons* at once beckon and challenge historical embeddings. For while the prose poems offer a genealogy of their surrounding terrain, their volatile ironies pulverize the ideological vectors that organize this terrain. Exploiting the contamination of poetic discourse by the prosaic agents of the "locutions vulgaires," *Le Spleen de Paris* unsteadily

grounds itself in the commonplaces, or *lieux communs,* of the postrevolution-
ary historical imagination and its field of cultural productions. The inscription
of such commonplaces presses into visibility the interwoven violences of the
social fabric. They also illuminate the *croisement de rapport* between a violence
intrinsic to art and the production of covert, symbolic violences in the social
field of the Second Empire.

The following analysis of "Une Mort héroïque" examines one particular
croisement, or transgression, that recurs in various poems such as "La Corde,"
"Les Foules," "Assommons les pauvres !" and "L'Invitation au voyage," where
the poetic and political spheres, so often divorced in Baudelaire's theoretical
writings, gradually contaminate and mirror one another. By challenging po-
etry's immunity to politics and ultimately unveiling art's potential complicity
with political power, such texts contest the absolute claims of both aesthetic
and ideological sovereignty. In "Une Mort héroïque," contamination, para-
doxically enough, is what opens up the ethico-political dimension of Baude-
laire's prose poetry. The refusal of an aesthetic that would remain autonomous
from the collective pathology, of a *poetically* depoliticized work, enables this
poem to point toward historical shifts in the representation of political sover-
eignty and to probe the paths that remain open to a contestatory poetics.

Conspiratorial Poetics in Baudelaire's "Une Mort héroïque"

"Une Mort héroïque" stages what appears to be an antagonistic struggle be-
tween the aesthetic and the political realms, embodied, respectively, in a jester
and a prince. Fancioulle, the prince's favorite jester and almost his friend, con-
spires against his sovereign and is denounced. He is commanded to perform
in a pantomime that may win him clemency. Yet at the moment the histrion
reveals himself to be a consummate artist, whose power exceeds that of his sov-
ereign, the prince orders one of his pages to blow a whistle so shrill that it in-
terrupts the performance and causes the artist to drop dead on stage. Despite
the apparent antithesis between despot and artist—or executioner and vic-
tim—that could be inferred from the poetic plot, the boundaries between the
aesthetic and the political are blurred, if not collapsed, throughout the poem.
Indeed, the opposition between the prince and Fancioulle systematically in-
verts the exigencies of the political and aesthetic domains. Fancioulle, the
court jester, is "voué par état au comique," a condition that "despotically" im-
presses political ideas of liberty and nation upon his brain, and leads him into
the conspiracy. The prince, himself an accomplished dreamer and aesthete, re-

verses the exigencies between the comic and the serious (a dichotomy that also opposes art to politics) by imposing a rule of "plaisir et étonnement" in his own state. The very conception of an "état," then, is defined entirely by its transgression: Fancioulle transgresses into the political domain just as the prince transgresses into the aesthetic realm. These transgressions define their identities and positions vis-à-vis both the stage and the state, presenting from the outset the stage and the state as parallel sites for the performance of power.

These reversals between the aesthetic and political states pivot upon the reiterated disjunction between one's "facultés" and one's "état." The emphasis on this recurrent disjunction is crucial, for it reveals the common goal of both artistic and political projects: the fusion of one's inner possibilities (or imagination) and one's outer circumstance. The artist's embattled relationship to a given empirical predicament strives toward the imaginary fusion of "facultés" and "états" in the work of art. This coincidence between inner possibility and outer circumstance has its political analogues, for example, in republican idealism. Indeed, the infinitely renewed reconciliation of one's faculties with one's social conditions in a republic whose sovereignty fully reflects the collective will is the very premise of the incurable political utopianism both repudiated and perversely celebrated by Baudelaire. Several poems in *Le Spleen de Paris* are satirical deflations of this idealism and point out the irreconcilable gap between one's "facultés" and one's "états." "Assommons les pauvres !" for instance, likens the beggar's impotent gaze, "un de ces regards inoubliables qui culbuteraient les trônes, *si l'esprit remuait la matière*," to both the poet's idealizing imagination and the socialist theories of 1848.[14] The poet's physical assault upon the beggar demystifies such utopian celebrations of the sovereign imagination or of mind's ability to move matter. In "Une Mort héroïque," the authoritarian despot and the conspiring artist share the conviction that imagination can materialize itself in the world. Yet both figures are defined by the discrepancy between their imagination and their empirical circumstance. The emergence of their identities through the tension between "faculté" and "état," rather than through identifiable roles and positions (subject and sovereign, victim and executioner, artist and despot, actor and spectator), complicates the distribution of power in the poem. The parallels between the prince and the artist-conspirator map a peculiar convergence of aesthetic and political forms of sovereignty.

Indeed, the prince initially occupies both the position of the artist who transfigures his empirical predicament into a stage for the play of his aesthetic faculties and, paradoxically, that of the disempowered political subject thwarted by the discrepancy between his inner possibilities and his finite outer circumstances: "Le grand malheur de ce Prince fut qu'il n'eut jamais un théâtre assez vaste pour son génie. . . . L'imprévoyante Providence avait donné à celui-ci *des facultés plus grandes que ses États*" (*OC,* 1: 320; emphasis added). A similar discrepancy defines Fancioulle, whose faculties lead him astray into a state that is not his own: "Mais pour les personnes vouées par état au comique, les choses sérieuses ont de fatales attractions" (319). Moreover, when the prince summons the jester to perform for his life, Fancioulle moves from the wings of conspiracy to the center of the stage—his proper domain—to demonstrate how his imaginative, *artistic* faculties will relate to his state as the prince's doomed *political* subject: "Il [le Prince] voulait profiter de l'occasion pour faire une expérience physiologique d'un intérêt *capital,* et vérifier jusqu'a quel point les *facultés* habituelles d'un artiste pouvaient être *altérées* ou *modifiées* par la situation extraordinaire où il se trouvait" (320; some emphases added). The dis*location* of art and politics in the poem foregrounds their equal status as competitors for agency and ascendancy over the givenness of empirical conditions, thus calling into question the very distinction between these domains.

If Fancioulle as conspirator is reminiscent of Baudelaire during the active phase of his republicanism in 1848, the prince incarnates the sovereign indifference and aestheticism of the poet as dandy. He is "Assez indifférent relativement aux hommes et à la morale" and *therefore* "véritable artiste lui-même." The prince thus offers a striking contrast to the alienated and impotent figurations of the artist in poems such as "Le Vieux Saltimbanque" or "Le Mauvais Vitrier." His domain is a powerful, albeit incomplete, attempt at realizing the aesthetic ideal of *surnaturalisme* and of *art pur.* Here, however, the vehicle for an ideal transcendence of empirical conditions is the *political* state.

Baudelaire's definition of pure art as a self-reflexive "magie suggestive contenant à la fois le sujet et l'objet, le monde extérieur à l'artiste et l'artiste lui-même" is radicalized in "Une Mort héroïque" as the inscription of the prince's desires ("facultés") upon his domain ("états"). The aestheticization of politics, implicit in the portrait of a state as a theater "governed" by the sovereign's imagination, is a powerful echo of Baudelaire's celebratory representations of the aesthetic process through the rhetoric of political sovereignty. In the Salon of 1859, for instance, imagination, "cette reine des facultés," is an absolute sovereign that creates and governs the world (*OC,* 2: 623). The political incarnation of imagination's power in "Une Mort héroïque," however, is a critical moment illuminating the absolutist violence of the artistic and political sovereign. The seamlessness of the prince's tyranny is explicitly established by the narrator's comment that "les efforts bizarres qu'il faisait pour fuir ou pour vaincre ce tyran du monde [l'Ennui] lui auraient certainement attiré, de la part d'un historien sévère, l'épithète de « monstre », s'il avait été permis, dans ses domaines, d'écrire quoi que ce fût qui ne tendît pas uniquement au plaisir ou à l'étonnement." Writing that does not conform to the royal text of pleasure and surprise and that may testify to the sovereign's monstrosity is occulted or erased just as Fancioulle's fellow conspirators are erased from life itself—"effacés de la vie."

Still, a conspiracy did manage to form within the fissures of the royal domain, and while Fancioulle's political opposition has failed, his symbolic opposition when he appears on stage challenges the sovereign's political authority precisely because the artist's own faculties (unlike the prince's) *do* momentarily transcend his state. The locus of opposition thus shifts from the wings of conspiracy to the center of the spectacle. The prince may not have been unstaged by the conspiracy, but he is symbolically upstaged by Fancioulle during the performance.[15] If aesthetic and political performances mirror each other in their common pursuit of the fusion between one's "facultés" and one's "états," Fancioulle's pantomime, a "chef d'oeuvre d'art vivant" is a triumph that eclipses the despot. The authority of his performance is even more powerful over his spectators than that of the prince over his subjects, who, after all, have conspired against him. The narrator points out the structural similarity between political and aesthetic performances when he speculates that the prince is envious of the histrion's despotic grip on his audience: "Se sentait-il vaincu dans son pouvoir de despote ? humilié dans son art de terrifier les coeurs et d'engourdir les esprits ?" Despotism, the absolute mastery over one's circumstances and subjects, is thus disclosed as common to both aesthetic and political constructions.

Fancioulle's consummate spectacle temporarily pits aesthetic mastery against political subjugation, and despite the contamination effected between these two realms, we now have a hierarchy that briefly ruptures the prince's "experience physiologique," for the subject performing under the threat of capital punishment here incarnates his own contestatory law. Fancioulle momentarily embodies the victory of the symbolic over the political, or, rather, the victory of one's "facultés" over one's "état." His pantomime is "une parfaite idéalisation." The absolute fusion between self and ideal turns the spectacle into a transcendental buffoonery in which the histrion soars above the conditions of his performance. Portrayed by the narrator in metaphysical terms as a defiant consciousness who infinitely recreates the world according to his own edicts, Fancioulle embodies a pure, untrammeled and unrepresentable self-invention: "Fancioulle introduisait . . . le divin et le surnaturel, jusque dans les plus extravagantes bouffonneries."[16] Yet this spectacular idealization is also a powerful gesture of political defiance. Fancioulle's bodily translation of a "paradis excluant toute idée de tombe ou de destruction" creates an imaginary state over which the prince's power has no bearing. Transfiguring temporality into infinity, mortality into the divine and the immutable, the jester's flawless mimesis of life becomes a contestatory fiction that masters death itself through irony ("qui bouffonnait si bien la mort"). This fiction challenges the basis of the prince's "expérience physiologique" by disregarding its very conditions (the sovereign's power over a subject's life or death). Fancioulle thus performs his own "expérience physiologique": the sublime enactment of a utopian state beyond the prince's law.

The central question raised by the pantomime, then, is whether art can provide a lasting symbolic contestation of the ruling order. Does Fancioulle's utopic fiction allegorize art's transcendence of official hegemony, or does it instead suggest that art's resistance to power is a mystification? Perhaps we should reframe the question and ask if Fancioulle's imaginative sovereignty matches the prince's real political power. The narrator, significantly, punctures the perfection of the pantomime's metaphoricity (in which being fuses with fiction) by displacing the *symbolic* representation of Fancioulle's body (as a seamless and absolute incarnation of freedom and aesthetic sovereignty) with an *allegorical* one. This subtle shift occurs in the allusion to the artist's halo, visible to the narrator alone, "où se mêlaient, dans un étrange amalgame, les rayons de l'Art et la gloire du Martyre." The amalgamation of art and martyrdom in what was until now a victory of metaphoricity over empirical conditions, marks a shift from symbolic to allegorical representation and interrogates the status of Fancioulle's symbolic transcendence.[17] However victorious the histrion's transfiguration of life into fiction may be, its price is death. The doubleness of the halo prefigures the doubleness of Fancioulle's position prior to the fatal whistle. The sovereign of his imaginary state on stage, he nevertheless remains the subject of the prince's own experimental stage *and* state. The fragility of the fictional world, its inextricable link to a broader frame of reference including its reception, is such that a whistle of disapproval ruptures the act and executes the actor. The poem thus offers a shimmering vision of aesthetic transcendence only to revoke it.

As in "L'Héautontimorouménos," an excursion into Edgar Allan Poe's work

opens up the full significance of Baudelaire's decision to establish a specular re-
lationship between artist and sovereign—hence unraveling the expected op-
position between victim and executioner—and yet, to end on the artist's
dethronement. Poe's "Hop Frog," published in 1849 and translated by the
French poet in 1855—eight years before "Une Mort héroïque" appeared in *La
Revue nationale et étrangère*—is a central intertext, if not even a "pre-text," for
Baudelaire's prose poem. One could argue that a more significant intertextual
translation occurs in the prose poem, which rewrites Poe's scenario in terms
that irrevocably dislocate the opposition between despot and conspirator.
"Hop Frog" narrates the conspiratorial revenge of a dwarf and court jester
upon a tyrannical king who has struck his companion. Compelled by the king
to devise an ingenious costume for his courtiers and himself for a masquerade,
Hop Frog disguises them as eight chained orangutans. During the festivities,
amidst the general panic caused by the appearance of the orangutans, a con-
traption lifts the king and his men up, and Hop Frog sets them on fire, before
escaping, presumably to his native land.

Hop Frog's origins and character are as enigmatic as Fancioulle's, yet unlike
Baudelaire's histrion, Poe's protagonist—a disfigured dwarf—is portrayed as
utterly foreign to the court's norms. Whereas Fancioulle, as "presque un des
amis du Prince," has an ambiguous proximity to power, Hop Frog, the king's
property, is only a commodity, whose monstrosity enhances his value: "Sa
valeur était triplée aux yeux du roi par le fait qu'il était à la fois nain et boi-
teux."[18] In Poe's tale, the opposition between "victime" and "bourreau" is ini-
tially absolute and then systematically reversed according to a carnivalesque
logic that is sustained to the last spectacular *dévoilement,* when the jester sets
the king and his courtiers alight as retribution for their cruelty. Although ini-
tially Hop Frog is but a hobbling dwarf, closer to beast than man, man and
beast exchange places in a neat inversion. Indeed, while the king promises the
dwarf humanity in exchange for his ingenious plot—"Hop Frog ! nous ferons
de toi un homme !" (177)—it is the dwarf who uses the orangutan costume to
unmask the king's bestiality and thereby reclaim his humanity for himself.
Baudelaire's translation of the text indicates his awareness of its ironies, for
whereas Poe merely writes that the buffoon tied the king and his men together,
the translation reads "On se procura une longue chaine. D'abord on la passa
autour de la taille du roi et on l'y *assujetit*" (178). Baudelaire italicizes the verb
assujetir in a brilliant swerve that illuminates the king's unsuspecting subjuga-
tion before the dwarf and suggests that his apish disguise discloses his true sta-
tus as subject.

Not only does Hop Frog engineer the script of this performance, but it is he who whistles and then vociferously asserts his status as conspirator, demystifier, and executioner before the stunned court: "Maintenant, dit-il, je vois *distinctement* de quelle espèce sont ces masques. Je vois un grand roi et ses sept conseillers privés, un roi qui ne se fait pas scrupule de frapper une fille sans défense, et ses sept conseillers, qui l'encouragent dans son atrocité. Quant à moi, je suis simplement Hop-Frog le bouffon, et *ceci est ma dernière bouffonnerie !*" (181).

Hop Frog's denunciation is as vocal as Fancioulle's pantomime is silent. The repeated assertion of his privileged vision and of his identity finds no echo in Baudelaire's text, where instead, opposition—both covert in the form of the conspiracy and spectacular in the form of the dumb show—has literally been silenced. The central distinction between these two parables is symbolized by Hop Frog's flight and conjectured return to the native land from which he was abducted. The histrion's flight indicates a separation of spheres between his own "state" and the sovereign's. Fancioulle, however, is part of the prince's nation and conspires for its sake, his powers as artist structurally mirror the sovereign's political power. Moreover, his very identity emerges only as a fluctuating tension between his "facultés" and his "états" within the prince's domain. It is hardly surprising, given Fancioulle's existence *as* his role, that the rupture of mimesis should lead to death. Much like the shock of laughter described in Baudelaire's "De l'essence du rire," the page's whistle shatters the mime's fictional self-representation and hurls him back into an empirical, intersubjective, and censored realm. The disjunction between "facultés" and "états," between the imaginary contestation and its historical frame, is absolute. Baudelaire's significant swerves from Poe's carnivalesque logic, his contamination of the aesthetic by the political, stage the loss of a prophetic mode of denunciation and suggest the absence of an autonomous or even a distinct sphere from which social reality can be rearticulated. The utopic state for which Fancioulle conspires and that he then embodies is so fragile, so inextricably bound to the context of the performance, that the whistle of a mere page suffices to destroy it. Representation cannot sever itself from the conditions of its articulation and of its reception. The mystification of a contestation that strives for autonomy is punished by death.

Fancioulle's fleeting metaphoric freedom is a vivid illustration of Baudelaire's conception of "art pur" and of imagination's absolute sovereignty over the empirical world. In sabotaging its triumph, the whistle seems to figure Baudelaire's own "dédoublement" into the executioner and victim of an aesthetics of *surnaturalisme*. One could even say that Fancioulle's death figures a kind of poetic suicide, transforming the prose poem into a "gibet symbolique où pendait mon image," to quote from "Voyage à Cythère" (*OC,* 1: 119). In what follows, I shall examine the alternative poetic voice that emerges from this self-decapitation and argue that the whistle interrupting Fancioulle's spectacle, like the Stendhalian "coup de pistolet au milieu d'un concert," ushers in the politics occluded by the prince's *régime.* I hope to show that the narrator refigures the oppositional politics so spectacularly—and suicidally—embodied by the mime into a conspiratorial poetics.

The narrator's ambiguous testimony reflects, *en abyme,* a general crisis of reading in the kingdom itself, where "truth" is the unreadable product of a performance of power. Indeed, the court's "esprits superficiels" are explicitly indicted for their naïve reading of the prince's plot, as a "signe évident" of his clemency. Even more striking is the audience's response to Fancioulle's performance. The mime's sublime convulsions are in turn mimed by the audience: "Les explosions de la joie et de l'admiration ébranlèrent à plusieurs reprises les voûtes de l'édifice avec l'énergie d'un tonnerre continu." The spectators' response is an immediate, visceral surrender to the performance's seduction. Their unquestioning, collective prostitution is underlined by the erotic vocabulary of *volupté, abandon, enivrement, convulsion:* "Chacun s'abandonna, sans inquiétude, aux voluptés multipliées que donne la vue d'un chef d'oeuvre d'art vivant."

The narrator himself participates momentarily in the court's submissive and deluded reception, for the mime's sublime incarnation of art precludes a detached and analytical reading. Significantly, the pantomime remains a mystery at the core of the text, and the narrator can only allude to the resistance of such an ineffable "physiological" experience to linguistic figuration: "Ma plume tremble, et des larmes d'une émotion toujours présente me montent aux yeux pendant que je cherche à vous décrire cette inoubliable soirée." It is an experience before which writing, and language itself, falters and is silenced, leaving the body's response (the infinitely renewed tears) as testimonies to its power.

Fancioulle's hyperbolic, unrepresentable performance and the narrator's own untranslatable witnessing, exemplify Baudelaire's conception of the *comique absolu,* a category that elucidates the competing oppositional positions in "Une Mort héroïque." Fancioulle's dumb show is a virtual reenactment of the English pantomime evoked in "De l'essence du rire." Just as the narrator's pen trembles before Fancioulle's ineffable performance, the analyst of the essay mourns his pen's inability to transcribe the spectacle's hyperbolic vertigo: "Avec une plume tout cela est pâle et glacé. Comment la plume pourrait-elle rivaliser avec la pantomime ?" (*OC*, 2: 540).

As discussed in the preceding chapter, Baudelaire's distinction between the *comique absolu* and the *comique significatif* hinges upon the question of legibility and translation. The absolute comic, denoting man's superiority over nature, is akin to *l'art pur*, for it marks imagination's transcendence of empirical conditions. The "ivresse terrible et irrésistible" performed both by the English Pierrot and Fancioulle engenders a rapturous vertigo in which the spectator is lost in the performance. Whereas the absolute comic "se présente sous une espèce une" and thus incarnates a symbolic fusion of signifier and signified that is intuitively grasped, the *comique significatif*, addressing man's superiority over man, is a hieroglyphic, analytical, and temporal expression requiring reflection and judgment from the viewer.[19]

Baudelaire's distinction between the *comique absolu* and the humbler *comique significatif* may be mapped onto the oppositional strategies of "Une Mort héroïque" to illuminate the historical significance of the narrator's conspiratorial voice. Baudelaire characterizes the absolute comic as "Les créations fabuleuses, les êtres dont la raison, la légitimation ne peut pas être tirée du code du sens commun" (*OC*, 2: 535).[20] Fancioulle's living masterpiece ("un chef d'oeuvre d'art *vivant*" [emphasis added]) opens a vision of absolute otherness. In bringing to life an experience that defies "le code du sens commun," he voids the prince's reign of its legitimacy and imposes his own self-legitimating sovereignty. Yet, the visionary "ivresse" is precariously located in a historical, political, and collective reality that shatters its contestatory power.

If Fancioulle's performance incarnates Baudelaire's celebrated *comique absolu*, the narrator, instead, offers a different oppositional discursive strategy modeled on the *comique significatif*, one attentive both to the conditions of its articulation and its reception. As we saw in Chapter 1, the *comique significatif* is characterized by doubleness—"l'art et l'idée morale," and by deferral—"le rire après coup." Not only a more analytical form of communication, the *comique significatif* also addresses a common frame of reference, *le code commun*. Whereas the absolute comic personified by Fancioulle indicates man's superiority over nature (the mime's ability to veil the abyss of death through art), the *comique significatif* is contextual, occurring in an intersubjective realm of power relations, and hence more suited to political negotiation. It is precisely through intertextuality and irony, both of which share the structure of doubleness and deferral characteristic of the *comique significatif*, that the narrator inscribes his contestatory testimony.[21]

In contrast to the symbolic fusion of Fancioulle's pantomime, the narrator articulates the gap between an act and its possible significances, as we saw in his allegorical presentation of Fancioulle's halo. His translation of the prince's physionomical shifts juxtaposes yet another frame upon the prince's "expérience physiologique": the sovereign subject observing the jester's body becomes the object of the narrator's gaze. The narrator's privileged insights, both into the recesses of the sovereign's mind and into the doubleness of Fancioulle's spectacle (as sovereign of his imaginary state and subject of the prince) turn him into an ambiguous accomplice for both figures. An impotent witness to the scenario that unfolds, he is nevertheless its sole agent of transmission, since neither historian nor histrion may record or denounce the prince's tyranny. Yet his pen falters at every turn, trembling before the spectacle and erasing its testimony in a repeated gesture of self-censorship. Indeed, the narrator's conjectures on the prince's motives are parodically voided by remarks such as "C'est un point qui n'a jamais pu être éclairci"; "Le Prince avait-il lui-même deviné l'homicide efficacité de sa ruse ? Il est permis d'en douter"; "De telles suppositions non exactement justifiées mais non exactement injustifiables." These self-erasing speculations suggest the complex negotiations of an oppositional voice striving to be heard in a censored domain.

The final conjecture is crucial in this regard, for, through the double voice of intertextuality, it performs a complicitous subversion of the prince's discursive rule. Amidst a tyrannical reign of "plaisir et étonnement," which either co-opts serious contestation or erases it, the narrator 's cautious rhetoric evokes yet another critical intertext: "[Le Prince] regretta-t-il son cher et inimitable Fancioulle ? Il est doux et légitime de le croire." The citation from Horace—"Dulce et decorum est pro patria mori"—is all the more powerful for its truncation. The gaping absence of both nation and death in this formulation ("il est doux et légitime de . . . croire," that the prince regretted his jester) denounce the travesty that the capricious sovereign's stage makes of the state. The translation of *decorum* into the politically loaded term "légitime" underscores what Virginia Swain has called the "legitimation crisis" performed by the poem, a crisis that ripples out to encompass the postrevolutionary body politic.[22] The fragmented Horatian intertext resurrects the "serious" national ideal for which the jester and his fellow conspirators die at the same time that the decapitation of politics is textually performed by the narrator's fragmented testimony. Such a double gesture restores the political opposition erased by the official discourse, just as the final italicized word of the poem, *faveur,* alludes to the *droits* denied to the prince's subjects ("Depuis lors, plusieurs mimes, justement appréciés dans différents pays, sont venus jouer devant la cour de *** ; mais aucun d'eux n'a pu . . . s'élever jusqu'à la même *faveur.*" The "expérience physiologique" conducted in the poem is indeed "d'un intérêt capital," for it fully implicates the head of the political body.

In his correspondence, Baudelaire makes two intriguing references to possible versions of "Une Mort héroïque." The first is in a letter to Gustave Rouland, where he alludes to a project entitled "Aperçu historique sur le Conspirateur et le Favori" (*Corr.,* 1: 405); the second, two years later, to Auguste Poulet-Malassis, announces: "Enfin j'ai fait une *nouvelle* basée sur l'hypothèse : découverte d'une conspiration par un oisif, qui la suit jusqu'à la veille de l'explosion, et qui alors tire à pile ou face pour savoir s'il la déclarera à la police" (*Corr.,* 1: 584). The prose poem retains the terms of these *ébauches,* yet departs from them at several points. The conspirator is *favored* by the prince, and the historical parameters of the tale seem erased. Moreover, the oscillation between complicity and denunciation described in the letter to Poulet-Malassis is presented from the stance of an absolutely disengaged flâneur, who bears no allegiance to the state or to the conspirators and yet can determine the destinies of both. The narrator of the prose poem, however, is denied any direct intervention. His speculative faltering seems to mimic Fancioulle's own dying convulsions. Yet as I have argued, the narrator inscribes his own oppositional stance through the tactics of the *comique significatif,* through complicity, irony, and intertextuality. In tracing the failure of absolute aesthetic sovereignty, personified by the mime, the political state as the incarnation of an individual's despotic consciousness, one structurally akin to artistic transcendence, is also shown in all its frailty and illegitimacy.[23]

"Une Mort héroïque" may be closer to the "aperçu *historique* sur le Conspirateur et le Favori" described to Rouland than it appears at first glance. The portrait of the prince's carefully crafted reign of censorship resonates with the Second Empire's tight system of surveillance (the discretionary measures of the Sûreté générale) and censorship to counter the threat of republican conspiracies.[24] It also puts on trial the republican ideological legacy. The utopic homology between "facultés" and "états," upheld by the revolutionaries as the cornerstone of a nascent democracy, is systematically evoked, only to be ironically suppressed in the poem. Moreover, the displacement of *droits* by the arbitrariness of *faveur* replaces the revolutionary promise of collective sovereignty with an ancien régime form of despotism, opposition to which costs the conspirators their lives. And it is precisely through a textual self-immolation, through the sabotage of aesthetic sovereignty and autonomy, that the narrator—with the deftness of a textual conspirator—resuscitates in fragments the utopian politics embodied by Fancioulle.

While "Une Mort héroïque" indicts the Second Empire's masked despotism and conspiratorially alludes to the republican ideals it co-opted or censored, the very definitions of despotism and resistance are considerably complicated. The structural complicities between aesthetic and political sovereignty collapses the very possibility of an oppositional stance toward the state's englobing power. The fissure made by Fancioulle's contestatory spectacle is sealed by his death, leaving the task of conspiratorial witnessing to the narrator. Yet, in an even more disturbing turn, the poem discloses a gaping absence at the heart of the mechanism of state power. Authority is cut loose from a governing agency, for both Fancioulle and the prince are ultimately subject to the vagaries of an indeterminate authority, an "imprévoyante providence." The prince is haunted by a law greater than his own, *Ennui:* "il ne connaissait d'ennemi dangereux que l'Ennui . . . ce tyran du monde." Similarly, Fancioulle is daemonically possessed by politics "bien qu'il puisse paraître bizarre que les idées de patrie et de liberté s'empare despotiquement du cerveau d'un histrion." *Ennui* fractures the desired equivalence between the sovereign's imagination and an aestheticized politics, just as the page's whistle shatters the jester's embodiment of a politicized fiction.

In light of this diffusion of intention and agency, it is crucial to remember that the free state beyond censorship and capital punishment performed by Fancioulle is "executed" (if indeed the whistle was of homicidal intent) not by the prince but by an unsuspecting young proxy, a blank page of sorts. This dislocation of agency also disrupts the opposition between artist and sovereign, or "victime et bourreau." Just as Fancioulle's political commitment is the result of floating ideological principles (of freedom and of nation) "despotically" capturing the histrion's brain, the prince's act of punishment is carried out without a clearly intending agent and executioner. The narrator's question, "Le sifflet, rapide comme un glaive, avait-il réellement frustré le bourreau ?" suggests that the shrill whistle preempts the hiss of the guillotine's blade, that censorship is akin to capital punishment. Yet the source of this punishment is displaced onto the lips of a blind executionary agent.

The displacement of individual agency by an unpredictable and mindless form of collective complicity can be traced from the beginning of the poem. The bewitched spectators' thunderous applause before Fancioulle's performance on stage echoes their absorption into the prince's state; their faith in the power of signs makes them unwitting accomplices to the perpetuation of absolute power, aesthetic or political. The pervasive complicity staged in the poem between the tyrant and his subjects mirrors the collective legitimation of Napoléon III's reign through a plebiscite that cloaked the empire with the mystique of popular sovereignty. The court's delighted passivity before the aesthetic and political performances of power recalls the consent of seven million Frenchmen to the legitimation of a régime whose "extraordinary measures," implemented by the discretionary powers of the Sûreté générale, led to 20,000 arrests and deportations.[25] Baudelaire's rage at his compatriots' blind consent to the empire's despotism is recorded in a passage that testifies to the eclipse of direct modes of opposition in the paradoxical context of an authoritarian democracy:

> En somme, devant l'histoire et devant le peuple français, la grande gloire de Napoléon III aura été de prouver que le premier venu peut, en s'emparant du télégraphe et de l'Imprimerie nationale, gouverner une grande nation.
>
> Imbéciles sont ceux qui croient que de pareilles choses peuvent s'accomplir sans la permission du peuple, — et ceux qui croient que la gloire ne peut être appuyée que sur la vertu.
>
> Les dictateurs sont les domestiques du peuple, — rien de plus, — un foutu rôle d'ailleurs, — et la gloire est le résultat de l'adaptation d'un esprit avec la sottise nationale. (*OC*, 1: 692)

For the poet, the dislocation, or quite literally, *decapitation* of power, its dissemination into the social field, dooms the possibility of a reflective and consensual democracy. Instead, politics, like the syphilitic contagion of republicanism, has been voided of all contestatory force and has mutated into an impersonal plague, whose circulation collapses any possible distinction between despot and subject, or "dictateur" and "domestique." Neither dictator nor subject is an agent in this social organism. They are blind participants in the construction of a mass delusion—"la sottise nationale"—in the fiction of a democratic nation. Baudelaire's paradoxical vision of this authoritarian democracy, where dictator and crowds converge through new systems of representation and communication, ominously foreshadows emerging forms of power, forms that can no longer be identified and contested from a vantage point of separation and knowledge.

The decentering of power and the intricate web of complicity in "Une Mort héroïque" suggest that the dissenting voice has no room for resistance or opposition. It must choose between suicidal defiance or conspiratorial complicity. The poem ultimately points to the erasure of politics as an arena for contestation. The catastrophic vision of history and progress recorded elsewhere in Baudelaire's notebooks is testimony to the poet's prescience. In his prophetic account of historical progress, Baudelaire describes the teeming urban crowds as blind accomplices to unforeseen strains of tyranny that breed in the ruins of an oppositional political culture:

> Ai-je besoin de dire le *peu qu'il restera de politique* se débattra péniblement dans l'étreinte de l'animalité générale, et que les gouvernants seront forcés, pour se maintenir et pour créer un fantôme d'ordre, de recourir à des moyens qui feraient frissoner notre humanité actuelle, pourtant si endurcie ? . . . — Ces temps sont peut-être bien proches ; qui sait même s'ils ne sont pas venus, et si l'épaississement de notre nature n'est pas le seul obstacle qui nous empêche d'apprécier le milieu dans lequel nous respirons !
>
> Quant à moi, qui sens quelquefois en moi le ridicule d'un prophète, je sais que je n'y trouverai jamais la charité d'un médecin. Perdu dans ce vilain monde, coudoyé par les foules, je suis comme un homme lassé dont l'oeil ne voit en arrière, dans les années profondes, que désabusement et amertume, et devant lui qu'un orage où rien de neuf n'est contenu, ni enseignement, ni douleur. (*OC,* 1: 666–67; emphasis added)

In 1939, Walter Benjamin's commentary on this passage elucidated its prophetic insight into the modern face of political tyranny: "Nous ne sommes déjà pas si mal placés pour convenir de la justesse de ces phrases. Il y a bien des chances qu'elles gagneront en sinistre. . . . Est-il trop audacieux de prétendre que ce sont ces mêmes foules qui, de nos jours, sont pétries par les mains des dictateurs ?"[26] The convergence of archaic despotism in "Une Mort héroïque" and a disseminated circulation of power that nevertheless *conserves* the prince's absolute sovereignty suggest that it would not in turn be too audacious to trace a similar foreshadowing in Baudelaire's prose poem.

The "expérience physiologique d'un intérêt *capital*" conducted in "Une Mort héroïque" probes the pathologies of power at multiple levels, implicating the political and poetic bodies while also tracing the convergences between old and new forms of authoritarianism. The *mise en spectacle* of symbolic authority, both held and lost by Fancioulle and the prince, is a powerful interrogation of the mythic autonomy of political and aesthetic constructions. The narrator's wily rhetorical shifts in conspicuously pressing to the margins the subversive political content of the tale suggest that if no separate symbolic sphere may exist for contesting such forms of power, the voice of conspiracy, relying on the contamination of art and politics, as well as of text and intertext, can craftily inscribe its opposition. This is indeed a "capital" experience, for that which is of utmost importance can only be uttered at the cost of one's head. If both symbolic opposition and covert conspiracy are doomed to failure, textual conspiracy, by intertwining the political and the poetic and sacrificing the dream of aesthetic autonomy, points the way to a new poetics of opposition, one that vigilantly traces the complicity between aesthetic and political performances.[27]

The Rhetorical Legacy of the Revolution

> *Toute révolution a pour corollaire le massacre des innocents.*
> Baudelaire, quoted above a portrait of him by Nadar in 1854

Baudelaire's oeuvre is suffused with allusions to the legacy of the Revolution. His ambivalence about his past republican fervor in 1848 manifests itself in vengeful outbursts that confront the utopianism of revolutionary rhetoric with the bankruptcy of actual social and political practice. The prose poems in particular ironically recollect the linguistic vestiges of the Revolution—its vocabulary of liberty, equality, fraternity, concord, and *patrie*—in order to expose their travestied afterlife in the bourgeois order of the Second Empire. The presence of such rhetoric has frequently been read as symptomatic of a failed attempt to transcend the omnipresent and omnivorous political vocabulary of his time. Linda Orr shows, for instance, how the poet's repugnance toward 1848 (a repugnance shared by Marx and Flaubert) was a fruitless attempt to exorcise the language of Robespierre, Proudhon, and Michelet. Orr argues that such ostentatious disavowal deflects from his actual engagement in—if not cooptation by—the revolution's shameful discursive legacy: "Baudelaire protests that he is an aristocrat of art, but he knows, as Vigny did before him, that the only language possible is the one that is steeped in Rousseau and the Jacobins, twisted by contemporary democratic literature . . . Baudelaire succeeds in making us forget the degree to which his words are saturated with the ubiquitous discourse of his century."[28]

Yet as I have tried to show, in "Une Mort héroïque" Baudelaire's ironic use of such rhetoric continually reminds us of this saturation. By displaying how even poetry is bogged down in the clichéd and defunct vocabulary of republican idealism, Baudelaire also insists on the Revolution's failure to make good on its promises.

This idiosyncratic and unreliable form of *engagement* is expressed *through* the idiom of poetic production. As Barbara Johnson puts it, Baudelaire's prose poem disfigures poetic language: "Le passage de la poésie à la prose correspond

79

à une amputation de tout ce qui, dans la poésie, s'érige comme unité, totalité, immortalité, puissance" (154). But these truncations of poetic discourse revive the rhetorical legacy of revolutionary history, albeit in disfigured form. Baudelaire's critique of history is conducted through a metapoetic reflection on the aesthetic process. The truncation of aesthetic unity simultaneously disrupts the illusion of social harmony perpetuated by the empire. The poems' narrators, like the *chiffonnier,* collect and ironically reframe the utopian rhetoric of 1848, showing how its legacy has been co-opted, homogenized, and short-circuited. Often this rhetoric resembles the platitudes in Flaubert's *Dictionnaire des idées reçues:* its recycled quality is made evident by italics pointing out the chasm between the blind promise of utopian rhetoric—become meaningless *lieux communs*—and the harsh realities of ongoing social and economic inequity. The *faveur* with which "Une Mort héroïque" concludes highlights the absence of rights in the prince's kingdom. In "Le Joujou du pauvre," the italicized reference to "equality" has a similar function. The poem portrays the separation between rich and poor as a barrier so impermeable that the children standing on either side of it appear to be made of an altogether different substance, for as the narrator says of the rich: "on les croirait faits d'une autre pâte que les enfants de la médiocrité ou de la pauvreté." Yet the wealthy boy briefly joins his poverty-stricken counterpart as they contemplate the latter's toy (a live rat in a box) through the property's bars: "Et les deux enfants se riaient l'un à l'autre fraternellement, avec des dents d'une *égale* blancheur"(*OC,* 1: 305). Their complicit, "fraternal" laughter and the equal whiteness of their teeth are obvious parodic references to the failure of equality and fraternity, and there is more than a hint of violence conveyed by teeth bared in a grin of symbolic communion over the rodent, a toy that "[l]es parents, par économie sans doute, avaient tiré . . . de la vie elle-même."[29]

The latent, structural violence opposing the rich and the poor is obliquely unveiled in "Les Yeux des pauvres" (1864). In this prose poem, the underlying violence of economic inequity is conveyed in the failure of amorous reciprocity. The poet and his recalcitrant beloved-muse sit down to eat and drink at the very threshold dividing the wealthy and the poor, on the terrace of one of those new boulevard cafés that had turned Paris into a spectacular site for literal and vicarious consumption. They observe a destitute family pressed up against the windows, whose reactions to the splendor of the café, reflected in their eyes, are read by the poet. Yet when he seeks out confirmation of his empathy in the beloved's eyes: "Je tournais mes regards vers les vôtres, cher amour, pour y lire *ma* pensée," the comfortable piety of this correspondence is ruptured by her snobbish response: "Ces gens-là me sont insupportables avec leurs yeux ouverts comme des portes cochères" (*OC*, 1: 318–19). She thus dismisses the entire hermeneutic circuit that emerges from the assumption that the eyes of the poor are readable texts, that the poet's eyes can decipher these texts, and that her own eyes may in turn mirror his reading. The utopia of readability is treated as both a domestic and public affair. Just as the poet expects his thoughts to be reflected in the eyes of his beloved, he similarly congratulates himself on his ability to step into the paupers' shoes. Such transparency, or intersubjective "correspondence," is steeped in the revolutionary mythology. It is "un rêve qui n'a rien d'original, après tout, si ce n'est que, rêvé par tous les hommes, il n'à été réalisé par aucun" (318). The interruption of dialogue between lovers voids the premise that the poet's negative capability overcomes the symbolic and material bars between rich and poor. The dream of communion and social harmony is fully co-opted by bourgeois consumerism, just as in the luxurious café, "toute l'histoire et toute la mythologie sont mises au service de la goinfrerie." After all, the poet-consumer indulges in this exercise of decipherment to assuage his conscience before turning to drink his thoughts in his beloved's eyes, and then returning—if reluctantly—to his overflowing glass of wine. The principle of *correspondances* is deployed both in its poetic and social form to unveil a structural inequity before which poetic empathy and bourgeois humanism are woefully inadequate.

The most violent mise-en-scène of this discrepancy between the idealism of revolutionary social thought and the ongoing reality of destitution is, of course, "Assommons les pauvres !" where the poet, bludgeoned into a theoretical stupor by the socialist literature of 1848, tumbles out of his ivory tower into the streets of Paris. He encounters a beggar, whose pleading eyes mirror both the idealist promises of utopian literature and the poet's own idealizing imagination, in a typically Baudelairean imbrication of poetic and social idealism: "un de ces regards inoubliables qui culbuteraient les trônes, *si l'esprit remuait la matière*" (*OC*, 1: 358; emphasis added). In a Nietzschean explosion of violence, the poet expels the theoretical nonsense of the "entrepreneurs de bonheur publique" by attacking the beggar and beating him until he fights back, thus actualizing the antagonistic social relations underlying the theoretical rhetoric of equality.[30] Such violence, our perverse philosopher suggests, must be resuscitated and acknowledged before the "partage de la bourse" may occur.

Baudelaire's prose poems illuminate a profound shift in the conceptualization of violence. No longer displayed in the bloody spectacles of revolutionary upheaval, violence is an invisible force woven into the very fabric of postrevolutionary social life. The physical blows that proliferate in the collection's explosive pieces can be read as attempts to resuscitate the hidden, structural violences that compose the social fabric: not only the "coup de poing" that initiates the cartoonish exchange of blows in "Assommons les pauvres !" but also the "coup de sifflet" that executes Fancioulle; the "coup de poing" delivered to the poet as he dreams over his soup; the "coup terrible, lourd" on the poet's door, received like a "coup de pioche dans l'estomac"; the flowerpot hurled on the glazier's windowpanes; the "coup de baton" administered to "la femme sauvage"; the "coup de tête dans l'estomac" delivered by one of the boys struggling for the remains of the poet's bread; and the violent stomp, or "coup de pied," that forever attaches the poet to "la fosse de l'idéal." These destructive blows systematically puncture each attempt at either poetic or political idealization. They stage the interlocking violence of aesthetic and political claims to mastery and closure.

Baudelaire's celebration of revolutionary destruction taps into the violence invisibly woven into the very fabric of postrevolutionary social life: "Je dis *Vive la Révolution !* comme je dirais : *Vive la Destruction ! Vive l'Expiation ! Vive le Châtiment ! Vive la Mort !*" (*OC*, 2: 961). The social violence so visibly displayed and acknowledged in times of radical historical crisis (the Terror, the June days) has become insidiously disarticulated under the authoritarian democracy of Napoléon III and the emergence of new modes of production and domination. In the face of this camouflaged perpetuation of violence, Baudelaire's declarations challenge the assumption that terror has ceded to collective legislation, suggesting instead that terror has taken on an altered, and perhaps even more virulent face. As the following reading of his prose poem "La Corde" suggests, Baudelaire's distorted allusions to the Revolution press into visibility the latent violence of the Second Empire and the unkept promises of the republican legacy. His critique of urban and political modernity is fully imbricated with a critique of art's own betrayal of the living, vulnerable bodies that move within the social—as well as the textual—corpus.

The Tie That Binds: Violent Commerce in "La Corde"

[L]a majorité trace un cercle formidable autour de la pensée.
Alexis de Tocqueville, *De la démocratie en Amérique*

Les illusions — me disait mon ami, — sont aussi innombrables
peut-être que les rapports des hommes entre eux, ou des hommes avec

*les choses. Et quand l'illusion disparaît, c'est-à-dire quand nous voyons
l'être ou le fait tel qu'il existe hors de nous, nous éprouvons un bizarre
sentiment, compliqué moitié de regret pour le fantôme disparu, moitié
de surprise agréable devant la nouveauté, devant le fait réel.*

Baudelaire, "La Corde"

Baudelaire's prose poem "La Corde" (1864), inspired by the suicide of Alexandre—the young model for Édouard Manet's *L'Enfant aux cerises*—recounts how a painter takes in a little boy to pose and to do minor chores around the *atelier*. The child's initially sunny disposition gives way to mysterious bouts of melancholy and an immoderate taste for sugar and liqueurs. After threatening to send the child back to his parents, the painter goes off to take care of some business. Upon his return, he discovers that the boy has hanged himself. The painter informs the mother of the tragic news, and she begs for the remains of her son's noose. Only when the painter receives letters of solicitation from his neighbors does it dawn on him that the mother, exploiting the superstition that to own a rope with which someone has been hanged brings luck, intends to sell its pieces as profitable consolation.

"La Corde" not only demystifies the "givenness" of maternal love, by suggesting that it too has its price, but examines the nature of art's attachment to its model, leading to a broader meditation on the threads that tie together the postrevolutionary community. Like "Une Mort héroïque," it attests to Baudelaire's profound political disillusionment in the aftermath of 1848 and to a general crisis in representing the contemporary political body through the symbolic legacy of the Revolution. The "unnatural" mother of the poem points to the emergence of an entirely different conception of the social family, one whose latent violence is again revealed through the idiom of artistic production.

The alleged purpose of "La Corde" is to show that even an emotion as immutable, sacred, and "natural" as maternal love cannot be taken for granted. Indeed, the painter defends his initial blindness to the nature of the mother's request for the rope by invoking the unquestionable naturalness of the maternal instinct, an instinct that provides the foundation for the nuclear and social family alike: "S'il existe un phénomène évident, trivial, toujours semblable, et d'une nature à laquelle il soit impossible de se tromper, c'est l'amour maternel." Yet this immutable given, "l'illusion la plus *naturelle*," as the painter calls it, turns out to be the deceptive product of established cultural assumptions about the "nature" of the maternal instinct. Natural instincts and empirical phenomena, as the poem gradually discloses, are culturally produced illusions that have acquired the status of nature over time. Initially a trial of the maternal instinct, the poem swiftly engages in a broader consideration of the natural grounds for filiation, of the *nature* of man's relationship to men and to things. From the outset, the bonds that tie the boy to the painter and to his parents are not natural or affective but economic and contractual. Seduced by the boy's appearance, the painter asks his parents to surrender their son to his care. His proprietary attitude toward the child suggests a repressed and denatured paternity, not unlike the mother's own travestied maternity: " je priai un jour ses parents, de pauvres gens, de vouloir bien me le céder." The violence of the maternal contract, it turns out, will be fully matched by that of the artistic contract.

At stake in the demystification of the "naturalness" of filial attachment, then, is a parallel demystification of the life-enhancing powers of art. Like biological reproduction, artistic production is animated by a blind, proprietary violence. The child's portraiture is an exercise in creating "l'illusion la plus naturelle," one that will have deadly repercussions on "le fait réel," the empirical fact of another's body. The violence of the aesthetic process is implicit from the very beginning of the text, when the painter recalls his initial attraction to the boy in acquisitive terms: "Ma profession de peintre me pousse à regarder attentivement les visages, les physionomies *qui s'offrent dans ma route,* et vous savez *quelle jouissance nous tirons* de cette faculté qui rend à nos yeux la vie plus vivante et plus significative que pour les autres hommes" (emphasis added). The aristocratic and appropriative thrust of the artist's perception is typical of the Baudelairean poet-flâneur of "Les Foules," who, under the guise of a poetics of charity, assumes the vacancy of all beings before his expropriating imagination: "Pour lui seul, tout est vacant" (*OC,* 1: 291).[31] A similar evacuation of the model's intrinsic properties occurs in his successive metamorphoses under the painter's brush: "je l'ai transformé tantôt en petit bohémien, tantôt en ange, tantôt en Amour mythologique. Je lui ai fait porter le violon du vagabond, la Couronne d'Épines et les Clous de la Passion, et la Torche d'Eros. . . . Cet enfant, débarbouillé, devint charmant." At once painted and unpainted, transformed into so many conventional cultural and religious icons (several of which invoke martyrdom), the boy is a mute, plastic body washed clean to receive the painter's allegorical imprint. No instance of reported speech breaks his conspicuous silence throughout the tale. The only details that rupture the proprietary, aesthetic economy established by the painter are the child's "crises singulières de tristesse précoce." These fits, significantly, remain uninterpreted by the painter, who merely notes their literal manifestations in the boy's excessive taste for sweets and liqueurs: "un goût immodéré pour le sucre et les liqueurs." Melancholy, as that which exceeds cultural assumptions about childhood ("précoces") and challenges the painter's representational authority ("crises singulières"), erupts as an immoderate taste for the superfluous ("le sucre et les liqueurs"). Such illegible excesses in the painter's artistic and domestic economy are immediately suppressed by the reestablishment of the implicit contract between artist and model, one resting upon the painter's right to dispose of the child as he deems fit: "je le menaçai de le renvoyer à ses parents."

The boy's suicide by hanging is a grim literalization of his previous commodification and aesthetic manipulation. His dangling body, described by the painter as "le premier *objet* qui frappa mes regards" (emphasis added), bears mute testimony to the underlying violence of a social and artistic process that puts real, living bodies into circulation for profit. The nature of the relationship between model and painter is conveyed in a near-pun, "Le dépendre n'était pas une besogne aussi facile que vous pouvez le croire." *Dépendre* is but a letter away from *dépeindre,* which is precisely what the painter does in his clinical account of the cadaver's "unhanging," suggesting the link between painting and hanging, representation and execution.

Yet the boy's mise-en-scène of his own death also endows his previously imprinted body with an undecipherable opacity, a weight that challenges the painter's representational mastery. From "mon petit bonhomme" and the "compagnon de ma vie," the child becomes a "petit monstre," a *monstrum,* or sign, that resists decipherment. It is only as a corpse that the boy is presented in active terms as excess, as opacity to the painter's gaze and manipulation. Baudelaire conveys the fleshy resistance of the child's body in vivid, tactile detail. Rigor mortis is so advanced by the time the painter discovers the gruesome scene that the clothes have to be cut from the child's body: "la rigidité cadavérique était telle, que, désespérant de fléchir les membres, nous dûmes lacérer et couper les vêtements pour les lui enlever." The puffiness of the boy's face, the folds of his neck, the stiff resistance of his limbs and the dense weight of his body are ironic counterpoints to the fluidity of his previous incarnations. The boy's implacable gaze, "ses yeux, tout grands ouverts avec une fixité effrayante," contrasts with his previous plasticity. The fixity of this gaze will embed itself in the painter's memory: "le fantôme me fatiguait de ses grands yeux fixes." While "l'illusion la plus naturelle" ostensibly demystified in the poem is maternal love, whose "fait réel" appears to be the more natural instinct of greed, it is a demystification that, unbeknownst to the painter, fully implicates the artistic process itself. For the "fait réel" that the painter fails to acknowledge throughout the poem ultimately designates the facticity of the child's body, its obdurate resistance to the "naturalizing" illusions that have been painted upon it.

The trial of maternal love thus fully implicates the process of artistic figuration. The underlying price of both the maternal and the artistic contracts is unveiled in all of its violence when the boy stages himself as his own *nature morte:* "le petit monstre s'était servi d'une ficelle fort mince qui était entrée profondément dans les chairs, et il fallait maintenant, avec de minces ciseaux, chercher la corde entre les deux bourrelets de l'enflure, pour lui dégager le cou." The painter's laborious extraction of the noose is mirrored by the mother's own extraction of the rope from the painter's home: "je compris pourquoi la mère tenait tant à *m'arracher* la ficelle" (emphasis added). The artist, however, disavows any responsibility for the boy's suicide, blithely dismissing a police officer's suspicious queries as motivated by "une habitude d'état de faire peur, à tout hasard, aux innocents comme aux coupables." Yet even after the necessary rites disposing of the cadaver, when the artist returns to his labors, he finds himself unable to extract the bothersome ghost from his conscience. The boy's corpse remains embedded in the folds of the artist's brain ("ce petit cadavre qui *hantait les replis* de mon cerveau" [emphasis added]) the way the rope itself was embedded in the folds of the child's flesh. That the painter is himself haunted by a repetition (*re-pli*) of the noose cutting into the boy's neck (*pli*) only reiterates the implicit connection between *peindre* and *pendre.* But the capture of matter by aesthetic form is never entirely complete, as the model's unyielding body and its continued life suggest. It leaves behind a stubborn residue that lingers in the recesses of the artist's imagination.[32]

Painting is not the only artistic discipline on trial, for "La Corde" provides a general meditation on the underlying price of all art forms that transfigure living bodies and things: "vous savez quelle jouissance nous tirons de cette faculté qui rend à nos yeux la vie plus vivante et plus significative que pour les autres hommes." What animates life into signification, it would seem, is the ability to extract the intensity and coherence of illusion from the living "fait réel." The painter confides this to the silent interlocutor and author of the poem (which retains its status as reported discourse until the very end). Poetry, too, is implicated in this representational violence. This ripple of complicity becomes all the more significant when we recall that at a gathering shortly after the death of Alexandre, where Manet was present, Baudelaire read "La Corde" aloud. Baudelaire thus uttered the words attributed to the painter-figure in the poem before a silent Manet, no doubt fully exploiting the interpellative power of the poem's narrative mode as reported discourse. He thereby reversed the relationship between the speaking painter and the silent poet in the text. This mise-en-scène of complicity conveys the ways in which poetry and painting converge in their potential violence toward a represented object. The *hypocrite lecteur* is here a *hypocrite spectateur.* If the painter resembles the poet, the rope also evokes the lyre's string and illuminates the violence of allegorical capture. What the boy's *nature morte* suggests is nothing less than the price of aesthetic production, the violence that art, as "l'illusion la plus naturelle," does to the body that inspires it, "le fait réel." "La Corde" is a biting parody of the vital chain of analogies between sights, sounds, and smells celebrated in *correspondances,* here frozen into a set of conventional allegorical equivalences (Christ, gypsy, and so forth) imposed on a vulnerable—though ultimately recalcitrant—human body.

"La Corde" thus reveals the discrepancy between "le fait réel" and "l'illusion la plus naturelle," between the body and its artistic representation, and between the ambiguous nature of the maternal instinct and its cultural construction. Yet the complicity established between painterly and poetic violence radiates outward to contaminate the social body itself. At stake in this demystification of art and maternity is the *corde* of *concorde,* the bonds of the social contract itself. As in "Une Mort héroïque," the critique of aesthetic production (along with human reproduction) is folded into a meditation on the implicit violence of the public sphere. The mother's betrayal of the umbilical cord radiates outward and implicates the *concorde* that binds together the larger social family. The thread weaving together the social family has quite literally fallen to pieces.

When the artist discovers the hanging body, his neighbors turn a deaf ear to his cries for help: "J'ai négligé de vous dire que j'avais vivement appelé au secours ; mais tous mes voisins avaient refusé de me venir en aide, fidèles en cela aux habitudes de l'homme civilisé, qui ne veut jamais, je ne sais pourquoi, se mêler aux affaires d'un pendu." Civilized man, Baudelaire suggests with grim humor, will only entangle himself in the affairs of the hanged in the most literal sense of the expression. For it is the rope (*l'affaire*) of the hanged, and the business (*affaires*) it enables, that define a new community, one bound (*mêlé*)—albeit anonymously—by the ritual purchase of the noose. "La Corde," then, not only puts on trial the metaphorical process through which the artist transforms his material—the bodies and things that nourish his art—but simultaneously questions the symbolic threads that bind together the postrevolutionary social fabric and the illusions they weave about the nature of man's bond with men and things.

Given Baudelaire's fascination with the bankruptcy of the Revolution's discursive legacy, it is not surprising that he found Robespierre's rhetoric, his "style de glace ardente, recuit et congelé comme l'abstraction" (*OC*, 1: 592) more worthy of interest than his actions.[33] Echoes of what the poet called his "style sentencieux dont ma jeunesse s'est enivrée" (ibid.) may be discerned in the most startling places. Consider, for instance, Robespierre's famous *Rapport du 18 Floréal* and its celebration of fraternal bonds tying together the universal human family: "Le véritable prêtre de l'Être suprême, c'est la nature, son temple l'univers, son culte, la vertu, ses fêtes la joie d'un grand peuple rassemblé sous ses yeux pour resserrer les doux noeuds de la fraternité universelle et pour lui présenter l'hommage des coeurs sensibles et purs."[34] It is tempting to hear reverberations of this imagery in the opening lines of Baudelaire's "Correspondances" and its hymn to an anthropomorphic nature: "La nature est un temple où de vivant piliers / Laissent parfois s'echapper de confuses paroles," a connection that may not be entirely fanciful if we recall that the principle of universal analogy professed in this sonnet is proposed by Robespierre as the foundation for fraternity.

The image of fraternity as a knot tying together the human family becomes particularly significant in the context of "La Corde" and its implicit scrutiny of the body politic. As the portrait of the parental figures and their neighbors suggest, "La Corde" attests to a crisis in representing a community through metaphors of natural filiation. Robespierre's "doux noeuds de la fraternité" mutate into a noose whose severed fragments, once put into circulation, foster a parody of universal brotherhood. The transparency of hearts, or Robespierre's "coeurs sensibles et purs" constituting both the etymological root and principle of *concorde,* is travestied into a cluster of anonymous transactions feeding greed and superstition.[35]

"La Corde" offers an ironic commentary on the bankruptcy of a unified body politic, one whose underlying corruption is figured through the mother's unnatural body, her loyalty to the economic chain rather than the umbilical cord. Could we then read the child's suicide as an allegory for the slain republic? Certainly the child-martyr who dies in suicidal loyalty for the *patrie* is a familiar figure in the iconography of the Revolution. The thirteen-year old Joseph Bara, for example, died opposing the Vendée rebels and became a cult republican figure extolled by Robespierre, along with the young Agricola Viala, shot by the federates in 1793. Both children, in their intransigent and literal espousal of the Jacobin motto "Liberté, égalité, fraternité ou la mort," incarnated the ideal of Terror. Their suicidal opposition, made in the name of the republic, and memorialized in paintings such as David's *Death of Bara*, was part of a symbolic legacy that may well have informed Baudelaire's portrait of Manet's boy model in "La Corde."[36]

Still another sacrificial figure and scene are invoked in the poem's final, ironic gesture toward the collective consumption of the noose: Louis XVI, his decapitation and the alleged distribution of his clothing and body.[37] As Lynn Hunt has shown, the parsing out of the king's body and possessions—his blood, hair, and clothing—was a rite intended to disseminate his sacredness onto the people. Louis-Sébastien Mercier gives a gruesome account of the festivity surrounding the king's decapitation and the alleged circulation of his body and belongings: "Son sang coule ; c'est à qui y trempera le bout de son doigt, une plume, un morceau de papier ; l'un le goûte, et dit : *Il est bougrement salé !* Un bourreau sur le bord de l'echafaud, *vend et distribue* des petits paquets de ses cheveux ; *on achète le cordon qui les retenait ;* chacun remporte un petit fragment de ses vêtements ou un vestige sanglant de cette scène tragique. J'ai vu défiler tout le peuple se tenant sous le bras, riant, causant familièrement, comme lorsqu'on revient d'une fête."[38]

In this spectacular rite, a community is symbolically founded and nourished by the distribution of its sovereign-victim's body. The cannibalistic imagery of Mercier's description, and the reference to the ribbon, or *cordon,* tying the king's hair, are details that resonate with the prospective circulation and consumption of the noose in "La Corde" (incidentally, we know that Baudelaire had read Mercier's *Tableaux de Paris* and found it "merveilleux" [*Corr.*, 2: 254]). Designated a "horrible et chère relique," the noose will serve as an ironic substitute for the sacred body, ushering in a community founded, not on symbolic parricide, but rather on symbolic infanticide, an anonymous community governed by the laws of commerce: "Et alors, soudainement, . . . je compris pourquoi la mère tenait tant à m'arracher la ficelle, et par quel *commerce* elle entendait se consoler" (emphasis added).

Like many of his generation, Baudelaire was fascinated by the sacrificial elements of the French Revolution, the spectacular reversibility of victim and executioner staged by the decapitation of the king. Consider for example, the following stanza from "Le Voyage," which could provide its own *pendant,* or gloss, on Mercier's account of the bloody feast consecrating the king's execution:

> Le bourreau qui jouit, le martyr qui sanglote;
> La fête qu'assaisonne et parfume le sang;
> Le poison du pouvoir énervant le despote,
> Et le peuple amoureux du fouet abrutissant.[39]

Extolling somewhat theatrically the festive carnage of the Revolution, such passages resurrect the violent origins of the postrevolutionary social contract, a violence that has become clouded by the apparently benign mediocrity of Napoléon III and his authoritarian democracy. The brutality of the *lien social* is latent throughout "La Corde," where the community, so conspicuously absent for most of the tale, virtually reconstitutes itself around the boy's dead body and seeks to appropriate the severed fragments of his noose in a cannibalistic ritual reminiscent of the king's execution.

Baudelaire's distorted allusions to the Revolution's symbolic legacy press into visibility the latent violence of the Second Empire. The poet's later works insistently implicate the utopian vocabulary of communion, fraternity, equality, and concord with the reality of collective violence, terror and ongoing economic inequity. Nowhere is the perversion of fraternity into fratricide more clearly staged than in "Le Gâteau" (1862), published two years before "La Corde." The prose poem details the poet's journey through an idealized, romantic landscape. In a beatific moment of lyric elevation, the voyager, soaring on the wings of *l'universelle analogie,* succumbs to Rousseauist reflections on the essential goodness of man: "dans mon total oubli de tout le mal terrestre, j'en étais venu à ne plus trouver si ridicules les journaux qui prétendent que l'homme est né bon" (*OC,* 1: 297–98). His epiphany is brutally interrupted, however, by a typically Baudelairean fall. Having offered some bread to an urchin on the street, another little fellow, "si parfaitement semblable au premier qu'on aurait pu le prendre pour son frère jumeau," surges out of nowhere and wrestles his "brother" to the ground. The unsuspecting narrator has engendered a vicious struggle in which the twins tear each other to pieces and literally "break bread" until only crumbs remain.[40] The poet concludes wryly, "Il y a donc un pays superbe où le pain s'appelle du *gâteau,* friandise si rare qu'elle suffit pour engendrer une guerre parfaitement fratricide !" An ironic allusion, no doubt, to the proverbial "Let them eat *brioche*" that Louis XIV's first wife, Marie-Thérèse of Spain (and not Marie-Antoinette, as it is commonly believed) allegedly declared in the face of all-too-real hunger.[41] The individual poet's fall from an edenic correspondence between men and things finds its historical correlative in the fall from the illusion of fraternity to the reality of fratricide, from the idealism of the Revolution to the reality of the Terror.[42]

Baudelaire's dictum "Toute révolution a pour corollaire le massacre des innocents" is an eloquent comment on the *price* of revolution and counterrevolution, and of the murderous rites of collective purification.[43] Yet "La Corde" also suggests that, unlike the bloody spectacles of revolution, the violence particular to the postrevolutionary epoch is insidiously woven into the social fabric by the mercenary logic of *commerce.* Attesting to a crisis in representing the postrevolutionary collective as bound by the harmonious threads of *fraternité* and *concorde,* "La Corde" points to the emergence of an order where the logic of the market, in service of superstition, fosters its own species of terror. A possession relinquished, if not sold, by his parents, figuratively consumed by the painter, his family, and neighbors, the boy symbolically refers to the bodies and beings that suffer the price of new social modes of production and consumption. Both at the center and the margins of the relations enabled by his body, he is—significantly—barred from consumption. His "immoderate and excessive" tastes are forbidden and threatened with punishment. His suicide, then, is a powerful demystification of the underlying logic governing both aesthetic and social production. As Baudelaire trenchantly says in his notebooks: "Le commerce, c'est le prêté-rendu, c'est le prêt avec le sous-entendu : *Rends moi plus que je ne te donne*" (*OC,* 1: 703; emphasis added). In keeping with the spirit of the market, then, a body acquires value when it yields more than has been invested in it. "La Corde" develops this implicit premise to its conclusion: the mother makes a profit off the death of her child; the painter's investment in his model(s) must have been amply repaid by his paintings if his "business" keeps him out for several hours at a time. As for the neighbors who solicit the rope, their everlasting good fortune will only cost them a few francs.[44] By staging himself as a *nature morte,* the boy literalizes his own reification and unveils the latent violence of a community in which a person's body only acquires value through its *symbolic* circulation.

Baudelaire fully grasped the consequences of revolutionary upheavals in the body politic for the living and vulnerable bodies within it. As a poet-dandy and an allegoricist, he knew such violence to be the material consequence of idealist systems imposing their form upon an embodied and differentiated social content. His sardonic remarks in the early days of the abortive Second Republic indicate a keen awareness of the human cost of revolutionary upheaval: "Lorsque Marat, cet homme doux, et Robespierre, cet homme propre, demandaient, celui-là trois-cent mille têtes, celui-ci, la permanence de la guillotine, ils obéissaient à l'inéluctable logique de leur système."[45] Such declarations about the bloody realities of revolution are more than the provocative *boutades* of an aesthete thrilling in the spectacle of history. They are unflinching assessments of the price of revolution. Revolutionary utopianism, in its vision of a body politic as matter to be shaped into coherence, is almost always associated with sacrificial terror in Baudelaire's thought. For the revolutionary—and in this he is truly kin to the despotic artist—necessarily turns a blind eye to the human cost of transformation, to the bodies that were once attached to the three hundred thousand heads requested by Marat, that is to say, to "le fait réel."

Even more unbearable than the spectacular despotism of the Terror for Baudelaire, however, was the headless, flabby despotism of the multitudes in postrevolutionary France. His outbursts against the formless hydra of democracy should not be dismissed as the histrionics of an aristocratic aesthete repudiating his dabbling in republican politics.[46] His disgust at the United States—described as a shapeless monster—is telling in this regard. It betrays an obscure yet prescient sense of the violences underlying a decentered, commercial metropolis: "mais *Cela !* cette cohue de vendeurs et d'acheteurs, ce sans-nom, ce monstre sans tête, ce déporté derriere l'Océan, État !" (*OC,* 2: 327). A social field governed by the fluctuating rules of the market, politically mystified by an apparent diffusion of class antagonism, and in which "cette cohue" blindly collaborates in its own subjection—this also seems to have been Baudelaire's thumbnail sketch of the brave new world inaugurated by the Second Empire.

In his portrait of Théophile Gautier, Baudelaire proposes a curious parallel between the utopianism of revolutionary thought and the conformism of its failed aftermath. He blames this "tyrannie contradictoire" on the fact that France and "le caractère utopique, communiste, alchimique, de tous ses cerveaux ne lui permet qu'une passion exclusive : celle des formules sociales. Ici, chacun veut ressembler à tout le monde, mais à condition que tout le monde lui ressemble" (*OC,* 2: 125). The utopian attempt to alchemically transform the world to the measure of its abstract formulae is echoed in the majority's desire to contemplate and consume its flattering self-images in art. The revolutionary's will to purification thus finds its degraded correlative in the bourgeoisie's attempt to hold the multiplicity of its social and cultural environment in its conformist grip. The violence of this narcissistic self-replication is conveyed throughout Baudelaire's poetry. The rope that hangs the boy and consecrates this anonymous community is but an example of the price of such collective transformation. The usurping twin brother of "Le Gâteau" and the malevolent, proliferating old men of "Les Sept veillards" also recover the disquiet occulted by the apparently benign cult of universal sameness.

Let us now return to Baudelaire's declaration that "Non seulement, je serais heureux d'être victime, mais je ne haïrais pas d'être bourreau, — pour sentir la Révolution de deux manières !" (*OC,* 2: 961). In a sense, his vocation as poet locked him into this contradictory historical predicament long before he chose to embrace it. For the poet-dandy is the despotic figure par excellence; his sovereign imagination "executes" a recalcitrant and fragmentary reality in its image. As Pierre Pachet remarks, "Dans une société qui ne possède plus de monarque sacré mais un Empereur bénin et médiocre . . . la tyrannie est accaparée par les artistes : ils ressentent avec plus de nervosité ce qu'il y a de despotique dans la réalité . . . et en même temps exercent, en tant que nouveaux princes, le plus magnifique et plus arbitraires des pouvoirs" (Pachet, *Premier venu*, 125). And yet, as Walter Benjamin has shown, the poet-merchant is also a victim at the mercy of the market's grip. The hanging boy of "La Corde," whose noose suggests voicelessness made visible, is a striking avatar for this predicament. An anterior version of the poem makes this parallel more explicit, for it concludes thus: "Un mètre de corde de pendu, à cent francs le décimètre, l'un dans l'autre, chacun payant selon leurs moyens, cela fait mille francs, un réel, un efficace soulagement pour cette pauvre mère."[47] The fate of the noose, the appraisal and circulation of its fragments, resonates with that of poetry and its circulation in the newspapers. As each decimeter of rope is worth one hundred francs, similarly, each line of Baudelaire's prose poems fetched roughly three sous apiece. The preface to *Le Spleen de Paris* fully acknowledges that the prose poems emerge out of these new conditions for literature's production and consumption. Advertised as a corpus that can be hacked into pieces (or *tronçons*), the format of these poems is designed to provide "admirables commodités" for the writer, editor, and reader alike as the text passes through their hands: "Considérez, je vous prie, quelles admirables commodités cette combinaison nous offre à tous, à vous, à moi et au lecteur. Nous pouvons couper où nous voulons" (*OC*, I: 275).

A textual body cut up into fragments in order to facilitate its circulation, the strings of the poetic lyre on sale for a few francs apiece, such metaphors capture some of the violence of the market's logic, and of literature's paradoxical implication in it. Poetry has relinquished its hieratic autonomy.[48] It is coopted and cut up by the demands of an urban consumer culture, victimized or prostituted by its readers' narcissistic investments. Yet, as Baudelaire also suggests throughout his oeuvre, art in its own way participates in the (dis)figuration of bodies, the capture and shaping of matter into symbolic form. Poetry's idealizing force resonates and even colludes with cultural logics of representation that imprint a mobile and differentiated social body. That Baudelaire was able to probe the complexity of poetry's imbrication within shifting forms of violence speaks to his ethical understanding of history. For to inhabit the oscillation between victim and executioner, alternatively and reciprocally, is deeply to understand the human cost of the revolutions—both spectacular and veiled—that unfold around us.

It is impossible to impose neat allegorical closure upon Baudelaire's poetry, and teasing out the possible historical significances of the poet's notorious ironies is risky business indeed. By applying pressure on the linguistic ambiguities of his prose poems and spinning out the political resonances of their imagery, I have tried to shed some light on the poet's prescient understanding of terror, not as a historical event, but rather as a force infiltrating every nerve of the postrevolutionary social body. The ritual public executions of the Terror exhibited the sacrifices that founded and consecrated a new social order. Besides sporadic resurgences that have failed to bring about the republic, these purgative violences, Baudelaire suggests, have sunk underground. A diffuse force nourishing a decapitated social organism, one of terror's most insidious new faces is commerce. The illusions bred by commerce are as innumerable as the relations between men and men, men and things, and men as things.

3 ▌ *Bodies in Motion, Texts on Stage*

Baudelaire's Women and the Forms
of Modernity

La femme a faim et elle veut manger. Soif, et elle veut boire.
Elle est en rut et elle veut être foutue.
Le beau mérite !
La femme est naturelle, c'est-à-dire abominable.

Baudelaire, "Mon coeur mis à nu"

Baudelaire is notorious for the violence of his representations of women. The unabashed misogyny of his declarations on female nature seems to require little commentary. Yet let us begin with this most damning of statements, "La femme est *naturelle,* c'est-à-dire, abominable," to consider the "nature" of this femininity in Baudelaire's poetry. The notion of woman as a regressive, instinctual organism, as many critics have shown, participates in a broader cultural disquiet about the female body, a fascinated repugnance for the unthinking materiality that this body represents. For Baudelaire, a woman who has not been transfigured through artifice—through fashion or cosmetics—appears to be the very incarnation of unredeemed materiality. But her aesthetic reincarnation is proof of art's power to redeem matter. In artistic terms, then, "woman" may function as a material body, a substance to be alchemically transformed by the creative process. Or, like the traditional muse, she may serve as a figure for poetry itself. In the *dédicace* of *Les Paradis artificiels,* Baudelaire declares that "La femme est fatalement suggestive ; elle vit d'une autre vie que la sienne propre ; elle vit spirituellement dans les imaginations qu'elle hante et qu'elle féconde" (*OC,* 1: 399). The category of "woman" is delivered here from its material content and redefined as pure metaphor, as a figure for figuration itself. Such conflicting definitions of woman—as "naturelle" and as "fatalement suggestive"—contradictorily posit the female body as both matter and figure, both resistance to and catalyst for aesthetic production.

Baudelaire is certainly not alone in harboring this ambivalence about the female body, as a plethora of late nineteenth-century writings attests. A woman's body is "*naturelle,* c'est-à-dire abominable" in Zola's *Nana* and her contagious sexuality or "*fatalement suggestive*" in Mallarmé's ballerina, whose body generates a series of signs (*glaive, coupe, fleurs*) that detach themselves from the swirl of her limbs and gauzes. In these representations, femininity stands in both for a regressive materiality upon which social and artistic processes are inscribed and as the figure for an open-ended semiotic drift.

This contradictory mapping of gender—as nature and as sign—opens a consideration of "woman" as the placeholder for aesthetic modernism's vexed relationship to reference. As Fredric Jameson has observed, the distinction between modernism and postmodernism is usually conceptualized in terms of a "dissolution of reference." High modernist art still retains the vestiges of faith in categories such as nature, being, depth, and authenticity, even if such concepts are on the brink of disappearance. Under the conditions of postmodernism, however, melancholy alienation cedes to a poker-faced celebration of glossy surfaces and artifice. For Jameson, Baudelaire is at the threshold between modernism and postmodernism. His poetry voices the eclipse of poetry's expressivist and referential vectors, ushering in the heterogeneous disjunction and textual free play of consumer society and its simulacra: "The whole drama of modernism will lie here indeed, in the way in which its own peculiar life and logic depend on the reduction of reference to an absolute minimum and on the elaboration, in the former place of reference, of complex symbolic and often mythical frameworks and scaffolding: yet the latter depend on preserving a final tension between text and referent, on keeping alive one last shrunken point of reference, like a dwarf sun still glowing feebly on the horizon of the modernist text."[1]

Jameson's reading of Baudelaire is attuned to the multiplicity of potential histories dormant in his poetry and actualized in its readings. It nuances Baudelaire's canonization (discussed in Chapter 1) as a melancholy witness of modernity by suggesting how the poet's scenarios of reification resonate with our postmodern culture of commodities.[2] In this chapter, I want to take this analysis one step further by exploring how the drama of modernism might have less to do with a vanishing point of reference than with staging the aesthetic and material conditions that produce the illusion of reference in the first place. As the preceding chapters suggest, the "crisis of representation" that continues to define historical modernity and aesthetic modernism opens a reflection on the production of reference itself. The human body is a key locus in the self-reflexive turn of French modernism. Its explicitly figural production in literary texts illuminates some of the material conditions of the body's inscription into form by social and cultural representations. The representation of bodies *through* this reflection on reference invites a reading of the ideological as well as aesthetic processes that make bodies "matter" (the processes that materialize the body and invest it with meaning and value).[3] Baudelaire's writing illuminates the cultural conditions that produce a body and invest it with value in the ideological map of the Second Empire. The body—as a site for the enactment of historical violences that are mirrored and critiqued by literary counterviolence—will also be the locus of my subsequent investigation of post-Baudelairean committed ironists.

My reading of the body through notions of performativity and violence does not strive to make Baudelaire our postmodern feminist contemporary. Rather, I suggest that Baudelaire belongs to a continuum of writers (including Gautier and Balzac) whose apparent retreat into textuality in fact explores the human body's contradictory status as vulnerable materiality and as cultural sign. Their representation of the body converges with the representation of writing to show how materiality itself is defined by cultural assumptions about the body's nature, ground, place, and performance. The horizon for this reading of Baudelaire's female bodies could thus extend to later representatives of literature's "disembodiment" such as Mallarmé (to whom I turn in the coda to this chapter), Valéry, Rachilde (discussed in Chapter 5), Colette, and other early and high modernists who map the poetic, economic, and cultural inscription of material bodies into form, thereby putting bodies in motion *and* texts on stage.[4]

As we have seen, Baudelaire's strategies of poetic counterviolence bring into relief the human body's fate as it circulates in the poetic and social field. In "La Corde," the violence of aesthetic production virtually "executes" the "fait réel," or facticity, of the child model's body. This allegorical violence is in turn embedded in larger social structures that reify, dislocate, and circulate bodies for aesthetic, economic, and symbolic profit. Baudelaire thus discloses the price of aesthetic representation and embeds the violence of allegory into the structural violence of a life-world dominated by commerce. Violence becomes a vehicle for the inscription of competing aesthetic, economic, and ideological contexts within the poem itself.

The following pages situate Baudelaire within broader nineteenth-century discourses on gender and modernity. I argue that "woman" becomes a site of contested meaning at the crossroads of aesthetic modernism and the material conditions of capitalist urban modernity. Since the prostitute is so central to this contradictory mapping of woman as matter, sign, and commodity object, my discussion will take us through a reading of prostitution in the nineteenth-century literary imagination, starting with Balzac (to whom Baudelaire pays tribute throughout his oeuvre) to consider Baudelaire's transformation of prostitution into a metaphor for the inscription of bodies into meaning in his prose poem "Les Foules." I then turn to a series of poems that put bodies in motion *and* poetry on stage, thereby disclosing the violence of signifying practices that constitute the very "nature" of femininity. The chapter concludes with a brief reading of Mallarmé in this vein, to consider how modernism's apparent "disembodiment" might offer a critical genealogy of the body's production in modernity.

The Prostitute as Body and Figure: Balzac's La Fille aux yeux d'or

For Baudelaire, woman is at once a regressive organic corporeality and a mobile, semiotic entity. As the latter, she is linked both to the creation of art and to commodity fetishism. In the famous pages of *Le Peintre de la vie moderne,* Baudelaire describes woman as one "pour qui, mais surtout *par qui* les artistes et les poètes composent leurs plus délicats bijoux" (*OC,* 2: 713), that is to say, as a vehicle for poetic transportation. Yet she is herself a *thing* of beauty, an object circulating in the marketplace of erotic, aesthetic, and consumer desire. Decked out in jewels and fabrics that billow from their limbs, "faisant ainsi des deux, de la femme et de la robe, une totalité indivisible" (*OC,* 2: 714), beautiful women harmoniously blend together flesh and fashion, matter and figure, nature and art. The clothes and ornamentation grafted onto the female body, like the idealizing impact of poetry itself, are "comme une déformation sublime de la nature, ou plutôt comme un essai permanent et successif de réformation de la nature" (*OC,* 2: 716).

The prostitute is a key figure for woman's cultural mapping as resistant matter and meaningful sign. As a body reduced to meat for sale, the prostitute incarnates a pathological animality. Yet she is also a performer transformed by fashion and cosmetics into a desirable commodity. She is thus at once "naturelle," "abominable," and "fatalement suggestive." As many cultural historians have argued, the nineteenth-century artistic fascination with prostitutes shared by Balzac, Baudelaire, the Goncourts, Barbey d'Aurevilly, Flaubert, Zola, and many others rehearses typically "modernist" anxieties about corporeality, organic matter, and temporal decay. For Charles Bernheimer, the artistic solutions to such a feminized understanding of organic life—artifice, self-reflexivity, autonomy—spell the very birth of modernism: "Confronted by this pathological erosion, the writer must construct art against nature, against woman, against the organic. Such constructions of artifice and reflexivity signal the birth of modernism, which . . . is inscribed on the prostitute's wounded body."[5] Yet the prostitute is also a symbol of money itself. Her mobility and semiotic expertise enact the circulation of commodities in economic modernity. While the obsession with the prostitute is obviously linked to her associations with the body as a diseased and decaying materiality, this anxiety is also profoundly *semiotic* and responds to a crisis of legibility within the social body. If women could circulate and cash in on their bodies as commodities in the public sphere, prostitutes were the incontrovertible evidence of the permeability of class and gender boundaries in the anonymous, market-driven context of the city.[6] The prostitute is figured as the "embodiment" of bourgeois capitalist modernity.

The prostitute and the kinds of femininity she represents become a powerful site of contest for the claims of gender, class, and art. At once *"naturelle, c'est-à-dire abominable"* and *"fatalement suggestive,"* she represents a conflict between the aesthetic imagination and its matter, between "form" and its "contents." She also articulates the tension between atavistic nature and urban modernity. An embodiment of what Baudelaire calls "la sauvagerie dans la civilisation," she is a point of resistance to narratives of historical progress and, as such, illustrates what Naomi Schor has described as an accepted "divorce between women and modernity" (*Breaking the Chain,* 145). Yet the venal female body enacts the very workings of capitalist modernity. To further tease out the points of conjunction that the prostitute allows us to discern between the female body, aesthetic modernism, and urban modernity, let us turn to Balzac's *La Fille aux yeux d'or,* a novella that Baudelaire recalls in *La Fanfarlo* (1847) and that plays out a series of cultural assumptions on women's "place" in modernity.[7]

In Balzac's tale, the body of the golden-eyed girl becomes the site of a struggle between the archaic, oriental way of life, and the circulation of commodities under modern industrial capitalism. Balzac's opening chapter, titled "Physionomies parisiennes," describes the multiple currencies of gold and pleasure that circulate within and between the city's layered socioeconomic spheres. In this introductory panorama, Paris is a hierarchical pyramid that, from its toiling workers to its corrupt bankers and lawyers, pulses to the uniform beat of *or et plaisir.* At the summit of this pyramid, we find the luxurious chambers of the aristocracy, where women live like rare flowers that blossom far from the city's tumult: "il se rencontre, dans le monde féminin, de petites peuplades heureuses qui vivent à l'orientale . . . elles demeurent cachées, comme des plantes rares qui ne déploient leurs pétales qu'à certaines heures, et qui constituent de véritables exceptions exotiques" (*Histoire des Treize*, 225). While these women are the final recipients of the upward surge of wealth in the city, they appear untainted by the capitalist machinery's cycle of labor, production, and expenditure. Aristocratic women live in a premodern, static, and "oriental" state that lies outside the Parisian economy of gold and pleasure, even though their exotic and oriental chambers are its final destination.

Balzac situates his girl with golden eyes at the heart of this paradox. Amidst the urban swirl of money and pleasure lies the timeless oriental interior in which Paquita is kept like a rare blossom by her jealous mistress, the marquise de San Réal. Baptized as "la fille aux yeux d'or" by her admirers, designated as "fille"—prostitute as well as girl—her association with the public circulation of money is stressed throughout the tale. A feeling and thinking embodiment of gold itself, her eyes are portrayed as commodities seeking a buyer and as metonyms for the living gold driving modern Paris: "deux yeux jaune comme ceux des tigres ; un jaune d'or qui brille, de l'or vivant, de l'or qui pense, de l'or qui aime et veut absolument venir dans votre gousset" (*Histoire des Treize*, 236). Yet, along with her incarnation as commodity fetish circulating in the modern metropolis, she is also emblematic of a static, preindustrial, "oriental" lifestyle, an exotic harem girl out of a Delacroix painting. Paquita is thus an overdetermined site of cultural inscription: as nature, art, oriental slave, and Parisian commodity fetish.

Balzac dedicated *La Fille aux yeux d'or* to Delacroix, after seeing the painter's luminous orientalist interior *Femmes d'Alger dans leur appartement* in 1834. His gestures to Delacroix in this ekphrastic novella explore art's relationship to a new urban economy of gold and pleasure. Paquita's body is explicitly described as a work of art. She is "un chef d'oeuvre de la nature" and also "l'original de la délirante peinture, appelée *la femme caressant sa chimère*" (*Histoire des Treize*, 237).[8] Her bloody end accomplishes her destiny as art. Ripped to shreds by her jealous keeper, the marquise de San Réal (who turns out to be the half-sister of Paquita's lover, Henri de Marsay), her death is a spectacular tableau that rivals Delacroix's *Death of Sardanapalus*. Her struggle to escape her keeper's fury is visible in the bloody imprint of her hands and feet on the walls and divan of her boudoir, imprints coldly described by de Marsay as so many traces of the marquise's *fantaisie*. The sensuous violence of these hieroglyphs attests to an orientalist aesthetic that situates itself above and beyond social law.

La Fille aux yeux d'or shores up an archaic figure of oriental despotism (the marquise as Sardanapalus) against the more disquieting flux of a postrevolutionary, market-driven society in which bodies anonymously circulate through economic transactions. The final chapter, titled "La Force du sang," reiterates the biological ties of blood over the circulating relationships of the market. This is conveyed in the image of the brother and sister's incestuous embrace over the bloody corpse of a mistress unwittingly shared. While Paquita is repeatedly embedded in a Parisian economy of bodies bought and sold, the conclusion displaces this reification onto the Orient. "Elle est d'un pays où les femmes ne sont pas des êtres, mais des choses dont on fait ce qu'on veut, que l'on vend, que l'on achète, que l'on tue, enfin dont on se sert pour ses caprices, comme vous vous servez ici de vos meubles" (*Histoire des Treize*, 289), the marquise declares, assuaging de Marsay's concern that Paquita's mother will denounce the murder. Paquita's incarnation as art, as she dies in a pool of blood, is explicitly tied to her status as a commodity sold by her mother. She is a decorative piece of furniture whose erasure from circulation will escape notice. Whereas the denaturalization of filial ties by economic transactions is initially established as a Parisian predicament, it is displaced into another place at the novel's conclusion. *La Fille aux yeux d'or*'s punishment, then, is an aesthetic redemption of social and sexual mobility. It relegates the disruption of filial ties characteristic of a market-driven society onto the Orient. By reversing the attributes traditionally opposing the archaic Orient to modern civilization, Balzac's narrative can be read as providing a symbolic solution of sorts to anxieties about capitalist bourgeois modernity.[9]

Naomi Schor has argued that whereas Flaubert's narratives operate a partial denaturalization of gender, in which the attributes of gender are considered as both anatomical and cultural accounts of the difference between men and women, Balzac's "univocal narrative voice . . . serves to naturalize, that is to feminize passivity."[10] Yet, as Schor notes, many of Balzac's most celebrated texts (*Seraphîta, Sarrasine, La Peau de chagrin*) attest to the instability of such natural determinations of gender. *La Fille aux yeux d'or* plays out the tension between Balzac's naturalization of the social (in Paquita's portrait as the essence of presocial, anti-modern femininity) and a partial denaturalization of the body (in her overdetermined representation as oriental art work and as commodity fetish).[11] The complex maneuvers in the narrative produce Paquita as both a regressive materiality and a crafted object upon which erotic, economic and allegorical desire are violently enacted.

Violence and Representation in Baudelaire

Baudelaire and the Prostitution of Poetry

Qu'est-ce que l'art ? Prostitution.

Baudelaire, "Fusées"

"[E]lle darde son regard sous son chapeau, comme un portrait dans son cadre. Elle représente bien la sauvagerie dans la civilisation," Baudelaire says of a courtesan's drawing by Constantin Guys. "Elle porte le regard à l'horizon, comme la bête de proie" (*OC,* 2: 720). The courtesan is a predatory beast pacing through the urban jungle; she is Juvenal's *foemina simplex,* reduced to aggressive biological facticity. Yet the flash of her eyes from beneath the rim of her hat is likened to a portrait in its frame, destabilizing the opposition between matter and figure, between the body and art, and between savagery and civilization. Baudelaire here rehearses the conflicting accounts of femininity observed thus far (as nature, art, commodity fetish, savagery, and civilization). Yet elsewhere in his work, "prostitution" is redefined as a dynamic metaphor for poetry, and more specifically, for the circulation of bodies and things in the poetic and social texts. In contrast to the contemporary discourse of containment found in texts such as Alexandre Parent-Duchâtelet's *De la prostitution dans la ville de Paris* (1836) and exemplified in the creation of the *maisons de tolérance,* Baudelaire uses "prostitution" to denote an explosion of psychic boundaries and a free circulation of subjectivities.[12] Poetic prostitution releases the body from its gendered and class determinations, thus calling into question the cultural processes of naturalization found in accounts of the venal body by authors such as Balzac, Zola, or Barbey d'Aurevilly. Baudelaire's "disembodiment" of the prostitute into a metaphor for semiotic exchange, however, is more than a symptom of some misogynist rejection of the female body.[13] Rather, in his work, poetic prostitution becomes a metaphor for the semiotic exchanges of allegory and commodity production, a heuristic tool for investigating the tension between body and form within interlocking processes of representation.

In the prose poem "Les Foules," the poet is figured as a prostitute driven by "le goût du travestissement et du masque" to plunge into the electric force field of the urban experience. This abdication of poetic sovereignty is extolled as "cette ineffable orgie . . . cette sainte prostitution de l'âme qui se donne tout entière, poésie et charité, à l'imprévu qui se montre, à l'inconnu qui passe" (*OC,* 1: 291). Yet Baudelaire's celebration of poetry as charity is sabotaged from the outset: the universal communion with the urban crowds is not an experience available to all; it takes place "au dépens du genre humain." The poet is an *âme errante* who possesses bodies in their unthinking materiality. This non-reciprocity dismantles the very idea of communion: "Multitude, solitude : terms égaux et convertibles pour le poète actif et fécond. Qui ne sait pas peupler sa solitude, ne sait pas non plus être seul dans une foule affairée" (ibid.). Multitude and solitude are indeed equal and convertible terms, not because of the poet's "conversion" to the collectivity, but because of the "convertibility" of otherness into sameness, of human material into poetic matter.

Walter Benjamin suggests that Baudelaire's poet-as-prostitute discovers the reification characterizing relations between people and things in a market economy. Inspired by Marx's definition of the commodity fetish as a "definite social relation between men that assumes, in their eyes, the fantastic form of a relation between things" (*Marx-Engels Reader,* 321), Benjamin examines the kinship between the poet-narrator of "Les Foules" and the commodity caught in the bustle of the urban *clientèle.* The poet-prostitute's fascinated identification with dead matter, his sterile and imaginary empathy for strangers, situates Baudelaire within the class of mystified petit bourgeois that had yet to fully grasp its reification by the forces of the market.[14]

Yet Benjamin's account of "Les Foules" as an example of ideological mystification misses the irony of the poem's conclusion, in which the underlying inter-subjective relations of domination that produce the commodity fetish-relations *do* surface: "Il est bon d'apprendre quelquefois aux heureux de ce monde, ne fût-ce que pour humilier un instant leur sot orgueil, qu'il est des bonheurs supérieurs au leur, plus vastes et plus raffinés. Les fondateurs de colonies, les pasteurs de peuples, les prêtres missionnaires exilés au bout du monde, con-naissent sans doute quelque chose de ces mystérieuses ivresses ; et, au sein de la vaste famille que leur génie s'est faite, ils doivent rire quelquefois de ceux qui les plaignent pour leur fortune si agitée et leur vie si chaste" (*OC,* 1: 291–92).

Baudelaire's poet-narrator links the aesthetics of prostitution—and its arbitrary assignment of value to others as empty sites—to the mystical foundations of ideological formations. In that sense, the poet-prostitute is kindred to shepherds of peoples, missionaries, and founders of colonies, all of whom taste the joy of generating communities from within and over which they reign with unquestioned authority. Like the artistic despot of "Une Mort héroïque," the founders of colonies, of religious orders, or of imaginary worlds reign "au sein de la vaste famille que leur génie *s'est faite*" (emphasis added). The reflexive form underlines the solipsism of these "imagined communities."

The conclusion of "Les Foules" takes the figure of the poet–prostitute–

commodity fetish out of the urban marketplace and locates its kindred spirits outside the dominant bourgeois order, in "premodern" social structures based on the sovereignty of the missionary, the colonizer, or the spiritual leader. The *convertibility* of things, established by their exchange value, is redeemed into their *conversion* by the authoritarian despot. In this regard, the final lines of "Les Foules" echo Balzac's *La Fille aux yeux d'or,* which also concludes on the oriental despot's will over Paquita's circulation as an object on the marketplace of aesthetic and erotic desire. Yet in an unexpected dialectical turn, the commodity's subjection and the subject's sovereignty are figured in "Les Foules" from the stances of both *victime* and *bourreau.* Baudelaire's poet-prostitute not only occupies the position of the commodity caught in the turbulence of a free market (as Benjamin describes it), he also embodies the despotism of rulers who found and legitimate communities by transforming their subjects into empty sites or dead matter to which value and meaning may be assigned. The poet-prostitute becomes both subject and object, victim and executioner—as well as symptom and critic—of prostitution's logic. Baudelaire thus releases prostitution from its gendered determination, transforming it instead into a dynamic principle of force that operates in aesthetic, sexual, economic, and, as I shall show, colonial systems. Prostitution enacts the violence of allegorical desire as it transforms bodies and things into poetic and cultural meaning.[15]

The preceding discussion of prostitution has traced a number of contradictory topoi structuring accounts of femininity in the nineteenth-century literary imagination. "Woman" is posited both as regressive materiality and as meaningful sign, as savagery and civilization. She is at once archaic or exotic nature, modern commodity object, and work of art. These contradictory determinations invite an inquiry into the female body as a site for competing symbolic violences in the Second Empire's vision of modernity. Baudelaire's rehearsal of these overdetermined accounts denaturalizes the very category of gender. This denaturalization opens up an analysis of "woman" as a key category for *l'art pour l'art,* that is to say, as a resistance to and catalyst for the derealizing tendencies of aesthetic modernism. It also enables a consideration of "woman" as a placeholder *and* token for conflicting accounts of modernity in the nineteenth century.[16]

The poems examined in the remainder of this chapter trace the conditions for a gendered body's emergence in the poetic and the broader sociocultural and colonial field. All three texts define woman as either "naturelle" or as "fatalement suggestive," and posit the female body as simultaneously matter and figure, as resistance to and catalyst for productions that are not only poetic, but also sexual, socioeconomic, racial, and colonial. These textual exhibitions of the female body are fully attuned to the Second Empire's spectacular displays of commodity culture (*expositions universelles,* department stores, panoramas, fairs, public morgues, and arcades).[17] Baudelaire's "Une Martyre" is an ornate, poetic *fait divers* that transforms the domestic interior into a spectacular crime scene; "La Femme sauvage et la petite-maîtresse" unfolds in a carnival fair, casting the poet as a sort of sideshow barker; and "La Belle Dorothée" takes on the glossy promise of an *invitation au voyage,* a cruise to tropical bliss that puts the "native" body of a colonial subject on display. In all three texts, a female body is exhibited as either allegorical or natural, and in each case, violence is ironically deployed to reveal the hidden violences of Baudelaire's nineteenth century, the price exacted by urban, imperial, and colonial modernity.

Losing One's Head to Things: "Une Martyre"

> La femme est fatalement suggestive ; elle vit d'une autre vie que la sienne propre ; elle vit spirituellement dans les imaginations qu'elle hante et qu'elle féconde.
> Baudelaire, *Les Paradis artificiels,* "Préface"

Balzac's evocation of Paquita's opulent boudoir, filtered through the colors and lights of Delacroix's orientalist paintings, set the stage for Baudelaire's "Une Martyre."[18] A poem that mysteriously escaped censorship in 1857 despite its extraordinary sexual violence and necrophilic overtones, "Une Martyre" is inspired by an anonymous masterpiece depicting a decapitated woman in an opulent apartment. It provides a vivid mise-en-scène of Baudelaire's conception of the female body as an aesthetic figure delivered from all material content, and as catalyst and muse for poetry itself. Yet in doing so, it also grasps the violence of this allegorical inscription of gender, for here the woman is "fatalement suggestive" in the most literal sense of the expression. It is only insofar as her body is dead and virtually in pieces that the process of allegorization and the parallel activities of detection, circulation, and consumption, can take place. As in "La Corde," where the violence of allegory is embedded in the structural violence of the postrevolutionary body politic and its ethos of commerce, "Une Martyre" links the allegorization of female bodies to their circulation as commodities in the modern city. Like the poems examined in the previous chapter, the self-reflexive features of aesthetic modernism open up a critique of the material conditions of urban modernity.

"Une Martyre" hovers at the margins of many passages in Walter Benjamin's essays on Baudelaire, even if explicit references to the poem are rare and no reading on the scale of "À une passante" is elaborated.[19] As the first chapter of this book proposed, Benjamin's reading of Baudelaire as a witness to the trauma of modernity has often been privileged at the expense of the more historical and materialist readings offered in earlier versions of his "On Some Motifs in Baudelaire." These earlier readings "embedded" Baudelaire into the broader cultural landscape of the nineteenth century by situating poetry within a spectrum of cultural artifacts (such as arcades, fashion, and photography) that, when scrutinized, reveal the mystifications of high capitalism and the phantasmagoria of the bourgeoisie. Yet, as my previous discussions have suggested, Benjamin's ambiguous positioning of poetry primarily as *witness* to the ideological contradictions of its historical moment and as a symptomatic inscription of historical trauma tends to eclipse the more active, contestatory, and political dimensions of Baudelaire's poetics.[20] The following reading of "Une Martyre" explores Benjamin's comments on the structural similarities between allegory and commodity fetishism. I take three Benjaminian motifs as guiding threads: the bourgeois interior, the poet as flâneur and prostitute, and the detective novel. All three motifs for Benjamin serve as *defensive* responses to the disappearance of the individual in the jostle of the modern city. My dialogue with these motifs strives to open up spaces for an account of the critical dimension of Baudelaire's engagement with the shocks of modernity *through* the category of gender. By applying pressure on a Benjaminian reading of "Une Martyre," I suggest that Baudelaire's allegory both mirrors and critiques the female body's reified circulation as a commodity.

From the reign of Louis-Philippe to the Second Empire, the bourgeoisie's growing investment in private spaces is a form of compensation for the erasure of the individual by the masses of the metropolis. Benjamin describes how the opulent apartment in the "Makart" style, for instance, was designed to faithfully reflect its owner's individuality and furnished a kind of membrane protecting this reified imprint from public view.[21] The spectacular interior of Baudelaire's "Une Martyre" is a fossil that retains the imprint of the victim's history. In this ostentatious décor, "nature" is represented as a "second nature"; it is fully commodified and transformed into so many luxury items. Dresses, jewels, bottles, paintings, pillows, furniture, and garter belts indiscriminately pile up, collapsing the distinction between the organic and the inorganic (hair mingles with jewelry), the organic and the synthetic (a flesh-colored stocking clings to the victim's leg), and between the vegetal and the human (the victim's

head is a "renoncule"). Nature is figured as a river of blood quenching a tex-
tiled field:

> Un cadavre sans tête épanche comme un fleuve,
> Sur l'oreiller désaltéré
> Un sang rouge et vivant, dont la toile s'abreuve
> Avec l'avidité d'un pré.

By the time the decapitated body is discovered by the reader in the third stanza,
it has become a decorative centerpiece displayed for public consumption, a
"renoncule" fated to join the dying flowers in their vases, a poetic *fleur du mal.*

While the human body is presented as an inert and petrified thing, inani-
mate objects are invested with human characteristics.[22] The objects on display
brim with significance and furtive vitality: flowers exhale in their vases, the pil-
lowcase (a "toile," or a canvas) thirstily drinks the victim's blood, a jeweled
garter casts a glimmering look. The victim's own gaze, however, is blank just as
her head, significantly, is "vide de pensers."[23] In this scenario, it is the rustle of
objects, the glint of a garter—that "ainsi qu'un oeil secret qui flambe / Darde
un regard diamanté"—that seduce, and even chain the spectator's eyes to the
dreadful spectacle. Objects are anthropomorphized as consumers, agents, and
witnesses to the crime. The mutilated body is both another "thing" in the
apartment's landscape and the necessary agent of transfer between nature,
commodity, and art.

"Une Martyre" stages the logic of commodity fetishism. The animation of
its objects illustrates the consumer's delirious identification with dead matter
in the marketplace. The anthropomorphic nature of correspondences yields to
a dense network of relations between dead—yet animate—things.[24] We have
entered a world in which objects are both allegorical and commodified: they
stand in for some "natural" counterpart and yet destroy the illusion of a real,
organic nature. For Benjamin, allegory and the commodity form were struc-
turally similar modes of representation. Just as the commodity on the market
is a sign invested with an arbitrary value, similarly allegory posits an arbitrary
relationship between a sign and its meaning. Allegory and commodity are rep-
resentational currencies whose origins are masked, erased, or forgotten. They
are processes that rip an object from its context of production, hollow it out,
and reify it in its circulation.[25] How, then, might Baudelaire's allegory of the
commodity form in "Une Martyre" also function as an allegory of allegory it-
self? How might the convergence of aesthetic, sexual, and urban economies
perform a critique of their overlapping violence?

"Une Martyre" enacts the poetics of prostitution of "Les Foules." The poet is a voyeur who, like the flâneur and poet-prostitute discussed above, wanders the streets of Paris (and its museums) in search of bodies, homes, and things to enter (along with anonymous masterpieces). The poet-voyeur slips into the painting/crime's framed interior and appropriates its objects through a process of identification. He turns the female body and the private interior inside out, displaying both for public viewing. The apartment or protective membrane containing its owner's consciousness is ripped aside and exposed. The victim's body bears a synecdochal relationship to this exposed interior, its decapitation figures, *en abyme,* the violation of the domestic space. Shamelessly splayed on the bed, she exposes the secret splendor of her "natural" endowments:

> Sur le lit, le tronc nu sans scrupule étale
> Dans le plus complet abandon
> La secrète splendeur et la beauté fatale
> Dont la nature lui fit don.

The body's commodification is conveyed in the verb *étaler*: to spread out one's wares at the marketplace or on the *étalage* of a *grand magasin.* Both the apartment and the body are private containers brutally opened by the poet-flâneur-voyeur and exhibited as objects on display. The human body's mutilation, and its parceling out into illegible pieces form the conditions of poetic identification, aesthetic representation, and, ultimately, public consumption.

Curiously, in the eleventh stanza, the poet-spectator wonders if the martyr's physical senses may have *opened themselves up* to, and welcomed in, pressing crowds of unspeakable desires:

> Et ses sens par l'ennui mordus
> S'étaient-ils entr'ouverts à la meute altérée
> Des désirs errants et perdus ?

The allusion to a thirsty mob of stray desires conjures an image of the body's penetration and possession by the *city's* wandering and aimless crowds, a suggestion that is reinforced in the penultimate stanza's allusions to the "monde railleur," "foule impure" and "magistrats curieux." Not a portion of this body, embedded and framed as it may be within the walls of a private apartment, has remained immune to or unclaimed by the public domain.

The body and the apartment are thus the sites of multiple violations: by the lover–assassin–suspected necrophiliac, by the crowds consuming the representations of the crime, by the poet-spectator of the "dessin d'un maître inconnu," and by the reader of the poem. This violence characterizes each interpretive gesture made by the poet-viewer, such that the attempt to decipher the crime scene becomes indissociable from a prurient reenactment of the crime itself. As aesthetic object and desirable commodity, the body is no "given" matter; rather, it is explicitly produced by the violence done to it.

For Benjamin, just as the opulent apartment serves as a defense against an impersonal urban chaos, the rise of the detective novel can be explained by the illusion it gives that an individual's trajectory leaves recoverable traces in the teeming metropolis.[26] The intrigue of "Une Martyre" reproduces key elements of the detective plot: the discovery of the body, the careful record of the crime scene, the cataloguing of forensic evidence, the reconstruction of the victim's moral history and of the possible motives for the murder, up to the fanatical courtroom interrogation before the gaze of the "foule impure" and "magistrats curieux." The poet-spectator is thus also a detective who reconstructs the crime with whatever clues the anonymous *dessin* gives him. Strangely enough, a painting *within* the drawing offers a key to the poetic investigation:

> Le singulier aspect de cette solitude
> Et d'un grand portrait langoureux
> Aux yeux provocateurs comme son attitude
> Révèle un amour ténébreux,
>
> Une coupable joie et des fêtes étranges
> Pleines de baisers infernaux,
> Dont se réjouissent l'essaim des mauvais anges
> Nageant dans les plis des rideaux;

The victim's history is injected into an object (a *portrait langoureux*), which—like the other objects in the room—is humanized and invested with the ability to look and to seduce. The painting contains, *en abyme,* elements of the poetic tableau itself, such as the teeming crowds of rejoicing witnesses (the "essaim des mauvais anges") repeated in the "meute altérée / Des désirs errants et perdus" conjured up by the poet in the eleventh stanza, and in the penultimate stanza's allusion to the "monde railleur," "foule impure" and "magistrats curieux." All of these framed representations and their crowds of witnesses—the portrait, the anonymous drawing, the poetic tableau, and the poet's own imaginary reconstructions—are competing testimonies that promise to unlock the mystery of the body's history, only to be set into a dizzying regress of failed embeddings. This failure to detect and consume the criminal scenario as one would a *fait divers* or a macabre *estampe érotique* is a curious volte-face after the graphic sensationalism of stanzas describing mutilation, orgies, and necrophilia. What is the significance of the poem's abortive gestures toward the detective genre's typical structure of disclosure?

In a discussion of the *roman policier,* Benjamin makes explicit reference to "Une Martyre" and provides a fascinating comment on the poet's failure to sustain the basic structure of the detective plot.

> The detective story, the most momentous among Poe's technical achieve-ments, was part of a literature that satisfied Baudelaire's postulate. Its analy-sis constitutes part of the analysis of Baudelaire's own work, despite the fact that Baudelaire wrote no stories of this type. The *Fleurs du mal* have three of its decisive elements as *disjecta membra:* the victim and the scene of the crime ("Une Martyre"), the murderer ("Le Vin de l'assassin"), the masses ("Le Crépuscule du soir"). The fourth element is lacking—the one that per-mits the intellect to break through this emotion-laden atmosphere. Baude-laire wrote no detective story because, given the nature of his instincts, it was impossible for him to identify with the detective. In him, the calculat-ing, constructive element was on the side of the asocial and had become an integral part of cruelty. Baudelaire was too good a reader of the marquis de Sade to be able to compete with Poe. (Benjamin, *Charles Baudelaire,* 43).

While Baudelaire clearly shows a disposition for the genre, his psychologi-cal makeup and its fundamental asociality, according to Benjamin, forbid the identification with the detective necessary for a successful criminal scenario. Yet what beyond an *instinctual* disposition toward the criminal, the sadist, and other such figures of abjection who resist the social order and its representative *magistrats* could account for the complex interplay of identification and resis-tance staged in this poem? The oscillating identifications with the commodi-ties, the dismembered body on the scene, and the criminal himself suggest that we are witnessing a typically Baudelairean mise-en-scène of the shifting relationships between *victime* and *bourreau,* one that refuses any stable identi-ficatory recuperation and that fully participates in the cruelty that is repre-sented. It is only through a rehearsal of the representational logics of allegory, commodity, and detection, from the standpoint of both *victime* and *bourreau,* that the violent underpinnings of such logics may be disclosed.

The convergence of the detective genre with the allegory of commodifica-tion ultimately unveils an allegory of the reading process itself, one that per-forms the link between violence and representation. This violence is recorded in the poetic form, with its incongruously deliberate, classical diction and its syntactical reenactment of the decapitation in the enjambment between the fourth and fifth stanzas ("La tête . . . / Repose.") The poet-witness, a "hypocrite lecteur" in his own right, enlists the reader's participation and complicity in the voyeuristic reading of the crime scene: as detective, as empathic dandy and aesthete, as prurient voyeur and avid *faits divers* reader, as moralist and finally, as both courtroom prosecutor *and* criminal lover. This delirium of identifications culminates with the apostrophes that imagine the assassin's necrophilic violation of the corpse:

> L'homme vindicatif que tu n'as pu, vivante,
> Malgré tant d'amour, assouvir,
> Combla-t-il sur ta chair inerte et complaisante
> L'immensité de son désir ?
>
> Réponds, cadavre impur ! et par tes tresses roides
> Te soulevant d'un bras fiévreux,
> Dis-moi, tête effrayante, a-t-il sur tes dents froides
> Collé les suprêmes adieux ?

The poem's abrupt suspension of these identifications comes as a shock, if not a betrayal to the reader (as detective, consumer, and necrophiliac accomplice). In the penultimate stanza, the caesura marks a sudden rupture with these sensationalist readings and a retreat before the body's irreducible otherness:

> — Loin du monde railleur, loin de la foule impure,
> Loin des magistrats curieux,
> Dors en paix, dors en paix, étrange créature
> Dans ton tombeau mystérieux;

The poetic investigation thwarts its will to representation and, in a protective—if belated—gesture, cordons the corpse from the public gaze, turning from the registers of detection and consumption to that of an epitaph's inscription.

"Une Martyre" discloses the concealed violence of each act of reading—a violence that binds the detective to the criminal, the executioner to his victim and the poet to the reader. It is only by being "an integral part of cruelty," as Benjamin puts it, that the poetic persona may disclose the overlap of sexual, aesthetic, economic, and readerly desire. Baudelaire's hyperbolic performance of cruelty explodes, from within, the appropriative motion of reading as consumption. The allegory of commodification and detection in the poem disrupts its own procedure by exposing this logic and showing its failure to assign a value to the body beyond its irreducible materiality. This poetic exercise in cruelty forces its readership, its "hypocrite lecteur," to falter in its consumption of the body in/of the poem.

"Une Martyre" displays a female body that has been produced through the interwoven violence of allegorization, prostitution, commodity production, and textual—as well as visual—consumption.[27] It stages femininity as "fatalement suggestive," as a figure for the process of figuration itself. Baudelaire's poem relinquishes the notion of a preexisting nature. It presents us with a world of glassy surfaces, a "new" or "second" nature that encases the mutilated human body as but another commodity for the reader as consumer. In that sense, "Une Martyre" gives a prescient illustration of what Jameson defines as the postmodern turn: "In modernism . . . some residual zones of 'nature' or 'being,' of the old, the older and the archaic still subsist; culture can still do something to that nature and work at transforming that 'referent.' Postmodernism is what you have when that modernization process is complete and nature is gone for good. It is a more fully human world than the older one, but one in which 'culture' has become a veritable 'second nature.'" (Jameson, *Postmodernism,* ix).

Baudelaire's poem deploys a critique of this "second nature," but not from a vantage point that retains an authentic nature or that rescues a relationship to the human body beyond the violence of reification. The demystifying moment emerges instead from the very cycle of commodity production and consumption, a cycle that fully implicates the writing and reading of poetry itself. We are now in a better position to examine the opposite pole of Baudelaire's conception of femininity—as natural, that is to say, abominable—in order to further explore how the conspicuous absence of a primary "nature" in such exhibitions of the body intervenes in the Second Empire's ideological narratives of sexual, racial, and colonial domination.

Whipped into Shape: *"La Femme sauvage et la petite-maîtresse"*

Baudelaire's prose poem "La Femme sauvage et la petite-maîtresse" describes a poet who, exasperated by his mistress's languid complaints and affected femininity, decides to teach her the meaning of "real" suffering by taking her to a street fair, where, for a couple of sous, spectators watch a savage woman in a cage as she tears into live animals and is beaten by her husband-keeper.[28] After a cursory meditation on the sorry state of conjugal mores, the poet turns to his mistress and reiterates his disgust for her "précieuses pleurnicheries," threatening to either beat her up like the savage woman or to throw her out the window like an empty bottle.

The poem initially appears as a straightforward sadistic pedagogical experiment designed to teach the poet's mistress of her good fortune in the hands of her generous keeper by showing the difference between real and simulated suffering, between the working-class fair and the comfortable bourgeois interior. Yet, this mise-en-scène of class difference is complicated by a reflection on the very nature of "femininity," raising questions of a different order altogether: what do these scenarios have in common? What corporeal reality underlies these performances of savagery and femininity, conducted, respectively, in the working-class fair and the opulent apartment? In other words, what is the "nature" of woman? And this question inevitably leads to another: how is the emergence of her "nature" conditioned by certain sanctioned forms of violence that are at once physical, rhetorical, and institutional? For as we shall see, both the physical brutality of the savage woman's treatment and the discursive beating to which the little mistress is subjected in fact *constitute* the so-called "natural" bodies put on display on the public scene and on the textual stage.

The alleged aim of the poem is to confront nature in all of its degraded animality ("la femme sauvage") with its simulation ("la petite-maîtresse"). But nature and its simulation coalesce so perfectly in the savage woman's performance that it becomes impossible to distinguish between them: "Voyez avec quelle voracité (non simulée peut-être !) elle déchire des lapins vivants et des volailles piaillantes." Either the savage woman is a consummate performer of savagery or her natural instincts have been unleashed by the performance itself.

What binds these two women together is not their female nature so much as their status as performers. Both of them are, after all, engaged in parallel— if contrasting—productions (of nature and its savagery, of culture and its affectation). These performances are not only parallel but continuous: the woman at the carnival apes the savagery of wild animals, her artificially bestial form vaguely imitates the mistress's own body, and the mistress herself mimics conventional attributes of femininity learned from novels ("toutes ces affectations apprises dans les livres"). So to ask that the mistress act more "natural" by showing her the woeful fate of her savage counterpart is bound to fail, since the performance itself sends any stable notion of nature into a kind of imitative regress.

In both scenarios, the "natural" bodies of the women in question are ultimately constructed through an exercise of violence over which they do not have control. In both, a violent process of figuration produces—or attempts to produce—the natural state that is supposed to exist prior to figuration. The poet-figure unveils this paradoxical mechanism with great relish: "Allons ! un

bon coup de bâton pour la calmer ! car elle darde des yeux terribles de con-
voitise sur la nourriture enlevée. Grand Dieu ! Le bâton n'est pas un bâton de
comédie, avez-vous entendu résonner la chair, malgré le poil postiche ? Aussi,
les yeux lui sortent maintenant de la tête, elle hurle *plus naturellement.* Dans sa
rage, elle étincelle toute entière comme le fer qu'on bat."

In this passage, the material body and its figuration—nature and its per-
formance—are implicated in an extraordinarily complicated way, for it is
through the theatrical blows inflicted by a real stick (masquerading as a fake
one) that the woman's naturalness, and her authenticating howls, are pro-
duced. In other words, it is through a hyperbolically artificial performance of
brutality that the category of "the natural" comes into italicized being: "elle
hurle *plus naturellement.*" But we have yet another turn of the screw, for the re-
turn to nature signaled by the woman's howls of pain is immediately followed
by her resurrection as art: "avez-vous entendu resonner la chair . . . ?"; "elle
étincelle toute entière comme le fer qu'on bat." The sheer violence of the
blows, in producing the natural body in all of its eloquence, also unleashes its
aesthetic potential, its "resonance" and "scintillation."

The significance of this aestheticized image raises some questions, especially
since it is only one in a poem that, after all, involves four artistic figures: two
performers, a "metteur en scène," and a poet. How might the violence exer-
cised on the savage woman's body be akin to the violence of aesthetic produc-
tion, an act that extracts *la beauté du mal*? More specifically, how does the
aberrant figuration of femininity at the fair suggest a parallel disfiguration in
poetry? The spectacular fate of the *femme sauvage* stages the effects through
which her nature is materialized as savage: the husband-showman's blows have
quite literally generated the "naturalness" of the body and its howls on stage.
This ability to bring (or beat) a body into existence through the suspension of
that body's referential status (is the wild woman a woman? is the little mistress
a beast?) is not unlike poetry's own suspension of reference. Its systematic con-
fusion of literal and metaphoric registers is staged as the confusion between
the body proper and its figurative guises. The very principle of "surnatural-
isme" on which Baudelaire founds the ideal of *poésie pure* is repeatedly de-
scribed in his art criticism as the despotic enhancement of natural phenomena
through a penetrating and almost alchemical alteration, one that releases these
materials from their natural state and into their hyperbolic, "surnaturel," and
properly poetic incarnation. The blows that transform the savage woman's
body into shimmering metal resonate with the very terms that Baudelaire,
along with his Parnassien contemporaries, such as Gautier, associate with po-

etic craft. Poetry is an *alchimie verbale* that sculpts and chisels resistant metals and minerals, forging a verbal artifact that is "belle come un rêve de pierre."[29] The ideal of beauty as a shimmering, metallic body forged and polished by poetry is invoked in an unpublished fragment as "cette beauté, sombre comme le fer / Est de celles que forge et que polit l'Enfer" (*OC*, 1: 189). The poet's task is precisely this alchemical transfiguration, which changes mud into gold ("J'ai pétri de la boue et j'en ai fait de l'or" [*OC*, 1: 188]). The savage female body undergoes just such a transfiguration: she is fashioned and struck to embody a hyperbolical naturalness, a "surnaturalisme" that turns her into a species of art.

"La Femme sauvage et la petite-maîtresse" proposes that the aesthetic process and the fairground performance are analogous in their violence toward the bodies they allegedly "represent." The act of poetic figuration—its transformation of bodies and materials—is parodically literalized as the beating of flesh into art. The homology between poetry and the public domain of mass entertainment is established from the outset in a series of ironic *correspondances* between the poet's domestic drama and the fairground's spectacle: the poet-*entreteneur* is as much a keeper and a showman as is his monstrous counterpart—the husband; the physical abuse of the savage woman doubles the poet's discursive abuse of his mistress; both explicitly male subjects put commodified bodies on display, and both produce—or attempt to produce—an ideal of nature through the exercise of violence.

The sequence of threats upon which the poem concludes flesh out the affinities between poetic violence, and the physical brutality of the fairground scene: "Si vous méprisez le soliveau (ce que je suis maintenant, comme vous savez bien), gare à la grue *qui vous croquera, vous gobera et vous tuera à son plaisir !*... et si vous me fatiguez trop souvent de vos *précieuses* pleurnicheries, je vous traiterai en *femme sauvage,* ou je vous jetterai par la fenêtre, comme une bouteille vide."

The mistress must be beaten out of her figurations of femininity to better embody a natural condition. Yet this "nature" exists neither in the books she reads nor in the "real world" of working-class spectacles. So she will be beaten, not until she can embody herself more naturally, but until she suffers with greater conviction and howls "plus *naturellement.*" Or if she is not beaten, she will be eaten like La Fontaine's frogs (who foolishly demanded a despot instead of a gentle sovereign). Failing that, she will be cast out the window, out of the very frame of representation. In this final threat, on which the poem closes, "ou je vous jetterai par la fenêtre comme une bouteille vide," the little mistress occupies all three contradictory and mutually reinforcing positions in which the poem places women. She stands in for an unintelligible body ("naturelle donc abominable"). She also figures as the impotent muse incapable of metamorphic mutation, unable to inspire the poet with meaningful signs (not "fatalement suggestive"). Finally, like the body of "Une Martyre," she becomes a prostituted commodity object that, once consumed, may be discarded.

The poet's struggle with his recalcitrant mistress-muse is but one of several sites for the production of gender. Others are the domestic sphere of the "petite-maîtresse" and its literary culture (the books that fail to teach her how to perform her nature adequately), the public domain of working-class fairs, and—as the poem points out—a much more vast administrative and juridical sphere. As the poet stresses with more than a touch of sadistic irony, the beating is legally sanctioned, since the savage woman's keeper is her husband: "Il a enchaîné sa femme *légitime* comme une bête, et il la montre dans les faubourgs, les jours de foire, avec permission des magistrats, *cela va sans dire*" (emphasis added). The savagery of this scenario is a parodic literalization of the institution of marriage—an institution that, with the promulgation of the Napoleonic Code, turned women into their husbands' property by according them the legal status of minors and the insane (and this would be another reason why the mistress is the more fortunate of the two by far). Baudelaire's text thus unveils the ideological underpinnings of the "cela va sans dire," that is to say, the unspoken consensus that legitimates the display, diminishment, and punishment of women by their brutal husbands and keepers.[30]

This vast network of mutually reinforcing determinations of gender and nature, however, still fails to fully domesticate the wild body on display. The poet's ostentatious effort to name this body is a case in point: "Ce *monstre* est un de ces *animaux* qu'on appelle généralement « mon *ange* ! » c'est-à-dire *une femme*" (emphasis added). The location of a natural female body is foiled by the very complexity of its production. The attempt to "raisonner la chair," to reason the body (and not simply make it resonate) through the allegory of "la femme sauvage" spins out of control, since the body fashioned for private or public consumption is so volatile and riddled with artifice that the very categories that define and control it as a gendered, natural entity break down. Neither the carnival scene nor the poet's ironic admonition contain the "monstre" within the confines of the "démonstration."

In disclosing the unstable ground of gender, the poem also sweeps away a host of related differences. The distinction between femininity and masculinity reveals a common monstrosity; the natural and artificial—and savagery and art—are put into an uneasy and reversible relationship; the private apartment collapses into the "faubourg"; the poetic struggle with the muse becomes a public beating to amuse. This corrosion also unravels the closure of traditional literary forms, forms that fail to contain the body's contradictory productions. The citations (or "sages paroles") that saturate the text—allusions to Marivaux's *Le Petit Maître corrigé*, maxims such as "Il ne faut pas manger tout son bien en un jour" (as the husband tells savage woman as she devours a live chicken) and La Fontaine's fable "Les Grenouilles demandent un roi"—are parodic references that underline the bankruptcy of these classical forms and proverbs and the irrelevance of their appeal to communicable notions of "morale," "mesure," or "nature."[31] It is hardly surprising, then, that Baudelaire gave up his initial plan to compose "La Femme sauvage et la petite-maîtresse" in verse. As we saw in Chapter 2, no genre could be further from the closure of classical forms than the prose poem, which emerges from the intersections of urban modernity and its jostling bodies and discourses.

Situating the female body at the crossroads of poetic figuration and other cultural sites for its production, then, "La Femme sauvage et la petite-maîtresse" and "Une Martyre" give a complex view of how poetic objects and social subjects are constituted and interpellated. Textual stage and social scene both violently produce the "nature" of bodies on display. Poetry's production of the bodies and beings that it names is tied into a critique of the competing régimes that violently constitute the category—or figure—of gender. The metapoetic reflection lays bare the violence of accepted cultural practices that make possible the equation between femininity and a materiality that is alternately malleable and regressively savage.

Baudelaire and the Exposition universelle of 1855: Ethnographic Spectacle, Imperial Display, and Visual Consumption

The demystification of the body's nature and ground in "La Femme sauvage et la petite-maîtresse" returns us to our opening discussion of "woman" as a key token in nineteenth-century narratives of modernism and modernity. Baudelaire's exhibition of the *femme sauvage* resonates against broader cultural preoccupations with the female body's place in the historical continuum between "sauvagerie" and "civilisation," one increasingly mapped along evolutionary and racial axes. What are some of the cultural investments in conceptualizing femininity as regressive materiality within the Second Empire's colonial imaginary? And how does Baudelaire's denaturalization of *la femme sauvage* intervene in contemporary narratives of savagery, modernity, progress, and imperial conquest? To tease out the ideological valences of Baudelaire's demystification of the savage body, let us return briefly to his initial portrait of the *femme sauvage:* "Considérons bien, je vous prie, cette solide cage de fer derrière laquelle s'agite, hurlant comme un damné, secouant les barreaux comme un orang-outang . . . imitant, dans la perfection, tantôt les bonds circulaires des tigres, tantôt les dandinements stupides de l'ours blanc, ce monstre poilu dont la forme imite assez vaguement la votre."

The zoological register of this description, and specifically the allusion to orangutans, recalls similar cultural displays of the female body in all of its spectacular otherness, such as the exhibition of the so-called Hottentot Venuses or female Khoisanids at fairs and salons in Paris and London earlier in the century. Georges Cuvier dissected the most famous of these, Saartjie Bartman, whom he described as a member of the "lowest human species" and likened to the most evolved of apes, the orangutan, in a presentation at the Académie de médecine in 1817. Her brain and genitalia were preserved in formaldehyde as specimens of primitive sexuality.[32] Another Khoisanid was exhibited nude in the drawing room of the duchesse du Barry as late as 1829. These exhibitions of the African body, as Sander Gilman and others have argued, confirmed racist agendas by exhibiting the difference between the savage dark bodies on display and those of their civilized, white—and clothed—spectators, between primitive abjection and civilized subjecthood.

As the converging iconography of the prostitute and the "Hottentot" suggest, pseudo-scientific representations of "unbridled" female sexuality later in the century became increasingly inflected and pathologized by racial categories. The Khoisanid is but one example of this equation of degenerate female sexuality with blackness. One thinks of Manet's Nana, whose protruding buttocks suggest the steatopygia for which Khoisanids were famed, or Zola's Nana, whose *fameux coup de hanche* catapults her into fame at the *théâtre des variétés,* or even Manet's Olympia, derisively called "that Hottentot Venus with a black cat," whose sexuality is underscored by the black maidservant behind her.[33] Baudelaire's own parallel between the *petite maîtresse* draped in fine silks and the raging creature in the cage captures this contamination of the civilized woman by her dark, savage sister ("ce monstre poilu, dont la forme imite assez vaguement la votre"). To read *la femme sauvage* along with such contemporary racializations of female sexuality is not so fanciful when we recall Baudelaire's long-standing relationship with his Creole mistress Jeanne Duval, the ostensible biographical source of his "Black Venus" poems and allegedly the inspiration for Olympia's black maidservant. Duval remained associated with a dark, exotic, and even pathological sexuality in the minds of Baudelaire's contemporaries. At the poet's death, for instance, the journalist Victor Noir evoked a purely imaginary trip to "Madras," where the poet "se lia avec une Indienne qu'à Paris on appelait : Le Monstre noir," and a few years later, Lautréamont would refer to Baudelaire as "l'amant morbide de la Vénus Hottentote."[34]

The joint reification of race and sexuality evident in the fascination with the "black Venus" is inseparable from the imperial enterprise of displaying the body of the "other" in a context of accelerating colonial expansion. The human zoos, or ethnographic spectacles of the Jardin d'acclimatation, for instance, displayed the bodies of various indigenous peoples amidst their "native" flora and fauna. Baudelaire's zoological depiction of the savage woman in a cage seems an uncanny foreshadowing of this phenomenon. After its inaugural exhibition of Nubians and Eskimos in 1877, the Jardin staged thirty such displays of "natives" from various parts of the world until World War I. These exhibits established the genre of the native villages that proliferated over the next half-century in *expositions universelles* and, later, colonial exhibitions. Such spectacular displays of indigenous bodies in their so-called native habitat helped to show the spoils of the empire, to figure and thereby domesticate—if not simply invent—the colonial subject and its place in the imperial design.[35]

Although the exhibition of "natives" as *tableaux vivants* in these human zoos did not begin until the 1867 Exposition universelle (the year of Baudelaire's death), representatives of most nations of the British Empire were present at the Crystal Palace as early as 1851, forming an imperial *tableau vivant* of sorts.[36] As Ann McClintock has observed, the Crystal Palace set the stage for subsequent world fairs and their phantasmagoria of historical progress as global conquest. It mapped a unified world time geographically, placing Western colonial power at the head of the evolutionary hierarchy: "The Crystal Palace housed the first consumer dreams of a unified world time. As a monument to industrial progress, the Great Exhibition embodied the hope that all the world's cultures could be gathered under one roof—the global progress of history represented as the commodity progress of the Family of Man. At the same time, the Exhibition heralded a new mode of marketing history: the mass consumption of time as a commodity spectacle" (McClintock, *Imperial Leather*, 57).

We can perhaps imagine what Baudelaire's reaction would have been had he strolled past the human displays of the later exhibitions and their phantasmagoria of industrial progress and imperial conquest. During his own time, the Paris exhibition and its heterogeneous display of merchandise and commodities from around the world already presented history as a geopolitical progress narrative of imperial expansion. The Paris Exposition universelle of 1855 boasted the first separate "Imperial Pavilion"—paid for by the government—to stage the gains of the empire, a pavilion that set the vogue for the colonial palaces of future world fairs. The emperor had initially envisioned it as an exhibition of industrial products, a veritable hymn to progress, but then decided to include a section on the *beaux-arts*. As Timothy Raser shows, citing from the imperial "Rapport sur l'exposition de 1855," the French exhibition sought to distinguish itself from the English model by integrating spiritual as well as material accomplishments: "il appartient spécialement à la France, dont l'industrie doit tant aux beaux arts, de leur assigner, dans la prochaine Exposition Universelle, la place qu'ils méritent."[37] This union of art and industry was to reflect the Exposition's universalist aims, and it accordingly included a two-floor Palace of Fine Arts in which works by French artists (such as Ingres and Delacroix) were prominently displayed. Prussia was well represented, and the galleries contained paintings from about thirty other nations. In keeping with the presentation of the Exposition as a modern consumer event, the metal and glass pavilion also contained a restaurant and an air-conditioning system. With its array of international merchandise and entry fee structure, the Exposition truly presented itself as a global stage for the display of the world's commodities.[38]

Baudelaire's writings on the Arts Pavilion of the 1855 Paris Exposition universelle famously reject "progress" as a natural principle guiding civilizations to their assigned state of supremacy.[39] His critique thus questions the Exposition's very basis, its propagandistic display of national progress and global conquest, as well as its transformation of history into a commodity spectacle available for mass consumption. Baudelaire explicitly denounced this narrative as an ideological sham designed to lull its bourgeois public into a fatuous stupor that announced France's imminent decline. Such faith in a historically determined collective evolution was fiction that stripped individuals of their agency and lucidity: "Cette idée grotesque, qui a fleuri sur le terrain pourri de la fatuité moderne, a dechargé chacun de son devoir, délivré toute âme de sa responsabilité, . . . et les races amoindries, si cette navrante folie dure longtemps, s'endormiront sur l'oreiller de la fatalité dans le sommeil radoteur de la décrépitude."[40]

These vitriolic denunciations of progress are usually read within a Catholic or de Maistrean framework of original sin and providentialism, in light of the poet's many proclamations that the civilizing process does not reside in technological or industrial progress but in the diminishment of the traces of mankind's fall ("Théorie de la vraie civilisation. Elle n'est pas dans le gaz, ni dans la vapeur, ni dans les tables tournantes, elle est dans la diminution des traces du péché originel" [*OC*, 1: 697]). Yet it is important to remember that Baudelaire's anti-progressivist stance consistently dislocates the Western civilizing mission to assert the value, dignity, and energy of preindustrial peoples and nations against the apparent supremacy of Western nations and their modes of production. The fragment on original sin in "Mon coeur mis à nu," for instance, concludes with the declaration that "[p]euples nomades, pasteurs, chasseurs, agricoles, et mêmes anthropophages, *tous* peuvent être supérieurs, par l'énergie, par la dignité personnelles, à nos races d'Occident" (*OC*, 1: 697). Baudelaire's celebration of the survival of dandies and of heroism among so-called "savage populations" such as Amerindians or African Americans are not simply sentimental gestures imbued with Rousseauist nostalgia but, rather, integral to his critique of capitalist modernity and its repressed savagery.[41]

Baudelaire's introduction to the Arts Pavilion in 1855 thus challenged the capitalist and colonialist ideology of progress at the heart of the Exposition universelle and discerned a central premise of the world fairs' ideology: that human evolution and historical progress are one and the same; that an identical teleology regulates the development of the species and that of a civilization:

> Demandez à tout bon Français qui lit tous les jours *son* journal dans son estaminet, ce qu'il entend par progrès, il répondra que c'est la vapeur, l'électricité et l'éclairage au gaz, miracles inconnus aux Romains, et que ces découvertes témoignent pleinement de notre supériorité sur les anciens ; tant il s'est fait de ténèbres dans ce malheureux cerveau et tant les choses de l'ordre matériel et de l'ordre spirituel s'y sont si bizarrement confondues ! Le pauvre homme est tellement américanisé par ses philosophes zoocrates et industriels, qu'il a perdu la notion des différences qui caractérisent les phénomènes du monde physique et du monde moral, du naturel et du surnaturel. (*OC*, 2: 580)

Far from being a bout of conservative rhetoric—as it may at first appear—Baudelaire here pinpoints the conflation of industrial progress with innate national superiority that guided evolutionary teleologies legitimating a hierarchy of nations.[42] He shows how this temporal narrative of progress (the moderns' superiority to the ancients) is mapped geographically to justify the supremacy of Western civilized nations. In his account, France cannot complacently count on a "natural" teleology of progress to stake out its imperial and artistic territory. France's centrality is but a temporary mirage that will be dissolved by the winds of time and by the emergence of other nations: "La prospérité actuelle n'est garantie que pour un temps, hélas ! bien court. L'aurore fut jadis à l'orient, la lumière a marché vers le sud, et maintenant elle jaillit de l'occident. . . . la vitalité se déplace, elle va visiter d'autres territoires et d'autres races" (*OC,* 2: 581–82). Baudelaire thus rejects the conflation of evolutionary accounts of the human species with historical narratives of progress, a conflation that formed the ideological crux of the *expositions universelles* as well as that of later colonial expositions, with their native villages displaying primitive bodies in natural habitats en route to modernization. His essay offers a prescient understanding of the ideological phantasmagoria embodied in these exhibitions.

The foreign products at the Exposition universelle were not simply showcased as curiosities, but as material evidence of the empire's expanding boundaries, as forms of the exotic literally "in-corporated" into the display of a growing imperial body. Baudelaire's opening remarks on the exhibition, however, reverse this process of incorporation and destabilize the armature holding these commodities in place. His essay does not open with a work of art or even with a French object but instead with an unspecified Chinese product that invites a new aesthetics of reception. Opposing the tyranny of neoclassicists, Baudelaire wonders what a modern Winckelmann would do if faced with an exotic object completely alien to his sensibilities:

> [Q]ue dirait-il en face d'un produit chinois, produit étrange, bizarre, contourné dans sa forme, intense par sa couleur, et quelquefois délicat jusqu'à l'évanouissement ? Cependant, c'est un echantillon de la beauté universelle ; mais il faut, pour qu'ils soit compris, que le critique, le spectateur, opère *en lui-même* une transformation qui tient du mystère, et que, par un phénomène de la volonté agissant par l'imagination, *il apprenne de lui-même à participer au milieu qui a donné naissance à cette florasion insolite.* (*OC,* 2: 576; emphasis added)

Far from passively occupying their assigned place and yielding to French viewers' consumption, for Baudelaire, the foreign objects on display actively reframed the terms and conditions of their viewing. In his account, it is the domestic subject who is transformed, if not reconstituted, by his encounter with the foreign object. The spectator's submission to its alchemical alteration reverses the habitual hierarchy of viewing subject and viewed object. We witness a dislocation of the familiar—and of Frenchness—under the despotic power of the foreign product, which now generates its context as well as the criteria by which it will be judged.[43] The French encounter with foreignness is described as a profound physiological and spiritual penetration that resists the assumed conversion and convertibility of a conquered nation "penetrated" by the colonial presence.[44] Thus, three main points emerge out of Baudelaire's interrogation of the ideology of the Exposition universelle: a critique of the concept of Western civilization's natural and inevitable progress, which is implicitly yoked to a critique of the regressive savagery of modern capitalism; a reversal of visual power in the exhibition of foreign merchandise; and a scrutiny of Frenchness as the universal model for aesthetic judgment.

Now just as Baudelaire is notorious for his general misogyny, some of his most celebrated poems exemplify the exoticism that we find both in imperial *expositions universelles* and in ethnographic spectacles and reproductions of native villages a decade or so later. The latter's reification of dark bodies, tropical landscapes, and oriental behaviors recall Baudelaire's own hymns to "la langoureuse Asie et la brûlante Afrique." But in what follows, I wish to complicate this take on Baudelaire's exoticist misogyny by reading his prose poem "La Belle Dorothée" against the concerns outlined above—against a context of imperial display in which exotic products, foreign habitats, and later, indigenous bodies were exhibited as commodities offered up for France's consumption. How might the demystification of the body's "nature" that we have observed thus far in "Une Martyre" and "La Femme sauvage et la petite-maîtresse" help us to reread such fictions of the racial and colonial body? How might Baudelaire's poetic displays destabilize the ethnographic and colonial gaze and, in doing so, open up a critical perspective on what Christopher Miller has called the "state-sponsored hallucination" of the French Empire?[45]

Exhibiting Black Venus: "La Belle Dorothée"

In 1841, Baudelaire spent a few weeks on the islands of Bourbon (now Réunion) and Mauritius on his way to India—a journey that his stepfather, General Aupick, deemed necessary to cure him of his excesses in matters of sex and money and to steer him back on track. Baudelaire did not make it beyond the Mascarene Islands of the Indian Ocean before turning back, but his brief sojourn there inspired poems such as "À une Malabaraise," "À une dame Créole," and "La Belle Dorothée," a prose poem written twenty years later (which he refers to as a "souvenir de l'île Bourbon"). "La Belle Dorothée" (like "La Femme sauvage et la petite-maîtresse," published that same year) was initially intended to be in verse. It also has its verse counterpart, "Bien loin d'ici," a steamy sonnet referring to a prostitute called Dorothée and rehearsing a gamut of exoticist tropes through which Baudelaire hoped to show "l'idéal de la beauté noire" or "l'idéal de la nature tropicale."[46] The prose poem, however, aimed to represent the geographical and racial specificity of this ideal tropical black body, as we can gather from Baudelaire's response to Charpentier, the editor of *La Revue nationale et étrangère,* who balked at the provocative anatomical description of Dorothée. Baudelaire protests the editor's censorious intervention thus: "Croyez-vous réellement que « *les formes de son corps* », ce soit là une expression équivalente à « *son dos creux et sa gorge pointue* » ?— Surtout quand il est question de la race noire des côtes orientales ?" (*OC,* 1: 1333). Christopher Miller reads this statement, and the poem more generally, as evidence of Baudelaire's ethnological, colonial gaze, and of his conflation of orientalism and Africanism in the creation of an imaginary exotic geography.[47] And to be sure, this desire to pin down the physical characteristics of a typical Creole female from the Mascarene Islands—with her combination of African and Asian features—seems to place Baudelaire squarely in the exoticist, ethnographic camp that represented an eroticized colonial "other" as a domesticated object of visual consumption. Yet my reading will take issue with the view that Baudelaire's exoticism perpetuates an imperialist tropology. I contend that "La Belle Dorothée" and its picturesque representation of a desirable exotic body exemplifies the ironic maneuvers I have been tracing thus far, maneuvers that disclose violence of allegorization in both aesthetic and colonial production and that unmask the price of putting the colonial body on display.

In "La Belle Dorothée," Baudelaire creates a visual masterpiece that we might be tempted to enjoy simply as a vital sample of the poet's celebrated "culte des images"(*OC,* 1: 701) As Yves Bonnefoy remarks, we are invited to experience the poem as "a painting that sticks to what the eyes see, without ever undertaking the deciphering of the figures that would make them significant," that is to say, as pure form and color, void of any allegorical dimension (Bonnefoy, "'La Belle Dorothée' or Poetry and Painting," 89). Yet it is this visual dimension, the purely formal properties of the poem's exhibition, that subtly indicates its allegorical dimension. The poem depicts an emblematic "black Venus" evolving in her natural habitat and describes her indolent progress toward an unknown destination in the stupefying heat of a tropical noon. A splendid specimen, exposed through violent contrasts of form and color, Dorothée is figured as a moving black stain against a glittering backdrop of sea, sun, and sand. The violence of this figure's composition sharply contrasts with the serene languor of her gait and immediately conveys an uneasy rapport between form and meaning, between the body and its allegorical inscription. The pink dress slashing against her dark body ("Sa robe de soie collante, d'un ton clair et rose, *tranche vivement* sur les ténèbres de sa peau" [*OC*, 1: 316; emphasis added]), for instance, is an image of disquieting erotic force. The expanse of Dorothée's flesh is visually cut up by her dress, itself suggested to have "flesh-colored" tones. And rather than protecting her from the sun's onslaught, the parasol she carries casts a bloody hue on her face. The explicitly corporeal resonances of the poem's color schemes (pink flesh, red blood, black skin) fully disclose the erotic violence of its mode of figuration.

The color scheme in "La Belle Dorothée" echoes the saucy quatrain that Baudelaire had written that same year under Manet's portrait of the part-Creole Spanish dancer Lola de Valence: "Mais on voit scintiller en Lola de Valence / Le charme inattendu d'un bijou rose et noir" (*OC*, 1: 168). Dorothée is completely eroticized throughout, with her protruding buttocks, glistening teeth, and serpentine gait. In a virtual peepshow, the breeze intermittently lifts up her skirt to reveal a glistening leg, exposing a foot so perfect, we are told, that it is equal to the white feet of the gods of classical statuary displayed in Europe's museums: "De temps en temps la brise de mer soulève par le coin sa jupe flottante et montre sa jambe luisante et superbe ; et son pied, pareil aux pieds des déesses de marbre que l'Europe enferme dans ses musées, imprime fidèlement sa forme sur le sable fin." The parallel between museum figures and Dorothée is perhaps not fortuitous, for as she unfolds poetically before our eyes, she is already something of a *tableau vivant,* the living embodiment of a primitive golden age that mirrors the classical era enshrined in Europe's museums. We thus see the spectacle of a body in motion, one that is as embedded in its natural habitat as her foot is faithfully—if briefly—imprinted on her native soil.

The lingering description of a black woman walking in the tropical heat, her head pulled back by the weight of her "enormous hair" (énorme chevelure) echoes other Baudelairean portraits of exotic bodies in motion, such as "Le Serpent qui danse":

> A te voir marcher en cadence
> Belle d'abandon
> On dirait un serpent qui danse
> Au bout d'un bâton
>
> Sous le fardeau de ta paresse
> Ta tête d'enfant
> Se balance avec la mollesse
> D'un jeune éléphant, (*OC*, 1: 30)

This fascination with the alien gate of the exotic body is an uncanny fore-shadowing of Felix-Louis Regnault's chronophotographic study of a West African woman walking with a weight on her head. Regnault's subjects were the Wolof performers at the 1895 Exposition ethnologique. His studies of African bodies in motion (jumping, running, walking) as Fatimah Tobing Rony has shown, functioned as a sort of evolutionary record comparing the African's "natural," primitive and authentic movements ("la marche primitive de l'humanité") to the stiffness of the constrictively civilized European body (Rony, *Third Eye,* 49). Contemplating Dorothée's discursive unfolding in Baudelaire's poem (as a striking black stain moving across a white, mineralized landscape) along with Regnault's chronophotograpic studies captures some of the implicit violence of our positions as readers as we visually consume the poetic ethnography of this specimen of "la race noire des côtes orientales" (*OC,* 1: 1333).

Dorothée is a parody of the luminous Baudelairean ideal of "correspondances," so seamlessly embedded in her habitat (the elements, her little hut by the sea) as to be virtually enshrined in her own analogy: "Elle s'avance ainsi, harmonieusement, heureuse de vivre et souriant d'un blanc sourire, comme si elle apercevait au loin dans l'espace un miroir reflétant sa démarche et sa beauté."[48] "L'Invitation au voyage" (prose) describes its utopic destination in identical terms, as a land where the beloved would be framed in her own analogy and reflected in her own correspondence ("Ne serais-tu pas encadrée dans ton analogie, et ne pourrais-tu pas te mirer, pour parler comme les mystiques, dans ta propre *correspondance ?*" [*OC,* 1: 303]) Yet, as this echo from the 1857 poem suggests, Dorothée is not so much framed by her landscape as she is by verbal shards, intertexts from the ideal poems of *Les Fleurs du mal.* The poem is an "invitation au voyage" in time and space, taking us to a "vie antérieure," where the native, wearing her "bijoux sonores" is fanned or languidly smokes in her idyllic hut by the sea, combing her heavy tresses as a stew of crabs sends its "parfum exotique" her way.[49]

Dorothée is not only an overly figured erotic and aesthetic body. Hers is also an ideal geographic body, an organism fully attuned to its milieu, much in the sense in which Baudelaire—in a declaration tinged with irony—describes nations as "vastes animaux dont l'organisme est adéquat à leur milieu" (*OC,* 2: 575). Just as Bernardin de Saint-Pierre's Virginie is described in "De l'essence du rire" as emerging out of nature's very hands, drenched with the winds and waters of her native île Bourbon, Dorothée's reflection in the surrounding elements suggest that she is not only the inhabitant but also the symbolic recapitulation of an idealized geography whose literary cartographers at the time of Baudelaire's trip included Bernardin de Saint-Pierre and George Sand, and would be followed by Alexandre Dumas (*Georges,* 1843) and Leconte de Lisle (*Poèmes barbares,* 1862).

However, the subtle irony imbuing this picture-perfect scene gives way to a Baudelairean fall into the historical conditions underlying this ideal racial and geographic body. Admired and cherished by all, Dorothée would be perfectly happy if it were not for the fact that she must labor and save to buy back her eleven-year-old sister, already pubescent and too lovely to remain safely in her master's house. We may recall that Baudelaire called this poem a "souvenir de l'île Bourbon," and that at the time of the poet's visit in 1841, it was still a slave-owning plantation culture that produced tobacco and coffee. Seven years later, it implemented abolition (with great resistance on the part of the French and *métis* plantation owners) only to import indentured laborers from India, Indochina, and South Africa. Indolent, naïve, vain Dorothée must laboriously pile "piastre sur piastre" to buy her sister's freedom, and thereby save her from the prostitution that Dorothée herself—with all the freedom of her status as "affranchie"—is compelled to embrace. Baudelaire thus offers us a luminous ideal only to reveal its basis in an interlocking system of sexual and colonial violence.

Dorothée's progress in the stupefying heat of a tropical noon, decked out in silks and jewels, needs to be reread not as a beatific communion with nature, but more prosaically, as a walk to the marketplace, where her tryst with the French officer will hopefully yield more than simply reports of Paris's beautiful women and nightlife ("Infailliblement elle le priera, la simple créature, de lui décrire le bal de l'Opéra, et lui demandera si on peut y aller pieds nus"). Where "La Femme sauvage et la petite-maîtresse" poses the question of a woman's productivity along with the production of gender (the savage woman as her husband's capital, the mistress as the poet's luxury), "La Belle Dorothée" complicates these matters by putting the body in the embedded economies of sexual *and* colonial labor. The poem's final allusions to money and its various currencies ("piastres," "écus," and, as it turns out, "beauté") unveil what actually animates both Dorothée and the island: that is to say, Dorothée's progression in the sun and Bourbon's progressive yield of products. If by the end of the poem, "la belle Dorothée" is converted to "la bonne Dorothée" and the narrator predicts the success of her mission ("elle réussira, la bonne Dorothée"), this is not because of the goodness of her natural state (the *simple créature* as a *bon sauvage*). Rather, as the poem hints wryly, her success will be thanks to a "conversion" operated by the colonial system itself, a system that expertly converts not only souls but also—and most profitably—bodies. The golden age offered up for our visual pleasure is always already an age of gold. And exile, it would seem, is the very condition of the native.

Baudelaire conjures up a tropicalist stereotype of native indolence, a world of noontime siestas from which all signs of labor are banished, except for Dorothée "working it" in the sun, only to sabotage this solar utopia.[50] As I suggested earlier, "La Belle Dorothée" and its luminous celebration of indolence is a Mascarene version of the "pays de cocagne," the luxurious utopia described in "L'Invitation au voyage," a utopia whose colonial underpinnings Baudelaire made quite explicit in the prose version: "Les trésors du monde y affluent, comme dans la maison d'un homme laborieux et qui a bien mérité du monde entier" (*OC,* 1: 302). In "La Belle Dorothée," the question of labor, and of the female colonial subject's labor in particular, is completely elided. But as the French officer's speculated reports on the beautiful balls of the Paris Opera might suggest, the flow of treasures will travel across the ocean and into the chests of the French capital.

"La Belle Dorothée" and its oscillation between idealization and kitsch, between *ekphrasis* and tourist brochure, tells us something about how a foreign body—its racial, cultural, and geopolitical alterity—is familiarized and consumed as a visual spectacle. Where "Une Martyre" and "La Femme sauvage et la petite-maîtresse" demystify the violent production of femininity as matter and figure, or as beast, art, and commodity, "La Belle Dorothée" discloses the violence of representing the black body as at once primordial nature and exotic commodity.[51]

It is standard to read Baudelaire as an exemplary voice for the nineteenth century's exoticist literary imagination and its symbolic collaboration with colonial conquest. His biographical position as a white male poet of the metropole celebrating the dark female body makes such an ideological assimilation all too easy.[52] My readings attempt to demonstrate that his poetry's ironic texture resists full cooptation by such critical scripts, and explore alternate possibilities opened up by its self-demystifying tropological constructions. Françoise Lionnet has also challenged readings of Baudelaire's masculine imperial gaze upon dark others of an exotic femininity. In a carefully contextualized reading of "La Belle Dorothée," she proposes that the poet's inclusion of the word *cafrine*—a specifically Creole word designating black women—reveals his attunement to the specificity of the Mascarene Islands and their actual historical subjects. She sees Baudelaire's poetry "as one of the first places for the emergence of the native Creole woman's voice."⁵³ While I agree with Lionnet that the complexity of Baudelaire's rhetorical structures resists the ideological erasure of such historical subjects, I am less certain that his poetry gives these subjects a voice. In "La Pipe," for instance (a mock-orientalist sonnet) *cafrine* describes the color of the talking pipe as it puffs tobacco, which may well have been harvested by a *cafrine* from Bourbon's plantations, but whose smoke conjures up the image of a cozy countryside cottage.⁵⁴ The migration of the word *cafrine*—from the designation of a Creole subject to the description of a circulating object whose final destination is rural France—exemplifies how the exotic is reified, circulated, and consumed in the homeland. It may be too hopeful to turn to Baudelaire for the "voice" of the other. I have attended instead to the construction of corporeal alterity in his poetry, rather than seeking signs of these bodies' subjectivity or voice. Yet, as I hope to have shown, his poetry discloses with unparalleled force the contours of an other's reification and the imbricated violences that make such "other" bodies matter, produce, and signify.

Violence embeds competing ideological contexts within the poem, all of which are in tense dialogue with one another and with the process of making, reading, and contextualizing poetry. It is precisely the collusion and the collision between different terms, such as "nature," "race," "the body," "commodity," "femininity," "figuration," and so forth—their *correspondance* and *dissonance*—that enable the poem to engage and challenge the competing ideological investments of its historical moment.

From Baudelaire to Mallarmé: Poetry's Diminishing Body

Mallarmé's symbolism is often read as a culmination of Baudelaire's *poésie pure,* its evacuation of reference and its autonomy from contextual determinations. His famous declarations on poetry's power to dissolve bodies and things into language are usually perceived as part of an idealist program that banishes all signs of the body, materiality, and history from the poem, inaugurating what we might call a "poetics of disembodiment." Yet Mallarmé's fascination with bodies, and with performing bodies in particular, is amply documented in his writings on ballet, pantomime, and fashion (*Crayonné au théâtre, La Dernière Mode*). It is true that these bodies are so intricately crafted, so "textual" in fact, that they could be read as simply perpetuating Baudelaire's legacy of representing femininity as pure figuration ("la femme est fatalement suggestive"). This view of femininity is particularly visible in Mallarmé's writings on dance, where the body of the dancer is transformed into a purely semiotic surface. Indeed, for Mallarmé, dance was a form of corporeal writing, an expression that—like the poem—constituted its own reality and *embodied* what it signified. In these texts, performers such as La Cornalba, Rosita Mauri, and Loie Fuller are treated not as bodies on stage but as instances of thought in motion. It follows that for Mallarmé, the dancer is not a woman but a sign. She does not dance, she produces poetry, and this poetry is located not in her body but in the viewer's imagination: "À savoir que la danseuse *n'est pas une femme qui danse,* pour ces motifs juxtaposés qu'elle *n'est pas une femme,* mais une métaphore résumant un des aspects élémentaires de notre forme, glaive, coupe, fleur, etc., et *qu'elle ne danse pas,* suggérant, par le prodige de raccourcis ou d'élans, avec une écriture corporelle ce qu'il faudrait des paragraphes en prose dialoguée autant que descriptive, pour exprimer, dans la rédaction : poème dégagé de tout appareil du scribe."[55]

We might assume that Mallarmé is interested in such bodies only insofar as they can be dematerialized and recast as vehicles for semiotic play in the viewer's imagination (a stance that is not free of misogyny, since the ballerina would be an infinitely suggestive *petite-maîtresse*). But let us follow up on the previous readings of Baudelaire and tease out another possible perspective on this vision of the human body as a series of productions rather than as an object of representation. When Mallarmé presents dance as a phenomenon that unfolds in the viewer's imagination, he suggests that what matters in dance or writing is not the representation of an object but rather, the representation of this object's effect. This shift from the theater on stage or page to the theater of the mind is famously put in his letter to Cazalis regarding *Hérodiade:* "j'invente une langue qui doit nécessairement jaillir d'une poétique très nouvelle, que je pourrais définir en ces deux mots : Peindre non la chose, mais l'effet qu'elle produit" (*Oeuvres,* 479). Are we to understand this shift from the visual to the virtual, from what is displayed to what is experienced by the viewer, as a ploy to abolish the represented body, to dissolve it into language in order to resurrect it as pure ideal? Or could we instead perform a Baudelairean reading of this shift as conveying something about the actual historical conditions of a body's construction (through desire, language, and spectatorship)? And how might this in turn challenge the thoughtless consumption of the body in a culture of exhibition?

Mallarmé's prose poem "Le Phénomène futur" gestures in this direction. Significantly, this poem—steeped in Baudelairean imagery—is also the only piece by Mallarmé that Baudelaire is known to have commented on. Although not published until 1875, "Le Phénomène futur" was composed much earlier and circulated in literary circles. Baudelaire summarized the poetic plot thus: "Un jeune écrivain a eu récemment une conception ingénieuse mais non absolument juste. Le monde va finir. L'humanité est décrépite. Un Barnum de l'avenir montre aux hommes dégradés de son temps une belle femme des anciens âges artificiellement conservée. 'Eh ! quoi ! disent-ils, l'humanité a pu être aussi belle que cela ?'" Always the pessimist, Baudelaire then reproaches Mallarmé's faith in mankind's ability to recognize and mourn beauty: "L'homme dégradé s'admirerait et appellerait la beauté laideur" (*OC*, 2: 831).

Mallarmé's poem is set in a bleached out, crepuscular Baudelairean landscape sometime in the future. A Shower of Things Past (Montreur de choses passées) claims to have in his tent a body that defies all description, a "femme d'autrefois," a glorious Venus emerged from the primordial sea with salt still clinging to her limbs. The living specimen of a bygone era of beauty, she has been preserved from the beginning of time by the miracle of science. As in Baudelaire's "La Femme sauvage et la petite-maîtresse" and "La Belle Dorothée," an archaic, anachronistic female body is displayed—or rather, advertised—as a vestige of primeval nature. She is no less than the original matrix of an evolutionary chain that ends in collective decay. Significantly, this state of decay is not embodied by the men in the crowd but by their wives, described as decrepit, bald women, whose diseased wombs carry the rotten fruits by which the world will perish. Once again the feminine is inscribed as the collective body's origin and end, its redemptive norm and pathological aberration. The blonde counterpart to Baudelaire's Black Venus, an *Eve future avant la lettre*, Mallarmé's female phenomenon is reified as a pure object of visual consumption. Like Baudelaire's *martyre*, whose sight is displaced onto the decorative belt of her garter, the primordial woman's gaze is located not in her jewel-like eyes, but as an emanation from her very flesh (the tips of her breasts): "et les yeux, semblables aux pierres rares ! Ne valent pas ce regard qui sort de sa chaire heureuse : des seins levés comme s'ils étaient pleins d'un lait éternel, la pointe vers le ciel." This is, at least, what the barker's titillating sales pitch, his "boniment," would have us believe.

Yet, just as the spectators crowd around the tent and the poem promises to deliver its splendid body—a *phénomène* is, after all, a thing to be seen—we encounter a blank space, an elision of the body (the famous Mallarméan *blanc*) and a description, instead, of its effect on the viewers. Our expectation of visual pleasure is thwarted as image is displaced by rhythm: "Quand tous auront contemplé la noble créature . . . les uns indifférents . . . mais d'autres navrés . . . les poètes de ce temps, sentant se rallumer leurs yeux éteints, s'achemineront vers leur lampe, le cerveau ivre un instant d'une gloire confuse, hantés du Rythme et dans l'oubli d'exister à une époque qui survit à la beauté." Between anticipation and remembrance, between the sales pitch and the review, then, the body is suppressed, its exhibition sealed off in the unlocatable time of the futur anterior. Like Mallarmé's suppression of the dance in *Hérodiade* (which he was beginning at the time), what is represented here is not the thing—or the body—but the effect it produces on its viewers. As in Baudelaire's "Une Martyre," what the reader witnesses is, not a body displayed in its "originary" state, but rather its verbal production as an exhibition piece saturated with economic, scientific, and cultural value: the myth of a vestigial Eve conserved by science for profitable sideshows and to which only poets can attest.

Mallarmé, like Baudelaire, makes explicit the body's verbal construction as a commodity on display, as a repository for conflicting cultural inscriptions. This attention to the semiotic fashioning of bodies (be it through language, electricity, or clothing) is hardly surprising from an author who single-handedly wrote twelve issues of a women's magazine called *La Dernière Mode*. Rather than dissolving the body into the autotelic language of poetry, then, Mallarmé shows us what the "nature" of this body owes to such languages. In texts such as "Le Phénomène futur," Mallarmé is not so much engaged in obliterating or abolishing the body and reference as in reframing this reference and body within a broader field of cultural productions.

Of course, Mallarmé and Baudelaire cannot be conflated in their attitudes toward the bodies staged in their poems. Where Baudelaire conducts a hyperbolic rehearsal of the cultural processes through which bodies emerge, Mallarmé proceeds by ellipsis and elision; his irony is far more gentle. His meticulous attention to the body's semiotic potential does not seem invested in the level of ideological critique that Baudelaire's works conduct. One formulation of the difference between them might be that whereas Mallarmé's primary objective is to "peindre non la chose mais l'effet qu'elle produit," Baudelaire's objective is to "peindre non la chose mais l'effet qui l'a produite," to paint not the thing but the effect—or nexus of effects—that have produced it.

In presenting women's bodies as exhibition pieces, Baudelaire and the modernist tradition he exemplifies call into question the very nature and ground of these bodies, pointing out instead the ideological investments that produce the feminine as "naturelle" *and* as "fatalement suggestive." Significantly, this demystification of the body's emergence is conducted by literary figures usually said to remove poetry from social and historical concerns and to inaugurate the aesthetic of self-reflexivity and autonomy that we generally associate with high modernism. As I have tried to show in the preceding chapters, the self-reflexivity that supposedly banishes history from Baudelaire's poetry is exactly what lets history back in.[56] The poems read in this chapter all capture the violence of an allegorical process at work in aesthetic *and* cultural productions. They expose the conditions of a subject's emergence in the broader cultural field, and this at a time when a body's performance—its value, productivity, visibility, and yield—were increasingly at stake. Their representations of women as corpse and ornament, as primitive savagery, as civilized artifice and as exotic commodity, disclose what Gordon Teskey describes as "capture," or the "point of contact between allegory and violence" (Teskey, *Allegory and Violence*, 6).

Teskey presents allegory as a rhetorical mode that "oscillates between a project of reference and a project of capture," one that exercises a figural violence upon the heterogeneous materiality of the world (ibid., 8). Allegory's imposition of meaning upon matter is disclosed in the moment of capture, which is "not so much a literary figure as it is a moment of revelation in which the origin of figures may be seen" (30). In all allegorical processes, there exists a point of disclosure that reveals as it conceals the violence done to the mobile heterogeneity of a world of bodies and things. Teskey's discussion of allegory and violence provides an eloquent commentary on Baudelaire's poetic practice: "It is more broadly characteristic of allegory—though by no means more true of it—for violence such as this to be concealed so that the female will appear to embody, with her whole body, the meaning that is imprinted on her. When this occurs, we have personification. But the violence inside personification is exposed when that figure is, by an act I shall refer to as capture, turned inside out. What the act of capture exhibits is the truth over which allegory is always drawing its veil: the fundamental disorder out of which the illusion of order is raised."[57]

I have addressed this capture as the moment of metapoetic reflection that, in Baudelaire, becomes a point of contact between the poem and a referential world of bodies and things. Baudelaire's degraded muses—the female bodies struck, dismembered, and displayed—spectacularly unveil the violence of a literary tradition and a contemporary set of cultural practices that converge to define "woman" as a substance either inviting or resisting the imprint of masculinized form.[58] In "La Femme sauvage et la petite maîtresse," the parodic beating of the mistress and muse generates the nature and substance—the *physis*—of a body that is then made to signify as regressively savage or as unintelligibly performative ("Et que peuvent signifier pour moi ces soupirs. . . ?"). In "Une Martyre," the body is an ornament that circulates in pieces. "La Belle Dorothée" turns the figure of the Black Venus inside out to disclose the violence of the colonial allegory (a violence that is visually discharged in the pink dress slashing across Dorothée's dark body). It is through the mutilation of such figures that Baudelaire unveils—from within—the forgotten and often violent transactions that produce poetic objects and cultural subjects.[59]

Let us return to Walter Benjamin's declaration (discussed in Chapter 2) that he aimed to show how Baudelaire lay embedded in the nineteenth century. For Benjamin, the imprint left behind would stand out clear and intact, like that of a stone. Yet, as his own writings on the poet attest, Baudelaire is as recalcitrant to historical embedding as his bodies are to allegorical closure. His imprint upon—and by—the nineteenth century, while certainly more lasting than the imprint of Dorothée's bare foot on her native soil, shares its volatility and critical charge. This is in part because his poetry imbricates so many different contexts at once, an imbrication that resists any one embedding and, in fact, questions the very ground of context. But it is precisely this imbrication that weaves poetry into a broader field of cultural practices, allowing us to read and reread Baudelaire's poems neither as hieratic expressions of pure poetry nor as symptomatic imprints of the shocks of modernity, but rather as contestatory and self-contestatory pieces that unveil some of the hidden violences of his historical moment. Just as Baudelaire continually invites and resists new theoretical and historical embedding, his poetry also solicits a constant reevaluation—and recontamination—of our own critical practice.

Unlikely Contestations

Baudelaire's Legacy Revisited

The preceding chapters situated Baudelaire within a reading of French modernism that attends to the ideological valences of literary form, and to irony as a mode of historical contestation. The representation of the body—and of womens' bodies in particular—emerges as a key locus for the converging violence of aesthetic modernism and historical modernity. Baudelaire's representations of the human body make visible the multiple symbolic forces that shape a subject's emergence into being. They offer a genealogy of the overlapping violence of poetry and ideology at a particular historical juncture. The body of the martyr, the conspirator, the sovereign, the artist, the dandy, the prostitute, the beggar, and the savage are sites of contest that reveal central—and often contradictory—cultural assumptions about the meaning of "modernity" itself. The fate of these bodies as they circulate in the poetic text and its cultural contexts opens up a critique of the Second Empire's ideologies of pacified class struggle, urban development, modern progress, and colonial conquest. "Woman"—in the writings of Baudelaire and others—functions as the site for an inquiry into the cultural processes that make an embodied subject matter and signify in economic, political, sexual, and aesthetic terms. The spectacle of bodies marked by competing values give insight into the consolidation of a postrevolutionary bourgeois capitalist and colonial modernity. The explicit production of "femininity" through the violence of allegory, spectacle, and commodity fetishism participates in a broader critique of the conditions that inscribe matter into form—and bodies into subjects—on the poetic scene and the historical stage.

Unlikely Contestations

My readings of Baudelaire strive to account for the volatile critical energy of his poetry in terms that make room for dialogic, differential, and even combative relations between text, reader, and historical horizon. Baudelaire's ironic counterviolences open up a range of positions for the reader—as victim, executioner, accomplice, and witness—toward the cultural logics rehearsed in the poems. The act of reading itself becomes a form of counterviolence, in which the reader is coerced into collusion with and resistance to the text's interpellations and exclusions. It makes sense, then, that Baudelaire's legacy continues to be revitalized in intertextual rereadings of his poetry, and that some of the most vital and compelling "counterviolent" readings are by those who are excluded by his intended readership, that is, women authors and committed intellectuals.

In "Assommons les pauvres !" Baudelaire gives us an allegory of reading itself as counterviolence, as a practice of violence not only against another but against oneself, as well as against past literature. Before turning from Baudelaire to some of his most unexpectedly provocative readers, it may be useful to return briefly to this poem. As we saw in Chapter 2, the poet-intellectual of "Assommons les pauvres !" suffers from an overdose of indigestible literature from his idealist past. He rushes outside and beats up a random beggar on the streets, until his victim finally retaliates and in turn beats him up. The reason for the blows remains mysterious but they have something to do with the nature of the literature the poet has swallowed—utopian theories that advise all paupers to turn themselves into slaves or persuade them that they are "tous des rois détrônés." The impotence of these texts before the material conditions of history is likened to the beggar's own impotent gaze, one of those unforgettable gazes that would topple thrones if only mind could move matter. What is at stake, then, is the idealist belief in the transformative power not only of theory but also of literature itself. Indeed, what is perhaps also at stake is poetry's power to "move matter" and to produce social change. Such alchemical transformations have woefully failed: the poet's ingestion of revolutionary thought was earnest but stupefying, the beggar's gaze is soulful but impotent. In the words of Marx, "the tradition of all the dead generations weighs like a nightmare on the brain of the living" (*The Eighteenth Brumaire of Louis Bonaparte,* in *Marx-Engels Reader,* 595). Yet the act of reading does rouse the poet from his torpor and into action. Ejected from his ivory tower, he tumbles into the city streets and confronts the beggar's solicitation. The ongoing impact of past writing is rehearsed as a collision between bodies that unfolds across historical time, for the poet's beating responds to texts written some sixteen odd years before. The shift from theory (or reading) to practice (or beating) is staged as a violent encounter between self and other in a particular historical moment that is woven out of unacknowledged relations of inequity and force. The poem thus gestures to the constant renewal of literature's energy as it is transferred from one subject to another: through reading, through blows, through retaliations and counterblows.

Baudelaire's allegory materializes the legacy of literature over time, insofar as the struggle between poet and beggar is a corporeal reenactment that tests the historical relevance of past theory (the republican promise of freedom and equality) through irony. As we have seen, Baudelaire's ironic violence actualizes latent relations of force that continue to structure postrevolutionary society. In "Assommons les pauvres !" as in the other poems studied thus far, these relations of force are restaged as a physical encounter between embodied subjects who inflict, suffer, and witness pain. In a characteristically dialectical maneuver, for Baudelaire, the discovery of agency is accompanied by the recognition of one's own fragility. Our philosopher-poet is himself turned into a body vulnerable to the beggar's multiplied blows. Theory is rehearsed through pain ("la théorie que j'ai eu la douleur d'essayer sur votre dos"). What emerges out of this parodic exchange of *douleurs,* leading to the *partage de la bourse,* is nothing less than a mutual recognition of one's vulnerability to the violence of history, whether this history is textual, figural, and symbolic, or empirical, corporeal, and material.

The politics of the poet-philosopher's intervention are, of course, open to conflicting interpretations. The exchange of blows has been persuasively read by different critics as a Nietzschean initiation into anarchist revolt, as a prefiguration of totalitarian power, and even a parody of Proudhon's theory of mutualism.[1] Yet, as a broader allegory of reading, Baudelaire describes the vital, often dolorous exchange that occurs between a text and its readers, which is irreducible to an ideologically determined agenda. Marie Maclean's reading of this poem eloquently captures this openness to combative resignification: "However, one fine day it may all become too much. The passive receiver may suddenly pick himself up and, with a look of hate, realize that two can play at the text game. The realization comes in two stages: first the transgressive reading of the authoritarian text and then the production of a new text, either mentally as an active reader or eventually as a reader turned writer. Beat certain readers over the head long enough and, to the consternation of many, they will produce *A Season in Hell, Ulysses. . . .*"[2]

The last two chapters of this book pursue this legacy of literary blows and counterblows in three French authors whose combative rereadings of Baudelaire illustrate the value and relevance of his poetics of irony for crucial historical junctures, including our own. I trace this intertextual dialogue in the work of the decadent woman writer Rachilde, in the contemporary writer–film director Virginie Despentes, and in Albert Camus's intervention in the postwar debate on literary commitment. These readings are not proposed as a history or genealogy of Baudelaire's influence on subsequent literary production but, rather, as beacons, or "phares ironiques," that illuminate his legacy of counterviolence in diverse cultural sites. In this regard, my selection of authors has not been motivated by a readily discernable or canonized relationship to Baudelaire but by the vectors of analysis their counterblows enable. Indeed, the very heterogeneity of these writers—decadent Rachilde, absurdist Camus, punk Despentes—is meant to suggest that productive engagements with Baudelaire are to be found in rather unlikely places. Given Baudelaire's centrality to modern literature, there are, to be sure, any number of other figures who might have been included here. My choice of these writers has been prompted by their continued—albeit easily overlooked—meditation on a constellation of Baudelairean themes. The experimental flights taken up in these pages pursue the lines of inquiry opened by the previous chapters: literary form as a site for ideological critique, writing as combative intertextual exchange, irony as a vehicle of aesthetic counterviolence to historical violence, and the body as locus for the claims of reference.

4 Matter's Revenge on Form

Bad Girls Talk Back

Ce livre n'est pas fait pour mes femmes, mes filles ou mes soeurs.
Baudelaire, *Les Fleurs du mal*

Baudelaire's readers are men. It is men who have made him famous; it is them he has redeemed.
Walter Benjamin, *The Arcades Project*

[W]e had some brilliant writers in the 19th century, brilliant intellects, especially about sex and love. Flaubert, Baudelaire, then Bataille, Genet. If I hadn't read French authors like this before, I don't think I'd have written Baise-Moi.
Virginie Despentes

This chapter examines two women writers who revisit Baudelaire and the canon of high literature he has come to represent. Their combative rewritings attest to the vitality of Baudelaire's legacy of counterviolence and its power to stimulate ethical and political critique in the most unlikely places (the work of an until recently marginalized decadent author, and that of a contemporary anarchist punk writer). My choice of these works, and of *Baise-moi* in particular, may raise skeptical brows. Yet an underlying impetus in this book is to open the canon to alternate readings. The following discussions of texts that may be considered "unliterary" or unworthy of scholarly interpretation is also motivated by a reconsideration of high literature and its fetishism of style and form. The preceding chapters have argued that even in Baudelaire, aesthetic form is subjected to scrutiny for its complicity with other regimes of power. Thus, while occupying the canonical position of *l'art pour l'art*, Baudelaire opens up a critical modernity that makes room for authors such as Rachilde and Despentes as points of relay in an ongoing meditation on art and violence.[1]

Rachilde and Virginie Despentes are women writers, that is to say, readers explicitly excluded from Baudelaire's intended readership. Their works both acknowledge and contest the cultural legacy traditionally associated with the poet: matter's redemption by form, the violence of allegorical inscription, the gendering of poet and muse, the supremacy of poetry over history. From their respective and very different historical vantage points, Rachilde and Despentes turn the tables on Baudelaire's legacy through counterviolent dialogues with its dominant topoi: the dandy, the flâneur, intoxication, *ailleurs,* and the woman as prostitute, beast, or vehicle for literary transports.[2] These counterviolent reappropriations enact what I call "matter's revenge on form."

Mlle Baudelaire: The Dandy and Prostitute Resignified in Rachilde's L'Animale *and* Monsieur Vénus

Rachilde was born Marguerite Eymery to a middle-class military family in 1860. In a bold and eccentric legitimation of her desire to write, she adopted her pen name from a dead Swedish man for whom she claimed to serve as a "medium" during occult séances. In the 1880s, she moved to Paris with her mother and was introduced to avant-garde literary circles. She contributed to Anatole Baju's magazine *Le Décadent* and was catapulted into notoriety with the publication of *Monsieur Vénus* (1884), a novel banned as pornographic in Belgium. Married to Alfred Valette, editor of *Mercure de France,* Rachilde remained active in literary circles until the 1930s as a prolific writer and reviewer. Her best-known novels include *La Marquise de Sade* (1887), *Madame Adonis* (1880), *La Tour d'amour* (1899), and *La Jongleuse* (1899).[3]

Rachilde's oeuvre continues to solicit controversial readings. Her resolutely anti-feminist stance, her decadent elitism, and general hostility to progressive social or political agendas, make it difficult to assign an emancipatory politics to her fiction. She was heralded as the "queen of decadents" by her peers, who included such figures as Jean Lorrain, Catulle Mendés, and Villiers de l'Isle Adam, and her works seem to embrace the apolitical tendencies of the decadent movement, with its radicalization of *l'art pour l'art* and its disdainful retreat from the democratic principles of the Third Republic. Rachilde rehearses the dominant motifs of decadence—the *femme fatale,* the dandy, the beauty of evil, the cult of artifice, the fascinated horror with organic decay, the aristocratic disdain for the masses.[4] Still, in recent decades, her work has become a point of reference for feminist readers who argue that the inversion of such motifs carves out a space for rethinking sexual difference. As critics such as Janet Beizer, Diana Holmes, Rita Felski, and others have argued, in the volatile sexual politics of the Third Republic, as feminist movements proliferated and a growing number of women gained access to education and joined the workforce, the fields of medicine, psychology, and the natural sciences coalesced in attempts to locate sexual difference in the body.[5] In the fin de siècle cultural imagination, the Commune's *pétroleuses* or Charcot's hysterics displace the prostitute as figures for the association of femininity with savagery and irrationality.[6] When read against this horizon, Rachilde's ludic inversions of gender roles challenge the givenness of sexual difference and open up a carnivalesque play that rubs against the grain of the regulatory norms for gender and sexuality. Her celebration of the semiotic, theatrical dimension of identity and desire even foreshadows such contemporary theoretical lenses as performativity, gender, and identity as masquerade. The fluid, textual nature of selfhood and desire are epitomized by the protean heroine of *La Jongleuse,* whose masterful juggling becomes a metaphor for the emergence of identity through performance and masquerade. Yet even when read through the critical apparatus of performativity and gender, the negativity of Rachilde's dystopias may prove disappointing to readers seeking a celebration of alternate forms of selfhood and desire. While her characters explore transgressive modalities of identification and desire in fantasies that celebrate the plastic, semiotic quality of the human body, these *femmes fatales* and their destructive agency often seem merely to reverse the existing relations of force in the erotic scenarios of decadent literature. Rarely does Rachilde present a utopian space of "free play" where alternate bodies and desires may be imagined and lived out.[7]

Rachilde's oeuvre poses a familiar critical bind to readings seeking to recuperate a progressive political agenda from an ostensibly reactionary text. She fails both in the realm of praxis and in the space of textuality, neither offering an explicit critique of women's oppression nor envisioning an imaginary *ailleurs.* Her negative dystopias offer little by way of consolation or critique. Yet this eminently Baudelairean negativity is precisely where we may maneuver to recover the critical force of her intervention in the decadent legacy. Like Baudelaire's, Rachilde's choreographed perversity enacts invisible social structures of power and makes legible underlying relations of force that crisscross the aesthetic, erotic, and social domains. The private dramas of the Third Republic's upper echelons are portrayed as a vicious battle between sexes and classes, waged between men and women, but also between the military, the bourgeoisie, the aristocracy, and a disempowered proletariat represented by passive ephebes. With Baudelaire, but also with other fin de siècle contemporaries, Rachilde envisions the social arena as a sacrificial space: the family and social order are a shifting network of victims and executioners, love and sexual desire are a battle in which sovereignty is maintained by inscribing one's will on the body of another and the price of one's life is the death of another.[8] As we shall see, Rachilde's engagement with the decadent legacy can be read as a vector of an ongoing critique of modernity that illuminates the cultural conditions that allow certain subjects to emerge by repressing others.

In his preface to the 1889 edition of *Monsieur Vénus,* Maurice Barrès famously baptized Rachilde as "Mlle Baudelaire." Professing his admiration for the refined perversity of the nineteen-year-old author, he cast her as the latest representative of literary lineage that included such figures as Sainte-Beuve and Baudelaire: "Ramenant gentiment ses jupons entre ses jambes, cette fillette se laissa gentiment rouler sur la pente de l'énervation qui va de Joseph Delorme aux *Fleurs du mal*" (13). Rachilde's literary production is pathologized as the physiological record of an ambient *mal du siècle,* and legitimated in its ventriloquism of established precursors.[9] Barrès illustrates the contradictory treatment of woman as both "naturelle" and "fatalement suggestive" that we have seen in Balzac, Baudelaire, and Mallarmé. Declaring that "la petite fille qui rédigeait ce merveilleux Monsieur Vénus n'avait pas toute cette esthétique en tête. . . . Simplement, elle avait de mauvais instincts" (13), he reads the novel as an expression of the body's instinct *and* as a textual point of relay for the decadent legacy. Once again the literary text is reduced to a symptomatic inscription of the cultural contradictions from which it issues.

In some sense, Barrès's disparaging assessment of Rachilde's debt to Baudelaire hit the nail right on the head. Yet Rachilde's engagement with such masculine precursors is irreducible to the docile mimicry suggested by the preface. Her incursions into the French literary heritage are counterviolences that appropriate and resignify some of its key topoi. In *La Marquise de Sade* (1887), which traces the descent of its young protagonist into sexual depravity, Rachilde not only provides a female counterpart to Sade's libertine but also rewrites a founding scene of French allegorical tradition: the plucking of the rose in *Le Roman de la rose.*[10] In the medieval romance, the pilgrim who represents masculine quest violently possesses the feminine virginal flower in the love garden of Déduit. In Rachilde's version, the naughty little marquise de Sade—Mary Barbe—frolics in a dreamy fin de siècle erotic garden with the young Sirocco. They come upon garden's most precious blossom, a perfect rose called *l'émotion.* Compared to a maid poised on the first blush of sensual awakening, the exquisite rose mirrors the pale and virginal, though not so innocent, Mary Barbe. The traditional allegorization of femininity as a rose to be ravished by the pilgrim, however, is overturned. Instead, it is the maid who plucks the rose and eats it: "Mary ne se lassait pas de respirer la rose. . . .

Soudain, elle y mit les dents et, dans un raffinement de plaisir, elle la mangea" (97). Mary devours the virginal rose to become instead an unruly *fleur du mal.* This moment of cannibalistic *jouissance* captures an essential feature of Rachilde's appropriation of her literary heritage. Her defiant intrusion into the rhetorical blossoms of predecessor texts do not merely reproduce their topoi through a simplistic inversion of gender that leaves the process of allegorization intact. Instead, Rachilde's curious reinscription of the rose discloses something about the sexual politics of allegory itself. It alerts us to the violence of a creative process in which a masculine subject inscribes its will upon a feminine matter, mistress, and muse.[11]

Rachilde engages in dialogue with dominant topoi from the literary tradition, as well as with more contemporary writings by Baudelaire, Huysmans, Villiers de l'Isle Adam, Barbey d'Aurevilly, and others. Characters such as Mary Barbe are female incarnations of the Baudelairean dandy. Androgynous, opposed to reproduction and maternity, plagued with ennui and disgusted at the tepid mediocrity of their times, Rachilde's female protagonists are aesthetes whose cruel and refined sexual practices extract *la beauté du mal.* Yet Barrès's theory of passive and ventriloquized influence is belied by Rachilde's often comical counterviolent treatment of her literary predecessors. In *La Jongleuse,* Baudelaire himself is unceremoniously dispatched as a decadent cliché. Indeed, the mysterious Eliante Donalger initially appears to be a typical Baudelairean female idol. Her body is seamlessly encased in black dresses, and her alabaster face is permanently painted into artifice. Léon, a medical student, thwarted in his attempts to seduce her, muses as she dances past him: "un tourbillon passait en rêve. Une valseuse noire dont les jupons s'envolaient comme de sombres feuilles d'acanthe autour du beau fruit défendu, d'un corps lisse et souple, que l'on rêvait plus blanc, plus lisse et plus souple parce qu'il était voilé de deuil. Deuil de qui ? Deuil de quoi ? Un affreux deuil prémédité avant la lettre, pour aguicher les pierrots dont l'imagination aigrie de bonne heure avait picoré le fumier de Baudelaire, les jours de pluie. Nom d'un chien !" (*Jongleuse,* 63). Through Léon's caustic eyes, Eliante momentarily embodies Baudelaire's marmoreal *passante,* her flying skirts recalls the woman mourning who walks by, "soulevant, balançant le feston et l'ourlet" (*OC,* 1: 92). Yet this intertextual incarnation is dismissed as a bit of clichéd rubbish lying in the Baudelairean dungheap. Baudelaire's *passante* is caricatured as "passing fashion" and trashed; the poet who would turn mud into gold is turned back into mud, his legacy mocked as an obsolete *charogne* curdling the imagination. Rachilde turns Baudelaire's polarized images of women (as material decay and as marmoreal ideal) against the poet himself. The character of Eliante both rehearses and eludes these images of femininity. The passing object of the poet's fascination in "À une passante" becomes, in *La Jongleuse,* a performing subject in her own right, one who deliberately cultivates her semiotic possibilities.[12]

"Mlle Baudelaire" is at her most Baudelairean in such contestatory rewritings of her precursor. Her dialogue with Baudelaire takes up the challenge of "Assomons les pauvres !" and its invitation to reading as counterviolence. This combative play with precursor texts also opens a meditation on the body's plasticity before the other's erotic and aesthetic gaze. Indeed, Rachilde rewrites the traditional opposition between female materiality and masculine form, between *femme sauvage* and dandy, in sexual scenarios that show the violence through which a body is turned into a meaningful semiotic object. In dislocating the gender positions associated with the creative process, she reveals how allegory itself is "engendered" through violence. As in Baudelaire, who serves as an intertextual thread in the following readings of *L'Animale* and *Monsieur Vénus,* violence and counterviolence are textual modalities that convey the vulnerability of the human body and the painful—as well as pleasurable—conditions under which certain bodies emerge, are empowered, or are cast into abjection.

"La femme est naturelle, c'est-à-dire abominable": Rachilde's L'Animale

As its title suggests, Rachilde's *L'Animale* ambiguously rehearses the decadent topos of the bestial woman. Whether *l'animale* of the title is the heroine or the feline pet that finally kills her is left ambiguous, but Laure Lordes is a parody of the Baudelairean *femme sauvage.* There is more than a hint of *charogne* to her loveliness even as a child. Born to parents who performed gastronomical experiments worthy of Huysmans's des Esseintes to increase their fertility, she is a hothouse plant, a *fleur du mal* whose beauty is on the verge of organic decay: "L'enfant n'était pas seulement avancée, elle était pourrie, d'une jolie pourriture de champignon blanc et brodé. Elle se montrait *naturellement* décomposée, comme les bulles qui s'arrondissent sur les ondes stagnantes, sur les mares où l'on a mis des chanvres à rouir, lesquelles bulles, très jolies, s'irisent de toutes les couleurs de l'arc en ciel et n'en sont pas moins montées de l'infection. . . . Nulle innnocence ne pouvait, du reste, égaler la sienne, puisqu'elle était née avec le germe du mal."[13] Rachilde's portrait of Laure Lordes's corrupt femininity rehearses a host of conventional Baudelairean motifs. The italicized reference to her "natural" decay echoes Baudelaire's view of woman as "naturelle . . . abominable"; the venom flowing in her veins recalls the venereal imagery of "À celle qui est trop gaie"; her long, fragrant tresses—a metonymic sign of her bestial disposition—invoke the musky sexuality of his exotic women.[14] Laure's bestiality will find its perverse expression in her passionate intimacy with a cat called Lion. This too seems a wink at Baudelaire, since it is well known that cats became the poet's signature, such that the black cat in Manet's scandalous *Olympia* served both as a metonym for the prostitute's genitals and as a bawdy hommage to the poet.[15]

Rachilde's protagonist is thus a caricature of the cultural logic that produces "woman" as "la sauvagerie dans la civilisation," a logic illustrated in the century's obsession with the prostitute's contagious sexuality (as we saw earlier). Laure Lordes's precocious, unbridled instincts and ennui drive her to corrupt the boys in her village. She then seduces her father's notary, the repulsive, one-eyed Lucien Séchard.[16] Her next victim is a young priest, whose religious fervor conceals an incestuous obsession with his sister. As the priest finally succumbs to Laure's advances, he mouths the opening lines of Baudelaire's "L'Invitation au voyage": "Oui mon enfant . . . ou mieux, ma soeur" (*A*, 101). Their fleeting communion is filtered through the ecstatic transports of Baudelaire's love lyric. Laure's tresses billow around him in a hot fragrant haze reminiscent of "la langoureuse Asie et la brûlante Afrique" slumbering in the aromatic forest of "La Chevelure":

> Ils demeurèrent une seconde enlacés ; Laure se fondait tout entière sur sa bouche, comme un fruit s'écrasant. Des odeurs de roses dans les cheveux . . . des bras nus, une forêt de bras nus, se nouaient à son cou ; il était caressé par une tresse de cheveux noirs flottants qui prenait la dimension d'une fumée d'incendie, et il ne pourrait plus s'echapper, car une mutine voix d'enfant lui criait
> — Porte moi, mon frère, porte-moi, emporte-moi ! (*A*, 103)

Given this parody of the love lyric's conventional scenario, it is perhaps not an accident that Rachilde called her heroine Laure Lordes. The echoing of "Laure" recalls Petrarch's Laura, the quintessential mistress and muse of the Renaissance love lyric. The protagonist's name is perhaps an ironic gesture toward a literary tradition that has constructed femininity as a passive erotic and aesthetic object and as the vehicle to an ideal destination. But Rachilde reverses the direction of poetic transportation, for in this passage and throughout the novel, it is Laure who turns her male beloved into a muse and vehicle to an ideal *ailleurs* ("Porte moi, mon frère, porte-moi, emporte-moi !").

This *ailleurs* however is systematically banalized and co-opted by the bourgeoisie. Instead of a land of "luxe, calme et volupté," the paradise promised by her fraternal priest turns out to be the confining platitude of a bourgeois marriage. Indeed, to ensure Laure's salvation (from his own desire and the consequences of her affair with her father's notary), the priest arranges her marriage to Henri Alban, a tepid bourgeois Parisian. The jilted and jealous notary tells the would-be groom of his affair with Laure before committing suicide. Laure is disowned by her family, abandoned by her fiancé, and cast out of the village. She flees to Paris, where she joins Henri and offers to serve as his *petite-maîtresse* instead of his legitimate wife, an arrangement that he accepts with orderly aplomb.

Henri Alban's mean and calculating spirit epitomizes the deadening conformism of an American-style status quo based on the reign of profit. Described as a "chef d'oeuvre de sa fin-de-siècle . . . apothéose du genre américain francisé . . . fier de la France, que la raison et un bel équilibre social momifiait honnêtement" (*A*, 169), he represents a cold, masculine, bureaucratic bourgeoisie invested in a purely transactional model of human relations. Sapped of vital force and nobility, worshipping at the altar of commerce, and incapable of any emotion that has not been scripted in advance for profit, he is a comic sample of Baudelaire's civilized man.[17] Henri's deadening—and deadly—conformism drives Laure into the madness and abjection he believes is intrinsic to her. Neglected by her lover, who wants to sell her off to one of his friends, treated like a lunatic, kept in solitary confinement like a harem girl, with only her cat for company, Laure slowly mutates into a feline creature.

Laure thus comes to embody the lunacy, bestiality, and prostitution that the social order (her family, the church, her village, and her fiancé) attributes to her essential nature. Embracing her social construction as abject and bestial, as the vital, feminized irrational principle repressed by the bourgeois life-world, Laure moves beyond the symbolic order and becomes a phantasmagorical nocturnal prowler who crawls around the rooftops of Paris, peering through windows in an indiscriminate quest for communion with men and beasts. After a brief affair with a young working-class boy, she is abandoned by Henri and sinks into a coma. When she recovers, she is a pauper, and she decides to prostitute herself in order to survive. On her first nocturnal excursion in search of clients, she meets an older man, who vows to take her away to Africa. Yet once again, the promise of the *ailleurs* or an escape route from dependency and abjection proves a mirage. Her beloved cat, Lion, who escaped during her illness, returns in a state of rage, starvation, and jealousy to attack his owner. Laure's spectacular combat with the feline monster is reminiscent of Balzac's *La Fille aux yeux d'or,* only the relations of power are reversed.[18] She is ripped to shreds by the animal she has kept, rather than by a pantherish "keeper" like Balzac's marquise. Yet no executioner is needed to kill Laure. She is, Rachilde ostentatiously points out, slaughtered by her own inner beast. At the end, a glimpse into the mirror will reveal "un félin diabolique, un monstre inconnu, effroyable. . . . À travers son voile de sang, Laure s'était vu dans la glace" (*A,* 268). Laure's metamorphosis into a beast is complete: her animal nature, materialized in Lion, devours her. The novel closes on woman and cat, locked in a grotesque embrace, hurtling from the roofs into the void below.

L'Animale opens with a meditation on the implicit violence of bourgeois masculine rationality, contrasting it to the instinctual, nervous, melancholic disposition of women. Laure's nocturnal bestiality is quite explicitly described as the repressed other of enlightenment rationality. As she contemplates Henri's oblivious slumber, she muses: "Si le jour, elle devenait raisonnable, est-ce que cela prouvait que la nuit, elle était toquée ? Du reste, la raison représentait une chose fabriquée par plusieurs générations d'hommes. Les gens savants avaient faits des philosophies à leur taille, tandis que surgissaient des femmes, spontanément, des instincts qui devaient être les naïves formules de la vérité" (*A,* 17). From the outset, rationality is presented as a masculine construction tailored to the diminutive size of men and their contingent frameworks for knowledge. Women are defined antithetically, as nocturnal visionaries, filled with melancholy spleen and attuned to the life of the body.

Rachilde's mimicry of conventional discourses on gender difference paradoxically makes legible the construction of female nature through the naturalist discourse of heredity whereby atavistic instincts determine one's destiny. In *L'Animale,* we discern the systemic social discourses that produce the protagonist's "essential" bestial disposition. As in Baudelaire's "La Femme sauvage et la petite-maîtresse," Rachilde presents a woman locked between two impossible incarnations: the docile, socially scripted *petite-maîtresse* whom Henri initially keeps under his thumb and the regressive corporeality of the savage beast he reviles and abandons. Laure's own body, like the performing savage of Baudelaire's poem, remains undecidable. She is perfectly capable of exploiting pathological stereotypes of femininity to her own ends, as when she feigns hysteria in order to seduce her priest, or as she reasons through her construction as either *toquée* or *animale.* In these instances, she performs the derogatory scripts assigned to her—as hysterical female—much the way Rachilde, as a writer, "performs" her stereotype as a precociously perverse female whose pen is governed by her instincts. Yet these performances do not lead to resignification. Rachilde closes off all escape routes to her protagonist and grants her no alternate scripts. Laure Lordes is condemned to play out her "nature" in terms of the abjection, madness, and animality ascribed to her.

Rachilde's representation of femininity as the repressed "animal" nature contained and scapegoated by the instrumental rationality of modern society closes off all utopian paths to the resignification of gender. Aside from her fleeting nocturnal trysts on the rooftops of Paris, there exists no *ailleurs* for Laure's desire. In the absence of utopian spaces for alternative identities and desires, the body itself becomes a crucial site for resistance to the dominant modes of production and reproduction. In other works by Rachilde, the female dandy (as opposed to the female animal embodied by Laure) is a key figure for imagining such an opposition. Yet, before examining how Rachilde rewrites the figure of the dandy to exploit its oppositional possibilities, let us briefly return to Baudelaire's remarks on the dandy as the quintessential "modern" hero.

Dandyism Revisited: Monsieur Vénus, *Shame, and the Embodied Experience of Violence.*

For Baudelaire, the dandy is an exemplary rebel against the rising tide of bourgeois capitalist modernity. This rebellion takes the body as a site for opposition and agency. In *Le Peintre de la vie moderne,* the dandy transforms his body into a semiotic surface whose codes for legibility remain purely internal and voluntaristic. His aesthetic self-fashioning is a *culte de soi-même* that signals his resistance to the status quo. The dandy harbors a latent fire within that refuses to spark action in the world or to burn outright, producing nothing beyond a punctual performance of his originality.[19] This autonomous creation of body, dress, and lifestyle defies the dominant bourgeois ideology of productivity, instrumentality, and conformity.

In a rarely discussed passage, Michel Foucault pays tribute to the oppositional force of the Baudelairean dandy. Unlike Sartre, Foucault does not dismiss dandyism as an abdication of freedom; rather, he sees it as a literary activation of modernity's spirit of permanent critique.[20] Dandyism, as part of "la modernité Baudelairienne," is perceived as a complex, ascetic labor upon the self, as "un exercice où l'extrême attention au réel est confrontée à la pratique d'une liberté qui tout à la fois respecte le réel et le viole" (Foucault, "Qu'est-ce que les Lumières ?" 570). Far from being a reactionary provocateur, then,

Baudelaire's dandy offers a kernel of resistance to the cultural and economic strategies that produce the bourgeois humanist subject as a natural interior to be discovered: "l'ascétisme du dandy, qui fait de son corps, de son comportement, de ses sentiments et passions, de son existence, une oeuvre d'art," calls into question the nature and ground of this subject (ibid., 571). Instead, the dandy elaborates a set of practices—technologies of the self—through which a certain set of identities and lifestyles are endorsed with a measure of choice and agency. Foucault's formulations foreground the dandy's body, affect, and sensation as sites for crafting one's opposition to the subjectivizing forces of the power-knowledge network. The dandy is defined by his capacity to exercise a degree of control over the material givenness of the body. This control is precisely what opposes dandyism to femininity in the decadent tradition. The distinction between dandy and woman rehearses an opposition between form and content, wherein the latter falls prey to the natural demands of reproduction, organicity and the deterioration of time.

Rachilde reworks the Baudelairean figure of the dandy in three important ways. She too opposes the hyperreflexivity of the dandy to the regressively materiality of the *femme sauvage* or the prostitute, but she dislocates the gendered underpinnings of this opposition. The sexual politics governing the opposition itself are shown to depend on highly unstable conceptions of nature and artifice (an instability found in Baudelaire's own works, as we saw in Chapter 3). Secondly, Rachilde suggests that the very opposition to corporeality on which dandyism depends is a violent fiction. Her female dandies are sadistic despots whose reflexive powers turn *other* bodies into tablets on which their fantasies are enacted. In her inversion of the decadent sexual scenario, the male body becomes a plastic form that bears the imprint of female desire. The violence of allegorical desire is given literal form. Finally, Rachilde's reworking of the dandy illuminates the relations of force that oppose the "form" of the dandy to the "materiality" of the body. By refusing to envision a textual space of free play in which a body is liberated from its material, sexual, and gendered determinations, her narratives nuance theoretical formulations that turn to the body as a site for agency and resistance. They focus instead the body's vulnerability, experienced as shame or painful recalcitrance to fashioning by oneself and another. This emphasis on the body's abjection points out the underlying violence of allegorical and cultural processes by which matter is redeemed into form.

Rachilde's most famous novel, *Monsieur Vénus,* is often read as denaturalizing the very category of gender and opening a space of play with material, sexual, and gendered determinations of identity.[21] In this reading, however, I shall focus on how the novel portrays—and at some points even gives voice to—the body's vulnerable recalcitrance before another's erotic, aesthetic, and social desire. Jacques Silvert, a lower-class ephebe, falls under the spell of the androgynous and wealthy Raoule de Venerande. Lulled into a hashish-induced stupor, kept like a mistress in a harem, Jacques is a mobile text shaped and reshaped by Raoule's desire. He frolicks about his apartment, "se jouant la comédie vis-à-vis de lui-même, se prenant à être une femme pour le plaisir de l'art" (109). Jacques's performance of femininity is matched by Raoule's masculine dandyism. Raoule explicitly likens herself to a modern Faustian figure of masculine quest. Complaining to her friend the baron de Raittolbe about her past experience with men, she declares that she will henceforth script her own body and rewrite the book of love:

> Il est certain, monsieur, reprit Raoule en haussant ses épaules, que j'ai eu des amants. Des amants dans ma vie comme j'ai des livres dans ma bibliothèque, pour savoir, pour étudier . . . Mais je n'ai pas eu de passion, je n'ai pas écrit mon livre, moi ! Je me suis toujours trouvée seule, alors que j'étais deux. On n'est pas faible, quand on reste maître de soi au sein des voluptés les plus abrutissantes. . . . À présent, mon coeur, ce fier savant, veut faire son petit Faust . . . il a envie de rajeunir, non pas son sang, mais cette vieille chose qu'on appelle l'amour ! (84)

A Baudelairean dandy in matters of sex, Raoule retains her sovereign mastery even in the convulsions of lovemaking. Yet, while her mysterious sexual practices appear to put her in a masculine position, the narrative resists the intelligibility of a sexual regime of mere inversion: the opposition between men and women, as well as that between hetero- and homosexuality, is systematically undone. Raoule confides to the perplexed Raittolbe: "Je suis *amoureux* d'un homme et non pas d'une femme !" (88); "Je veux qu'*elle soit* heureuse comme *le filleul* d'un roi !" (91). The alternation of gender pronouns for the object of her desire (as "elle" and then as "le filleul") point to the instability of Jacques's body. The italics underscore the mutability of "his" gender, disrupt the binary classification on which sexual regimes rest, and cause some confusion: "Un homme semblable peut-il exister ? balbutia le baron abasourdi, entraîné dans une région inconnue où l'inversion semblait être le seul régime admis" (89). The baron comically begs his "ami" Raoule to limit the havoc caused by her ambiguous use of pronouns: "Tâchons de nous entendre ! Si je suis le confident en titre, mon cher ami, adoptons il ou elle afin que je ne perde pas le peu de bon sens qui me reste" (90). Jacques's plasticity, his fluid incorporation of masculine and feminine attributes, is thus matched by Raoule's many inversions. The final image of Raoule alternately dressed as a man and a woman, making love to a human turned into an automaton by a German scientist, illustrates this volatile fusion of nature and artifice, masculinity and femininity, heterosexual and homosexual desire.

Jacques's mutable and ultimately textual nature is addressed as a pathological threat to the Third Republic's social structure and its determinations of gender, sexuality, and class. Like Zola's Nana, the *mouche dorée* whose sexuality spreads like a plague among the upper circles of the Second Empire and emasculates the most powerful representatives of the régime, Jacques's plastic mobility disrupts the hierarchies of both sex and class in Raoule's social circles. His presence causes a ripple of undefined desire in Raoule's salon; it is a contamination that both Raoule and Raittolbe will attempt to contain. Initially turned into a harem girl by Raoule, Jacques is then trained by Raittolbe to perform the functions of aristocratic masculinity when Raoule decides to marry him. Raittolbe teaches Jacques how to ride a horse, wield arms, and regain his lost virility at brothels. Yet taming Jacques's body proves a vain task. The aristocratic, masculine Raittolbe will indeed lose his mind, or "le peu de bon sens qui me reste" over the young man's enticing ambiguity. He ends up having an affair with Jacques's sister, a prostitute whose proletarian vulgarity serves as a reminder that Jacques's circulating body disrupts class—as well as gender— distinctions.[22] Later, bewildered by his own homoerotic desire for Jacques, Raittolbe savagely beats him up. The logic of scapegoating (whereby Jacques's sexual and social hybridity is both desired and reviled) is taken to its logical conclusion when Raoule has Jacques killed by Raittolbe in a duel and makes a wax replica of his body, thus fixing into meaning a text that—when alive— eluded established sexual and social scripts.

Rachilde reworks the myth of Pygmalion to expose the violence by which a pliable human body becomes the incarnation of another's desire. Raoule reads Jacques's very nudity as an awe-inspiring poem to be rewritten throughout the narrative. A failed artist, Jacques knows that his body is a work of art more eloquent than his own words could be. Instead of writing to Raoule after Raittolbe's attack, he waits for her to read the marks left on his body: "Jacques, dont le corps était un poème, savait que ce poème serait toujours lu avec plus d'attention que la lettre d'un vulgaire écrivain comme lui" (139). Raoule contemplates his scars, "reads between the lines," and discerns the homoerotic desire that led to the baron's attack. In her rage, she reopens Jacques's wounds, and re-marks him as her own. The young boy's body becomes a palimpsest, bearing witness to the various desires he provokes and yet cannot control.[23] His final incarnation as a wax mannequin on which human hair and nails have been grafted parodies Pygmalion's statue come to life. It is also an ironic gesture to the marmoreal Parnassian ideal of feminine beauty ("belle comme un rêve de pierre") and its modern, technological incarnations such as Villiers de l'Isle Adam's *L'Eve future,* published two years later.[24]

However, in a striking departure from her decadent precursors and contemporaries such as Baudelaire, Barbey d'Aurevilly, or Huysmans (for whom the object of violent desire retains her silent opacity), *Monsieur Vénus* offers fragmentary glimpses into the forms of subjectivity that emerge out of the experience of corporeal dispossession. Jacques's pliant emasculation and lack of agency in his body's performance are repeatedly perceived by himself and by others as vile, abject, and shameful. Jacques obscurely perceives how deeply others' desires have shaped the most intimate recesses of his being. He intuits this objectification with a mix of pleasure and disquiet. In a rare flash of lucidity, he observes that "On l'avait fait si *fille* dans les endroits les plus secrets de son être, que la folie du vice prenait les proportions du tétanos !" (220). At critical junctures in the narrative, this lucidity erupts as shame. As Raoule watches him bathe, for instance, Jacques is "troublé subitement par la honte de lui devoir aussi la propreté de son corps" (54). Conscious of his passivity, "navré, tout pale de honte" (57), he surrenders to Raoule's gaze and lets the bathrobe slip off his body. His pallor and then flush before Raoule's gaze signals his sense of corporeal dispossession. When Jacques then bursts into tears of shame, a voice that could be his, his spying sister's or the narrator's explains that "Jacques était le fils d'un ivrogne et d'une catin. Son honneur ne savait que pleurer" (58). This unlocated voice of social opprobrium and its naturalist allusion to heredity interrupts and contains the emergence of Jacques's subjectivity, much like the previous allusion to vice as a *tétanos.* In such moments, the narrative voice briefly evokes Jacques's subjective experience of shame but then returns to a more citational mode that relies on the pathologizing *doxa* of heredity, class, and morality.

What might these flashes of shame convey about a subject's experience of violence? Shame is often addressed as an affect that signals subjectivity's sense of dispossession from itself. It is the response to a rupture in the circuit of communication with another, to the refusal or breakdown of an interpersonal contact through which we position ourselves in the world.[25] As our sense of being bounded and intact slips away before the gaze (or the averted eyes) of another, we awaken to a sense of inner otherness in which we are at once subject and object, oneself and another.[26] This may be why shame is also described as a form of hyperreflexivity that makes us see ourselves as fragile and changeable, exposed to the violence of a world that does not recognize our contours. The experience of shame is akin to having the intimate lining of one's being turned inside out and exposed, while sensing that the forces outside of us are imprinted into our core. Understood in this light, shame is an affective state that stands at the polar opposite of the self-possession of the dandy, whose cultivation of surface and contour forms a protective glaze that parries the shocks of the external world. Shame erupts when that protective glaze is pierced by forces that both escape us and yet inflect our very sense of ourselves as other, dispossessed, or permeable. The emergence of subjectivity *through* the experience of shame, as it is registered by the body, will be the subject of the following pages. For now let us simply note that the repeated shaping and laceration of Jacques's body throughout the text enacts this double movement of subjectification and desubjectification. Jacques feels his innermost self to be at once intimate and alien. The forces shaping him are perceived as an exteriority that reaches into "les endroits les plus secrets de son être" and yet remains quite literally in another's hands.

Monsieur Vénus delivers in fragments an intuitive experience of shame as vulnerability to another's random violence. At the novel's conclusion, Jacques's duel with Raittolbe (arranged by Raoule) is recounted—exceptionally—from Jacques's point of view. His innocent musings drift in and out of the depiction of the duel's preparations. Obscurely aware—and ashamed—of having betrayed Raoule by visiting Raittolbe in drag with the vague intent to seduce him, Jacques nevertheless trusts Raoule's assurance that the duel is a performance from which he will emerge unscathed. Yet his body signals the danger that awaits him. His neck retains the memory of Raittolbe's hands, and his childlike refrain "Pourtant cet homme lui avait fait bien mal au cou" (221) conveys a hazy, somatic awareness of his vulnerability to impending violence. This vulnerability and dispossession take center stage at the novel's close, when Jacques's flesh yields like a newborn's to the point of Raittolbe's sword and his dead body is stripped of its hair and nails so that they may be grafted onto a wax replica.

Rachilde's text conveys something of the subjective experience of violence as it is registered in the body. Her allusions to Jacques's intuitive experience illuminate the embodied sense of vulnerability that I have addressed here as shame. Shame may be understood as an affective state that emerges through an experience of self-dispossession. It occurs when we feel alien at our most intimate core and experience that strangeness as a vulnerability to the violence of the world around us. Rachilde deploys the motif of the body as matter and figure that we previously examined in Baudelaire's definition of femininity as both blind materiality and pure, disembodied metaphoricity. Her swerves from precursor texts expose the "engendered" nature of representation, through overdetermined citation in *L'Animale* and the inversion of gender in *Monsieur Vénus*. Yet her analysis exceeds the framework of identity politics, in that her portrayal of subjection crosses the lines of gender. It also resists a purely performative reading of gender and desire by reminding us of the vulnerability of the human body to the violence of another. As such, Rachilde offers a bracing corrective to contemporary celebrations of the body's utopian textuality. Her intervention in the legacy of decadence is most compelling at points that disclose the fragile materiality of the human body. This vulnerability emerges paradoxically, through the enactment of violence upon a desired or reviled body.

I have read Rachilde as a point of resistance to the narrative of modernism as the evacuation of content by form. The previous chapters on Baudelaire showed how violence becomes a textual modality that both critiques existing material and symbolic violences and, in doing so, signals the vulnerability of bodies scripted by a nexus of cultural investments. An author such as Rachilde—and, as I shall suggest, Virginie Despentes—intervenes in a symbolic legacy that opposes empirical matter to the transformative power of form. Their textual counterviolences exploit and explode the systemic violence of idealization itself. Over a century after Baudelaire, a generation of women writers and directors continue their combative engagement with a cultural imaginary that persistently redeems recalcitrant bodies through the idealization of form. Through intertextual dialogues with Baudelaire, among other established cultural icons, their representations enact what could be called the revenge of matter on form. Their rehearsal of symbolic violence opens up spaces for the representation of affects such as shame and abjection, affects that characterize a subjectivity's emergence through its vulnerability to bodily violence.

Accursed Poets, Damned Women, and Bad Girls: Trashing Baudelaire in Virginie Despentes's Baise-moi

Baise-moi, a novel written by Virginie Despentes in 1994, was transposed to film by Despentes with her co-director, the former porn star Coralie Thrinh Thi, in 2001. Censored by the Conseil d'état in France after the right-wing association Promouvoir intervened and claimed it was pornographic, the film re-

ceived an X rating and had its *visa d'exploitation* temporarily withdrawn, lead-
ing to protests led by several filmmakers, such as Catherine Breillat in France
and Atom Egoyan in Canada. "Il est temps pour les femmes de devenir des
bourreaux, y compris par la plus extrême violence," Despentes has pro-
claimed,[27] and the film's brutal depiction of rape, sex, and murder provoked
violent, even traumatic, responses in spectators. During a screening of the
movie in Montreal, for instance, one viewer broke into the projection room
and ripped the film out of the projector. Critics have dismissed *Baise-moi* as
amateurish, sensationalist, gratuitously violent, vulgar, and pornographic. Yet,
as a novelist, Despentes belongs to a significant wave of contemporary writers
such as Michel Houellebecq, Maurice G. Dantec, Marie Darrieussecq, and
Vincent Ravalec, whose dystopic or apocalyptic visions of contemporary
French society are often rendered in shocking, hypernaturalist prose.[28] The
bleak negativity of their portrait of France (its rising unemployment, racism,
crime, and sexual violence) has branded them as nihilists who betray the pro-
gressive mission of literature. Nourished by Stephen King, trash and "gore"
genres, B movies, and other such popular cultural references, these writers are
cast as rebels making a definitive breach with traditional modes of representa-
tion and ushering in a new modernity. Marion Mazauric, literary director of
J'ai lu until 2000 and publisher of Despentes's works, describes the novelty of
this emerging generation in the following terms:

> Nous sommes en face d'une réappropriation critique du réel par ceux qui ne
> reconnaissent ni les modes de représentation ni les modèles antérieurs
> comme pertinents pour représenter, comprendre, changer ou simplement
> survivre dans le monde d'aujourd'hui. Et nous voyons aujourd'hui dans le
> même mouvement, renaître le roman de classes moyennes nées dans la crise
> générale des valeurs d'un système qui les abandonne. Dans ce grand bras-
> sage des formes se redéfinit ainsi une modernité des langages littéraires, mu-
> sicaux, cinématographiques. Modernité: réappropriation et subversion des
> grandes figures symboliques fondatrices de notre civilisation.

Despentes's rebellious blending, or *brassage,* of literary and linguistic forms has
branded her as an *écrivain rock,* or as a representative of punk art's anarchistic
rebellion.[29] Yet despite claims that this generation of writers emerged out of a
complete repudiation of preceding modes of representation, Despentes herself
has no qualms inscribing her fiction in a canonical tradition of "moderns" that
includes such prestigious classics as Baudelaire and Flaubert. She thus claims
as her own the French classical canon and acknowledges its ongoing resonance
in contemporary life and literature. In her prose, references to established lit-

erary figures such as Baudelaire, Rimbaud, and Breton provocatively jostle alongside the language of American rap, French punk, heavy metal, and *banlieue* slang. This strategy does more than simply "trash" the canon and level out distinctions between high and low culture. It recovers the critical energy and relevance of classics by recasting them in the contemporary urban slum belt, the *zone.* Yet, as in Rachilde's resignification of decadent topoi, Despentes's ludic allusions to the canon also challenge a cultural tradition that has cast women as aesthetic and erotic objects of desire in its celebration of form over matter. Unlike Rachilde, however, Despentes focuses on the predicament of women in the urban underclass and claims as her territory the abjection and vulnerability glimpsed in Rachilde's *Monsieur Vénus.* Hers is an ironic, postmodern brand of decadence, *version trash.*

Despentes's *Baise-moi* conducts an unruly dialogue with the repertoire of motifs traditionally associated with Baudelaire. This is not to say that Despentes had Baudelaire in mind as her novel's implied reader, but that she intervenes polemically in a cultural legacy that has been partially—and often paradoxically—shaped by the Baudelairean aesthetic imaginary. Her urban underworld of pimps, prostitutes, and gangsters is a postmodern incarnation of Baudelaire's nocturnal Paris and its vagrant population of ragpickers, prostitutes, and criminals. The losers who people her literary imagination are those left behind by modernity's narrative of consumerism and progress. Despentes also invokes familiar Baudelairean and decadent topoi: the evil woman, the *femme sauvage,* the poet, the dandy, the vengeful poor, and the lesbian. But she dislocates them from the canon of high literature and relocates them in the grim realities of the urban slum. As in Rachilde, such reinscriptions illuminate the iterability of these figures, their openness to unceremonious resignification. Most relevant to the following discussion, however, is her broader affiliation to the tradition of irony, counterviolence, and critique I have traced thus far. Despentes's sensationalist depictions of violence mimic existing violence in what Stéphane Spoiden has described as "une répétition désespérée, hard et destroy."[30] Her scenes of sex, rape, and murder, crystallize a violence endemic to contemporary urban life: economic marginalization, alienation from the labor force, racial violence, police brutality, and sexual exploitation. They are phantasmic stages on which victims and executioners act out the structural violences shaping their daily life.

These darkly comic reenactments of quotidian traumas offer neither consolation nor critique. Like Baudelaire and Rachilde, Despentes portrays the social world of her protagonists as a perpetual war between victims and executioners, as an inextricable web that knows no outside or *ailleurs* and offers no alternate positions beyond those of predator and prey, executioner and victim. Her characters replicate the violence that has victimized them in brutal scenarios of revenge that are part and parcel of Despentes's punk aesthetic. Yet, as we have seen in the case of Baudelaire and Rachilde, the "hard et destroy" tactics of counterviolence can have a critical function. *Baise-moi*'s trashy scenarios of revenge expose the underlying logics of systemic oppression—by race, class, and sex—through what can be call a process of corporealization. Like Rachilde, albeit in a completely different literary and historical register, Despentes challenges an aesthetic tradition that derealizes matter and fixes it into form by probing into the layers of aggression, shame, and abjection that condition a woman's emergence into being.

In an interview with Catherine Breillat in 2000, Virginie Despentes herself suggested that it is through the deployment of violence that the dignity of abject bodies may be reclaimed:

CATHERINE BREILLAT : Le carcan des lois a placé les femmes en état d'ignorance, les a vouées à être le ventre destiné à procréer. Elles n'ont pas eu de conscience, on ne peut pas le leur reprocher . . . *on commence à être la proie de l'homme dès que physiquement il apparaît qu'on devient une femme* [emphasis added].

VIRGINIE DESPENTES : Il faudra bien qu'elles deviennent plus fortes. J'ai le sentiment d'avoir une mission à remplir, j'allais dire une mission de vengeance, mais ce n'est pas tout à fait ça. Il faut faire éclater les choses, rendre de la dignité, de l'humanité.[31]

As was the case with Rachilde's oeuvre, the vengeful negativity of *Baise-moi* vexes feminist readings of book or film as an intelligible statement "about" the pervasion of sexual violence in contemporary society.[32] Yet this rejection of consolation or critique is part of its power to "faire éclater les choses." It is this *éclatement* that the next few pages pursue through the Baudelairean *éclats* of *Baise-moi* and its meditation on the body's vulnerable and destructive materiality, as well as its social sexing through shame, negativity, and abjection.

"Ailleurs, moi j'y crois pas"

In his "Salon de 1846," Baudelaire celebrated the *héroïsme de la vie moderne* captured by Balzac's representation of the city's underbelly and defended the lyrical potential of contemporary Parisian life, where "[l]e merveilleux nous enveloppe et nous abreuve comme l'atmosphere ; mais nous ne le voyons pas" (*OC*, 2: 496). His own Parisian tableaux in "Les Sept vieillards" and "Les Petites Vieilles" mapped the "fourmillante cite" and the "plis sinueux des vieilles capitales" teeming with drunks, prostitutes, criminals, the elderly, and the insane. In *Baise-moi*, Virginie Despentes paints what could be read as a hypernaturalist contemporary version of the *tableau parisien,* one that incorporates the *banlieue* and its underclass. But her bleak world of prostitutes, drug dealers, small-time crooks, killers, and aimless marginals attests to what she calls "un héroïsme dans la déchéance" (*BM*, 62). Her underclass is poor, uneducated, crude, and jobless. Its constant struggle to survive abject material conditions is bereft of "illumination" or the "merveilleux." The very concept of an *ailleurs,* an alternate space outside or beyond the degradation of everyday life is a mirage. Her protagonists seem fully resigned to the realities of police brutality, racism, sexual violence, drug dealing, and gang warfare. They are explicitly described as defeated, permeable entities in osmosis with the ambient violence of their surroundings.

The intractable violence of this social world is conveyed in the opening pages of the novel, when Manu, a working-class porn actress, hears about the death of her best friend Camel, who was probably the victim of racist police brutality. The adolescent who brings her the bad news is an idealistic lefty student who wants to spur Manu into sharing his indignant protest of this injustice. Manu, however, dismisses his verbiage as hypocritical posturing: "Il reproduit ce qu'il dénonce avec une inquiétante tranquillité d'esprit. Petit-fils de missionnaire, il entreprend de convertir les indigènes du quartier à son mode de pensée" (*BM*, 17). Any denunciation of injustice is dismissed as a replication of the very violence that is contested. Numbed by drugs and alcohol, Manu is reconciled to the idea that she belongs to history's losers: "D'ici peu de temps, elle sera trop déchirée pour que cette histoire l'affecte. Elle finit toujours par bien se faire à l'idée qu'il y a une partie de la population sacrifiée ; et dommage pour elle, elle est tombée pile dedans" (*BM*, 16).

If this vision of the sacrificial underpinnings of the status quo is reminiscent of Baudelaire, Manu's apathy is a far cry from the poet's revolt. Despentes debunks all basis for such heroism in her characters. The disheveled, vulgar Manu is a parody of the purely appetitive Baudelairean female. A gleeful illustration of Baudelaire's "La femme a faim et elle veut manger. Soif et elle veut boire. Elle est en rut et elle veut être foutue. Le beau mérite ! (*OC*, 1: 677), Manu speaks in barks and grunts, gorging on candy, alcohol, and sex throughout the novel.[33] Despentes's portrait of Manu echoes the famous poem

"Enivrez-vous," in which Baudelaire invokes intoxication as a flight from the burden of time, the body, and materiality ("enivrez-vous sans cesse ! De vin, de poésie ou de vertu, à votre guise"): "Il n'y a strictement rien de grandiose en elle. À part cette inétanchable soif. De foutre, de bière ou de whisky, n'importe quoi pourvu qu'on la soulage . . . elle est en relative osmose avec le monde" (*BM*, 14). The intoxication that wrests the poet out of the body and into idealization here becomes just another way of stuffing the body with matter.

This state of perpetual osmosis with the ambient violence of one's surroundings is also reminiscent of Baudelaire's poet-prostitute, whose subjectivity empties itself out into the world: "Ivresse religieuse des grandes villes. . . . Moi, c'est tous ; Tous, c'est moi. Tourbillon" (*OC*, 1: 651). Yet for Baudelaire, the poet retains some sort of agency throughout this process. The motion of self-vaporization is followed by a recuperative moment of self-crystallization: "De la vaporisation et de la cristallisation du *Moi*. Tout est là" (*OC*, 1: 676). Even when the Baudelairean poet submits to the jolts of modern life, cleaving through the city and parrying its shocks, "roidissant mes nerfs comme un héros" (*OC*, 1: 87), he never fully surrenders his contours or agency. In "Le Peintre de la vie moderne," the glaze that seals the contours of the poet also characterizes the female body, redeemed as art through the veneer of fashion and cosmetics.

Despentes opens her book with a clear message that such buffers and resistances to external shocks are irrelevant to her female protagonists. The violence of their surroundings registers at the very core of their being. Far from releasing them from the body's limitations, their *paradis artificiels* only exacerbate their unquenchable thirst and enhance the permeability of their psychic and physical boundaries. Throughout their flight across France, Manu and her partner in crime Nadine gorge on junk food, guzzle down bottles of Four Roses and Jack Daniels, and find fleeting satiation in random sexual encounters. A far cry from Rachilde's refined dandy heroines and their exquisite palette of food, drink, and sexual perversion, evasion in this text is not the enhancement of experience or a gateway into the aesthetic. The *ailleurs* promised by intoxicants is declared a chimera from the outset, since we enter into a social space that has no boundaries separating "ici" from "là-bas," no place within the interlocking structure of economic and sexual violence from which an "elsewhere" or an "outside" is imaginable. As Nadine puts it, "Ailleurs, moi j'y crois pas" (*BM*, 184).

In Despentes's narrative, the body is denied any transcendence. Its vulnerable or gross materiality always wins out. This point is brutally made in the instants preceding Manu's rape, when she drink a six-pack with her friend Karla on the banks of the Seine. The intoxicated, expansive Manu urges Karla to widen her horizons, to think about the spirit rather than the body: "Faut te dilater l'esprit, faut voir grand, Karla, sérieux . . . Faut s'écarter les idées" (*BM,* 51). At that precise moment, some men approach. "Nous, les filles, c'est pas les idées qu'on vous ferait bien écarter," one says, and they rape the two women. Manu's brief and drunken flight into her "idées larges" is precisely when she is hurled back into her body as the site of violation.

Baise-moi depicts the female body as an abject, vulnerable thing that harbors the scars of social violence at its very core. Manu's sense of osmosis translates a fractured, permeable subjectivity that emerges through violation (an embodied awareness of vulnerability conveyed as shame in *Monsieur Vénus*). This constitutive dispossession of one's own body is blatant in the gruesome depiction of the rape. Dehumanized, treated like trash, her genitals likened to a garbage disposal, Manu dissociates from her body altogether. It is precisely her obstinate refusal to acknowledge the pain and humiliation inflicted upon her personhood that thwarts her rapists' desire: "Elle a même pas pleuré celle-là, regarde-là. Putain, c'est même pas une femme, ça" (*BM,* 55). Her absence from a body that is being so forcibly expropriated ("ça"), and her refusal to show signs of distress are precisely what make her rapists claim that she is not a woman. This explicit linking of "real femininity" with tears or cries is reminiscent of Baudelaire's "La Femme sauvage et la petite-maîtresse," where the savage woman's shrieks under her husband's blows guarantee the authenticity of her femininity ("Avez-vous entendu résonner la chair malgré le poil postiche ? Les yeux lui sortent de la tête, elle hurle plus *naturellement*" [*OC,* 1: 290]). Despentes makes visible what remains implicit in Baudelaire's poem: the unspoken premise that a woman's very "nature" is something to be produced through physical violation (in one case, howls, in the other, tears).

Manu's impassivity during her rape is defended in a memorable response: "Je peux dire ça parce-que j'en ai rien à foutre de leur pauvres bites de branleurs et que j'en a pris d'autres dans le ventre et que je les emmerde. C'est comme une voiture que tu gares dans une cité, tu laisses pas des trucs de valeur à l'intérieur parce-que tu peux pas empêcher qu'elle soit forcée. Ma chatte, je peux pas empêcher les connards d'y entrer et j'y ai rien laissé de précieux . . . On n'est jamais que des filles" (*BM,* 57). Manu's portrayal of her body as a vehicle parked in the projects, and from which all valuables have been removed, conveys the expropriation that Despentes suggests to be constitutive of her sense of being in the world. *Baise-moi* depicts women's bodies not as commodities but rather as a materiality already turned into a waste product or debris. Manu's conclusion, "On n'est jamais que des filles," illustrates the extent to which sexual violence shapes the emergence into "femininity."

Manu's crassly eloquent declaration raises a central and provocative question: what does it mean to survive and circulate in the world as an embodied subject who feels fundamentally expropriated from herself, and indeed, defines herself as a "fille" through this expropriation? What forms of subjectivity emerge—or are foreclosed—in a social environment where rape is experienced as the life-threatening eruption of an ongoing, systemic condition, as just another "coup de queue" equivalent to the "coup de poing" Manu receives with equal equanimity from a boyfriend? Her response suggests that no psychic cohesion or corporeal integrity existed prior to her sexual violation. Her dissociation during the incident turns out to be a constitutive condition of her existence as a woman in the systemic violence of her milieu.[34]

Despentes's portrait of the rape scene as continuous with the layers of sexual and economic violence characterizing Manu's underground, underprivileged *banlieusard* environment illustrates what feminist psychologists now call "insidious trauma."[35] Insidious trauma has emerged as a category in recent years in order to redress the gender bias of the American Psychiatric Association's *Diagnostic and Statistical Manual*'s definition of posttraumatic stress disorder as the response to "an event that lies outside the range of human experience." As Laura Brown and others have argued, since the nineteenth century, "trauma" has designated public, visible events such as war, genocide, natural disasters, and other crises that have taken as their normative point of reference the experience of educated white middle-class men. Such a definition ignores a host of private forms of violence such as rape, battery, incest, and other kinds of interpersonal violence. Insidious trauma recognizes the everyday experiences of (often sexual or sexist) violence and forges connections between punctual traumas such as rape and more systemic forms of oppression and violence. The sense of dispossession Manu feels toward her own body illustrates the erosion of selfhood in an environment of constant sexual, racial, and economic abuse. "[E]n relative osmose avec le monde," the violence of her everyday experience registers at the deepest levels of her somatic and sensory being.[36]

From the outset, then, Despentes forges links between punctual acts of brutality such as rape and murder and the everyday, lived reality of social violence. Yet, oddly enough, her narrative rejects the psychological register we might expect from a murderous rampage that opens with a rape scene. No further allusion is made to this rape, as if to withhold its status as an explanatory force for the carnage that follows. Manu herself becomes an automaton, whose gestures take over and lead her through a series of unpremeditated killings, as if her body were a passive vehicle carrying out a predetermined script of violence. Immediately after her rape, Manu finds out that her Arab friend Radouan has been beaten up and disfigured in a drug dealers' squabble. She steals a gun to shoot the gangster who beat up Radouan and executes the policeman responsible for the death of her other Arab friend, Camel. It is interesting to note that insofar as a revenge narrative exists in this text, the initial targets of revenge are not the rapists themselves but other perpetrators who brutalize the "population sacrifiée" to which Manu avers allegiance. Manu's unthinking revenge makes explicit the implicit links between economic marginalization, gang warfare, racist police brutality, and sexual violence.

Despentes's rejection of psychology is implicit in her refusal to make Manu's rape the governing or explanatory course for the remainder of the plot. The revenge narrative explodes into a random sequence of automatisms that fold the characters into an ever-expanding web of violence. The protagonists' drive to kill is not addressed in psychological terms but manifests itself as a corporeal automatism. After their first joint premeditated murder of a middle-aged woman retrieving cash from the bank machine, for instance, a bemused Nadine reflects on the spontaneous efficiency of their killing: "Jusqu'à ce moment, elle n'a pas réfléchi, les gestes sont venus, automatiques. De drôles de gestes, d'une effarante efficacité. Automatiques" (*BM,* 117). "(E)n osmose avec le monde, " the protagonists' bodies take over and become conduits for the forces around them.

Despentes portrays a world in which the response to one's violation is an automatic replication of violence. Her heroines become executioners whose gestures repeat the physical and material expropriation that victimized them in a dizzying cycle that ends with their capture and death. Unlike Ridley Scott's *Thelma and Louise,* to which *Baise-moi* is often compared, the two protagonists have no agency over their demise. Thelma and Louise manage to flee an oppressively patriarchal world, symbolized by a fleet of police cars, by grasping each other's hands and defiantly driving off a cliff. In *Baise-moi,* there are no cliffs or exits to the cycle the protagonists are born into and mechanically perpetuate. While they plan their suicide throughout the novel, Manu is shot in a gas station, and Nadine is captured by the police just as she is about to pull the trigger on herself. Like Rachilde, Despentes forecloses any escape routes for the heroines, any *ailleurs* or any alternative response to their milieu beyond a replication of its violence.

Literature Recycled, and the Body Reclaimed as Waste

Despentes opens her heroines' murderous flight across France with a gesture to Baudelaire. She thus acknowledges a filiation with the canonical poet and the transgressive figures associated with his literary heritage: the outlaw, the lesbian, the savage woman, the damned poet(ess), and the dandy. Nadine's meeting with Manu is introduced by an excerpt from Baudelaire's poem "Femmes damnées : Delphine et Hippolyte," one of the six poems banned in 1857, for portraying the sapphic loves of Delphine and Hippolyte. Despentes's choice of this poem makes sense, given her admiration for Baudelaire and Flaubert, figures who, like herself, faced judicial pursuits for their transgressive representations. In fact, she mentions them both when discussing the banning of her film in France.[37] Yet her selective quotation of "Femmes damnées," like Rachilde's intertextual interventions, open up Baudelaire's literary legacy to re-signification. Here I have bracketed verses from the original poem left out or altered by Despentes:

> Ombres folles, courez au but de vos désirs;
> Jamais vous ne pourrez assouvir votre rage,
> [Et votre châtiment naîtra de vos plaisirs.]
>
> [Jamais un rayon frais n'éclaira vos cavernes;
> Par les fentes des murs des miasmes fiévreux
> Filtrent en s'enflammant ainsi que des lanternes
> Et pénètrent vos corps de leurs parfums affreux.]
>
> [L'âpre stérilité de votre jouissance
> Altère votre soif et roidit votre peau,
> Et le vent furibond de la concupiscence
> Fait claquer votre chair ainsi qu'un vieux drapeau.]
>
> Loin des peuples vivants, errantes, condamnées,
> À travers les déserts courez comme des loups
> Faites votre destin, âmes désespérées [désordonnées]
> Et fuyez l'infini que vous portez en vous. (*OC*, 1: 155)

Despentes alludes to Baudelaire's infernal vision of lesbian love and rebellion throughout her novel but subjects his vision to significant swerves. Her citation of "Femmes damnées" excises the dank, pestilential imagery of the lesbians' lovemaking and ignores their "châtiment." Despentes's heroines may be *condamnées*, but they are not *damnées*. Avatars of the *héautontimorouménos*, Baudelaire's lesbians are at once "la plaie et le couteau, la victime et le bourreau" of their infinite and unnatural desire. Although they heroically forge their own destiny, their conscience condemns them to despair. Despentes's epigraph misquotes Baudelaire and substitutes "âmes désordonnées" for "âmes désespérées" ("Faites votre destin, âmes désespérées"), replacing despair with disorder. She thus dismisses the psychological register of internalized opprobrium that reigns in Baudelaire's poem. The fierce exhilaration of her heroines on their killing spree is a sharp contrast to the desperate flight of their Baudelairean counterparts. Instead of portraying heroines racked by inner conflict, Despentes externalizes the dialectic between predator and prey, or victim and executioner. Whereas Delphine and Hippolyte are cast as exiled wolves running through the desert ("À travers le désert courez comme des loups"), Manu and Nadine joke about "catching wolf," or men, for sex. Their road trip turns predatory men/wolves into objects of sexual, murderous, and even artistic satisfaction. This latter point is illustrated in their slaughter of a literate architect, who quotes Baudelaire's very same poem in an unsuccessful attempt to disarm them: "Vous devez avoir beaucoup souffert pour en venir à ces extrémités, à ces ruptures. *Je ne sais quel désert vous avez traversé,* je ne sais ce qui me pousse à avoir confiance en vous" (*BM,* 222; emphasis added).

As the novel progresses, Nadine and Manu come to embody the idealized fusion described in Baudelaire's poem, where Delphine calls out to her lover:

> Hippolyte, ô ma soeur ! tourne donc ton visage,
> Toi, mon âme et mon coeur, mon tout et ma moitié.

So perfectly do Nadine and Manu come to mirror each other that they are described as "une bête à deux têtes, séduisante au bout du compte" (*BM,* 189). Yet the absence of lesbian sexuality in *Baise-moi* curiously departs from Baudelaire's poem. While the two women remain in close proximity, watching each other during their lovemaking with other partners, and even pleasuring themselves as they do so, they never sexually engage with one another. Despentes's foreclosure of same-sex desire is reminiscent of Rachilde's and has led to accusations of homophobia or, at the very least, an incapacity to imagine sex outside of the heteronormative order. This is surprising, given her gesture toward Baudelaire's poem, and the importance of the lesbian as a figure of rebellion in the poet's oeuvre.[38] For Baudelaire, the lesbian's heroism is her refusal of the "natural" drive of organic life. Like the poet and dandy, the lesbian cultivates artificial pleasures and crafts her destiny in exile. The amoral abyss of her desire is akin to the poet's thirst for the infinite. The poem "Lesbos," for instance, celebrates "la mâle Sappho, l'amante et le poète," linking lesbianism, masculinity, and creativity in terms that transcend the specificity of the female body. We could entertain the hypothesis that Despentes wants nothing to do with such a masculinist dismissal of the female body and its organic specificity. But her foreclosure of lesbianism is perhaps better explained as a refusal to entertain alternate forms of desire that would give her heroines a way out. Insofar as Despentes ascribes a cause for her protagonists' rebellious carnage, it is a resolutely heteronormative environment of sexual trauma, in which rape and prostitution are the extreme manifestations of the underlying violence of the "natural" order of social sexing.[39] Despentes's narrative suggests that it is only by banning sex from their connection that the idealized fusion between her protagonists occurs. As one of the characters observes, the absence of sex between Manu and Nadine is precisely "ce qu'elles ont trouvé de mieux pour se dire qu'elles sont soeurs" (*BM,* 191). When Despentes's "femmes damnées" touch each other—and this in spite of the brutality of their contact with others—it is with fleeting tenderness, such as when Nadine gently dyes Manu's hair, or at the end, bears her corpse out into the forest.

Yet *Baise-moi* does not foreclose lesbian desire altogether. Instead, desire between women passes through channels usually reserved for male heterosexual consumption. Nadine's obsession with pornographic images of women is a case in point. Much like Rachilde's marquise de Sade, who eats the rose symbolizing a virginity destined to be deflowered by a man, Nadine consumes images destined for heterosexual male viewers. She gazes at photos of a blonde porn model whose bejeweled genitals and provocative stances recall Baudelaire's "Les Bijoux," another banned poem that may have caught Despentes's interest. "Les Bijoux" portrays the poet's beloved and muse naked save for her jewels, which shimmer and tinkle as she assumes provocative poses for his pleasure:

> La très chère était nue, et, connaissant mon coeur,
> Elle n'avait gardé que ses bijoux sonores,
> Dont le riche attirail lui donnait l'air vainqueur
> Qu'ont dans leurs jours heureux les esclaves des Mores. (*OC,* 1: 158)

Nadine contemplates a contemporary and most prosaic version of Baudelaire's "slave to love." Unlike received ideas about pornography as the degradation of female agency, the woman in the photo appears in full control of her body's display. As Nadine observes her genitals glittering like the entrance sign to a bordello, she thinks: "Transgression. Elle fait ce qui ne se fait pas avec un plaisir évident. Le trouble vient en grande partie de l'assurance tranquille avec laquelle elle se dévoile. Nadine la contemple longuement, impressionnée et respectueuse comme devant une icône" (*BM,* 139). The model's assured display of her "entrejambe scintillante" is a sharp contrast to the Baudelairean exhibitions examined in the previous chapter. "Une Martyre," and its caricature of commodification, for instance, portrays a decapitated woman sprawled on the bed, with her garter flashing a "regard diamanté" while her actual head stares sightlessly from the nightstand. In Despentes's pornographic image, however, the woman's gaze accompanies the sparkle of her jewels and elicits a desiring and even worshipful response from a female viewer. *Baise-moi* wrests the erotic and pornographic image away from its usual connotation and destination. No longer the sign of the female body's degradation, pornography provides an index of its power, one that is respectfully acknowledged by a woman who evolves in a milieu where the dispossession of one's sex is the norm, both in the most literal sense of rape and in the more figural guises of commodification.[40]

Despentes's heroines are entrenched in physiology, in the organic experience of the body and its appetites. As women who have come to an experience of their body—its pleasure and pain—though shame, violence, and humiliation, her protagonists celebrate the abjection of their experience *as* beauty. Nadine's back is scarred with whiplashes sought out in masochistic encounters over the *minitel.* Although one of her clients demands that she lower her prices because she is damaged goods, the narrative revalorizes what the client depreciated with unusual lyricism: "Des traînées sombres lui éclaboussent tout le dos, comme une fresque rageusement raturée. Inquiétants hiéroglyphes déchaînés dans la chair" (*BM,* 98). In a similar revalorization of what is socially deemed shameful, Manu drips menstrual blood in their hotel room, leaving behind a blood-spattered scene reminiscent of an entire tradition of aesthetic tableaux depicting the beauty of the dead female body. In these passages, the shameful or disgusting materiality of the female body is redeemed as art.

In an interview with Virginie Despentes and Coralie Thrin Thi, Catherine Breillat explains why writers and directors such as herself and Despentes focus on the organic experience of the body: "Il faut changer les codes esthétiques. On peut se mettre à aimer et trouver beau le coulant, le suintant. Le dégoût moral est d'ordre esthétique. Il faut affronter le fait que l'organique effraie" ("Trois femmes s'emparent du sexe"). Despentes's heroines may be read as rebellious artists who stage the victory of organic content over aesthetic form, thereby rejecting the disembodied formalism associated with masculine models of creativity. In this sense, Despentes can be seen as changing aesthetic codes like her precursor Baudelaire, whose "Une Charogne" presented his contemporaries with an equally shocking aesthetic celebration of organic decay, or "le coulant, le suintant."

However, Despentes's protagonists displace the traditional figure of the *poète maudit* with a trash and "bad girl" version of the *femme damnée*. Significantly enough, the novel opens with a male *poète maudit* figure. Nadine's friend Francis is a drug-addicted, penniless marginal poet and small-time crook on the run: "Il est poète, au sens très mâle du terme. À l'étroit dans son époque, incapable de se résoudre à l'ennui et au tiède. Insupportable" (*BM*, 34). Nadine serves him with unflagging devotion as his friend, muse, and scribe, forging prescriptions for the drugs that "inspire" him. Despentes unceremoniously dispatches this Baudelairean poet-figure early on in the novel, when he is shot, fittingly enough, buying his dose of artificial paradise at a pharmacy with a prescription forged by Nadine.

Nadine's encounter with Manu—which opens with Baudelaire's epigraph—displaces the figure of the *poète maudit* with that of the *femme damnée*. Their killing spree is self-consciously treated as performance art that follows André Breton's famous dictum: "L'acte surréaliste le plus simple consiste, révolvers au poings, à descendre dans la rue et à tirer au hasard, tant qu'on peut, dans la foule" (Breton, *Manifestes du surréalisme*, 74). The gun-toting heroines quote and trash the vocabulary of high art. "L'art pour l'art" becomes "le mauvais goût pour le mauvais goût" (*BM*, 186); Manu refers to their slaughters as "du grand spectacle" (*BM*, 112) and "choréographies de rêve" (*BM*, 136–37). Annoyed at the discrepancy between the form and content of their killings, she complains: "Faudrait que dialogues soient à la hauteur. Moi, tu vois, je crois pas au fond sans la forme" (*BM*, 121). Expounding their commitment to a Kantian exercise of disinterested violence, Nadine explains to one of her victims: "Je trouve ça effroyablement vulgaire, avoir un mobile pour tuer. C'est une question d'éthique. J'y tiens. J'y tiens énormément. La beauté du geste, j'accorde beaucoup d'importance à la beauté du geste. Qu'il reste désintéressé" (*BM*, 219).

This darkly comic self-reflexivity, along with Despentes's unbeautiful brand of hypernaturalism, rejects the hypocrisy of aesthetic conventions that soar above or sterilize the messiness of the real. The gross, "trash" scenes of violence parody the vocabulary of high art and its irrealization of what violence does to real bodies. *Baise-moi* enacts a revenge of content over form: it refuses the aesthetic comforts of distance and embeds the narrative in the concrete realities of the body's vulnerability, desire, and death.

The final slaughter both parodies and destroys aesthetic celebrations of *la beauté du mal.* To enter the home of an architect they plan to rob and kill, Manu and Nadine pretend to conduct a survey of "consommation des ménages en matière de culture" (*BM*, 214), a bourgeois enterprise par excellence. Their entry into the architect's home confronts the "high culture" of the intellectual bourgeoisie with the trash culture of the proletarian *femme sauvage.* With grim irony, this scene stages the transformation of "culture" into "matière" and classifiable consumption into waste. The architect is a modern-day dandy *embourgeoisé;* he is fastidious, literate, and unflappable, even with a gun pointed at him: "Il fait exception à la plupart des règles, il jongle au-dessus de la mêlée. Désinvolte et précieux" (*BM*, 215). He exemplifies the cool self-possession of the Baudelairean dandy, who must live and breathe before a mirror and surprise without ever succumbing to surprise (*OC*, 2: 710). The architect wields the symbolic arsenal of high culture, with art on the walls, the complete works of Sade, Dostoyevsky, and doubtless Baudelaire in his library. As Manu tartly observes, he is a literary flâneur, a bourgeois consumer of sensationalist prose who classifies decadence in alphabetical order: "Ça vit enterré dans des bouquins, ça croule sous les disques et les cassettes vidéo. C'est sordide. Ça aime les auteurs déjantés et les putes dégénérées . . . Ça apprécie la décadence classée par ordre alphabétique. Bon spectateur, en bonne santé. Ça sait apprécier le génie chez les autres, de loin quoi. Avec modération, surtout" (*BM*, 232).

The architect's *frisson* upon discovering that Manu and Nadine are killers is a purely aesthetic thrill. As Nadine holds a gun to his head, she imagines that he sees her as art come to life rather than a threat *to* his life: "Fantasque et délicieusement violent, tellement littéraire justement" (*BM*, 219). Confident in his mastery over the literary script of this encounter, the architect approaches the killers with an aesthete's delight in *la beauté du mal:*

> Je n'ai jamais rencontré de femme qui vous ressemble. Vous ne ressemblez sans doute à personne. Ce que vous faites est . . . terriblement violent. Vous devez avoir beaucoup souffert pour en arriver à ces extrémités, à ces ruptures. Je ne sais quel désert vous avez traversé, je ne sais ce qui me pousse à avoir confiance en vous. Comme vous dites, le marché est simple, et je vous fais confiance, aveuglément. Je vous vois si belle, jusqu'au plus profond de vous.
> Il a un petit éclat de rire terriblement raffiné, et secouant la tête:
> — Vous êtes un tel personnage. Nous nous sommes à peine croisés, mais il s'agit là d'une rencontre. Je ne peux m'empêcher d'être . . . terriblement fasciné. Il est d'autres pactes que je passerais volontiers avec vous. (*BM*, 222).

The architect rehearses the entire repertoire of decadent tropes, many of which are virtual citations of Baudelaire: the Faustian poet's pact with satanic beauty, the celebration of violence as pure rupture and excess, the admiration of the evil woman and her absolute singularity, the *femme damnée* as a wolf running in the desert, and finally, the explicit allusion to Nadine as a literary character ("vous êtes un tel personnage"), as a Baudelairean *passante* whose eyes contain "la douceur qui fascine et le plaisir qui tue" ("À une passante"). The architect is the smug recipient of a literary tradition that he believes ensures interpretive mastery. In this sense, he exemplifies the delusion of a cultural legacy that separates life from art by giving its readers the comforts of form over content, the spectacle of perversity without the embodied experience of violence.

The architect and Nadine compete for mastery over an incongruously literary *badinage*. Nadine casts herself as the mad intellectual and Manu as the unthinking beast, while the architect plays seductive host to both. As Nadine peruses the architect's library, she peppers her speech with subjunctives and precious turns of phrases. Despite her verbal mastery of the script, ensured by the physical power of her gun, however, Nadine is disarmed by her victim's elegant poise. As she realizes her physical attraction to him, she is hurled back into a shameful awareness of her own body and its social marking as gross and undesirable: "Elle aurait honte de son corps contre ce corps-là. Sous les caresses dispensées par un amant de cet acabit, sa peau deviendra grasse et pleine de poils commes des cafards, rugueuse et rouge. Écoeurante" (*BM,* 223). Nadine's queasy desire for the architect's recognition briefly reverses the hierarchy between gun-toting executioner and helpless victim to unveil a more familiar scenario in which "woman" embodies shameful materiality before masculine self-possession (Baudelaire's "La femme est naturelle. . . . La femme est le contraire du dandy"). As we saw in Rachilde, shame erupts when the hostility of the world registers within the body as vulnerability to another's (mis)recognition. Nadine imagines that her body will mutate into an alien and disgusting thing under the caress of privilege. The shame of social difference thus registers within her body as a sense of intimate dispossession.

Yet as in Despentes's revision of "Femmes damnées" in which the psychological register is dismissed in favor of action, here again internalized shame erupts as violence. Nadine interrupts the comedy of manners and her desire for the architect's recognition by beating him into terrified acknowledgement of his own physical vulnerability. This return to brute physiology culminates in the depiction of the victim's body after he has been shot: "Le corps se secoue puis s'apaise complètement. Il se répand comme un sac à ordures malencontreusement déchiré qui laisserait échapper des ordures rouges et brillantes" (*BM*, 226). The designation of the body as a garbage bag recalls the incident of Manu's rape, when her genitals are likened to a garbage disposal. It also resonates with other moments in the narrative where the two women are treated (and treat themselves) as human waste. In a final defilement of this symbol of male economic and cultural power, Manu urinates on the dead body chanting, "Toi, on va t'apprendre ce que perdre veut dire" (*BM*, 224). "Ce que perdre veut dire," in this context, is to be reduced to abject fear and helplessness before the arbitrary violence of another. The architect, whose profession it is to organize space and matter into form, is reduced to brute matter. His dehumanization is a ritualistic enactment of Manu's quotidian reality, where one's body becomes a vulnerable materiality divested of any value, a species of human waste.

The architect's execution is inspired by a tradition of ritualistic executions of the bourgeoisie, from Genet's *Les Bonnes* to Claude Chabrol's film *La Cérémonie*. It uncovers the relations of force that maintain the economic and sexual status quo. As Despentes has indicated, the intersection of sex and class struggle is central to her work: "Dans *Baise-moi*, on ne s'est pas donné de limites. Les héroïnes appartiennent à un milieu social précis, une bonne prol' et une fille de classe moyenne blanche. A partir de là, tout est rapport de force. Et comme ce sont des femmes, ça se cumule. Elles éprouvent une colère contre tout ce qui est dominant, qui écrase, asphyxie. L'homme et son sexe, mais aussi son poids économique" ("Trois femmes s'emparent du sexe").

The confrontation between these Baudelairean *femmes sauvages* and the dandy-architect recalls Baudelaire's "Assomons les pauvres !" As we saw, Baudelaire stages the ongoing reality of class warfare in a seemingly pacified society as an embodied combat between a bourgeois intellectual and an old pauper. Yet Despentes's scene departs from Baudelaire in a significant way: Baudelaire's poet initiates the violence that will awaken the pauper to his fundamental human worth, an awakening that occurs, paradoxically, by reducing the pauper to abject materiality. The poet grabs a branch and beats the pauper "avec l'énergie obstinée des cuisiniers qui veulent attendrir un beefteack" (*OC*, 1: 359). It is only when the poet-intellectual has reduced the pauper to meat that his victim retaliates by seizing the very same branch and reducing the poet to pure matter: "le malandrin décrépit se jeta sur moi . . . et avec la même branche d'arbre, me battit dru comme plâtre." The mutual recognition of equality takes place through the reciprocal treatment of the other as matter, as meat or as plaster. One's physical vulnerability to another's random violence (a phenomenon I have addressed as shame) is the negative ground for this recognition of humanity. Yet while "Assommons les pauvres !" discloses the underlying physical vulnerability of poet and pauper alike, Baudelaire nevertheless maintains the superiority of the poet-intellectual—who, after all, enacts his theory on the pauper's back.

In "Assommons les pauvres !" and *Baise-moi,* the hypocrisy and dangerous irrelevance of high literature and theory are disclosed by returning to humanity's lowest common denominator, that is to say, the vulnerable materiality of the body itself. Only in Despentes, the architect-dandy and the high literature he consumes are fully co-opted by the bourgeoisie. Literature and theory have deteriorated into classified consumption, hence the irony of the killers' fake survey on the "consommation de ménages en matière de culture," which lets them into the dandy's abode. Despentes's protagonists mock the futility of the architect's library and its books on the psychology of the serial killer. The ensuing carnage makes clear that neither psychological nor literary perspectives on *la beauté du mal* have any bearing on the brute reality of class and sex warfare. Instead, the struggle between intellectual and female proletariat is one for an acknowledgement of "ce que perdre veut dire," that is to say, the raw violence of physical—as well as material and symbolic—dispossession.[41] In Baudelaire, the body (turned to meat or plaster) is momentarily freed of its class determinations; it becomes the site for a recognition of essential parity and agency. In *Baise-moi,* the body (turned to waste) becomes a site for the mutual recognition of inhumanity. The conventional celebration of *la beauté du mal*—its fetishism of form over content and its evacuation of quotidian violence—is repudiated; the body—in its vulnerable abjection—emerges as the only place from which an aesthetics and a politics can begin to be imagined. *Baise-moi* stages an infinite repetition of violence with no exit. The novel neither provides a therapeutic narrative of psychic or social integration nor gives a consistent critique of oppression by gender, race, or class. Its denunciation lies in its "hard et destroy" replication of violence, and in its mise-en-scène of abject bodies whose agency is exercised *as* matter's revenge on form.

In her interview with Breillat, Despentes argued that *Baise-moi* was censored because cinema, unlike books, is a medium available to the masses: "On peut aller plus loin en littérature, car le livre appartient à la classe bourgeoise, alors que le cinéma est accessible à tous : la peur est là. Je suis censée prendre des précautions avec l'image, alors qu'on rend les gens complètement ignorants, qu'on les laisse dans la misère."[42] Despentes points out the hypocrisy of confusing social violence with its filmic representation. For her, the scandalized response to *Baise-moi* was but another way of masking the class interests that maintain the bourgeoisie's economic and cultural privilege. This argument against the conflation of representation with violence is also made in terms of sex in her novel's tacit refusal to condemn pornography itself as the source of women's sexual degradation. Despentes thus reminds us that what is at stake in her phantasmic representations and their apparently gratuitous sensationalism is an ongoing, yet often invisible, reality of social and sexual warfare.

Baudelaire, Rachilde, and Despentes were censored for their transgressive representations of sex and violence. They were considered outrageous to public mores because of the "gratuitous" or "excessive" quality of their representations. Yet as I hope to have shown, it is the very excess of their violence that taps into a repressed nexus of institutional forces producing sexual, economic, and artistic subjects at the cost of abject others. Their hyperbolic scenes of perversity make legible the implicit and systemic violence of the bourgeois status quo. All three turn to literature not as a space of imaginative emancipation but as a privileged site for the sustained examination of the role of representation itself in the production of historical violence. The negativity of their critique and their resistance to clear political readings challenge straightforward ideological recuperations of their works. Yet this very resistance opens up new horizons for thinking about the body's fragility and resistance in literature, theory, and history.

I have attempted to demonstrate the value of irony as a strategy that radically "depositions" the reading subject by forcing her to listen to the reverberations of violence in texts, and to recover a level of ideological critique that refuses the comforts of identification or vicarious victimization. Rachilde's and Despentes's portraits of bodies in all of their unruly and vulnerable materiality participate in the alternate modernism I have attempted to trace from Balzac to Mallarmé. Their carnivalesque play with the figures of the dandy and the *femme sauvage* dislocate the conventional gender assigned to these figures. Yet such dislocations do more than recuperate high culture from a woman's perspective. Their enactment of "matter's revenge on form" pursues Baudelaire's meditation on the underlying violence of the human body's inscription in art and history, a meditation that takes one of its most compelling forms in the works of Albert Camus.

5 ▌ *Broken Engagements*

Albert Camus and the Poetics of Terror

J'ai essayé plus d'une fois, comme tous mes amis, de m'enfermer dans un système pour y prêcher à mon aise. Mais un système est une espèce de damnation qui nous pousse à une abjuration perpétuelle. Baudelaire, "Exposition universelle (1855)"

Je ne suis pas un philosophe. Je ne crois pas assez à la raison pour croire à un système.
Camus, interview in *Servir,* December 20, 1945

In his youth in Oran, Algeria, Albert Camus recited Baudelaire's prose poem "L'Étranger," alternating voices with a friend:

« Qui aimes tu le mieux, homme énigmatique, dis ? Ton père, ta mère, ta soeur, ou ton frère ?

—Je n'ai ni père, ni mère, ni soeur, ni frère.

—Tes amis ?

—Vous vous servez-là d'une parole dont le sens m'est resté jusqu'à ce jour inconnu.

—Ta patrie ?

—J'ignore sous quelle latitude elle est située.

—La beauté ?

—Je l'aimerais volontiers, déesse et immortelle.

—L'or ?

—Je le hais comme vous haïssez Dieu.

—Eh ! Qu'aimes-tu donc, extraordinaire étranger ?

—J'aime les nuages . . . les nuages qui passent . . . là-bas . . . là-bas . . . les merveilleux nuages ! »

The figure of the *étranger* may have returned to haunt Camus in postwar Paris as he struggled to circumvent the Manichean polarities defining the French intellectual and political landscape.[1] Camus came out of World War II as an exemplary *intellectuel engagé.* He had been editor of the resistance journal

173

Combat and wrote *Lettres à un ami allemand* and portions of *La Peste,* his alle-
gory of resistance, under the Nazi occupation. He thus emerged as a guiding
moral, political, and literary voice for postwar France. Yet in the decade fol-
lowing France's liberation, Camus's commitment to the absolute value of hu-
man life repeatedly pitted him against the political solutions endorsed by the
Left. His inability to adopt a course of action in which the end justified the
means alienated him from his allies and friends on more than one occasion. In
the matter of the postwar purges, for instance, Camus's initial support gave
way to disgust and fear that the *épuration* of collaborators was perpetuating the
spirit of Nazi eliminationism.[2] Camus's rupture with Sartre and his subse-
quent alienation from the intellectual circles of *Les Temps modernes* also
occurred over a question of ends and means, when he denounced Marxist
messianic violence in *L'Homme révolté* and called into question the French
Left's political ideal. And to this day, Camus's ambivalence about an indepen-
dent Algeria—in part because of his refusal to legitimate the FLN's terrorist
tactics and its toll on French Algerians—brands him as an apologist for French
colonialism, or at the very least, as an idealist who eschewed the moral com-
promises of political praxis.[3] As Sartre put it in his ambiguous *hommage* to his
erstwhile friend after his death in a car accident, "Son humanisme têtu, étroit
et pur, austère et sensuel, livrait un combat douteux contre les événements
massifs et difformes de ce temps. . . . Son silence même, ces dernières années,
avait un aspect positif : ce cartésien de l'absurde refusait de quitter le sûr ter-
rain de la moralité pour s'engager dans les chemins incertains de la *pratique*"
(*Sit.,* 4: 127). Camus's ambivalence about the politics of his time has con-
tributed to his lasting canonization as a *clerc* who refused to tread the muddy
paths of praxis and plunge his hands into the "shit and blood" of history.[4]

While it may seem paradoxical to conclude a study of Baudelaire, the ex-
emplary *poète dépolitiqué,* with a reading of Camus, the postwar *intellectuel en-
gagé,* it is nevertheless a fitting end to this book's broader exploration of irony
as resistance to the violence of modernity. Indeed, upon closer scrutiny, several
striking similarities emerge in these authors' critiques of modern experience
and analyses of the connections between literature, history, and terror. Al-
though inhabiting different historical junctures, both wrote in the aftermath
of great political upheavals (1848 and World War II respectively) and struggled
to articulate an oppositional politics and poetics when such positions either
risked co-optation by the logic of empire or seemed doomed to irrelevance.
For Camus, as for Baudelaire, postrevolutionary secular conceptions of collec-
tive identity inaugurated the age of ideology, or what Camus called "les reli-

gions horizontales de notre temps" (*E,* 601). These ideological systems (bourgeois capitalism and imperialism for Baudelaire, modern totalitarianisms of the Left and Right for Camus) were intractably violent, since they were founded on the sacrifice of vulnerable, suffering bodies to an idealized future. Camus's refusal of abstract solutions to particular historical crises echoes Baudelaire's rejection of aesthetic and philosophical systems. From Meursault's *acte gratuit* to the critique of teleological history in *L'Homme révolté,* Camus's work is a passionate meditation on the limits of theory before the unjustifiable fact of human suffering *and* the unpredictable vitality of human agency. For both authors, secular ideological systems are realized in the world of things as terror, as the sacrifice of living beings to a unified end. Baudelaire's dictum, "Toute révolution a pour corollaire le massacre des innocents" is echoed, almost a century later in Camus's indictment of purgative, revolutionary violence. Camus, the postwar humanist—like Baudelaire, the self-proclaimed postrevolutionary anti-humanist—refused the murderous abstraction of philosophical and political progress narratives. Confronted with the particularity of lived experience (and specifically the lived experience of violence), both chose the ambiguous refractions of aesthetic form over the "perpetual abjurations" of philosophy and political theory.

The following pages situate Camus within the legacy of committed ironists examined thus far. I begin with an overview of Camus's *L'Homme révolté* that attends to a neglected but central aspect of this essay: its meditation on the links between art, history and terror. Camus's reflection on the overlapping violence of these fields connects him with the authors discussed in the previous chapters and belongs to a long-standing preoccupation with literature's complicity with other regimes of power. His own position as a committed intellectual wrestling with the dilemmas of postwar French politics provides an exemplary elucidation of irony's value in a political—as well as aesthetic—exploration of violence.

The Diagnosis of Terror in L'Homme révolté

L'Homme révolté and its critique of contemporary deifications of History constituted an intervention in the heated debate following the disclosures of the Soviet labor camps. When the testimonies and narratives of Arthur Koestler, David Rousset, and Victor Kravchenko were met with cautious silence and skepticism, Camus publicly declared, as early as 1949, his belief that the labor camps were fully entrenched in the Soviet state apparatus.[5] In the aftermath of

Merleau-Ponty's *Humanisme et terreur* (initially published by Sartre's *Les Temps modernes* in 1946) and de Beauvoir's *Pour une morale de l'ambiguité*, essays that contemplated the legitimation of historically specific abuses for the sake of world revolution, *L'Homme révolté* instead called into question the very foundations of the French Left's political ideal.[6] In such a polarized Cold War context, it is not surprising that Camus's denunciation of the discourse of ends and means should have estranged him from the intellectual circle of *Les Temps modernes*. For his critique did not just target Marxist-Hegelian *doxa*. It became a sweeping denunciation of all utopic political and philosophical forms of messianism—irrespective of their ideological affiliation—that sacrifice living and suffering bodies to their idealized ends. In Camus's account, the French postwar political mentality was still blindly locked into a conceptual legacy built on the historical union of revolution and terror.

The genealogy of the Western revolutionary tradition proposed in *L'Homme révolté* casts the totalitarianisms of the twentieth century as the culmination of one hundred and fifty years of philosophical and political terror, beginning with the French Revolution. For Camus, secular postrevolutionary conceptions of identity and polity deified the individual, and by extension, the body politic, thereby displacing metaphysics with history. This fatal hypostasis of individual and state power inaugurated the age of ideology, the "religions horizontales de notre temps" (*E*, 601). Camus's genealogy of terror thus begins with 1789 and tracks its deployment through nineteenth-century philosophy, political theory, and literary production. In his discussion of historical forms of rebellion, the chapter entitled "La Prophétie bourgeoise" traces a direct line from the technocratic utopias flourishing in Baudelaire's time under Napoléon III's market authoritarianism to the modern police state.

Camus's indictment of the nineteenth-century bourgeois myth of progress echoes Baudelaire's denunciations of modernity's violence. A century earlier, Baudelaire's "Salon de 1846" portrayed the emerging capitalist state as an exquisitely regulated organism in which knowledge, property, science, and political power converged to suppress all forms of dissent: "Vous vous êtes associés, vous avez formé des compagnies et faits des emprunts pour réaliser l'idée de l'avenir avec toutes ses formes diverses, formes politiques, industrielles et artistiques. Vous n'avez jamais en aucune noble entreprise laissé l'initiative à la minorité protestante" (*OC*, 1: 875). By the time of *L'Homme révolté*, Baudelaire's vision of an amoral technocratic society whose ethos of production would be maintained by "des moyens qui feraient frissonner notre humanité actuelle" (*OC*, 1: 666) had been realized in the modern police states of Hitler,

Mussolini, and Stalin. Baudelaire's prophecy of a seamlessly policed social totality finds an uncanny echo in Camus's narrative of the emergence of state terror in the nineteenth century's technocratic utopias:

> Une société dont les savants seraient les prêtres, deux milles banquiers et techniciens régnant sur une Europe de cent vingt millions d'habitants où la vie privée serait absolument identifiée avec la vie publique, où une obéissance absolue "d'action, de pensée et de coeur" serait rendue au grand prêtre qui régnerait sur le tout, telle est l'utopie de Comte qui annonce ce qu'on peut appeler les *religions horizontales de notre temps*. Elle est utopique, il est vrai, parce que, convaincu du pouvoir illuminant de la science, il a oublié de prévoir une police. D'autres seront plus pratiques ; et la religion de l'humanité sera fondée, effectivement, mais sur le sang et la douleur des hommes. (*E*, 601; emphasis added)

Camus's genealogy of terror echoes Baudelaire's prophecy. Terror is not only a historical moment and specific consequence of the French Revolution; conceived more broadly, it is an imperial logic of domination that emerged out of the postrevolutionary deification of individual and state power. Modernity's enthronement of history and progress was intractably violent and nihilistic. Its premise was the sacrifice of a vital, immediate, and differentiated social content to a unified future totality. For Camus, dialectical materialism was but another avatar of modernity's political and philosophical messianism. A sweeping, imperialistic, and virtually cannibalistic force, the dialectic's end is the relentless absorption of difference and alterity: "En ce sens, il est juste de remarquer que la dialectique n'est pas et ne peut pas être révolutionnaire. Elle est seulement, selon notre point de vue, nihiliste, pur mouvement qui vise à nier tout ce qui n'est pas lui-même."[7]

The originality of *L'Homme révolté*—one significantly ignored in the ensuing debates—lies in Camus's treatment of violence as a *formal* principle that could be deployed in the distinct fields of philosophy, politics, and aesthetics. Violence erupts when the human desire for unity in a secular world (a central feature of rebellion) manifests itself as a will to totality. Camus's critique of the excesses of rebellion—as revolution and terror—thus fully implicates aesthetic production with political violence: "La révolte . . . est fabricatrice d'univers. Ceci définit l'art aussi. L'exigence de la révolte, à vrai dire, est en partie une exigence esthétique" (*E*, 659). Rebellion and art share an identical desire for unity and build compensatory fictions that contest the dissonance of historical experience. This desire for unity always risks mutating into a will to totality. Tracing the evolution of political messianism from the literary self-deification of Sade or Baudelaire to the revolutions that gave birth to the modern totalitarian state, Camus proposes that an identical violence animates art, philosophy, and politics. The totalitarian state is a political incarnation of the totalizing *forms* structuring modern Europe's aesthetic and ideological imagination. In this continuum, "l'étrange et terrifiante croissance de l'état moderne" is the historical and material outcome of a metaphorics of closure structuring the Western postrevolutionary imaginary:

> Toutes les pensées révoltées, nous l'avons vu, s'illustrent dans une rhétorique ou un univers clos. La rhétorique des remparts chez Lucrèce, les couvents et les châteaux verrouillés de Sade, l'île ou le rocher romantique, les cimes solitaires de Nietzsche, l'océan élémentaire de Lautréamont, les parapets de Rimbaud, les châteaux terrifiants qui renaissent, battus par un orage de fleurs, chez les surréalistes, la prison, la nation retranchée, le camp de concentration, l'empire des libres esclaves, illustrent à leur manière le même besoin de cohérence et d'unité. Sur ces mondes fermés, l'homme peut régner et connaître enfin. (*E,* 659)

Camus thus situates literary tropes of ascension and closure on the same conceptual spectrum as prisons, concentration camps, and empires. In this account, Sade's carceral imaginary, taken up and culminating in the explosive violence of surrealism's imagery, finds its historical and political correlatives in modern state terror.

No doubt there is something questionable in Camus's conflation of rhetoric and practice, of imagined and real violence. The sweep of his indictment, the enumeration of textual and political exercises of power, may initially strike the reader as an idealist blind spot in his thought. Yet it is the slippage between literary figuration and historical violence in this passage and throughout the essay that I find most compelling in Camus's understanding of art and terror. As we have seen in the preceding chapters, the treatment of violence as a formal operation that takes place in literature and history is central to Baudelaire's poetics and politics. By situating metaphorical and literal violence on the same conceptual continuum, Camus, like Baudelaire and the other authors examined thus far, suggests that figuration possesses a performative force that shapes and inflects historical reality. Violence and representation are fully imbricated, and this imbrication operates in overlapping areas of thought and life.

Baudelaire's poems map analogous figural operations in poetry and other fields of social and political power; his practice of counterviolence exploits the complicity between poetry's allegorical violence and existing cultural regimes of representation. The poet's formal understanding of violence anticipates Camus's aesthetic genealogy of terror. This shared vision of the irrealizing violence of aesthetic form might explain why Camus's discussion of metaphysical rebellion traces the origins of literature's complicity with terror back to late romanticism. Camus reads the gradual eclipse of literature's referential function in the nineteenth century (the standard account of "art for art's sake" discussed in Chapter 2) in light of a deification of form that collaborates with the origins of modern terror. The autonomy, closure, and irrealization celebrated in literary works by Sade, Lautréamont, and the surrealists, find their material incarnation in the reifying brutality of the totalitarian state. For Camus, the logic of empire is akin to the romantic imagination in its assumption of the plasticity of reference itself: "L'Empire suppose une négation et une certitude : la certitude de l'infinie plasticité de l'homme et la négation de la nature humaine. . . . S'il n'y a pas de nature humaine, la plasticité de l'homme est, en effet, infinie. Le réalisme politique, à ce degré, n'est qu'un romantisme sans frein, un romantisme de l'efficacité" (*E*, 640).

Camus designates as "romantic" aesthetic and political performances of absolute mastery that negate the irreducible difference and givenness of the material world and its subjects. Such unbridled romanticism necessarily assumes the materiality of the world to be infinitely malleable. Romanticism and realpolitik converge in their assumption of referential plasticity, of the sovereign imagination or empire's power to shape reality in its image.

Against such murderous ideologies and their aesthetic correlatives, Camus argued for the resuscitation of some fragment of humanity that escaped historical determination and resisted the claims of ideological and aesthetic representation alike. If literature was to contest the plasticity or erasure of the individual by larger historical processes, it could only do so by communicating the living texture of human suffering, the body's fragility when confronted with the force of history. As we shall see, Camus's portrayal of the body as a vulnerable site on which competing allegorical claims are exercised belongs to an ongoing reflection on literature's referential debt to the bodies it represents.

Despite the remarkable affinities between their understanding of violence as a formal principle deployed in aesthetics and politics, ironically enough, in *L'Homme révolté*, Camus positions Baudelaire as yet another point of relay in the conceptual continuum of terror. The chapter on metaphysical rebellion presents Baudelaire's dandy in light of the romantic subject's dangerous self-deification in a secular world. The Baudelairean dandy creates "sa propre unité par des moyens esthétiques" (*E*, 462). This self-unification through form attempts a personal askesis that is driven by the same impulse as the self-deifying collective ascensions of modern totalitarianisms. This view of dandyism could not be further from Foucault's, which, as we saw in the preceding chapter, cautiously envisions corporeal self-fashioning as a form of resistance to the subjectivizing forces of the state and market. Camus envisions dandyism as "une forme dégradée de l'ascèse" (*E*, 461), as the sterile, nihilistic manifestation of individual rebellion. Yet, having situated Baudelaire in terms of terror and its metaphorics of closure, Camus concludes his portrait of the poet with an enigmatic swerve: "Son vrai drame, qui l'a fait le plus grand poète de son temps, était ailleurs. Baudelaire ne peut être évoqué ici que dans la mesure où il a été le théoricien le plus profond du dandysme et donne des formules définitives à une des conclusions de la révolte romantique" (*E*, 463).

To what extent did Camus reevaluate Baudelaire's oeuvre after writing *L'Homme révolté*? Did he look for the *ailleurs* that he saw as the forum for the poet's true drama? Could we read Camus's later explorations of the dark side of commitment as a return to Baudelaire, in an attempt to find a way out of the apparent impasses of aesthetic rebellion? As early as 1940, Roger Quillot hazarded a reference to Baudelaire when discussing the title of Camus's *L'Étranger* (which is also the title of the opening prose poem of Baudelaire's *Le Spleen de Paris*), but Camus responded that the allusion was no doubt unconscious.[8] Four years after the publication of *L'Homme révolté*, however, Camus's enigmatic *La Chute* came out. Its distinctly Baudelairean resonances suggest that Camus may have returned to the poet in the course of the novel's writing. The famous rupture with Sartre over *L'Homme révolté* might have prompted a rereading of Baudelaire, who, it should be remembered, was also harshly condemned by Sartre in 1947, and on very similar grounds. Throughout the prosecutorial exchange that followed the hostile review of *L'Homme révolté* in *Les Temps modernes* in 1952 by Sartre's young colleague Francis Jeanson, Sartre and Jeanson cast the former *résistant* as a Baudelairean dandy, a failed rebel whose sullen withdrawal from praxis had led to a self-righteous, aestheticist, and ultimately terroristic stance.[9] In a ferocious caricature, the writer of *Les Mains sales* attacked Camus's tentative pokes into the ambiguous waters of historical action: "Tout comme la fillette qui tâte l'eau de l'orteil en demandant : « Est-elle chaude ? » vous regardez l'Histoire avec défiance, vous y plongez un doigt que vous retirez très vite et vous demandez : « A-t-elle un sens ? »."[10] For Sartre, Camus's denunciation of revolutionary violence in *L'Homme révolté* was blind to the writer's inextricable situatedness in history. Instead of participating in constructive political projects, Camus had relegated himself to a purely negative, condemnatory stance ("vous vous êtes condamné à condamner, Sisyphe" (*TM,* 345). Even Camus the *résistant* was denounced as a purely reactive rebel rather than a genuine revolutionary, one who had bravely defended the status quo before the madness of Hitlerism but had abdicated before the exigencies of postwar reconstruction. The only option for such exalted moral intransigence was, according to Sartre, exile from history itself: "je ne vois qu'une solution pour vous : les îles Galapagos" (*TM,* 343).

In 1947, Sartre had dismissed Baudelaire's rebellion (against his family, the Second Empire, and his historical epoch) in similar terms. For the philosopher of praxis, the nineteenth-century poet's *révolte* was far too invested in existing structures of authority to open up genuine revolutionary insight. Baudelaire's withdrawal into the reified language of poetry and into strategies of "loser wins" or *qui perd gagne* through figures such as the dandy and the *héautontimorouménos,* exemplified the nineteenth century's retreat into the sterile narcissicism of "art for art's sake." In the scathing exchange over *L'Homme révolté,* Camus is assigned to the class of *littérateurs* who, like Baudelaire, abdicate from the demands of history, serving instead the terroristic abstraction of literature: "La Terreur est une violence abstraite. Vous êtes devenu terroriste et violent quand l'histoire—que vous rejetiez—vous a rejeté à son tour : c'est que vous n'étiez qu'une abstraction de révolté. . . . Votre morale s'est d'abord changé en moralisme, aujourd'hui elle n'est plus que littérature, demain elle sera peut-être immoralité."[11]

Sartre's prophecy that *L'Homme révolté* was but literature on the verge of immorality, was fulfilled, not "demain" but a few years later, with the publication of *La Chute.* Ironically enough, Camus's novel earned high praise in Sartre's posthumous tribute: "On vivait avec ou contre sa pensée, telle que nous la révélaient ses livres—*La Chute,* surtout, le plus beau peut-être et le moins compris—mais toujours à travers elle" (*Sit.,* 4: 127). Did Sartre himself understand the extent to which its protagonist incarnates the caricature of Camus in *Les Temps modernes?*[12] A *juge-pénitent* who is "condemned to condemn" and longs for the edenic innocence of islands (Cipango instead of Galapagos this time), Jean-Baptiste Clamence exemplifies the moral terrorism that Sartre had imputed to Camus. Even the caricature of Camus's tentative pokes into history's chilly waters is echoed in Clamence's inability to dive into the Seine and save a drowning woman. Sartre's praise of the novel is all the more ironic when we consider that *La Chute* stages the very argument he had dismissed in 1952, for its protagonist's monologue is a brilliant illustration of the logic of totality and terror described in *L'Homme révolté.* Did Sartre discern the Baudelairean resonance of Camus's novel—its crepuscular lyricism, the *dolorisme* of its lucidity, its journey into *la conscience dans le mal*?[13]

Sartre's portrait of Camus as a dandy in revolt may thus have prompted a return to Baudelaire. Yet we could also speculate that the genealogy of terror in *L'Homme révolté*, as Camus's most systematic attempt to grapple with art's relations to politics and ethics, led him to reassess Baudelaire and the tradition of "art for art's sake" he represented and to consider the poet's exploration into art, history, and the problem of evil. *La Chute* deepens the meditation undertaken in *L'Homme révolté* on the complicity between literature and other regimes of power. Clamence's confession illustrates Baudelaire's strategy of irony as counterviolence, for it is at once a symptom and a critique of terror.[14] Haunted by the knowledge that contestation is fraught with ambiguity, that resistance is always on the verge of renewing the violence that is denounced, Camus's text explores the possibilities of commitment in a medium complicit with violence.

La Chute is an eminently Baudelairean text in its atmosphere, themes, tropes, and characters. Yet it is also an investigation of art's responsibility at a particular historical juncture—in the aftermath of war, occupation, collaboration, and genocide, and in the midst of complex, if not even paralyzing, choices for the intellectual: the fate of the Left in France and abroad, its reckoning with state-sanctioned or insurgent terror in Stalin's Gulag archipelago and Algeria respectively. Camus's novel reflects upon the intellectual's complicity with the violence of history and probes for alternatives to the dominant Sartrean model of commitment in terms that resonate with the Baudelairean engagements this book has traced thus far. In the following pages, then, Baudelaire will serve as a *phare ironique* as we navigate the ironies of *La Chute*. His poetry will illuminate Camus's journey into *la conscience dans le mal* and the paths left open for commitment in postwar France.

Narrative Terror, Irony, and Ideology in La Chute

> *Ces transformations progressives caractérisent le monde de la terreur rationelle où vit, à des degrés différents, l'Europe. Le dialogue, relation des personnes, a été remplacé par la propagande ou la polémique, qui sont deux sortes de monologue. L'abstraction, propre au monde des forces et du calcul, a remplacé les vrais passions qui sont du domaine de la chair et de l'irrationnel.*   Camus, *L'Homme révolté*

> *Par exemple, vous avez dû le remarquer, notre vieille Europe*
> *philosophe enfin de la bonne façon. Nous ne disons plus, comme*
> *aux temps naïfs : « Je pense ainsi. Quelles sont vos objections ? »*
> *Nous sommes devenus lucides. Nous avons remplacé le dialogue*
> *par le communiqué. « Telle est la vérité, disons-nous. Vous pouvez*
> *toujours la discuter, ça ne nous intéresse pas. Mais dans quelques*
> *années, il y aura la police, qui vous montrera que j'ai raison ».*
>
> Camus, *La Chute*

For Camus, one of the greatest challenges facing postwar Europe was the restitution of a dialogical structure of communication. The age of ideologies, culminating in the atrocities of twentieth-century's totalitarianisms, had coerced entire populations to actively or passively endorse murder through various forms of propaganda masquerading as fact or logic. Monologue, abstraction, propaganda, communiqué: this was the ideological artillery of terror. These weapons had delivered individuals to the violence of what Georges Perec called "l'Histoire avec sa grande hache," not only as victims but also as executioners and accomplices. The abstract monologues of ideology banished alternative sources of value such as the human body and nature, both of which precede, exceed, and posit a limit to, the violence of history itself. *La Chute* is a narrative inquiry into the ideological strategies of terror. It performs the violence of ideology itself, but also gestures toward the limits posed by the reality of human suffering. This reading will begin by mapping the ideological valences of the novel's structure before turning to its ethical reflection on the human body ("le domaine de la chair et de l'irrationnel") as the site upon which the violence of history is enacted, and in whose name this violence must be resisted.

L'Homme révolté defined terror as "une subjectivité interminable qui s'impose aux autres comme objectivité." If this was, as Camus asserted, "la définition philosophique de la terreur" (*E*, 646), the seamless first-person monologue of *La Chute* provides its narrative enactment. Jean-Baptiste Clamence, who describes himself as a "juge pénitent," has exiled himself to Amsterdam and converts those he encounters to his reign of "lucid culpability." A Lermontovian hero of our times, his duplicitous confession bears witness to the failure of bourgeois humanism in the face of the great ethico-political challenges of the century: colonial oppression, class warfare, totalitarianism, and genocide. Once a successful and athletic Parisian lawyer and lover, a specialist in noble causes, his personal fall into self-division and bad faith marks a collective fall into the ambiguous violence of historical modernity.

Clamence is a failed rebel, a degraded Baudelairean poet who has tumbled from edenic plenitude into the modern heart of darkness. Like the poet of "Perte d'auréole" who haunts the taverns of Paris after losing his auratic halo to "la fange du macadam," Clamence plays prophet in a seedy bar called "Mexico City" and complacently assumes Baudelaire's descent into ironic lucidity, described in the poem "L'Irrémédiable":

> Tête-à-tête sombre et limpide
> Qu'un coeur devenu son miroir !
> . . . .
>
> Un phare ironique, infernal,
> Flambeau des grâces sataniques,
> Soulagement et gloire uniques,
> — La conscience dans le Mal ! (*OC,* 1: 80)

La Chute exemplifies the fall into Baudelairean irony examined in the first chapter of this book. Its protagonist once basked in moral righteousness and social entitlement of the one who laughs in "De l'essence du rire" (Baudelaire's "*Moi* je ne tombe pas"), and yet is tripped up and falls into duplicity, abjection, and bad faith.[15] A kindred spirit of the dandy and *héautontimorouménos,* he is at once knife and wound, subject and object, of his *mal du siècle.* As we shall see, however, Clamence's fall does not lead to the lucid irony of rebellion, which for both Baudelaire and Camus required maintaining the reversals of authority proper to an ironic consciousness. Instead, his confession puts irony in service of terror.

While the origins of Clamence's ontological fall remain mysterious, it consistently occurs in *La Chute,* as in Baudelaire, under the sign of laughter. The first incident signaling Clamence's fall is trivial enough. At the height of his professional, social, and sexual prowess, he is caught in a traffic jam caused by a motorcyclist. He asks the man to remove his vehicle, thus provoking his ire. In the confusion that ensues, not only is Clamence accused of mistreating the biker, but he is also slapped by the man in question and retreats "sous les regards ironiques de la foule." For the first time he becomes the *object* of laughter and experiences the subjection of another's derisive gaze. Thereafter, laughter is indissociably linked to his fall before another's eyes: "Oui, ils étaient là, comme avant, mais ils riaient. . . . J'eus même l'impression, à cette époque, qu'on me faisait des crocs-en-jambe. Deux ou trois fois, en effet, je butai, sans raison, en entrant dans des endroits publiques. Une fois même, je m'étalai." Clamence becomes subject and the object of a typical Baudelairean *dédoublement.* The fall into lucidity is accompanied, as in Baudelaire, by the explosion of laughter: "Du jour où je fus alerté, la lucidité me vint, je reçus toutes les blessures en même temps et je perdis mes forces d'un seul coup. L'univers entier se mit alors à rire autour de moi."[16] Yet unlike Baudelaire's ironic philosopher, who maintains these reversals of authority by ironizing his own sense of superiority, Clamence reverses his fall into a new ascension, which, we belatedly realize, governs the course of his confession.

For Camus as for Baudelaire, irony and rebellion are lucid oppositions that nevertheless harbor within them the seeds of mystified authoritarianism. As *L'Homme révolté* argued, rebellion is always threatened by a compensatory self-deification, be it through aesthetic means (as in the dandy) or the more dangerous collective ascensions of the state. In Baudelaire, this authoritarianism is represented by the *Homme dieu* of "Le Poème du hashisch," who in his drug-induced fantasy, imagines that all things are created by and for him.[17] Jean-Baptiste Clamence betrays the origins of rebellion, which for Camus lie in the unresolvable tension between self and world, as well as self and other. Ignoring the dynamic reversals that form the ethical core of ironic lucidity, Clamence freezes his fall and establishes an authoritarian fiction of universal culpability. His sly confession moves from a "Je" who has fallen to the "nous" of a community that is equally fallen but unaware of it. The silent interlocutor-reader is turned into Baudelaire's "Hypocrite lecteur, — mon semblable, — mon frère": "Le réquisitoire est achevé. Mais du même coup, le portrait que je tends à mes contemporains devient un miroir. . . . Je suis comme eux, bien sûr, nous sommes dans le même bouillon. J'ai cependant une supériorité, celle de le savoir, qui me donne le droit de parler."[18]

Clamence emerges as an authoritarian ironist, the thwarted idealist heir to such Baudelairean figures as the despotic prince of "Une Mort héroïque," the ironic consciousness of "L'Héautontimorouménos," and the poet-philosopher of "Assommons les pauvres !" He displays both the triumph of one who has seized epistemological power in a world divested of given values and the anguish of a psyche locked into the sadomasochistic repetition of its fall into lucidity. As a figure for the artist, Clamence radicalizes the despotism of Baudelaire's sovereign imagination. A modern-day allegoricist, Clamence is not content with hollowing out the city around him, as the flâneur-poet of "Le Cygne" does when he declares that "tout pour moi devient allégorie" (*OC,* 1: 86). Nor do his allegories bear witness to the victims of history by resurrecting those who have fallen out of modernity's frame of reference ("Je pense aux matelots oubliés dans une île, / Aux captifs, aux vaincus ! . . . à bien d'autres encor !" (*OC,* 1: 87). Instead, Clamence seeks out blank spaces for a purely specular exercise of imaginative sovereignty. As he contemplates the livid horizon of the Zuyderzee, drenched in fog and spleen, Camus's flâneur celebrates a landscape from which all traces of the human have been expunged:

> Voilà, n'est-ce pas, le plus beau des paysages négatifs ! Voyez, à notre gauche, ce tas de cendres qu'on appelle ici une dune, la digue grise à notre droite, la grève livide à nos pieds et, devant nous, la mer couleur de lessive faible, le vaste ciel où se reflètent les eaux blêmes. Un enfer mou, vraiment ! Rien que des horizontales, aucun éclat, l'espace est incolore, la vie morte. N'est-ce pas l'effacement universel, le néant sensible aux yeux ? Pas d'hommes, surtout, pas d'hommes ! Vous et moi, seulement, devant la planète enfin déserte. (*T,* 1512)

The most beautiful negative landscape, for Clamence, is one that empties real places, people, and events of content and materiality. This transformation of a heterogeneous reality into closed allegories of identity surfaces numerous times in *La Chute,* and in terms so Baudelairean that they are virtually quotations. Baudelaire's poet-prostitute and his narcissistic relationship to the crowd in "Les Foules" ("Pour lui seul, tout est vacant" [*OC,* 1: 291]) finds its echo in Clamence's desire that "sur toute la terre, tous les êtres, ou le plus grand nombre possible, fussent tournés vers moi, éternellement vacants, privés de vie indépendante, prêts à répondre à mon appel à n'importe quel moment, voués enfin à la stérilité jusqu'au jour où je daignerais les favoriser de ma lumière" (*T,* 1510). In "Les Fenêtres," Baudelaire's narrator defends the priority of his fiction over the reality of another being: "Peut-être me direz-vous : « Es-tu sûr que cette légende soit la vraie ? » Qu'importe ce que peut être *la réalité placée hors de moi,* si elle m'a aidé à vivre, à sentir qui je suis et ce que je suis ?" (*OC,* 1: 339; emphasis added). This radical subjectivism is echoed in Clamence's defense of lies as a route to truth: "Et mes histoires, vraies ou fausses, ne tendent-elles pas toutes à la même fin, n'ont-elles pas le même sens ? Alors, *qu'importe qu'elles soient vraies ou fausses, si, dans les deux cas, elles sont significatives de ce que j'ai été et de ce que je suis ?*" (*T,* 1537; emphasis added). Baudelaire's *légende* and Clamence's confessions are instances in which a narrator proudly and anxiously asserts the legitimacy of his self-narration while gesturing to its referential instability. Yet Baudelaire's poet-narrators demystify their fictions and disclose the underlying violence of allegory itself, thus remaining faithful to irony's self-critical dynamism. Clamence, however, performs an act of allegorical closure when he freezes his fall into a theology of guilt. In this sense, he enacts the violence of ideology identified in *L'Homme révolté* (the transformation of a vital, heterogeneous world into a fixed allegory of culpability). His discourse is both a symptom and a critique of the disincarnated logic of terror. It erases all traces of contestation so that his word, like that of his namesake "John the Baptist," can resonate uncontested and inaugurate his reign of lucid culpability. Thus, while Clamence accuses modern politics and philosophy of eradicating dialogue in favor of the communiqué, his monologue itself functions as a communiqué. Clamence is a prophet of cynical reason and an exemplary narrator, whose methodical demonstration of individual and collective fallenness enacts the violence of ideology itself: "l'idéologie, qui substitue à la réalité vivante une succession logique de raisonnements" (*E,* 742).

Yet the narrative structure of *La Chute* sabotages the authority of Clamence's ideology at several points and incites the reader to vigilance. The status of his confession as a tour de force in rhetorical manipulation is made explicit in many cautionary asides such as "Ne vous fiez pas trop, d'ailleurs, à mes attendrissements, ni à mes délires. Ils sont dirigés" (*T,* 1550). The reader-interlocutor is warned to treat this discourse not as mimetic but as rhetorical and performative. While Clamence coerces his silent interlocutor (and the reader) into mirroring his guilt, the possibility that the interlocutor will like the beggar of "Assommons les pauvres !" in turn contest his rhetorical subjection and laugh *at* Clamence is suggested at several points: "Ne riez pas ! Oui, vous êtes un client difficile, je l'ai vu du premier coup. Mais vous y viendrez, c'est inevitable."[19]

The Proximity of Violence and the Politics of Guilt

What is the historical significance of Clamence's theology of guilt? And how does this theology resonate with the postwar climate of terror diagnosed in *L'Homme révolté?* Clamence's doctrine of universal culpability is derived from interconnected personal, historical, and religious sources. In recreating a genealogy of Western guilt that indicts Christ himself, he does not merely reiterate a disenchanted theology of the Fall but exploits slippages between personal, spiritual, and historical fallenness that are charged with political significance. The sliding frames of references inscribe his individual reflections within a broader collective trajectory. Clamence's failure to rescue a drowning woman becomes analogous to Christ's culpable survival of the massacre of Judea's children, which itself is implicated in Europe's passive collusion with the atrocities of colonial violence and genocide.[20] Clamence functions simultaneously as a symptom, critic, and apologist for past and current manifestations of terror. His condemnation of himself and of his contemporaries res-

onates with multiple instances of historical culpability, particularly France's re-
fusal to reckon with the ongoing reality of the concentration-camp universe
(or *le fait concentrationnaire*), of torture, terrorism, and state-sponsored terror
in Stalin's Russia and war-torn Algeria.

Clamence has embraced the knowledge that, just as Amsterdam is at once
the center and the extreme point of the continent, similarly, the heart of mod-
ern historical experience, its new ground and norm, hovers at the extreme
limit of the thinkable: "Mais vous comprenez alors que je puis dire que le *cen-
tre* des choses est ici, bien que nous nous trouvions à l'extrémité du continent"
(*T,* 1483). His confession illuminates the proximity of violence in everyday life,
drawing his interlocutor into complicity with what Hannah Arendt called the
"banality of evil."[21] As readers of his monologue, we are solicited to decipher
the historical resonance of his imagery and to fill in the blanks of a confession
that could be our own. When Clamence skips over the description of a con-
centration camp in Tripoli, then, it is only because we, his contemporaries,
share his fallen condition of *spleen:* "Nous autres, enfants du demi-siècle,
n'avons pas besoin de dessin pour s'imaginer ces sortes d'endroits. Il y a cent
cinquante ans, on s'attendrissait sur les lacs et les forêts. Aujourd'hui nous
avons le lyrisme cellulaire" (*T,* 1539).

The novel's oscillating frames of reference (Paris, Amsterdam, Jerusalem,
Auschwitz, Hiroshima, North Africa) underscore the pervasion of this *lyrisme
cellulaire,* or carceral imaginary, to disclose its dormant presence in the every-
day practices of even a liberal democracy. Clamence deploys a thematics and
rhetoric of hygiene to bring home the reality of terror.[22] Just as Camus's essay
on rebellion links seemingly disparate aesthetic and historical contexts through
its metaphorics of closure, similarly, the rhetoric of hygiene in *La Chute* links
bourgeois values to genocide, social grooming to ethnic cleansing, to point out
the violence underlying all social structures built on the premise of a unified
totality:

> N'avez-vous pas remarqué que notre société s'est organisée pour ce genre de
> liquidation ? Vous avez entendu parler, naturellement, de ces minuscules
> poissons des rivières brésiliennes qui s'attaquent par milliers au nageur im-
> prudent, le nettoient, en quelques instants, à petites bouchées rapides, et
> n'en laissent qu'un squelette immaculé ? Eh bien, c'est ça leur organisation.
> « Voulez-vous d'une vie propre ? Comme tout le monde ? » Vous dites oui,
> naturellement. Comment dire non ? « D'accord. On va vous nettoyer. Voilà
> un métier, une famille, des loisirs organisés. » Et les petites dents s'attaquent
> à la chair, jusqu'aux os. Mais je suis injuste. Ce n'est pas leur organisation

qu'il faut dire. Elle est la notre après tout : c'est à qui nettoiera l'autre. (*T,* 1479)

Clamence denounces the repressed savagery of the liberal bourgeois state, its regulation of public and private spheres, its emphasis on organization, homogeneity and the family. The individual's willingness to abdicate agency sustains this standardization ("Vous dites oui, naturellement"), an abdication that for Clamence—as for Baudelaire's poet-narrators—mutates into a murderous conformism that sanctions state terror.[23]

To better probe this modern heart of darkness, Clamence chooses to make his home on the site of one of history's greatest crimes: "Moi, j'habite le quartier juif, ou ce qui s'appelait ainsi jusqu'au moment où nos frères hitlériens y ont fait de la place. Quel lessivage ! Soixante-quinze mille juifs déportés ou assassinés, c'est le nettoyage par le vide. J'admire cette application, cette méthodique patience. Quand on a pas de caractère, il faut bien se donner une méthode" (*T,* 1481). The reference to this cleansing will be echoed later in an elliptical allusion to the Final Solution as a "grande entreprise de blanchissage" (*T,* 1532). Clamence points out the infection of a logic that draws the French, and the European community, into alliance with "nos frères hitlériens," their organization being but a distorted mirror image of our own: "Elle est la notre après tout : c'est à qui nettoiera l'autre."

Baudelaire's meditation on the violence of modernity (explored in the murderous ties of commerce in "La Corde" and the mutation of fraternity into fratricide in "Le Gâteau," as well as in other poems addressing the legacy of revolutionary terror) is echoed in Camus's postwar vision of Europe's ongoing complicity with the logic of extermination. By charting the continuities between the hygienic social rites of a bourgeois liberal society, the terror of the police state, and the eliminationism of the concentration camp, Clamence turns his interlocutor, the reader, the bourgeois, and all of modern Europe into accomplices. The narrative thus refuses to polarize "us" against "them," "victims" against "executioners," thereby also undoing the opposition between center and extreme. Europe has fallen into the violence of modernity, and its inhabitants are bound together by *la conscience dans le mal.*

One of the interpretive difficulties posed by *La Chute* is the irony of its narrative mode. Clamence is a demystifier whose insights ring true and false at once. He offers a damning critique of terror, illuminating its presence in all areas of thought and life, and yet his own confession exemplifies its logic. He illustrates the oscillation between victim, executioner, and witness characteristic of Baudelairean irony. This oscillation, however confusing, is essential to the novel's critical power. As we have seen in our discussion of other authors, irony retains its critical edge by performing the very state it condemns and opening a range of positions for the reader as victim, executioner, and accomplice of the violence that is represented. The displacement of referential frames and of subject positions in Clamence's confession performs this collapse into general culpability in a manner reminiscent of Baudelaire's address to his reader as a complicitous "hypocrite lecteur." Yet this performance of complicity, while central to the political (self-)interrogation in Camus's novel, is *itself* ironized and shown to be complicit with terror.

Clamence's theology of guilt has concrete historical precedents in the totalitarian police state. His rhetoric of culpability replicates what Camus understood to be one of the most terrifying features of modern terror. The obliteration of innocence both lamented by Clamence and yet reinstated in his theory of absolute culpability was, according to Camus, a central aim of Nazi Germany, and more generally, of totalitarian ideology:

> La propagande, la torture, sont des moyens directs de désintégration ; plus encore la déchéance systématique, l'amalgame avec le criminel cynique, la complicité forcée. Celui qui tue ou torture ne connaît qu'une ombre à sa victoire : il ne peut pas se sentir innocent. Il faut donc *créer la culpabilité chez la victime* elle-même pour que, dans un monde sans direction, la culpabilité générale ne légitime plus que l'exercice de la force, ne consacre plus que le succés. Quand l'idée de l'innocence disparaît chez l'innocent lui-même, la valeur de puissance règne dans un monde désespéré. C'est pourquoi une ignoble et cruelle pénitence règne sur ce monde où seules les pierres sont innocentes. *Les condamnés sont obligés de se pendre les uns les autres.* (*E*, 589; emphasis added)

The totalitarian state creates its subjects in its own image and legitimates terror through the imposition of universal guilt. This obliteration of innocence collapses all distinction between executioner and victim and creates the seamless fiction of a community of accomplices. Camus cites the example of a Greek mother asked by a sadistic Nazi officer to choose which of her sons will be shot, an anecdote that, significantly enough, is repeated by Clamence in *La Chute* as proof of the methodical inhumanity exercised in recent history and of the impossibility of claiming to be innocent of its atrocities.[24] Yet even as Clamence denounces such forms of torture, his confession rhetorically reproduces their underlying ideology of complicity and subjection. The invocation of collective guilt is the first step in Clamence's discursive replication of a state of terror in which force and manipulation masquerade as logical consistency to create a community of accomplices bound by an identical fallen condition. Clamence participates in the state he denounces, as both symptom and critic, passive collaborator and apologist for the violence of modernity. His peculiar position as at once victim, executioner, *and* witness exemplifies Camus's vision of the intellectual's abdication of lucidity vis-à-vis the faits accomplis of history. The surrender of oppositional thought, considered irrelevant to the course of history, dooms the intellectual to participate in forms of oppression seen as structurally inevitable and to become complicit in the violent workings of power.[25]

"Les yeux du corps": *Embodied Injustice in* La Chute

> *Les vrais artistes. . . . sont les témoins de la chair, non de la loi.*
> Camus, "Le Témoin de la liberté" (1948)

> *Ce n'est pas la logique que je réfute, mais l'idéologie qui substitue à la réalité vivante une succession logique de raisonnements.*
> Camus, "Entretien sur la révolte" (February 15, 1952)

For Camus, the ethical imperative of postwar writing was to commemorate the tangible fact of individual suffering, an irreducible reality threatened, overlooked, or betrayed in an age of murderous abstraction. Camus thus shares with his Baudelairean predecessors a preoccupation with the lived experience of the body, its fragility and excess vis-à-vis the forces of history. Against the murderous ideologies that reify the body for a "higher" purpose, and their aesthetic correlatives, Camus called for the resuscitation of the concept of a human nature that exceeds or resists the claims of history, ideology, and representation. "Nous vivons dans la terreur parce que la persuasion n'est plus possible, parce que l'homme a été livré tout entier à l'histoire et qu'il ne peut plus se tourner vers cette part de lui-même, aussi vraie que la part historique, et qu'il retrouve devant la beauté du monde et des visages ; parce que nous vivons dans le monde de l'abstraction, celui des bureaux et des machines, des idées absolues et du messianisme sans nuances," his 1946 article "Le Siècle de la peur" declares (*E,* 332). From the postwar articles collected under the heading of *La Chair* to the passages in *Le Premier Homme* describing his father's nausea upon witnessing the horror of capital punishment, Camus's thought consistently returns to the materiality of the body, the irreducibility of its contact with others and with nature. The writer was to bear witness to this fragile "nature humaine" that is always in excess of historicity and yet forever threatened by it.

In 1944, prior to his disillusionment with the *épuration*, Camus asserted that the crime for which the collaborator Pierre Pucheu had been executed was his lack of *imagination*, his inability to see beyond the abstraction of his bureaucratic functions and to understand the corporeal reality of the laws passed under the Vichy régime: "Pour ce genre d'hommes, c'est toujours la même abstraction qui continue et je suppose que le plus grand de leurs crimes à nos yeux est de n'avoir jamais approché un corps . . . avec les yeux du corps et la notion que j'appellerai physique de la justice" (*E*, 1469). This embodied understanding of justice, and the almost somatic apprehension of the other it presumes, was all the more urgent in a time when philosophers and politicians collaborated in a historical logic that justified the unjustifiable fact of human suffering.

The previous chapters turned to representations of the body in Baudelaire, Balzac, Mallarmé, Rachilde, and Despentes that probe its vulnerability before aesthetic and historical violence. Baudelaire's poetry illuminates how a body marked by class, economic value, gender, and race functions as a symbolic site upon which a series of violent cultural logics are performed to define the experience of modernity. His mise-en-scène of overlapping forms of allegorical violence offers a genealogy of how bodies come to signify (in terms of meaning and value) in historical modernity and aesthetic modernism. By putting bodies on display, Baudelaire also put poetry on trial, and explored the complicity between aesthetic and real life discourses that "produce" the body as savage nature and as meaningful sign. Rachilde and Despentes's interventions in the Baudelairean legacy continue this demystification of the body's aesthetic and cultural construction. Their scenes of violence rehearse and reverse the gender politics of the decadent imagination and beyond. Not only do they challenge the opposition between the body's materiality and its semiotic inscriptions. Their enactment of matter's revenge on form takes Baudelaire's counterviolence one step further and offers glimpses into a subject's embodied experience of violence. In these Baudelairean approaches, irony recovers the violence of a body's inscription into representation.

Camus's preoccupation with the body's precariousness, its vulnerability before the aesthetic and ideological imagination, is explicitly addressed in *L'Homme révolté*. The suffering of those who are subjected to historical processes—and objectified in literature—is central to the essay's reflection on the violence of representation.[26] Camus believed that the writer's allegiance was to those who endured history, and not to those who made it: "Par défini-tion, il [l'écrivain] ne peut se mettre aujourd'hui au service de ceux qui font l'histoire : Il est au service de ceux qui la subissent" (*E,* 1072). Yet if the author was to bear witness to those silenced and disempowered by history, it would not be by "speaking for" them but rather by rehearsing the very structures of oppression that erase them out of history's frames.[27] We saw how this irony operates at the level of the narrative structure in *La Chute,* where Clamence in-carnates the abstract terror and historicism decried in *L'Homme révolté.* My concluding reflections will suggest that the self-demystifying structure of *La Chute* also performs a revenge of matter on form. The disincarnated force of Clamence's confession breaks down at key points to reveal an embodied expe-rience of violence that challenges the text's representational authority. Despite the narrator's discursive mastery, the text's irony allows the reader to recover an apprehension of the other with the "les yeux du corps, et la notion . . . physique de la justice."

The presence of the other, of the body, and of its pain resurface in uncanny fragments throughout *La Chute.* The weight of human suffering erased by re-cent history, an erasure duplicated by the text's own abstraction, glimmers in allusions to an unrepresented, omnipresent pain. This pain is recorded by Cla-mence's body but disavowed by his confession. The woman whom Clamence failed to rescue, and whose cries mutate into his internalized self-derision, is a central figure for this suffering. The fusion of her cries with his laughter yields a *rire-cri* that repeatedly threatens to collapse the narrative's frame of reference.

Clamence ostentatiously points out that the episode on the Pont des Arts is the heart of his confession, a shameful truth that stands naked amidst all the artificial devices of his self-narration. It is "cette aventure que j'ai trouvé au centre de ma mémoire et dont je ne puis différer plus longtemps le récit, mal-gré mes digressions et les efforts d'une invention à laquelle, j'espère, vous ren-dez justice" (*T,* 1510). After an evening of lovemaking, Clamence's body is in perfect concord with his surroundings, as it has always been prior to this inci-dent. He passes by the dark silhouette of a woman who blends in with the night as she stands on a bridge. Yet a startling detail is recalled by Clamence's sensual eye: "Entre les cheveux sombres et le col du manteau, on voyait seule-ment une nuque, fraîche et mouillée, à laquelle je fus sensible" (*T,* 1511).

The crash of the body as it presumably hits the water vertiginously pos-sesses Clamence: "Je tremblais, je crois, de froid et de saisissement" (*T,* 1511). His helpless trembling—"je sentais une faiblesse irrésistible envahir mon corps"—translates into a discursive faltering, which interrupts the course of his narrative at several points. The cries of the woman as she is evidently carried away by the river will continue to ring in his ears, mutating into an internalized laughter that marks the belated recognition of his connection to a stranger's unknown fate. Indeed, years later, when Clamence once again finds himself poised over a body of water, celebrating his regained mental and physical integrity, he sees a black piece of flotsam, a *point noir* that instantly resurrects the scene of the drowning. The piece of debris left behind by a ship resuscitates the memory of a wet nape and the body Clamence has attempted to leave behind. This corporeal shard and its reminder of another's suffering becomes an embodied point of resistance to Clamence's self-referential discourse. The convergence of these separate moments (of trembling or passivity and recovery) also signals the convergence of Clamence's self-ironic laughter and the cry of the victim. The suffering body that cries out for a response emerges as a rupture or *rire-cri* escaping the narrative economy of the confession while functioning as its repressed structural principle.

Yet despite the central place accorded to the scene of the drowning, Camus's text refuses to deliver one foundational "trauma" around which the confession is symptomatically organized. Instead, the "fall" is decentered and lends itself to multiple allegorical readings. In a similar passage at the close of the text, as he lies bedridden and feverish, Clamence once again evokes the residual effects of a moral fall that his body has recorded: "Ce n'est rien, un peu de fièvre que je soigne au genièvre. J'ai l'habitude de ces accès. Du paludisme, je crois, que j'ai contracté du temps que j'étais pape" (*T,* 1537). He later discloses that his crime as "pope" in a North African concentration camp was to drink the water of a dying comrade.[28]

In Camus's fiction, as for the other authors examined thus far, consciousness often discloses its secrets through the body's somatic expressions.[29] In Rachilde's *Monsieur Vénus,* Jacques's blushes of shame express his intuitive sense of physical expropriation vis-à-vis Raoule's economic and sexual mastery. *Baise-moi* describes its protagonists' murders as corporeal automatisms that replicate the structural violence of their environment. In Camus's novel, Clamence's body also records events that are repressed in his narration. When he refuses to cross a bridge at the close of the first chapter, foreshadowing the disclosure of the drowning, he refers to the residual aches symptomatic of his past inability to dive into the Seine: "Supposez, après tout, que quelqu'un se jette à l'eau ? De deux choses l'une, ou vous l'y suivez pour le repêcher et, dans la saison froide, vous risquez le pire ! Ou vous l'y abandonnez et *les plongeons rentrés laissent parfois d'étranges courbatures*" (*T,* 1483; emphasis added).

Clamence's encounter with and subsequent internalization of another's suffering manifests itself physically as residual fevers or aches, which partially record the full violence of the event. His body becomes the repository for a remembrance that his consciousness seeks to discard through his rationalization of collective guilt. The unassimilated experience that the mind seeks to obliterate, but that the body stubbornly resuscitates, inscribes a point of resistance to the narrative's totalizing abstraction. Clamence's shame at his inaction is reminiscent of Jacques Silvert's shame at his passivity in Rachilde's *Monsieur Vénus*. In both cases, the body registers an awareness of vulnerability to the violence of the world, only for Clamence, it is the vulnerability of another that causes him shame. His confession is an attempt to exorcise this shame by turning it into a collective ethos of culpability, and yet is exposed by the narrative as an untenable form of bad faith.

As we see in the permutation of both an "original event" (the woman's fall from the bridge, the dying comrade whose water is drunk) and its symptomatic return (the laughter and cries), the specificity of the event is never confirmed. Indeed, the anonymous woman's cries rising from the Seine find their echo in Rachel's inconsolable wails, Christ's seditious outcry (censored by Luke) over the massacre of the innocents, and the protestation of the little Frenchman at Buchenwald, whose claim to innocence is met with the derisive laughter of his fellow inmates.[30] The fall unfolds over a series of contextual displacements that implicate a private scene of suffering (Clamence's somatic remembrance of the drowned woman's cries) within a broad frame of reference that is haunted by terror.

Clamence's allusions to the various forms of harm inflicted upon the body throughout history obsessively return to the human body's plasticity before another's violence. The medieval *cellule du malconfort*, a cell whose dimensions were just small enough to impede either sitting or standing, which, like Kafka's harrow, forced prisoners into a corporeal apprehension of guilt, finds its recent incarnations in identical cells in Nazi death camps, but also conjures up Stalin's Gulag archipelago *and* French torture in Algeria.[31] As Clamence points out, inmates of the medieval cells were forgotten for life, a fate that resonates not only with his own belated encounters with past forgettings but also with postwar France's multiple forms of amnesia, bad faith, and silence. As a *bourreau-philosophe* of sorts, Clamence's specious reasoning is a form of "historicism" that condones a state of affairs simply because it exists. If a human being is tortured and confined, then surely that person is guilty: "Quoi ? On pouvait vivre dans ces cellules et être innocent ? Improbable, hautement improbable ! Ou sinon, mon raisonnement se casserait le nez" (*T,* 1531). Clamence collaborates with historical terror in rationalizing injustice through "mon raisonnement" and refusing the call of imagination or "les yeux du corps."

Clamence colludes with history's erasure of the body and yet is compelled to resuscitate its suffering through temporal slides and intertwined metaphors. *La Chute*'s metaphor of hygiene resonates with a number of historical contexts, invoking the *épuration* and its sacrificial cleansing of France's body politic, but also the Nazi genocide, Stalin's labor camps, civilian France's attempts to turn away from or wash its hands of its governments' repressive measures in Algeria, and also, for Camus, the dissenting intellectuals' sacrifice of French Algerians in expiation of the "sins" of colonialism.[32] The *rire-cri* is a figure for the real cost in human suffering exacted by these political measures. The horror of collective, state-sanctioned violence, as well as insurgent terror, and the intellectual's complicity in their legitimation, finds a paradoxical testimony in Clamence, whose confession is haunted by the practices of terror even as he replicates their eliminationist logic.

The kaleidoscopic treatment of the body in *La Chute* embeds points of resistance into the self-reflexive terrorism of Clamence's confession. These narrative blind spots disclose a corporeal condition of suffering irreducible to narrative and ideological appropriation. Clamence's faltering allusions to the body's untheorizable suffering illuminate his contradictory position as simultaneously critic, apologist, and symptom of history's ongoing violence. His confession is thus also burdened with a troubling affective charge that lingers within the reader as it foils the narrative's closure. As Camus put it in his enigmatic preface to the novel, "Une seule vérité en tout cas, dans ce jeu de glaces étudié : la douleur, et ce qu'elle promet" (*T,* 2015). The promise of pain is intimately tied to imagination's capacity to "see" history through the eyes of the body. Yet it also emerges out of the hall of mirrors that constitutes a genuinely self-reflexive project of critique.

Camus's attempt to yoke a self-reflexive analysis of violence to an affective and even somatic apprehension of pain mediates between the interventionist claims of *engagement* and the testimonial force of literature. Our historical experience continues to lend credence to Clamence's pessimistic pronouncement, "Chère planète ! Tout y est clair maintenant. Nous nous connaissons, nous savons ce dont nous sommes capables" (*T,* 1499). The concept of commitment requires a measure of faith in the political as a field for the exercise of agency, critique, and transformation. At certain historical junctures, we witness an erosion of belief in the individual's capacity to intervene in the course of history or to justly apprehend the suffering of others, as Clamence's feverish confession, made from the ruins of Amsterdam's Jewish ghetto, attests. Yet Clamence's *dolorisme,* his melancholy abdications before the many faces of terror, retain their relevance as a cautionary parable about the fate of critique. As we face emergent forms of terror and their visible and invisible costs—in different histories and geopolitical sites—Camus's negotiations between a self-reflexive, ironic inquiry into systemic violence and his passionate commitment to the absolute value of human life help to better define the challenges of theory before the ongoing fact of suffering.

The escalating violence of our century calls for discourses of commitment that forge connections between distinct eruptions of violence and their underlying structural causes, discourses that open up spaces for the recognition of our vulnerability and power in relation to histories and bodies other than our own. The project of critique is inseparable from imagination and the ability to look at history with the "eyes of the body" so that an "embodied notion of justice" can emerge. A self-reflexive inquiry into historical violence, Camus suggests, needs to retain the capacity to imagine another's pain.

Throughout his life, Sartre came to different conclusions about the necessity and legitimacy of violence. Although he believed—with Camus—that the intellectual's responsibility was to denounce all forms of terror, nevertheless, as a "compagnon de route" of communism and a committed supporter of the wars of decolonization, he came to sanction its inevitability, and even to celebrate its emancipatory, purging, or humanizing effects.[33] Sartre saw violence as an inextricable component of political life. In the aftermath of France's liberation, he declared that the writer's responsibility was not to speak from a fictitious vantage point of peace but to provide a theory of violence that would provide the grounds for a praxis of counterviolence: "Il faut savoir au nom de quoi on condamne la violence. Il faut d'abord savoir que nous vivons dans un univers de violence, que la violence n'a pas été inventé par les gens qui s'en servent, que tout est violence. Mais, dans ces conditions, il faut d'abord que l'écrivain essaie de faire, pour lui-même, une théorie de la violence, qu'il comprenne qu'il y a plusieurs espèces de violences, qu'il y a la violence contre la violence."[34]

If "all is violence," for Sartre, one had to choose between just and unjust violence, between passivity and an active compromise with the exigencies of political action, between quietism and "counterviolence." Sartre's notion of "la violence contre la violence" takes "counterviolence" into the realm of political practice, as a recuperable or justifiable violence deployed toward the end of freedom. I should clarify that my use of the term "counterviolence" in this book has been exclusively limited to the sphere of representations. The current global escalation of terror in the name of competing projects of liberation makes it difficult to endorse Sartre's defense of a legitimate counterviolent praxis. Yet his inquiry into the visible *and* invisible structures of domination that give rise to such counterviolence retains its power today.[35]

Camus's wartime experience also led him to realize that, as a historical agent, an individual needed to choose between courses of action with injurious consequences. Yet, as an intellectual, he adamantly refused to offer a theoretical sanction to violence, regardless of the justness of the cause. His fiction returns to the forms and dangers of such legitimations, suggesting that literature's ethical imperative is to create the grounds for refusing our consent to the logic—as well as the fact—of terror.

My reading of Camus's oeuvre has foregrounded the importance of irony for a critique of violence that remains attentive to its own potential violence, and that opens the imagination to human pain and vulnerability in different times and places. As we have seen throughout these readings, irony takes the shape of the enemy; its weapons are fashioned out of the same metal as the edifices it contests. The ironic critique is necessarily an impure path that fully contaminates the position of the ironist. Yet it is this impurity that gives the ironic critique its ongoing relevance and energy. The reenactment of "terror" as a dynamic operation in *La Chute* beckons the reader to wrestle with the multiple positions s/he occupies in the continuing reality of historical violence. For Camus, as for the Baudelairean committed ironists whose legacy this book has traced, it is only when we grapple with the complexity of our historical embedding, as alternately—and even simultaneously—victim, executioner, accomplice, and collaborator in the violence that we witness, that the possibility of a just community can emerge. Irony is the first step toward a more differentiated understanding of our own historical positioning, and toward a community whose members can claim to be "ni victime, ni bourreau."

Afterword

My readings in French modernism through irony and counterviolence have been an effort to understand "modernity" by means of a critique of its violence rather than a testimony to its trauma. The violence harbored in the self-reflexive forms of the modern aesthetic experiment attunes us to the dynamic force of representation, and to the complexity of our historical embedding. The strategies of counterviolence this book has pursued in Baudelaire and some of his unlikely heirs forge important connections between the affective modes of trauma and the political possibilities of rebellion. Such textual interventions continue to invigorate the spirit of contestation before the fact of violence.

Camus's meditation on terror in our age of ideologies, or *les religions horizontales de notre temps* (*E*, 601), returns me to this book's opening concerns. The dominance of trauma and crisis as models for reading experience tends to mute or otherwise diminish the contestatory dynamism of representations, with considerable costs for our readings of the past and the present. The critical fate of *La Chute* has been exemplary in this regard. In the past decade, Camus's novel has been consecrated as an exemplary narrative for modern times, as the traumatized testimony to an ever-present crisis of representation inaugurated by the Holocaust. Shoshana Felman's influential reading, for instance, has argued that Camus's novel attests to a new ethical imperative for all narrative written "after Auschwitz":

> In bearing witness to the witness's inability to witness . . . *The Fall* inscribes the Holocaust as the impossible narrative of an event without a witness, an event eliminating its own witness. Narrative has become the very writing of

> the impossibility of writing history . . . I would suggest, now, that the cryptic forms of modern narrative and modern art always—whether consciously or not—partake of that historical impossibility of writing a historical narration of the Holocaust, by bearing testimony, through their very cryptic form, to the *radical historical crisis in witnessing* the Holocaust has opened up. (Felman and Laub, *Testimony,* 201)

Felman contributes to a broader meditation on the Holocaust as modernity's limit-event and defining crisis of representation. In this view, the Holocaust forces us to rearticulate the relationship between language, narrative, and history and to attend to what Cathy Caruth has called "unclaimed experience," experience that remains unrecorded by the dominant narratives of modernity. Felman's reading of *La Chute* suggests that Jean-Baptiste Clamence's failure to save the drowning woman figures the historical betrayal of such "unclaimed experience." Clamence's missed encounter with the drowned is an allegory of the Allies' blindness to the Nazi concentration camps, as well as to Sartre's blindness to Stalin's Gulag. Yet in this account, the historical specificity of Clamence's "betrayal" evaporates into a universal ontological condition of trauma: since the Holocaust collapses the very possibility of witnessing, any attempt to understand and transmit the event will fall short of—and betray—the experience. "Betrayal" thus functions as a historical fact (the failure to "see" the camps), an epistemological proposition (the impossibility of "seeing" or understanding the camps even for those who experienced them), *and* an ethical imperative to bear witness to the impossibility of bearing witness to the camps. Adorno's pronouncement on the impossibility of poetry after Auschwitz now encompasses narrative, which, in the aftermath of the Shoah, "has thus become the very writing of the impossibility of writing history."

Our current emphasis on historical experience as crisis of representation, however, runs the risk of treating history itself as a "contentless form." Indeed, the discursive construction of the Holocaust as modernity's exemplary trauma positions it as both a catastrophic, singular event *and* a recurrent condition that continues to unfold and to uniformly affect the generations that emerge in its wake. This erases the historical specificity of the Holocaust by conflating the event and its aftermath, survival and spectatorship, while also blurring distinct experiences of the event itself by victims, perpetrators, accomplices, witnesses, survivors, writers, and readers.[1] In the name of its irreducible singularity, the Holocaust is transformed into a transhistorical symbol for the violence of history *and* the trauma of modernity.

As I argued in the introductory chapters of this book, the hermeneutic of trauma can be deployed uniformly in an analysis of the shocks of the nineteenth-century metropolis, the Holocaust, or our contemporary climate of terror. The dislocation of a traumatic event's particularity and of a subject's distinct position in relation to it fosters a catastrophic vision of history that may become a cultural master narrative in its own right. As an interpretive paradigm, trauma tends to conflate different sites of symbolic, historical, and geopolitical violence, contributing to a melancholy, disempowered and ultimately aesthetic view of history *as* terror.

Authors such as Baudelaire and Camus have been central to formulations of modernity as an epochal crisis that banishes "history" to the limits of representation. Yet, as I have argued, an exclusive focus on trauma in readings of cultural production yields a symptomatic view of the subject and the text as passive sites on which the violences of history are enacted. This short-circuits the contestatory powers of representation before historical violence. I hope to have shown what is missed in reading modern literature exclusively as testimony to unspeakable trauma. In the case of *La Chute*, it is the novel's own reflection on the ideology of its narrative mode, its critique of the conditions that make certain forms of speech heard and others not, certain bodies worthy of testimony and others not. I have proposed more generally that Camus's ironic performance of terror belongs to a model for *engagement* that performs the ideological valences of its representation. By exploiting literature's collaboration with other régimes of power, Baudelaire and Camus open up a dynamic and differentiated approach to history that speaks back to their belated canonization as traumatized witness. Camus's ironic portrayal of traumatic complicity as a melancholy abdication before historical violence illuminates the costs of a critical methodology that places such a high price on victimization. A figure such as Clamence, with his haunting but suspect mixture of *douleur, terreur,* and *mauvaise foi,* points to the violence inherent in the notion that we are all victims of a traumatic history.

My critique of our current propensity for "trauma" as a framework for investigating cultural representations in no way questions the reality of traumatic experience itself, of the terrible pain it inflicts on the body and the psyche. Pain is, in some fundamental sense, language-defying, and trauma may strain, and even shatter, the boundaries of representation.[2] Yet it is also our obligation to understand the interlocking systems of representation that make certain forms of pain visible and others not. Instead of an unwavering paradigm of victimization, we need nuanced and dynamic paths of inquiry into the distinct lived realities of trauma endured under different historical times and in particular geopolitical sites. As historical agents rather than mere witnesses, we also need different languages that clarify our own knowing or unknowing participation in the unequal, often unseen, distribution of vulnerability within the violence of history.

The literary experience opens a space for the critique of historical violence through dynamic relations of complicity and resistance. I have attempted to map such a critique through a strand of modern literature that explores the links between violence, representation, and human vulnerability. The authors I have considered teach us how to read violence at multiple levels: symbolic, material, structural, and corporeal. They remind us that violence is not an abstract or monolithic force, but an operation that implicates us in different ways. Their representations connect historical eruptions of violence to systemic forms of terror in art, politics, and everyday life. Such interventions constitute a critical, and even ethical, engagement with violence that acknowledges how we can alternately, and even simultaneously (or as Baudelaire puts it, "alternativement et réciproquement" [*OC*, 1: 275]) take the position of victim, executioner, witness, bystander, accomplice, and rebel in a given historical moment.

The committed ironists examined in this study show an attunement to the performative operations of representation in the private and public arenas. They open up a tropological analysis of power that speaks to us with renewed relevance today. As we saw in Chapters 2 and 3, Baudelaire's writings identified new networks of power and representation that enable the seizure, legitimation, and expansion of the logic of empire. His indictment of Napoléon III—*le premier venu*—whose market-oriented authoritarian regime retained the fiction of legitimacy through media such as the telegraph and the national printing house, resonates with our own era of embedded journalism and manufactured consent.[3] The disruption of established systems of representation in his poetry (through irony, citationality, and intertextuality) attempts to reinvigorate discursive forms of opposition to collectively sanctioned despotism.

Baudelaire's manipulations of the nineteenth century's rhetorical legacy might inspire us to reclaim a language for critique from within our existing vocabulary. As we witness the muting of dissent in the American public arena, the increased pressure to align our language and politics along manichean axes of good and evil, civilized and barbarian, freedom and terror, it is all the more necessary to pry open these binaries, to resituate them within their distinct contexts, and to point out the gaps between their theoretical deployments and strategic uses. An ironic, situated, and differential understanding of the politics and poetics of language—as performative, mediated by competing ideological investments, susceptible to the challenge of multiple resignifications—opens up the possibility of an energized critique that does not immediately fall into ready-made ideological scripts.

As Walter Benjamin famously observed, Baudelaire is the poet of high capitalism. The self-conscious production of violence in his poetry invites an ever-actual inquiry into the hidden structures of sacrifice in capitalist, imperial modernity. In a prescient diagnosis of commerce as an order of terror, maintained by methods that would make humanity shudder ("par des moyens qui feraient frissonner notre humanité actuelle"), Baudelaire attests to nascent structures of domination in a life-world governed by commercial investments and the quest for new markets. His poems offer a fractured but legible genealogy of reification. They perform the logic of commodification in shifting arenas, moving from the private spaces of the bourgeois interior into the urban and even global display of commodities.

Baudelaire's preoccupation with the tangible fact of violence—occluded by structural dispositions of power, and by the derealization of allegorical processes—glimmers throughout his scenes of modern life. His spectacle of bodies that are mutilated, reified, circulated, and consumed captures the dehumanizing impact of commerce on human relations at home and abroad. Even his most cool, ironic portrayals of reification afford glimpses into the cost of real suffering exacted by such symbolic mediations. They afford a recognition of what is damaged or extinguished in the name of revolution, progress, and conquest. Throughout his poetry, we are reminded of the *violence* of such teleologies, their sacrifice of a vital, differentiated, and vulnerable human reality to an ideal aesthetic and political end. Baudelaire's appraisal of modern historical experience finds an amplified echo a century later in Camus's indictment of ideological systems that sacrifice human lives on the altar of history. The "horizontal religions of our times" continue to reap their cost in human life and dignity. I have ended this book with a discussion of the affinities between Baudelaire and Camus in the hopes of bringing their insights on terror to bear on our own historical horizon. The escalating conflicts we currently witness between irreconcilable visions of progress, freedom, and civilization require a self-reflexive genealogy of terror that remains attuned to its distinct eruptions, its systemic operations, *and* to its visible and invisible costs in human suffering.

When represented in literature and theorized in scholarly discourse, the tangible costs of violence itself risk evaporating into abstraction. Discussions of structural or systemic force, or of the derealizing violence of allegory, perform their own species of *terreur.*[4] It becomes easy to forget that, in a fundamental sense, violence is about a dangerous touch that exposes the vulnerability of bodily life itself.[5] It designates an encounter with the other that, despite multiple mediations, yields an uncontrolled relationality that confronts us with our power *and* our fragility before proximate and distant others. We are never beyond or outside violence, but are historically situated in volatile, contradictory relations to its causes, deployments, and effects. We are therefore always connected to the power and vulnerability of others in history, by virtue of "being there," but also by our resistance, complicity, blindness, insight, denunciation, surrender, or engagement.

The embodied experience of violence as a touch that dispossesses, expropriates, and extinguishes human beings, our universal and unforeseen vulnerability to this violence, our participation in it, and, most important, the relationality of violence itself, bind us to proximate and distant others through actions and effects that ideology, aesthetics, and institutional structures can render invisible. This book has been an effort to pursue one aspect of such a meditation on violence and its vexed relations to representation. The self-reflexive legacy of counterviolence conveys the ways in which representation engenders and perpetuates injury to bodies and to selves. The ironic interventions of Baudelaire, Rachilde, Camus, and Despentes make legible occulted, naturalized, and structural dispositions of power that turn the human body into a site of inscription—or extinction—in the name of "modernity," "culture," and "progress." Their works offer no utopian moment of resolution, no thematic reconciliation of injury with reparation, no imagined "elsewhere" in which bodies and subjects are released from their bondage to another's immediate or mediated violence. Yet, to rephrase Adorno, even their most stark depictions of violence harbor a hidden "it should be otherwise" that "points to a practice from which they abstain: the creation of a just life."[6] Theirs is a labor of reflexive critique that disrupts established systems of representation and gives rise to a sense of the human body's fragility to another's touch when that touch is dangerously mediated by institutions, currencies, and symbolic systems.

▌ Notes

Introduction

1. See Seltzer, *Serial Killers,* for an analysis of the emergence of a traumatized, "pathological public sphere" in the United States, as well as Geoffrey Hartman's discussion of the desensitizing effects of the media, leading to attempts at self-definition *through* injury: "It is in pursuit of such defining memories that we abandon the issue of representational limits and seek to 'cut' ourselves, like psychotics who ascertain in this way that they exist. As if only a personal or historical trauma (I bleed therefore I am) would bond us to life" (Hartman, *Longest Shadow,* 152). For important work in this vein, also see Wendy Brown, *States of Injury.* Fredric Jameson's essay on 9/11, "Dialectics of Disaster," examines how the trauma of the event has led to the emergence of a homogeneous national affect operating according to the principle of a "lost innocence" that America should mourn. See also Judith Butler's essays on the links between mourning and violence in the aftermath of 9/11 in *Precarious Life,* as well as Jacques Rancière's analysis of the American war on terror in *Malaise dans l'esthétique.* From different vantage points, these thinkers investigate the ideological ramifications of our contemporary turn to the therapeutic registers of mourning and melancholy. Their voices are part of a broader critical scrutiny of the United States as a "trauma culture."

2. This formulation is borrowed from Raymond Williams, *Marxism and Literature.*

3. This point was brought home to me in an exchange with an undergraduate student who, when given the choice between discussing Flaubert and going to a teach-in and rally, chose literature over politics because her reading of Foucault led to the belief that personal resistance to political injustice was futile.

4. After an initial period of skepticism about the value of his oeuvre (rehearsed in the 1857 prosecution of *Les Fleurs du mal*), Baudelaire then became France's representative poet. Nowhere is this official redemption more obvious than in his prominent place in the prestigious *Anthologie de la poésie française* (Paris: Hachette, 1961, 1974, 2000) edited by Georges Pompidou. See Elisabeth Ladenson's forthcoming book on obscenity and censorship for a trenchant reading of the cultural significance of Baudelaire's consecration as France's national poet.

5. "J'ai essayé plus d'une fois, comme tous mes amis, de m'enfermer dans un système pour y prêcher à mon aise. Mais un système est une sorte de damnation

qui nous pousse à une abjuration perpétuelle ; il en faut toujours inventer un autre, et cette fatigue est un cruel châtiment." Baudelaire, *Oeuvres complètes*, ed. Pichois, 2: 577. Claude Pichois's edition of Baudelaire's *Oeuvres complètes* is hereafter cited in the text and notes as *OC*.

6. There is an enormous body of critical literature around the terms "modernity" and "modernism." As Fredric Jameson recently argued, the concept of modernity is itself a trope: " '[M]odernity' is then to be considered a unique kind of rhetorical effect, or, if you prefer, a trope, but one utterly different in structure from traditional figures as those have been catalogued since antiquity. Indeed, the trope of modernity may in that sense be considered as self-referential, if not performative, since its appearance signals the emergence of a new kind of figure, a decisive break with previous forms of figurality, and is to that extent a sign of its own existence, a signifier that indicates itself, and whose form is its very content. 'Modernity' then, as a trope, is itself a sign of modernity as such . . . the theory of modernity is little more than a projection of the trope itself" (Jameson, *Singular Modernity*, 34). Bearing these caveats in mind, my operative definition of modernity in this book is the nexus of historical conditions characterizing post-1848 industrial capitalist France and modernism as the aesthetic movement responding to these upheavals by withdrawing into formal preoccupations. This latter view (of literature's retreat into form) is interrogated throughout my analyses. For more extensive discussions of the concept of modernity, see Chapter 1. For an overview of dominant accounts of modernism that see Baudelaire as an inaugural figure, see the introduction to Chapter 2.

7. Reading Baudelaire as the poet of an ongoing traumatic modernity has unprecedented appeal in a contemporary urban culture haunted by the specter of terror. In "Les Sept Vieillards," for instance, the poet-flâneur wanders through a squalid metropolis, his consciousness braced to parry the intrusions of a hostile world. He comes upon a decrepit old man whose gaze seems to distill the malevolence of the world. The old man replicates himself seven times before the poet's transfixed eyes, like so many identical, menacing images serially unfolding on a television screen. The poet's vulnerability to the forces of a hostile, incomprehensible world manifests itself as an epistemological crisis that leaves him in a state of boundless trauma, his soul dancing on a monstrous and shoreless ocean. This immobility before the old man's replicated image finds an echo in our own sense of immobility before the monotonous unfolding of images of global violence. It may even resonate with our lived experience as we walk through cities with a heightened sense of the violence behind benign façades, of the fragility of our most solid monuments and landmarks. However, Baudelaire's own reversals of power both in this poem and in others examined in this book challenge such a positioning of the subject as a passive victim, focusing instead on the ethical and political agency made possible by this experience of generalized vulnerability.

8. For an overview of "trauma" as a category that operates as a way of reading

history and literature, see LaCapra, *Writing History, Writing Trauma*. There are a number of scholars (especially feminists) currently deploying "trauma" as a political category that bridges the personal experience of psychic pain and the public realm of representation and praxis. See, e.g., Cvetkovitch, *Archive of Feeling*, who recognizes the risks of "taking on a discourse that has been dominated by medical and pathologizing approaches" but seeks to deploy trauma because "it opens up a space for accounts of pain as psychic, not just physical. As a name for experiences of socially-situated political violence, trauma forges overt connections between politics and emotion" (3).

9. Rancière, *Malaise*, supports the parallel I suggest throughout this book between the construction of modernism as a self-reflexive aesthetic of autonomy and the theorization of modernity as a crisis of representation to which literature bears a testimonial relation. Indeed, Rancière proposes that the "ethical turn" recently characterizing art as testimony to unrepresentable catastrophe is, paradoxically, an even more depoliticized version of modernism's aesthetic autonomy. Art for art's sake and its aesthetic promise of future emancipation has been displaced with a conception of art as testimony to an unrepresentable and ongoing catastrophe: "le tournant éthique n'est pas une nécessité historique. Pour la simple raison qu'il n'y a pas de nécessité historique du tout. Mais ce mouvement tient sa force de sa capacité à recoder et à inverser les formes de pensée et les attitudes qui visaient hier à un changement artistique ou politique radical. Le tournant éthique n'est pas le simple apaisement des dissensus de la politique et de l'art dans l'ordre consensuel. Il apparaît bien plutôt comme la forme ultime prise par la volonté d'absolutiser ce dissensus. La rigueur moderniste adornienne qui voulait purifier l'élément émancipateur de l'art de toute compromission avec le commerce culturel et la vie esthétisée devient la réduction de l'art au témoignage éthique sur la catastrophe irreprésentable" (172).

10. Chapter 1 traces the ongoing influence of de Manian reading strategies in current models that invest textual undecidability with historical weight and ethical value. This nexus of assumptions needs to be interrogated for a more nuanced view of how undecidability functions as a mode of critique and commitment.

11. This project is informed by and indebted to a generation of scholars who have worked between textual analysis and historical contextualization in powerful yet nuanced discussions of Baudelaire, modernism, and oppositionality. My readings of Baudelaire are implicitly (as well as explicitly) in dialogue with critical terms and reading procedures developed by critics such as Ross Chambers, Barbara Johnson, Marie MacLean, Suzanne Nash, and Richard Terdiman.

12. Sartre's psychobiography of Baudelaire rehearses this split between poetry and prose. In Sartre's view, Baudelaire abdicated his lucidity before the contingency of existence and values, choosing to retreat into the compensatory fictions of poetic form. Baudelaire thus stands in not only for the nineteenth century's failure to meet the historical demands of its readership but for modernism's retreat from the claims of historicity and praxis, a judgment that includes Camus.

13. This has become a standard account of Sartre's distinction between poetry and prose and, by extension, between aesthetic experience and political commitment. For an important reevaluation of the relations between aesthetic form and engagement, see Guerlac, *Literary Polemics*, who reconfigures the twentieth-century French critical landscape and dismantles the traditional opposition between poetry and action, under which a number of other oppositions stereotypically adhere. In a close reading of Sartre that uncovers proximities with the thought of Bergson, Valéry, and Bataille, Guerlac identifies at the heart of Sartre's theory of engagement a formulation of freedom that is grounded specifically in aesthetic experience: "Engagement is not opposed to belief in an absolute value of art. On the contrary, an equation of literature and the absolute is itself the very mechanism of engagement, and not just of literary commitment" (94).

14. The question of poetry's relationship to ethico-political claims remains a vexed issue in criticism. Since Bakhtin's theorization of dialogism and the novel, narrative tends to be privileged over poetry as a form suitable for an ethical relation and political commitment. See, e.g., Newton, *Narrative Ethics*, which posits the relation between narrative and ethics as a defining feature of prose fiction: "The fact that narrative ethics can be construed in two directions at once—on the one hand, as attributing to narrative discourse some kind of ethical status, and on the other, as referring to the way ethical discourse often depends on narrative structures—makes this reciprocity between narrative and ethics more binding, more grammatical, so to speak, and less the accident of coinage" (8). Newton provides an admirable account of narrative as an intersubjective and ethical armature, but several of his claims could be extended to lyric and prose poetry.

15. It should be noted that for Adorno, irony could not provide an adequate oppositional stance in our age of ideology: "Irony's medium, the difference between ideology and reality, has disappeared. . . . There is not a crevice in the cliff of the established order into which the ironist might hook a fingernail" (*Minima Moralia*, 211). See my discussion of irony in Chapter 1 for an overview of irony's vexed relations to critique, from Friedrich Schlegel to Paul de Man.

16. I borrow this distinction from LaCapra, *Writing History, Writing Trauma*.

17. As Thomas Trezise has noted in an important reassessment of Adorno's declaration and its fate in recent theory, the very use of "Auschwitz" in this interdiction of figural representation is self-consciously figural, since "Auschwitz" functions as a synecdoche for the Nazi genocide. See Trezise, "Unspeakable."

18. In his important recent work, Ross Chambers offers an account of testimony that—in its focus on the contestatory power of figuration and on testimony's performative transmission of a knowledge repressed—resonates with Adorno's view. *Untimely Interventions* suggests that testimonial texts bear a residual, inaudible message often banished to the margins of a culture (the ob-scene) in a disavowal or repression of these testimonies' constitutive belonging to the scene

they haunt. In a series of readings of texts attesting to distinct historical traumas (AIDS, World War I, the Holocaust), Chambers identifies common features of testimonials' power to haunt a dominant culture, such as the infractions of figural language and the disruption of temporality (the slippage, for example, between event and aftermath). The referential lack that testimonials represent through various forms of catachresis induces an interpretive excess, activating the "phantom pain" of a knowledge (of survival and aftermath) that is simultaneously feared and grasped by the reader. For Chambers, then, testimony rewrites "insignificant residuality" (that which culture wants to forget) into a "hypersignificant liminality" (xxiv), thereby agencing an ethical project: "Such an ethics is grounded in acknowledgment of culture's constitutive difference from itself, and consequently, in an understanding of phantom pain as a manifestation of the mutual *relevance,* the pertinence one to the other of culture and the cultural obscene, civilization and disaster. Figuration actualizes that relevance in the form of rhetorical manifestations that, as interventions of the im-pertinent and the untimely (the untimely and the un-timely), function as reminders of such pertinence. And conversely, the untimely and im-pertinent now turn out to be describable as names for the existential manner of being, within an aftermath culture, of the communitarian ethos, its haunting parasocial presence" (320).

19. The exclusive focus on the category of "victimization" in discussions of historical violence masks the ways in which a subject or state harbors complex links to the violence at stake. Such a view forecloses more complex inquiries into the underlying conditions that precipitate violence. As Judith Butler pointed out in the aftermath of the September 11 attacks, the recent deployment of terms such as "terror," "terrorism," and "terrorist" has posited America as an injured victim whose retaliation is not addressed as violence but as legitimate retribution and self-protection: "The United States, by using the term [terrorist], positions itself exclusively as the sudden and indisputable victim of violence, even though there is no doubt that it did suffer violence. But it is one matter to suffer violence, and quite another to use that fact to ground a framework in which one's injury authorizes limitless aggression against targets that may or may not be related to the sources of one's own suffering" (Butler, *Precarious Life,* 4). The following discussions of literary violence also attempt to point out the ethical and political limitations of such frameworks of injury and victimization in an effort to open up a more nuanced inquiry into the causes, effects, and representational logics of historical violences.

20. The opposition between Sartre and Adorno has been interrogated and rethought in a different direction by Susan Blood, who uncovers in Sartre's notion of "bad faith" a point of slippage between ethical and rhetorical questions that reopens an inquiry into the formation of the modernist canon: "bad faith must be understood in terms of the tension between engagement and aestheticism that Adorno regretted losing" (*Baudelaire and the Aesthetics of Bad Faith,* 4).

Chapter 1: Baudelaire's Victims and Executioners

Epigraphs: Baudelaire, "Le Peintre de la vie moderne," in *OC,* 2: 690; Victor Hugo, letter to Baudelaire, October 6, 1859, cited in *OC,* 1: 1011; complete text at www.chronologievictor-hugo.com/pages/corp1859(4,1).htm (accessed July 11, 2005).

1. I shall not rehearse the enormous body of criticism and theory that turns to Baudelaire as a key point of reference for theories of modernity. Some by now classic formulations are Habermas, *Philosophical Discourse of Modernity;* Calinescu, *Five Faces of Modernity;* Compagnon, *Cinq paradoxes de la modernité;* and Berman, *All That Is Solid Melts into Air.* See Jameson, *Singular Modernity,* for a genealogy of the concepts of modernization, modernity, and modernism. Also see de Man, "Literary History and Literary Modernity" and "Lyric and Modernity" for a critique of continuous, developmental models for modernist poetry through readings of Baudelaire.

2. See de Man, "Rhetoric of Temporality," an essay that I discuss at greater length later in the chapter, and Newmark, *Beyond Symbolism.* More recently, Ulrich Baer has argued that Baudelaire and Celan bookend the modern tradition in their testimony to singular experiences of trauma that "seem to exceed all existing frames of reference" (Baer, *Remnants of Song,* 1).

3. Leo Bersani, for instance, rereads Freud's theory of narcissism to argue that Baudelaire's poetry conveys the self-shattering *jouissance* of primary narcissism through which the ego itself is formed. See Bersani, *Baudelaire and Freud* and *Culture of Redemption* (47–102).

4. For the former, historical reading of modernism through the trauma of revolution, see in particular Dolf Oehler, Nathaniel Wing, Ross Chambers, and Richard Terdiman. For some readers, the treatment of 1848–51 as the traumatic crucible for literary modernism raises questions about the historical specificity of such periodizations. As Susan Blood points out, "if literary modernism originates in trauma, the trauma has already begun with Rousseau and its specific connection to the 1848–1851 period therefore needs to be rethought" ("Modernity's Curse," 148).

5. A dichotomy that LaCapra's *Writing History, Writing Trauma* addresses as having traditionally been cast as one between "trauma" and "history." Klein, "On the Emergence of *Memory* in Historical Discourse," 27–150, recasts this polarity as one between "memory" and "history" in what he terms our contemporary "memory industry."

6. Benjamin records early responses to Baudelaire's person in terms of a "physiology" of shock that foreshadowed his status as a modern precursor. "His utterances, Gautier thought, were full of 'capital letters and italics.' He appeared . . . surprised at what he himself had said, as if he heard in his own voice the words of a stranger. . . . I do not even criticize his jerky gait . . . which made people com-

pare him to a spider. It was the beginning of that angular gesticulation which, little by little, would displace the rounded graces of the old world. Here, too, he is a precursor" (Eugène Marsan, *Les Cannes de M. Paul Bourget et le bon choix de Philinte* (1923), quoted in Benjamin, *Arcades Project,* 248).

7. Benjamin, "On Some Motifs in Baudelaire," 194. Fencing provides an image for the parrying of external shock, which is deflected and sterilized for composition into poetry. For Benjamin, to write poetry as a city dweller in the Second Empire is to undergo a traumatic series of encounters that can even unravel subjectivity altogether: "Baudelaire has portrayed this condition in a harsh image. He speaks of a duel in which the artist, just before being beaten, screams in fright. This duel is the creative process itself. Thus Baudelaire places the shock experience at the very center of his artistic work" (ibid., 163).

8. "Consciousness is not the only distinctive character which we ascribe to the process in that system. On the basis of impressions derived from our psychoanalytic experience, we assume that all excitatory processes that occur in the *other* systems leave permanent traces behind in them which form the foundation of memory. Such memory-traces, then, have nothing to do with the fact of becoming conscious; indeed they are often most powerful and most enduring when the process which left them behind was one which never entered consciousness" (Freud, *Beyond the Pleasure Principle,* 27).

9. "That the shock is thus cushioned, parried by consciousness, would lend the incident that occasions it the character of having been lived in the strict sense. If it were incorporated directly in the registry of conscious memory, it would sterilize this incident for poetic experience" (Benjamin, "On Some Motifs in Baudelaire," 162).

10. In a cogent meditation on Flaubert and Baudelaire's treatment of time that is informed by Benjamin's perspective on the shock experience and the decline of aura, Elissa Marder examines how "the trauma of the shock experience can account for important aspects of the structure of memory loss in Baudelaire" (*Dead Time,* 95). Her first chapter attends to representations of women in Baudelaire's poetry and argues that women serve as "shock absorbers," as buffers, defenses, or containers for the alienation and loss of the modern experience of time. My third chapter, "Bodies in Motion, Poetry on Stage," offers a different account of the representation of women in Baudelaire, not as "shock absorbers," but, rather, as sites for a rehearsal of dominant—and often violent—cultural logics that are demystified in his poetry. Marder gives a compelling account of the modalities of anxiety and disavowal (fetishism, addiction, misogyny) through which Baudelaire seeks to contain temporal and sexual difference. While I admire the elegance and reach of her analyses, such an approach sustains the portrait of a melancholy Baudelaire whose poetry reactively, even therapeutically, attests to the shock(s) of modernity, at the risk of overlooking his ironic engagement with the structures of power that create, sustain, and disguise the violence of modern experience. Furthermore,

while Baudelaire and Flaubert may indeed elucidate aspects of the "dead time" that Marder sees as central to the modern and postmodern historical experience, an important aim in my project is to show that the contestatory resonances of Baudelaire's poetry also posed a productive challenge to contemporary views of temporality (as modernity and progress), and that his legacy continues to be "reanimated" by his readers across temporal horizons.

11. See Freud's "The Aetiology of Hysteria" for an account of childhood sexual abuse in women as reactivated in later life and manifested through the symptoms of hysteria. Freud later repudiated this traumatic theory of hysteria and saw the hysteria of patients as signs of fantasy and desires rather than as symptoms of actual abuse. For a discussion of the therapeutic consequences of this repudiation, see Herman, *Trauma and Recovery,* 10–20.

12. Benjamin, "On Some Motifs in Baudelaire," 167. Cohen, *Profane Illumination,* challenges this reading of Baudelairean trauma as symptomatic of a repressed encounter with the crowd that is unrepresented yet constitutive of poetry. She rightly notes that, on the contrary, representations of the crowd abound in Baudelaire, and particularly in the prose texts of *Le Spleen de Paris.* She also observes that Benjamin's discussion of Freud and trauma is more relevant to the modern materialist encounter of Breton's *L'Amour fou* and *Nadja* than to Baudelairean subjectivity. Also see Marder, *Dead Time,* 68–87, for an illuminating discussion of Benjamin's commentary on "À une passante."

13. Benjamin's portrait of the poet as a "traumatophile" acknowledges this dialectical relation between poetry and history and the demystifying force of shock itself. His initial essay on "Paris of the Second Empire" opens with the image of Baudelaire as a kind of conspiratorial putschist, whose rhetorical jolts can be read parrying the unpredictabilities and contradictions of the Second Empire. Indeed, Benjamin points to Blanqui and Louis-Napoléon Bonaparte as political analogies for Baudelaire's poetic practice. Yet it is precisely this type of homology drawn between poetic and social texts that led to Adorno's famous critique of Benjamin's lack of "mediation" in his presentation of the Second Empire.

14. Margaret Cohen's analysis and comparison of the different stages of Benjamin's writings on Baudelaire (including an excellent account of the divergence between Benjamin and Adorno) provide an important corrective to this tendency. Noting the "torsions" to which Benjamin subjects Baudelaire's poetry for it to represent the "shock experience" in the revised and more psychoanalytic version of "On Some Motifs in Baudelaire," she redirects critical attention to "The Paris of the Second Empire in Baudelaire" while underscoring the complexity of Benjamin's treatment of representation (Cohen, *Profane Illumination,* 208–26).

15. Kevin Newmark suggests that, while Baudelaire brings into visibility hitherto undetected violence in figural structures that may be at work in the literary and social realms, the greatest critical violence might be the belief that rhetorical insight may be injected into social constructions in order to discover their hidden

violence. With de Man, he warns against investment in "pseudo-historical terms of resistance and nostalgia" that are "at the farthest remove from the materiality of actual history" (*Beyond Symbolism,* 222). In a more recent essay, however, Newmark is more explicit about the political possibilities opened up by Baudelaire's rehearsal of representational violence. Reading *Le Peintre de la vie moderne* as a critique of the idea of representation as mimesis, Newmark suggests that Baudelaire's portrait of Constantin Guys makes visible the violence of allegorical capture and, in doing so, offers a glimpse into the violence endemic to all systems of representations—since these are founded on operations of memory that inevitably abbreviate, diminish, and even erase, the particularity of the phenomena they represent. Poetry's failure to fully represent itself and its other and its call to the violence of memory, rather than the force of history, interrupt systems of representation and open up unknown contestatory possibilities, or "the incognito of genuine revolt" (84). Yet Newmark cautions against a stable and univocal recuperation of such a tactic: "It is a violence, though, only in the sense that, always as an *image écrite,* it can strike all that it touches with a force of displacement powerful enough, as in the case of Baudelaire and Benjamin, to make other forces legible, and thus to enable anything whatsoever to happen, even nothing at all. It is therefore a real revolt and not a real revolt" (Newmark, "Off the Charts," 84). See also Ellen Burt's subtle deconstructive reading of Baudelaire, which argues that poetry's appeal— and force—lie in its capacity to disintegrate reference, form, memory, and agency, to become—as Burt says of the censored poem "Les Bijoux"—a "self-toppling symbol" (*Poetry's Appeal,* 217). Poetry's power to unleash the disintegrating force of memory, for Burt, opens the possibility of unbinding history and politics from totalizing structures of intention, rhetoric, and ends.

16. Benjamin, "On Some Motifs in Baudelaire," 194. Compared to Wordsworth's treatment of the shock experience, for de Man, Baudelaire's poetry forgoes the continuities and closures of narrative emplotment: "in Baudelaire, such moments appear only by instants as isolated shocks that can never be incorporated into a larger temporal duration" (de Man, "Allegory and Irony in Baudelaire," 118).

17. To do justice to such moments of insightful blindness, Baer suggests, we must avoid the temptation of either violently historicizing the poem by locating "reference" in its blind spots or insisting on the radical indeterminacy of such moments: "In order to prevent the effacement of such moments, it is imperative to stress the variation in moments wherein history's rumble is halted and wherein other voices—in the form of contested readings—can be heard" (Baer, *Remnants of Song,* 152). For Baer, then, "What is defeated and exposed in these poems is the ability to recognize a defeat as defeat (and thus to celebrate, endorse and appropriate it): to experience the failure of attributing meaning without instantly attributing meaning to it" (ibid., 65). This Beckettian Baudelaire is not so far from Sartre's condemnation of the poet's passive bad faith and surrender to the comforts

of a loser-wins strategy, although in Baer's account this irrecoverable "failure" constitutes the ethical triumph of Baudelaire's poetry. For an alternate analysis of Baudelaire's "bad faith" and the value of failure in his poetry, see Susan Blood. In a reconsideration of Sartrean engagement, Blood reads the self-negating, "loser wins" impulse rehearsed in a poem such as "Le Guignon" and its many intertextual borrowings in light of a theory of human agency wherein poetry's self-negation and the failure of instrumental language bear witness to "the self-destructing character of human action on the largest of scales" (Blood, "Modernity's Curse," 155).

18. The paradoxes of modernism's retroactive periodization through the Holocaust are also noted by Jacques Rancière: "[O]n dit que l'événement inouï de l'extermination appelle un art nouveau, un art de l'irreprésentable. On associe alors la tâche de cet art avec l'idée d'une exigence antireprésentative normant l'art moderne comme tel. On établit ainsi une ligne droite depuis le *Carré noir* de Malevitch (1915), signant la mort de la figuration picturale, jusqu'au film *Shoah* de Claude Lanzmann (1985), traitant de l'irreprésentable de l'extermination" (*Malaise,* 164–65). Both Thomas Trezise and Jacques Rancière examine how the rhetoric of unrepresentability surrounding the Holocaust marks the convergence of an epistemological proposition and ethical injunction (see Trezise, "Unspeakable"). Rancière argues further that this fusion of impossibility and interdiction has yielded a totalizing concept of modern art as the testimony to unrepresentable experience: "Cela suppose une construction du concept de la modernité artistique, qui loge l'interdit dans l'impossible en faisant de l'art moderne tout entier un art constitutivement voué au témoignage de l'impensable" (*Malaise,* 167).

19. Giorgio Agamben's *Remnants of Auschwitz* illustrates the paradoxes of rereading the literary canon in light of the Holocaust. Agamben turns to Keatsian negative capability or the shame experienced by Joseph K. at the end of Kafka's trial as offering prophetic insight into the complex affective responses of the inmates of the concentration and extermination camps of Nazi Germany, but also as indications of a transhistorical condition inherent in human subjectivity. Comparing Keats, Kafka, and, elsewhere, Rilke's evocation of shame, to the blush of a young student from Bologna who is selected for arbitrary execution in Auschwitz (reported by Robert Anthelme), Agamben collapses an experience (the imminent execution of a youth) with literary precursors of this experience's purported affect (shame), while also conflating the atrocity of the real event's historical specificity (Nazi brutality toward Jews) with an affect constitutive of subjectivity itself.

20. Hanssen, *Critique of Violence,* 9. For an extensive and illuminating discussion of the distinction between violence, force, and power in Arendt, Foucault and Benjamin, see ibid., chaps. 1–2.

21. In Baudelaire's work, the oscillation between *victime* and *bourreau* does not, however, suggest these to be interchangeable positions that may be collapsed into one another. My reading of Baudelaire's "L'Héautontimorouménos" will clarify the distinction between irony and trauma as models for reading this oscillation.

22. There is an enormous body of work on the notion of "structural" or "institutional" violence, which I shall not rehearse here. Among the central texts informing this particular project are Foucault's *Surveiller et punir*, Camus's *L'Homme révolté*, and Butler's *Bodies That Matter* and *Excitable Speech*.

23. The term "counterviolence" resonates with the work of other Baudelaire critics who have teased out the modulations of oppositionality in nineteenth-century literature, and in particular, with Richard Terdiman's important work on counterdiscourse as "discursive systems by which writers and artists sought to project an alternative, liberating *newness* against the absorptive capacity of those established discourses," which nevertheless "are always interlocked with the domination they contest" (*Discourse/Counter-discourse*, 13, 16). Counterdiscourses such as irony disrupt systems of representation from within. I am particularly interested in pursuing the contestatory dimensions of ironic discourses that deliberately *fail* to offer consolation or critique, that close off the very possibility of distinction or newness, attending instead to the complicity between their expression and other discursive forms of power. My focus is thus on counterviolence as Sartre understood it, that is, as a violence against violence, but that is conducted in the sphere of representations (Sartre, *Responsabilité de l'écrivain*, 54).

24. Judith Butler alerts us to the critical possibilities opened up by the citation and possible resignification of an injurious representation. In a discussion of hate speech, she suggests that "[a]n aesthetic reenactment of an injurious word may both *use* the word and *mention* it, that is, make use of it to produce certain effects but also at the same time make reference to that very use, calling attention to it as a citation, situating that use within a citational legacy, making that use into an explicit discursive item to be reflected on rather than a taken for granted operation of ordinary language. Or it may be that an aesthetic reenactment uses that word, but also *displays* it, points to it, outlines the arbitrary material instance of language that is exploited to produce certain kinds of effects. . . . The possibility of decontextualizing and recontextualizing such terms through radical acts of public misappropriation constitutes the basis for an ironic hopefulness that the conventional relation between word and wound might become tenuous and even broken over time" (Butler, *Excitable Speech*, 99–100).

25. Pierre Pachet's *Le Premier venu* opens an important line of inquiry into Baudelaire's political thought that has stimulated my approach to the poet's scenarios of violence. Pachet attends to the conceptual operations by which the poet's treatment of sacrifice (in the form of capital punishment, suicide, and solitude) unveils "la présence dans le monde contemporain d'une violence qui résulte de la mise en présence brutale de postulations individuelles incompatibles" (203). For Pachet, the resurgence of sacrificial topoi in Baudelaire unveils the arbitrary structures of distinction that characterize postrevolutionary market capitalism. The modulations of this archaic ritual in Baudelaire rehearse the mechanism through which social differences are constituted and legitimated: "On peut trouver ces

principes à l'oeuvre dans la pensée de Baudelaire : unité de la création, échangabilité des individus. Peut-être à cause de son caractère barbare, anachronique et
figé, le sacrifice (guerre, suicide, peine de mort) prend pour lui la valeur d'une mise
en scène révélatrice. Par la publicité du sacrifice, la société se tient plus près du
mystère qui la perpétue, du mécanisme par lequel elle sanctifie les différences entre ses membres" (129). My readings of "Une Mort héroïque" and 'La Corde" in
Chapter 2 pursue this line of inquiry in dialogue with Pachet's work, while drawing out the challenge that Baudelaire's ironic repetition of hidden sacrificial structures poses to postrevolutionary configurations of power.

For a suggestive essay that theorizes the violence of Baudelaire's irony as a reconfiguration of the pain embedded in the discourse of the dominant, see Ramazani, "Writing in Pain." There are a number of resonances between our views
of Baudelaire's irony as an oppositional discourse that meets violence with violence, although Ramazani's focus seems to be on the representation and reception
of pain rather than on the rehearsal of violence. Ramazani speculates that pain and
its fissured transmission from text to reader in Baudelaire might be read as an activation of the social wounds of Haussmann's Paris and as a desublimation of fictions of absolute power. This activation/desublimation opens a reading "that allows us to feel the other's pain, to feel it as our own, and to desire to suspend
it—only insofar as the suspension of pain is not a forgetting of pain's aversiveness,
not a conflation of the relative absence of pain with the presence (the 'presentation') of sheer invulnerability. Oppositionality in *Le Spleen de Paris* consists neither
in textual violence, nor in the reader's interpretation of that violence as pain but in
the resistance of the idea of pain thus constructed to appropriation as an idea of
absolute power" (ibid., 223). Another extensive inquiry into violence and representation in Baudelaire is Thélot, *Baudelaire*, which brings René Girard's work to
bear on select poems and the often-neglected corpus of *Pauvre Belgique !* and argues that Baudelaire's writings rehearse an originary sacrificial violence from which
all language and social forms proceed. Thélot defines poetry as a language that assumes and reflects upon a violence inherent in language: "Appelons *poésie* la
recherche, dans un poème, par laquelle celui-ci accède à la compréhension de lui-
même, découvre son meurtre, et amèrement l'assume. Réalisation mais révélation
du mal, la poésie est ainsi, soucieuse de vérité, un mouvement de compassion pour
la victime du poème" (434). Thélot begins and ends his study with a reflection on
Baudelaire's silence at the end of his life. He considers the poet's aphasia as a
willed, meaningful return to an originary source of meaning, one that opens language up to alternate and nonviolent ends such as love and communication (233).
There are some affinities between our readings of Baudelaire's poetry as a self-
reflexive interrogation of linguistic and social violence (a phenomenon I shall address in terms of allegorical violence). Yet, while Thélot's view of violence as an
originary condition yields insightful readings of the thematics of sacrifice in
Baudelaire, his reading of the poet's aphasia as an invitation to imagine language

as a site of love rather than violence is carried out in a mythic, poetic, and trans-historical register that differs from the historical impetus of this inquiry.

26. For a discussion of the function of metaphor as transportation between lexical codes and the implications of such transfers for the relationship between rhetoric and history, see de Man's reading of "Correspondances" in id., "Anthropomorphism and Trope in Lyric." See also Newmark's illuminating commentary on this essay in *Beyond Symbolism*, 201–30.

27. We could also read "L'Héautontimorouménos" through the lens of sadomasochism. As Gilles Deleuze puts it, "The fact that the sadist has no other ego but that of his victims explains the apparent paradox of sadism, its pseudo-masochism. The libertine enjoys suffering the pain he inflicts on others; when the destructive madness is deflected outwards it is accompanied by an identification with the external victim. The irony of sadism lies in the twofold operation whereby he necessarily projects his dissolved ego outwards and experiences what is outside of him as his only ego" (*Sacher-Masoch*, 107). See also Blin, *Sadisme de Baudelaire*. For a discussion of the uncanny that reads the play of difference in the Baudelairean sadomasochistic scenario through Nietzsche, see Mehlman, "Baudelaire with Freud." For an analysis of sadomasochism as a manifestation of Freudian narcissism, see Bersani, *Baudelaire and Freud*.

28. In that sense, irony, like beauty, has no locus. Both are dislocated processes that act upon other selves and things: "Car j'ai, pour fasciner ces dociles amants, / De purs miroirs qui font toutes choses plus belles" (Baudelaire, "La Beauté").

29. Poe, *Complete Tales*, 270. Poe's text describes a palace that once stood proudly in "the Monarch Thought's dominion," and whose serene and ordered hierarchy made all things move musically "to a lute's well-tuned *law*" (270). The palace is then invaded by a spectral and discordant throng of laughers, a fall that is echoed in Baudelaire's representation of the sovereign subject as a discordant note in the divine symphony, and as one who belongs to the damned who are laughing in exile. For a de Manian reading of the Poe intertext in this poem, see Harter, "Divided Selves, Ironic Counterparts." For a discussion of the paradoxes of Baudelaire's canonization as practitioner of pure art (by Valéry) *through* his encounter with and translation of Poe, see Blood, *Baudelaire and the Aesthetics of Bad Faith*, 42–46. Also see Suzanne Guerlac's analysis of Baudelaire's translation of de Quincy's *Confessions of an Opium Eater* for a reading of translation/rewriting as the performance of an "amalgamation of poet and critic" essential to Baudelaire's reworking of the sublime (Guerlac, *Impersonal Sublime*, 85–93).

30. The image of a throng that laughs but cannot smile is most poignantly illustrated by the figure of Melmoth in the essay "De l'essence du rire": "Et ce rire est l'explosion perpétuelle de sa colère et de sa souffrance. Il est, qu'on me comprenne bien, la résultante nécessaire de sa double nature contradictoire, qui est infiniment grande relativement à l'homme, infiniment vile et basse relativement au Vrai et au Juste absolus. Melmoth est une contradiction vivante. Il est sorti des conditions

fondamentales de la vie ; ses organes ne supportent plus sa pensée" (*OC,* 2: 531). Modernity, as figured by Melmoth, is a living, insoluble paradox. Baudelaire's "double postulation" echoes Pascal's "grandeur et misère de l'homme," a doubleness that, in a fallen world, can only express itself as irony: the lucid appraisal of one's fallenness wedded to the persistent vision of a possible transcendence.

31. For a reading of the ambiguities of Baudelaire's ironic address in "Au Lecteur," see Chambers, "Baudelaire's Dedicatory Practice."

32. For a lucid critique of this slippage between victim and executioner in Cathy Caruth's account of trauma, see Ruth Leys: "But her [Caruth's] discussion of Tasso's epic has even more chilling implications. For if, according to her analysis, the murderer Tancred can become the victim of the trauma and the voice of Clorinda a testimony to his wound, then Caruth's logic would turn other perpetrators into victims too—for example, it would turn the executioners of the Jews into victims and the "cries" of the Jews into testimony to the trauma suffered by the Nazis" (*Trauma,* 297).

33. By "traditional" I refer to definitions of irony faithful to its etymological root. *Eironia* (dissimulation) is exemplified by Socrates, the consummate *eiron,* who, feigning ignorance, demystified his disciples' assumptions and brought out the contradictions in his opponents' arguments. Traditional irony—termed "stable irony" by Wayne C. Booth, "normative irony" by Gary Handwerke, and "specific irony" by D. C. Muecke—designates the creation of incompatible meanings in an utterance with a corrective aim that is both intended by the ironist and intelligible to the reader. For a useful overview of theories of irony in relation to politics and ethics, see Hutcheon, *Irony's Edge.* For a history of the term from Aristotle to the present, see Dane, *Critical Mythology of Irony;* Knox, *The Word Irony and Its Context.* Behler, *Irony and the Discourse of Modernity.* Booth, *Rhetoric of Irony* and Muecke, *Compass of Irony* exhaustively define the structure and significance of irony and offer nuanced taxonomies of the many forms of this trope. For a history of the reception of romantic irony in nineteenth-century French literature, see Bourgeois, *Ironie romantique;* Furst, *Fictions of Romantic Irony;* and Bishop, *Romantic Irony in French Literature.*

34. Literature is conceptualized by Schlegel as producing itself as it produces its own theory, as poetry and the poetry of poetry: "And it [romantic poetry] can also more than any other form hover at the midpoint between portrayer and portrayed, free of all ideal and real interest, on the wings of poetic reflection, and can raise that reflection again and again to a higher power, can multiply it in an endless succession of mirrors. . . . It alone is infinite as it alone is free; and as its first law it recognizes that the arbitrariness of the poet endures no law above him." Schlegel thus places the French Revolution, Fichte, and Goethe on equal footing: "The French Revolution, Fichte's *Theory of Knowledge* and Goethe's *Wilhelm Meister* are the three greatest tendencies of the age. Whoever takes offense at this combination, and whoever does not consider a revolution important unless it is bla-

tant and palpable, has not yet risen to the lofty and broad vantage point of the history of mankind" (Willson, *German Romantic Criticism,* 126).

35. Kierkegaard, *Concept of Irony,* 257, 283. For the French response to Fichtean idealism and romantic irony, see Madame de Staël, "La Philosophie et la Morale," in *De l'Allemagne.*

36. Hegel, *Aesthetics,* 64. Both Hegel and Kierkegaard thus seek to rescue a dialectical, Socratic irony from the nihilism of Schlegel's formulations. For an account of the importance of Hegel and Kierkegaard's reading of Schlegel in the transmission of a "myth" of irony as a manifestation of Fichtean idealism into current theories of this trope, see Dane, *Critical Mythology of Irony,* chap. 4.

37. De Man, *Allegories of Reading,* 301. Gary Handwerke terms de Manian irony "epistemological irony" and gives a critique of its misprision of Schlegel's irony, which in Handwerke's account, inaugurated an intersubjective theory of "irony of consensus" (*Irony and Ethics,* 1–17). The tension between irony and ethics is rehearsed in Rorty, *Contingency, Irony and Solidarity.* Although Rorty celebrates irony's powers of redescription for awakening our imaginative identification with what is foreign to the self (an identification necessary for the avoidance of cruelty), he nevertheless views irony primarily as an aesthetic and nihilistic mode of self-perfection and advocates its "privatization."

38. Terdiman discusses the nineteenth century's turn to irony as a response to the erosion of utopian thought and elucidates the dialogical, contextual, and oppositional features of irony itself: "As deployed in the counter-discourses of the nineteenth century, irony can be understood as a rhetorical figure of the *dialogic.* It materializes the counter-term which any dominant usage seeks to suppress. Its function is to provide an alternative through which any element of the here-and-now may be shown as contingent, and thereby to subject the whole configuration of power within which it took its adversative meaning to the erosive, dialectical power of alterity" (*Discourse/Counter-discourse,* 76).

39. For a different approach to the structure and function of irony in Baudelaire, see Kaplan, *Baudelaire's Prose Poems,* which examines the modalities of "Socratic irony" that inform the esthetic, ethical, and religious dimensions of *Le Spleen de Paris.*

40. Ecclus. 21:23, "vir sapiens vix tacite ridebit," translated by Bossuet as "rit à peine à petit bruit d'une bouche timide." The source in the Vulgate is thus significantly erased by Baudelaire.

41. See Claude Pichois's note and reproduction of the Chennevières passage in question (*OC,* 2: 1344–45).

42. Pagan idols, for instance, remain sacred only because laughter is banished from their midst: "Je crois que l'antiquité était pleine de respect pour les tambours-majors et les faiseurs de tours de force en tous genres, et que tous les fétiches extravagants que je citais ne sont que des signes d'adoration, ou tout au plus de symboles de force, et nullement des émanations de l'esprit intentionellement comiques" (*OC,* 2: 533).

43. The allusions to "horizons" and "thresholds" in the essay are numerous and suggestive: e.g., the "singuliers horizons" that a theological account of laughter would reveal, the "créations fabuleuses, les êtres dont la raison, la légitimation ne peut pas être tirée du code du sens commun" (*OC*, 2: 535). Melmoth's very identity emerges from the tension between two thresholds: "Melmoth, l'être déclassé, l'individu situé entre les dernières limites de la patrie humaine et les frontières de la vie supèrieure" (*OC*, 2: 534). Finally, describing the *comique féroce* of English pantomime, the narrator explains its poor reception by the French public with the assertion that "Le public français n'aime guère être dépaysé . . . les déplacements d'horizons lui troublent la vue" (*OC*, 2: 538). The comic thus transgresses and exceeds conventional conceptual and perceptual borders, opening up a world of dizzying possibilities. In the absence of a providential telos, however, in the historical time of modernity, which Baudelaire addresses, such an experience is not devoid of anxiety, as the author's own vertigo suggests.

44. For an important analysis of the centrality of the comic in Baudelaire's poetics of modernity that also contextualizes "De l'essence du rire" in terms of theories of the grotesque, the comic, and the sublime, see Hannoosh, *Baudelaire and Caricature.* Although Hannoosh focuses on Baudelaire's art criticism and particularly the essays on caricature, there are a number of affinities between our readings of "De l'essence du rire," especially her view that the essay is an inquiry as well as a performance of the comic that implicates the reader in the fall into duality: "Clearly, irony does not lead to synthesis or a stable recovered unity, nor is this in the Baudelairean scheme, its purpose; but as the recognition and realization of dualism, it may, like *dédoublement,* open the boundaries of the self, becoming the means by which others reach the same level of understanding and adopt the same course of action" (73).

45. The formulation is borrowed from John MacInnes.

46. Indeed, Schlegel's conception of transcendental poetry holds as its telos an ultimate synthesis of ideal and real: "There is a poetry whose One and All is the relationship of the ideal and the real: it should thus be called transcendental poetry according to the analogy of the technical language of philosophy. It begins in the form of satire with the absolute disparity of reality and ideality, it hovers in their midst in the form of the elegy, and it ends in the form of the idyll with the absolute identity of both" (Willson, *German Romantic Criticism,* 130).

47. De Man, "Rhetoric of Temporality," 214. There is a certain existential and romantic register characteristic of de Man's earlier work in this claim to locate the "authentic" voice of romanticism in irony.

48. For further discussion of the *interplay* between the "comique significatif" and the "comique absolu" in Baudelaire's writings on caricature, see Hannoosh, *Baudelaire and Caricature,* and Stephens, *Baudelaire's Prose Poems,* 108–59. The opposition between these two forms of the comic recapitulates broader tensions in Baudelaire's aesthetic theory. Essays such as "Le Poëme du haschisch," "L'Art philosophique," and "Puisque réalisme il y a" oppose autonomous art to "l'hérésie

de l'enseignement," only to dismantle such oppositions and propose a more nuanced view of analytical critique in relation to visionary art. Baudelaire's "L'Art philosophique" recasts this opposition as one between "L'art pur selon la conception moderne" and "l'art philosophique." Like a primitive hieroglyph, philosophical art is legible and applicable to everyday life. Its antithesis is Kantian pure and disinterested beauty. Yet the author then argues that truly allegorical art (treated as legible and hence "pedagogical") is not simply a literal translation of ideas into images but a fluid corpus of poetic meanings, which the *reader* must actualize: "D'ailleurs, même à l'esprit d'un artiste philosophe, les accessoires s'offrent, non pas avec un caractère littéral et précis, mais avec un caractère poétique, vague et confus, et souvent c'est le traducteur qui invente *les intentions*" (*OC*, 2: 601). This activity of readerly translation distinguishes the *comique significatif* from the absolute comic. Baudelaire's understanding of the creation and reception of the artistic text as an act of translation that must invent the work's intentions, fully implicates the *comique absolu* with the *comique significatif.*

49. An example of this misprision is de Man's reading of a pantomime performance in the essay as exemplifying the pathological vertigo of the *comique absolu.* Baudelaire's account of this scene in no way indicates its affect to be pathological, mad, or even anxious. He describes an enchanting performance in which the characters' careless, graceful actions are regulated by a magical providence that choreographs their every move from above: "Tous leurs gestes, tous leurs cris, toutes leurs mines disent : La fée l'a voulu, la destinée nous précipite, je ne m'en afflige pas ; allons ! courons ! élançons nous !" (*OC*, 2: 541).

50. "Ses conceptions comiques les plus supra-naturelles, les plus fugitives, et qui ressemblent souvent à des visions de l'ivresse, ont un sens moral très visible : c'est à croire qu'on a affaire à un physiologiste ou à un médecin de fous des plus profonds et qui s'amuserait à revêtir cette profonde science des formes poétiques, comme un savant qui parlerait par apologues et par paraboles" (*OC*, 2: 543). The demystifying role of the ironist is particularly pronounced in Hoffmann's *Daucus Carota,* where a father whose daughter is smitten by the fabulous display of military splendor shows her "l'envers de toutes ces splendeurs," the seamy underside of an army sleeping in the barracks.

51. As de Man puts it, "it is a historical fact that irony becomes increasingly conscious of itself in the course of demonstrating the impossibility of our being historical" ("Rhetoric of Temporality," 211). Yet, this forceful separation is never clearly substantiated and justified: "at the very moment that irony is thought of as knowledge able to cure and order the world, the source of its invention runs dry" (218). "Both modes [the ironic and the allegorical] are fully demystified when they remain within the realm of their respective languages but are totally vulnerable to renewed blindness as soon as they leave it for the empirical world" (226).

52. "Extended by Baudelaire to encompass the entirety of the individual subject as well as of the nations and their mobile links, laughter comes to name the

fallen mode of all experience; it thus becomes another name for the radically sec-
ular, that is to say, nonteleological and indeterminate, mode of history" (New-
mark, "Traumatic Poetry" 244).

53. Thus both Newmark and Baer criticize Benjamin for situating Baude-
lairean shock in a historical continuum that relies on chronological models of pro-
gression and change, since such models are precisely what the unlocatable nature
of trauma calls into question. As Newmark states, "Reading Baudelaire's own es-
say on the essence of laughter helps to disclose how even this picture of the more
or less recently produced shock of modernity may have its roots in a traumatic ex-
perience that ultimately eludes temporal and spatial determinations even though
these determinations remain inextricably bound up with it" ("Newmark, Trau-
matic Poetry" 253).

54. Our author obviously enjoys imagining the sorts of caricatures Virginie
could have encountered in Paris on the eve of the Revolution: "un Gavarni de ces
temps-là, et des meilleurs, quelque satire insultante contre les folies royales,
quelque diatribe contre le Parc-aux-Cerfs, ou les précédents fangeux d'une grande
favorite, ou les escapades de la proverbiale Autrichienne" (*OC*, 2: 529).

55. To be sure, writing, like trauma, escapes intentionality and historical
grounding even as it reveals the linguistic, and hence fractured and differential,
status of the subject itself. Yet one need not assign a specific intentionality to the
essay's voice to see that it performs (rather than symptomatically reveals) the con-
tradictions of its conceptual categories.

56. Dominick LaCapra has also criticized the binarisms deployed in de Man's
reading of Baudelaire (irony/history, "comique significatif" / "comique absolu").
He points out that de Man's "two world theory" situates what is excluded from so-
cial life within a "separatist" sphere of literature and culture and fails to address the
dialectical relationship between text and praxis. Such a separation "conceals the
role of 'fiction' in 'actual life.' More generally, it provides no critical, non-reductive
basis on which to raise the question of the actual or the desirable interaction be-
tween literature or art and social life. Rather, it leads to the ideological conception
of the status of the literary text that may (mystifyingly) see itself as the demystifi-
cation of ideology—a conception that is a displaced, perhaps abortive form of
transcendental metaphysics in the guise of pure figurality, or fiction. The result in
criticism is to generate a seemingly impenetrable barrier between texts and con-
texts that, insofar as they are not literary or linguistic in a formal sense, are either
ignored or deemed exotopic" (LaCapra, *Soundings in Critical Theory*, 105).

57. The caricaturists most praised by Baudelaire—Daumier and Goya—are
those who mesh the visionary and fantastic with a contextual critique of historical
and political reality. On Daumier's *Massacre de la rue Transnonain*, Baudelaire says:
"Ce n'est pas précisément de la caricature, c'est de l'histoire, de la triviale et terrible
réalité" (*OC*, 2: 552). Similarly, Goya's work lies at the threshold of the *comique
absolu* and the *comique significatif*, meshing the pathological with the analytical

and creating a "monstrueux vraisemblable" in which "[l]a ligne de suture, le point de jonction entre le réel et le fantastique est impossible à saisir" (*OC,* 2: 570).

58. After surviving the guillotine, the Pierrot of English pantomime who is "bien plus avisé que le grand saint-Denis" (539), stuffs his head in his pocket instead of carrying it around. In an anecdote that makes its way into Alexandre Dumas's *La Comtesse de Charny* and *Blanche de Beaulieu,* Camille Desmoulins allegedly said of Saint-Just, "Il porte sa tête avec respect sur ses épaules comme un Saint Sacrement," to which Saint-Just is said to have responded, "Bien, et moi je lui ferai porter la sienne comme un saint Denis." Desmoulins was executed with Danton on April 5, 1794. Baudelaire's "English" Pierrot is thus nationalized and ironically embedded in the French revolutionary legacy. My thanks to Peter Dreyer for alerting me to this reference.

Chapter 2: Passages from Form to Politics

Epigraph: Baudelaire, "L'Art philosophique," *OC,* 2: 598.

1. For a rigorous analysis of the paradoxes of Baudelaire's consecration—from misunderstood poet of the nineteenth century to rehabilitated modernist hero—see Blood, *Baudelaire and the Aesthetics of Bad Faith,* which identifies an allegorical structure in the history of Baudelaire's reception that allows us to rethink the relationship between aestheticism and engagement in terms of Sartrean bad faith. This bad faith, she observes, is operative in Baudelaire's poetry and essential to modernist consciousness itself: "Modernism requires both the recognition and the refusal of historical location. If there is no refusal of history, there can be no modernism, no production (however mystified) of the irreducibly new . . . the historical consciousness of modernism must be in bad faith" (27). Blood thus traces the structures of bad faith in Baudelaire's canonization, teasing out the mutual implication of aesthetic and historical conditions that allowed Baudelaire to emerge as exemplary modernist. As she suggests in a reading of Valéry's "Situation de Baudelaire," the poet's canonization was itself a performative process that concealed its historicity. For Blood, then, "Other histories of Baudelaire may be told, remain open for the telling. The canonical story of Baudelaire's aesthetic success is rigorously an allegory, since it retains the potential to reverse its own narrative. Put another way, the story cannot transcend its own temporality: it itself is engaged in a temporal predicament even as it recounts the flight of Baudelaire's poetry from the temporal into the symbolic realm" (*Baudelaire and the Aesthetics of Bad Faith,* 13). Blood's notion of the "caricatural mechanism" of Baudelaire's poetry (94–122) has some resonance with my use of irony. Blood defines it as a self-alienating mechanism that confronts the subject with its ontological ambiguity, and by which the poems acknowledge and disavow their historicity, point out the failure of symbolic totalization, and open a relation between aesthetic and ethical responses.

2. Friedrich, *Structure de la poésie moderne,* 70. For Friedrich, Baudelaire artic-

ulates the historical shift from things to words, an irrealization that will find its consummate practitioner in Mallarmé. Friedrich's genealogy of modernism thus situates Baudelaire at the origins of a developmental process in which the loss of representational reality and the loss of self go hand in hand. See Paul de Man's critique of Friedrich and literary historians of the Konstanz school for the teleological investment of their "assumption that the movement of lyric poetry away from representation is a historical process that dates back to Baudelaire as well as being the very movement of modernity" in "Lyric and Modernity" (de Man, *Blindness and Insight,* 183). For a dialectical reading of de Man's essay and its value for teasing out the challenges of periodizing modernity, see Jameson, *Singular Modernity,* 106–18.

3. Two distinct views are found in Claude Pichois's and Jean Ziegler's biography of the poet, which considers Baudelaire's republican fervor at the barricades as primarily a personal rebellion against his stepfather, General Aupick; and Burton, *Baudelaire and the Second Republic,* who offers a detailed account of the political influences leading to Baudelaire's early radical republicanism.

4. These facts and testimonies are recorded by Pichois and Ziegler in their thorough biography, *Baudelaire.* In a letter to Eugène Crépet, Jules Buisson recalls his encounter with Baudelaire on February 24, 1848, in the following terms: "Il portait un beau fusil à deux coups luisant et vierge . . . je le hélai, il vint à moi simulant une grande animation : « Je viens de faire un coup de fusil ! » me dit-il. Et comme je souriais, regardant son artillerie tout brillant neuve — « Pas pour la République par exemple ! » — Il ne me répondait pas, criait beaucoup ; et toujours son refrain : il fallait aller fusiller le général Aupick" (Pichois and Ziegler, *Baudelaire,* 257). Pichois is thus skeptical of readings that argue for a genuinely republican or revolutionary Baudelaire, and declares "Ce n'était pas pour la République qu'il se battait ; pas même pour la révolution. C'était pour assouvir son instinct profond de révolte. Sa fureur n'est pas politique ; elle est métaphysique" (257). This portrait of the poet as apolitical rebel has been challenged by a number of critics such as Dolf Oehler and Richard Burton. More recently, Virginia Swain's *Grotesque Figures* has traced Baudelaire's dialogue with Rousseau throughout his works in terms of an ongoing engagement with political utopianism. Her discussion of the continuities—as well as differences—between Baudelaire and Rousseau (particularly on allegory) writes Rousseau back into a historical period that either disavowed or recontained his subversive legacy. This account importantly nuances the historical shift Rousseau and Baudelaire have come to represent and brings into relief the political resonances of Baudelaire's theory and practice of allegory in the prose poems.

5. See Burton, *Baudelaire and the Second Republic,* for an impressively documented historical study of Baudelaire's political activity in 1848. Burton carefully maps the political influences informing the poet's thought in the 1840s and gives a detailed chronological account of his actions and writings during the Second Re-

public. On Baudelaire's fascination with Proudhon in 1848 and the significance of his republicanism, see Clark, *Absolute Bourgeois,* 141–77.

6. See Cohen, *Profane Illumination,* 220–26, for an excellent discussion of this image, and of the reciprocity it implies for the relations between Baudelaire, his historical terrain, and our perception of that terrain. Cohen's treatment of this image is part of an important argument that brings to the fore Benjamin's "Paris of the 19th Century" (which, as noted in Chapter 1, tends to overlooked in favor of "On Some Motifs in Baudelaire") by reassessing the grounds of Adorno's objections to it. Cohen points out that, far from establishing unmediated relations between base and superstructure in his readings of Baudelaire, Benjamin in fact explores the relations between social fact and representational form: "He asks, that is, not how Baudelaire's work reproduces existing material conditions but rather how it inscribes reactions to material conditions in current representational circulation" (Cohen, 225).

7. See also Baudelaire's comment, "existe-t-il. . . quelque chose de plus charmant, de plus fertile, et d'une nature plus positivement *excitante* que le lieu commun ?" (*OC,* 2: 609).

8. "« Eh ! quoi ! vous ici, mon cher ? Vous dans un mauvais lieu ! Vous le buveur des quintessences ! . . . Je puis maintenant me promener incognito, faire des actions basses, et me livrer à la crapule, comme les simples mortels. Et me voici, tout semblable à vous, comme vous voyez" (*OC,* 1: 352).

9. Sonya Stephen's illuminating study of irony in Baudelaire's prose poetry overlaps with the concerns of this book at several points, particularly on the contextualizing power of irony or self-reflexivity: "It is the self-reflexivity, the self-referentiality of the prose poem and its discursive strategies which is most powerfully oppositional, since these engage the reader in the perception of otherness without overt social confrontation" (*Baudelaire's Prose Poems,* 75). I concur with Stephens, moreover, on the subversive effects of Baudelaire's citation of commonplaces and the interpretive instabilities caused by his intertextualities. While there are similarities in our approaches to Baudelaire's prose poetry, particularly in the terms we use (irony, citationality, self-reflexivity), however, Stephens's focus is on the oppositional possibilities opened up by Baudelaire's transformation of genre and his emphasis on low discursive forms such as prose poetry, the "lieu commun," "poèmes-boutades," and caricature. My own approach seeks to foreground the oppositional force of Baudelaire's re-citation of specifically political vocabulary and to examine the convergences Baudelaire maps between art, politics, and violence.

10. I fully agree with Terdiman's analysis of the perpetual absorption of counterdiscourses by the dominant discourse, and his focus on the energetic plurality of Baudelaire's oppositional discourses, "as Baudelaire had sensed in his original characterization of the prose poem, there can be no decisive directionality in a guerilla combat waged under these conditions. The only omnipresent, omnitem-

poral reality is the constancy of the struggle itself" (*Discourse/Counter-discourse*, 339). My readings seek to recover modalities of this struggle specifically through Baudelaire's exploitation of the complicities binding dominant discourses to their "oppositional" others.

11. For a thorough and suggestive reading of the historical significance and class politics implicit in Baudelaire's use of the ragpicker, see Burton, *Baudelaire and the Second Republic*, 220–75.

12. *Les Français peints par eux-mêmes*, 190. L. A Berthaud's portrait in this "Encyclopédie morale du dix-neuvième siècle" explicitly describes the *chiffonnier*'s quest for detritus as the search for a "poétique chenille." His catalogue of waste that will acquire market value resonates with Baudelaire's own parodic allusions to poetry as a degraded commodity object: "Les débris de vaisselle, les lambeaux de torchons, les talons de bottes, les tessons de bouteille . . . tout est marchandise, tout a une valeur, tout est de bonne prise pour le chiffonnier. Avec ces ordures, il fera de l'argent, ce pauvre alchimiste, et avec cet argent, il trouvera de quoi se repaître ; et il ne crèvera pas de faim" (ibid., 192).

13. For powerful readings of "Le Cygne" through the categories of memory, melancholy, and semiosis, see Chambers, *Writing of Melancholy*, 153–73, and Terdiman, *Present Past*, 110–47. Terdiman examines the conjunction between memory, history, and the sign in this poem as what he suggestively terms a "mnemonics of dispossession," showing how the allegorical drift of "Le Cygne," its nexus of intertextualities, attests to a historically situated anxiety about the stability of reference itself. Baudelaire's bid for aesthetic autonomy is thus subverted by his poetic practice, which both asserts and denies the social determinations of art: "Absolutizing the present (the characteristic gesture of modernism) and absolutizing the cultural object (the effect of nineteenth-century formalism) are moves that seek to undo the instability of the sign. But for Second Empire culture such instability inevitably carries the mark of the conjunctural, of history. It is this *differentia specifica* that defines this period. So it should come as no surprise that Baudelaire, while forcefully asserting the aesthetic ideology that denies the links between a text and its social determinations, at the same time (though always in a different register) powerfully subverted precisely this position" (135). For Chambers and Terdiman, "Le Cygne" stages historical change under the sign of melancholy and nostalgia. Their attention to the conjunction between the aesthetic and the historical informs my readings of the self-reflexive turn in Baudelaire's poetry. However, I wish to counterbalance the emphasis on melancholy, mourning, and nostalgia by attending to more active, contestatory, and ironic reinscriptions of the past in Baudelaire's poetry. As I suggest in Chapters 2 and 3, Baudelaire's rehearsals of the imbricated violence of social and aesthetic transformation can be read as active contestations rather than symptomatic inscriptions of historical change. For a reading of "Le Cygne" as a poem that remaps political space by staging incompatible visions of history and myth, see Burt, *Poetry's Appeal*, 32–40. In the compelling

parallel she proposes between poetic and urban space, Burt views the critical gesture of "Le Cygne" as its refusal to subsume or repress the heterogeneity of the city: "Unlike narratives, which have to feign the narrator's claims to have gone beyond an error, the poem takes everything the poet-as-garbage collector finds and dumps it in our lap—trash gilded along with lilies. It recollects all the chances refused in the appropriation of the city, and returns them in a last-chance speculation concerning the readability of the system and the crowd, forgotten in its heterogeneity" (37). For an alternative reading of allegory in "Le Cygne," see Gasarian, *De loin tendrement*, 97–120, which treats the mobility, diversity, and theatricality of the poet's identifications with his figures as signs of a lyric subject whose "self" is exiled into multiple metaphoric figures that emerge from writing itself rather than from historical loss. For Gasarian, Baudelaire mobilizes allegory, not to mourn the loss of the past, but to pursue multiple self-figurations and to create, through poetry, a reservoir of imaginary affects, intensities, and relations (259).

14. *OC,* 1: 358; emphasis added. See also "Les Dons des fées," where the utopian homology between self and state inherited from 1789 is parodied as the fairies' incongruous gift of "l'amour du Beau et la Puissance poétique au fils d'un sombre gueux, carrier de son *état,* qui ne pouvait, en aucune façon, aider les *facultés,* ni soulager les besoins de sa déplorable progéniture" (*OC,* 1: 306; emphasis added).

15. Wing, "Poets, Mimes, and Counterfeit Coins," persuasively argues that the explosive novelty of Fancioulle's performance constitutes a subversive interruption of the sovereign's power and hence opens the possibility for a shift in the implicit consent upon which hegemonic power is based. I agree with Wing on several points: the partial complicity suggested between art and power, the spectacular originality of Fancioulle's oppositional stance and its disruptive implications for the discursive contract upon which both artistic and political power is based. However, I believe the poem to offer two distinct modes of opposition: the defiance provided by idealist art, embodied by Fancioulle, and the conspiratorial, complicitous poetics modeled on Baudelaire's *comique significatif.* The development of this contextual and ironic mode of contestation (as *self*-contestation) is central in "Une Mort héroïque" and other texts that similarly contaminate poetic idealism and political rhetoric, such as "Le Gâteau," "Le Joujou du pauvre," and "La Corde."

16. Friedrich Schlegel's treatment of irony as transcendental buffoonery is vividly embodied by Fancioulle's performance: "There are ancient and modern poems that breathe, in their entirety and in every detail, the divine breath of irony. In such poems there lives a transcendental buffoonery. Their interior is permeated by mood, which surveys everything and rises above everything limited, even above the poet's own art, virtue and genius; and their exterior form by the histrionic style of an ordinary good Italian *buffo*" (Willson, *German Romantic Criticism,* 115). "Une Mort héroïque" also provides an uncanny echo of Schlegel's portrait of

"English wit" in an aphorism that tersely associates wit with madness, absolute freedom, and martyrdom, suggesting the irrevocable gap between idealism and reality. The absolute freedom claimed by the ironist-wit will lead him to commit suicide rather than surrender to the empirical conditions his stance negates: "In England, wit is at least a profession, if not an art. . . . They [the wits] introduce into reality absolute freedom, the reflection of which lends a romantic and piquant air to wit, and thus they live wittily, hence their talent for madness. They die for their principles" (Willson, *German Romantic Criticism*, 116).

17. Swain reads "Une Mort héroïque" in terms of Baudelaire's revision of Rousseau's "realist" conception of allegory into a more generative, open-ended figure for the grotesque (*Grotesque Figures*, 130–32). Chambers, *Writing of Melancholy*, 10–11, suggests that Fancioulle's death provides an allegory of art's defeat and self-censorship before the conformism of the bourgeoisie.

18. Poe, *Contes, essais, poèmes*, 171. Subsequent citations from Poe refer to this edition.

19. For readings of Fancioulle's failure to perform the doubling characteristic of a truly comic art, see Hannoosh, *Baudelaire and Caricature*, 53–58, and Stephens, *Baudelaire's Prose Poems*, 151–59.

20. The response to Fancioulle's performance closely follows Baudelaire's analysis of *le comique absolu*, which induces in the viewer "une hilarité folle, excessive, et qui se traduit en des déchirements et des pâmoisons interminables" (*OC*, 2: 535). Baudelaire will insist on the Englishness of this phenomenon in his national taxonomy of comic forms. His essay on English caricature addresses the hyperbolic violence of, for instance, Seymour's caricatures, as such an example of "l'explosion dans l'expression" (*OC*, 2: 566).

21. According to Baudelaire, *le comique significatif* is also a specifically French phenomenon, reflecting a national predilection for analysis. On several occasions, Baudelaire alludes to the French sacrifice of beauty on the altar of politics and philosophy. Philosophical art appeals to the nation's interpretive, analytical bent, as he states in "L'Art philosophique": "La France aime le mythe, la morale, le rébus ; ou pour mieux dire, pays de raisonnement, elle aime l'effort de l'esprit" (*OC*, 2: 601). The French passion for analytical and decipherable art forms also indicates an obsession with politics. In his essay on Gautier, for instance, Baudelaire views the French thirst for legible allegories as the sacrilegious demand for a politicized aesthetic: "pour la France, le beau [n'est] facilement digestible que relevé par le condiment politique . . . le caractère utopique, communiste, alchimique, de tous ses cerveaux, ne permet qu'une passion exclusive : celle des formules sociales" (*OC*, 2: 125). In light of the repeated connection between rational analysis and political reading, the *comique significatif*, translated as a poetic mode of opposition, acquires complex political significances. The strategies of the *comique significatif* found in "Une Mort héroïque" mark an ironic concession to the poet's readership, since the *comique significatif* promises the intellectual satisfaction of hermeneutic

disclosure and political legibility. Yet the narrator's elliptical and ironic statements both point toward an unrealized political content in the tale and thwart its legibility. Instead, we are presented with a wavering between the absolute, or symbolic (embodied by Fancioulle and untranslated by the narrator), and the significant, or allegorical—a contamination of poetic and political modes performed by the very narration of the poem.

22. In "The Legitimation Crisis: Event and Meaning in 'Le Vieux saltimbanque' and 'Une Mort héroïque,'" Swain has addressed the truncated Horatian intertext as the symptom of a "legitimation crisis," an undoing of cognition that occurs at all levels of the poem and to which the narrator's own self-censorship contributes, and she concludes that the undecideability of the poem's closure is characteristic of radical irony (as de Man defines it in his "Rhetoric of Temporality"). I propose a distinction between irony as a mode of (self-)representation doomed to its own cognitive unraveling, and irony as a performance, which preserves the contestatory force traditionally attributed to this trope.

23. For an illuminating discussion of conspiracy and suicide in Baudelaire's political thought, see Pachet, *Premier venu*, 25–58. Baudelaire intertwines suicide and conspiracy in a curious note: "Qui donc niera le droit au suicide ? J'ai cependant voulu lire, tant j'ai l'esprit critique et modeste, tout ce qui a été écrit sur le suicide. . . . Si les conspirateurs lâchent pied, plus d'intérêt dans ma vie. Je suis donc intéressé à ranimer la conspiration" (*OC*, 2: 592). Pachet suggests that the poet's obsession with conspiracy and suicide opens a reflection on the impossibility of contractual relations between individuals in the public sphere of a postrevolutionary, democratic community. The turn to occult or unreadable exercises of power (the illegibility of suicide, the secrecy of conspiracy) signals a crisis of individuation within the collective, one that can only be captured by negative articulation: "Suicide et conspiration se rejoignent comme les deux incarnations d'une même position de l'individu, d'un individu qui n'est ni totalement solitaire, ni vraiment lié aux autres hommes" (Pachet, *Premier venu*, 54).

24. Indeed, Baudelaire himself suffered from this censorship as he was publishing "Une Mort héroïque." Two poems had already been refused by the *Revue nationale et étrangère* because of their potentially subversive political content. For an excellent reading of the political context of "Une Mort héroïque," see Murphy, "Scène parisienne." There are many affinities between our readings, particularly regarding Baudelaire's understanding of political intervention as a series of tactical positions that are always susceptible to mutating into their opposite, and of the poet's ambivalence about the collective—which, according to Murphy, dooms the poet's oppositional stance to a "révolte individuelle larvée" (57). It is also interesting to note that a large portion of the issue publishing "Une Mort héroïque" hotly denounces the excesses of the "pouvoir indépendant et irresponsable de la sûreté générale," specifically the censorship of the press through the taxing of political journals (*Revue nationale et étrangère*, October 10, 1863).

25. The empire's discretionary police powers dramatically increased after the Carbonaro Orsini's attempt on the emperor's life in January 1858.

26. Benjamin, *Charles Baudelaire,* 15, conference on Baudelaire under the auspices of the Décades de Pontigny cited by the translator, Jean Lacoste. All subsequent references to Benjamin's work in French refer to this Payot edition.

27. I am certainly not alone in pursuing the thematics of sacrifice in Baudelaire. The importance of this archaic ritual for the poet has been treated with unparalleled insight by Pierre Pachet, who, inspired by Bataille and Girard, identifies an anthropology of sacrifice in Baudelaire's thought that reveals the unanimous violence at the genesis of all community, a violence that goes unrecognized in modern industrial societies: "Or, la caractéristique des sociétés industrielles modernes—dont le Second Empire, avec son mélange de brillant et d'efficacité un peu brouillonne, est peut-être bien l'illustration, tient sans doute à ce que l'unanimité sacrificielle y est inconnu : sinon dans les accès barbares que Baudelaire avait anticipé, dans lesquels le ressort sacrificiel, entièrement dénudé dans son mécanisme, ne peut que s'exacerber jusqu'à ce qu'une intervention extérieure en dénoue le charme. Dans les autres cas, c'est dans l'individu et autour de lui que se joue la scène de la mise à mort, c'est entre l'individu et la société restreinte qui rend sa vie possible que se décident continûment les exclusions et les répartitions que la grande machine sociale se charge de consommer et d'inscrire dans ses réseaux" (Pachet, *Premier venu,* 204). See also Jérome Thélot's Girardian approach to "Le Vieux Saltimbanque" as emblematic of a community's emergence through the ritual murder of the scapegoat (Thélot, *Baudelaire,* 43–69).

28. Orr, *Headless History,* 30. See Swain, *Grotesque Figures,* which contests this assessment in a thorough investigation and revision of Baudelaire's debt to Rousseau.

29. "Just as Baudelaire adopts linguistic *lieux communs,* so he adopts the generic commonplaces of such newspaper and publishing items, which themselves adopt a clichéd discourse," Sonya Stephens observes. "All of this contributes to the effect of the citational, itself often used for parodic purposes by connecting and contrasting the parodic text with its model" (*Baudelaire's Prose Poems,* 89). For more detailed readings of citationality and its ironic effects in the prose poems (particularly in "Le Gâteau," "Les Yeux des pauvres," and "Le Joujou du pauvre"), see 86–107. Also see Hiddleston, *Baudelaire and "Le Spleen de Paris,"* 33–61, for an astute reading of Baudelaire's ironic deployment of commonplaces, aphorisms, and moral maxims in the prose poems.

30. See Chapter 5 for a more extensive reading of the poem with Camus's *La Chute.* For a reading of this poem in light of the Commune, which happened two years after its publication, see Terdiman, *Discourse/Counter-discourse,* 316.

31. For a fuller discussion of Baudelairean prostitution, see the introduction to Chapter 3.

32. This notion of an excess that disrupts the bounded and utilitarian economy of the family and of the creative process lends itself to a reading through

Bataille's conception of the "excess" at the heart of poetry itself. See Bataille, *Littérature*, 27–47.

33. "Robespierre n'est estimable que parce qu'il a fait quelques belles phrases," Baudelaire declares (*OC*, 1: 680), repudiating any substantive affiliation to revolutionary politics. Yet during the active phase of his republicanism, Baudelaire actually joined the Société républicaine centrale founded by Blanqui in 1848. Claude Pichois notes that Baudelaire saw in Blanqui a Robespierre of the nineteenth century: "Blanqui, par la pureté et l'intransigence de son républicanisme, par la flamme révolutionnaire dont il était animé, devait être pour Baudelaire un Robespierre du XIXe siècle" (Pichois and Ziegler, *Baudelaire*, 260). For an analysis of Robespierre as a mediation between Rousseau and Baudelaire that attunes the poet to the tyranny of "freedom," see Pachet, *Premier venu*, 38–47.

34. Cited in David, *Fraternité et Révolution*, 127.

35. See Baudelaire's "La Solitude" for another instance in which fraternity is associated with commerce and violence. The poet figure derisively describes "les belles agapes fraternelles" as the collectivity's attempt to *co-opt* individual thought as if it were an economic category, a common good to be homogeneously distributed and consumed. In the 1855 version, the poet figure responds to the chattering and appropriating throng by ironically reifying his vision of the sublime as inalienable private property—"ce coup d'oeil lui a conquis une propriété individuelle inaliénable"—thus mimicking the discourse he derides.

36. See Baudelaire's *Le Musée du Bazar Bonne-Nouvelle* for his appraisal of David's work, including *Marat* and *La Mort de Socrate*. No mention is made of *La Mort de Bara*, but the description of *Marat* is full of admiration, and it is suggestively called a "don à la patrie éplorée" (*OC*, 2: 410). For a discussion of the cult of Bara, see Crow, *Emulation*. It is interesting to note—in the context of "La Corde" and its perversion of the relationship between mother and son—that Joseph Bara joined the army to support his widowed mother and was commemorated as an exemplary son.

37. Could we read an allusion to the guillotine's blade in the chilling detail of the painter's scissors cutting into the boy's neck? Baudelaire in fact, rather than *cou*, initially wrote *col*, which directly invokes *décollation*—beheading.

38. Mercier, *Nouveau Paris*, 3: 4. For a discussion of the cannibalistic connotations of Mercier's description and more generally, of the psychosexual dimension of revolutionary symbolism and its rearticulation of the family as a paradigm for politics, see Hunt, *Family Romance of the French Revolution*. My thanks to Susan Maslan for pointing out this passage.

39. *OC*, 1: 132, a stanza to compare with Baudelaire's conflation of the bourgeoisie and the *peuple* in his description of the violence of the June days: "Les horreurs de Juin. Folie du peuple et folie de la bourgeoisie. Amour naturel du crime" (*OC*, 1: 679). The reference to "le peuple amoureux du fouet abrutissant," like the portrait of the blind, consenting audience of "Une Mort héroïque," conjures up

the poet's disillusionment with the overwhelming majority who supported the plebiscite legitimating Louis-Napoléon's coup d'état.

40. The allusion to the boys as twin brothers locked in vicious combat seems to parody familiar representations of "fraternité" as two cherubic boys locked in an embrace. See, e.g., the illustrations in David, *Fraternité et Révolution,* plates 17–18.

41. See Rousseau, *Confessions,* 1: 306 "Enfin je me rappelai le pis-aller d'une grande princesse à qui l'on disait que les paysans n'avaient pas de pain, et qui répondit : Qu'ils mangent de la brioche." Vicomte Louis de Roubiac quotes this very line in a letter to Marie-Antoinette from London in August 1793: "Il faut savoir que les misérables qui colportent cette infamie n'on même pas le mérite de l'avoir inventée : ils l'ont prise mot pour mot chez Jean-Jacques Rousseau, au Livre VI des « Confessions » ; . . . C'était donc un lieu commun qui circulait avant même votre naissance et que des misérables ont ramassé dans la boue où il était né" (www.dialogus2.org/MARI/quilsmangentdelabrioche.html [accessed August 21, 2005]). My thanks to Peter Dreyer for this reference.

42. Dolf Oehler reads this poem as an ironic meditation on the republican slogans of 1848 in the face of ongoing hunger and inequity, citing Pierre Dupont's *Chant du pain* as an intertext. I fully concur with Oehler's powerful, political reading of Baudelaire's textual provocations as "une protestation ciblée contre la banalisation du mal dans le quotidien bourgeois" (311), and as aiming to "mettre à nu la morale publique par le moyen d'une autodénonciation"(314), although I have some reservations about the one-to-one correspondences he sometimes draws between text and event, such as his reading of "Le Gâteau" as "une apologie secrète de la révolte de Juin" (328).

43. Baudelaire claimed that Joseph de Maistre (and Edgar Allan Poe) taught him how to reason. No doubt his readings of the ultra-Catholic de Maistre attuned him to the sacrificial dimensions of the French revolutionary experience (see Vouga, *Baudelaire et Joseph de Maistre*). Yet as we have seen throughout the readings of his poetry, Baudelaire's own resistance to the closure of systems and his fidelity to the sensuous particularity of lived experience were antithetical to a theological view of history as sacrifice. It is more likely that de Maistre attuned him to the sacrificial structures of secular modernity and its ideologies. I explore this notion further in Camus's own vision of history as terror in Chapter 5.

44. See Swain, *Grotesque Figures,* 132–38, for a divergent reading of allegory's significance in "La Corde." I agree with Swain's point that "La Corde" conveys Baudelaire's fascination with "the process by which allegory, arising out of death or loss, generates a supposedly meaningful and therefore marketable sign" (137). However, Swain reads the conversion of the rope into religious artifact and commodity not as a meditation on the converging violence of art and the market, but as a confirmation that "allegory is a valid escape from the misery and death that characterize the real. Converting 'la corde' from a suicidal instrument into a source

of fortune and good luck, allegory appeals to humanity's real, basic needs. . . . Baudelaire, I believe, finds welcome relief or solace in the escape it provides" (137–38). I have sought to convey instead Baudelaire's nonredemptive vision of allegory as a violent conversion of matter into meaning and value that operates in art, commerce, and the political imagination. I pursue the link between allegory and violence further in Chapter 3.

45. Pichois and Ziegler, *Baudelaire*, 269. See also Baudelaire's sketch for a prospective prose poem: "Poemes en prose (pour la guerre civile) : Le canon tonnne . . . les membres volent . . . des gémissements des victimes et des hurlements des sacrificateurs se font entendre . . . c'est l'humanité qui cherche le bonheur" (*OC*, 1: 371).

46. Linda Orr argues that Baudelaire's turn to violence in his poetry and notebooks is a vengeful and fruitless exorcism of his generation's past republicanism and its discursive debt to Robespierre, but also, more shamefully, to Proudhon and Michelet: "The Terror was wandering or erring in the nineteenth-century in the form of these misreadings, as errors that produced this gooey mess, worse than the terror itself, as far as Baudelaire was concerned. In fact he fantasized about resorting to his own terror as the only way of getting out of the twisted legacy of the Terror" (*Headless History*, 28). I concur with the general thrust of Orr's argument but would underscore that Baudelaire's ironic rewriting of that discourse deftly punctures its legitimacy in order both to critique the failure of republican idealism and to show how the misuses of its rhetorical legacy are precisely what blind people to the latent violence of their everyday practices, as the example of *commerce* suggests in "La Corde."

47. *OC*, 1: 339. My thanks to Jared Stark, who discusses this anterior version in the chapter in his dissertation on Baudelaire's "La Corde." Stark notes a pun on *réel* in the suppressed paragraph—as a unit of currency, *un réel*, and as "real," and reads Baudelaire's decision to excise the final paragraph as a resistance to the logic of the marketplace and as a gesture toward a reality that cannot be reduced to a commodity. My reading is also indebted to conversations with John Mackay. The parallel suggested by Baudelaire between the poet and the hanged (which gestures back to Villon) transforms the poem into a symbolic scaffold of sorts, a "gibet symbolique où pendait mon image" ("Un Voyage à Cythère"). For a political reading of "Un Voyage à Cythère" that sees the "pauvre pendu muet" of the 1855 version as an allegory of the ritual killing of the Second Republic, see Burton, *Baudelaire and the Second Republic*, 312–19.

48. Barbara Johnson has formulated this predicament beautifully in a reading of the preface to Houssaye: "Ce qui vient en tête de l'ouvrage, c'est l'absence de tête ; oeuvre décapitée dont la tête n'est jamais là où on la cherche. Oeuvre décapitée, mais qui se situe justement dans la 'capitale,' la grande ville où le 'croisement d'innombrables rapports' tient lieu de centre, où la linéarité, toute serpentine qu'elle soit, se retourne et se recoupe pour n'aller nulle part, pour n'avoir pas de sens,

labyrinthe dans lequel « on s'égare précisément parce qu'on se retrouve au même point », le point de la plus grande insécurité" (Johnson, *Défigurations,* 28).

Chapter 3: Bodies in Motion, Texts on Stage

Epigraph: Baudelaire, "Mon coeur mis à nu," *OC,* 1: 677

1. Jameson, "Baudelaire as Modernist and Postmodernist," 255. As I argued in the opening chapter of this book, Baudelaire is a pivotal figure for such accounts of modernism and its "crisis of representation."

2. In his more recent thinking, Fredric Jameson has pointed out the instability and ideological valences of categories such as modernism and modernity, while suggesting the inevitability of these periodizing narratives. Aesthetic autonomy is further historicized as the product of late-modernist reading practices that coalesce in the mid twentieth century. See Jameson, *Singular Modernity,* pt. 2, "Modernism as Ideology," 141–210

3. The allusion to Judith Butler's important work on the performative force of discourse is deliberate. See Butler, *Bodies That Matter* and *Excitable Speech.* One strand of my argument is that the self-reflexivity or irony we associate with high modernism is an instance of literature reflecting on the power of its own discourse, its "production" of reference, and that this reflection on aesthetics can in turn be situated within broader institutional and cultural practices that interpellate bodies and subjects. Mallarmé aimed to paint not the thing but the effect that it produces. I suggest throughout this chapter that Baudelaire paints not the thing but the effects that produce *it.*

4. See, e.g., Valéry, *Degas, danse et dessin* and *L'Âme et la danse,* which offer compelling meditations on the translation of the human body across different media and performances.

5. Bernheimer, *Figures of Ill Repute,* 2, Bernheimer demonstrates how authors such as Balzac, Baudelaire, Flaubert, Zola, the Goncourts, and others rehearse such contradictory mappings of the prostitute—as contagious abjection and as exemplary semiotic performer: "Balzac gives prostitution a variety of figural meanings based on processes of circulation and exchange among men alone. Perhaps the most radical of these processes involves the metaphorization of gender and genealogy so that the biological can be constructed and circulated as a male invention" (70). In Bernheimer's account, the prostitute exemplifies what elsewhere Naomi Schor has described as the status of femininity itself in nineteenth-century realism: "woman, that mobile unit, that empty square par excellence, wanders about the entire critical landscape . . . woman can be equated with the people, the body, or money, with all that circulates and/or is repressed" (*Breaking the Chain,* 29). Schor thus rightly cautions us against overdetermined readings of gender that replicate the very forms of reification that are under scrutiny.

6. For more on the iconography of the prostitute and her relations to capital-

ist modernity, see Clark, *Painting of Modern Life*, 79–146, and Matlock, *Scenes of Seduction*. For a reading of the female nude and the construction of "woman" in the nineteenth century as biological facticity, art object, and commodity fetish, see Brooks, *Body Work*, 123–61.

7. In *La Fanfarlo*, Baudelaire alludes to Balzac and to de Marsay's cavalier dismissal of Paquita after a night of passion. Samuel Cramer feels none of the *ennui* of Balzac's hero upon leaving La Fanfarlo's abode: "jamais . . . il n'éprouva cette jouissance égoïste du cigare et des mains dans les poches, dont parle quelque part notre grand romancier moderne" (*OC*, 1: 578).

8. De Marsay invokes this original as a contrast to the many copies of this fresco, turned into commodity by "un tas de bourgeois qui ne voient dans ce camée qu'une breloque" (Balzac, *Histoire des Treize*, 237). There is more than a little irony here in de Marsay's celebration of Paquita as an authentic original to a fresco Balzac himself derived from Latouche's *Fragoletta*.

9. On Balzac's sociological inquiry into the nineteenth-century's forms of sexuality, see Lucey, *Misfit of the Family*, which reads the conclusion of *La Fille aux yeux d'or* and the recognition of Paquita's fidelity to the bloodline by both de Marsay and the marquise as superseding other considerations, such as her threat to de Marsay's masculinity or infidelity to the marquise. Fidelity to the bloodline, then, invokes an alternate frame of values. It assumes that "[t]here is a possible place for and a possible way of recognizing and assimilating same-sex practices within an aristocratic ethos, especially when the family (with its 'identité pleinement consciente') is threatened from the outside" (Lucey, 122). For a discussion of oriental despotism in Baudelaire as a metaphor for the Second Empire and its repressed tyranny, see Chambers, "Poetry in the Asiatic Mode," in id., *Writing of Melancholy*, 118–52.

10. Schor, *Breaking the Chain*, 136. Balzac's famous description of the pension Vaucquer exemplifies this naturalization of the social, locating the characters' essence in the body and its "natural" embedding in its milieu, such that Madame Vaucquer's repugnant physique recapitulates her mores, beliefs, history, and fetid surroundings. Yet Schor has also observed the extent to which Balzac, along with the nineteenth century generally, "rehearses an interminable 'crisis of distinctions,' which is made manifest by the proliferation of effeminate male characters and viriloid female characters, not to mention the multiplication of borderline cases: androgyns and castrati" (30).

11. I use the term "commodity fetish" here in the classic Marxian sense, as an instance in which a relationship between men has taken the form of a relationship between things. This will be discussed further in my reading of "Une Martyre."

12. For a discussion of the regulatory measures taken against prostitution and of salient cultural articulations of the topos of the prostitute in this context, see Corbin, *Filles de noce*, and Parent-Duchâtelet, *Prostitution à Paris au XIXe siècle*.

13. Baudelaire's poet-prostitute enacts the principle of "De la vaporisation et de la centralisation du *moi*. Tout est là." Gretchen Schultz reads this aphorism as a

code for sexual difference operative at all levels of Baudelaire's writing. The productive mingling or cooperation of these poles (which are also transcribed along the sexual polarity of masculine singularity and feminine dispersal) in figures such as the *thyrse,* for Schultz, opens "a new definition of the subject, in a specific prosodic context" (*Gendered Lyric,* 194). Her fine reading of Baudelaire's "La Musique" attends to the formal features of the poem (its heterometricity, spatial imagery, and rhythm) to suggest that Baudelaire's position in literary history (at the juncture between the Parnasse and symbolism) needs to be rethought in light of his dislocation of the gendered poetic subject: "Baudelaire's poetic ruminations on dispersal and constraint surpass fixed dichotomies and create a space for difference. By reaching back to an unlocateable subject, Baudelaire elides sexual categories and creates the possibility of a lyric practice free of confining oppositions, a possibility pursued by subsequent Symbolist poets" (207).

14. Benjamin, *Charles Baudelaire,* trans. Zohn, 58. "To be sure, insofar as a person, as labour power, is a commodity, there is no need for him to identify himself as such. The more conscious he becomes of his mode of existence, the mode imposed upon him by the system of production, the more he proletarianizes himself, the more he will be gripped by the chill of the commodity economy and the less he will feel like empathizing with commodities. But things had not reached that point with the class of the petty bourgeoisie to which Baudelaire belonged" (ibid.).

15. The narration of "Les Foules" thus follows the ironic principle of textual production identified in "De l'essence du rire": "l'essence de ce comique est de paraître s'ignorer lui-même et de developper chez le spectateur, ou plutôt chez le lecteur, la joie de sa propre supériorité et la joie de la supériorité de l'homme sur la nature"(*OC,* 2: 543). For Baudelaire, laughter is a symptom both of one's sense of superiority and of lucidity with respect to the mystification upon which that superiority rests. The self-irony that opens the text up to laughter is the sign of the "esprit philosophe" who resists the temptation of superiority and stages the fall of the poet-prostitute as both "victime" and "bourreau" of his own superiority. For an alternative reading of prostitution in Baudelaire as a pleasurable disruption of gender and genre, see Wing, *Limits of Narrative,* 19–40.

16. My approach to the female body as a key token for narratives of modernity is informed by Peter Brooks's wide-ranging and stimulating work on the body in modern realist narrative. In *Body Work,* Brooks introduces his inquiry in the following terms: "While resisting the (impossible) task of saying exactly what the body is, throughout I ask why and how bodies have been imagined and symbolized, and particularly how they have been made *key tokens in modern narratives*" (xii; emphasis added). Although my approach is not psychoanalytic, this chapter is in dialogue with important work by Schor, Brooks, Matlock, Ender, and Beizer on the semioticization of bodies and the somatization of representation and seeks to extend their analyses to a discussion of poetry.

17. Classic studies on the emergence of "visual culture" in late nineteenth-

century Paris include Schwartz, *Spectacular Realities,* Barrows, *Distorted Mirrors,* Bowlby, *Just Looking,* Buck-Morss, *Dialectics of Seeing,* and Clark, *Painting of Modern Life.*

18. Baudelaire's comments on Delacroix's *Femmes d'Alger* (a painting that motivated Balzac's dedication of *La Fille aux yeux d'or* to the artist) announces his own exercise of *ekphrasis* in "Une Martyre": "Ce petit poème d'intérieur, plein de repos et de silence, encombré de riches étoffes et de brimborions de toilette, exhale je ne sais quel haut parfum de mauvais lieu qui nous guide assez vite vers les limbes insondées de la tristesse" (*OC,* 2: 440).

19. See in particular Benjamin's *ZentralPark,* fragments 5, 14, 19, and 20, collected in id., *Charles Baudelaire,* trans. Lacoste.

20. The literary text's capacity for ideology critique remains a difficult and vexed issue in Benjamin studies. The split between psychoanalytic and materialist readings of Baudelaire via Benjamin is addressed in the opening chapter of this book. Here I point out that both readings limit the levels of textual agency and ethical-political contestation found in the poetry itself. These layers are difficult to theorize and can only be discerned, I believe, through close readings that attend to what is present—as well as absent—in the text, and to the dialectical reversals typical of Baudelaire's irony.

21. "Since the days of Louis-Philippe the bourgeoisie has endeavoured to compensate itself for the inconsequential nature of private life in the big city. It seeks such compensation within its four walls. . . . For the Makart style, the style at the end of the Second Empire, a dwelling becomes a kind of casing. This style views it as a kind of case for a person and embeds him in it together with all his appurtenances, tending his traces as nature tends dead fauna embedded in granite" (Benjamin, *Charles Baudelaire,* trans. Zohn, 46). For a cultural history of the apartment in nineteenth-century Paris and London, see Marcus, *Apartment Stories.*

22. Benjamin describes this as an empathetic identification that fetishizes the commodity and invests it with a soul: "If the soul of the commodity which Marx occasionally mentions in jest existed, it would be the most empathetic ever encountered in the realm of souls, for it would have to see in everyone the buyer in whose hand and house it wants to nestle" (*Charles Baudelaire,* trans. Zohn, 55).

23. In his reading of "La Mort des amants," Fredric Jameson portrays a "postmodern" Baudelaire through these very categories: the disappearance of a human subject, of nature, and of referential frames, and their replacement with kitschy commodities, hyperbolically artificial interiors, and glossy surfaces that refuse to yield to depth. These elements create what he calls a "hysterical sublime" ("Baudelaire as Modernist and Postmodernist," 255). "Une Marytre" vividly displays the characteristics attributed by Jameson to a postmodern sensibility, while simultaneously returning to the price paid (both material and ethical) for this vision and experience, in an uneasy blending of registers that resists any one periodization.

24. An 1844 caricature by Grandville, *La Pêche à la ligne* (a title translated by

Susan Buck-Morss as "Fish fishing for people, using various desirable items as bait"), captures the scrambled configuration of humans, nature, and commodity (of anthropomorphism and reification) under high capitalism. In this drawing, a school of grinning fish, helped by a tree, dangle wine bottles, subscriptions, and watches over the heads of grasping consumers who are up to their shoulders in a river (reproduced in Buck-Morss, *Dialectics of Seeing,* 155).

25. The diminishment of things in both the process of allegorization and of commodification is repeatedly underlined by Benjamin. See, e.g., his statement, "La dépréciation du monde des choses dans l'allégorie est dépassée par la marchandise dans le monde des choses lui-même" (*Charles Baudelaire,* 215). For a fascinating analysis of Benjamin's conception of allegory and commodity in relation to Grandville, Baudelaire, and the representation of history, see Hannoosh, "Allegorical Artist."

26. The rising popularity of the *roman policier* during the Second Empire was in part due to Baudelaire's translations of Edgar Allan Poe. "Une Martyre" itself contains echoes of "The Murders of the Rue Morgue," where the Madame l'Espanaye's body is found virtually decapitated in her apartment.

27. For an intriguing treatment of women and sexual violence in Baudelaire, see Gasarian, *De loin tendrement,* chap. 1, "Les Femmes de Baudelaire," which reads scenes of violence and violation as poetic attempts to communicate to women and to the "other" through wounds that dislocate the identity of both the masculine poetic subject and feminine object, muse, and reader: "Le sadisme du poète, en dernière analyse, serait d'ordre non pas érotique mais poétique: il aurait à voir avec le désir du poète de forcer la femme—mais aussi bien « l'autre », comme dit Deguy, c'est-à-dire tout lecteur—à entendre la poésie" (36). While Gasarian's discussion of lyric self-figuration leads in a direction quite different from my project, his view of violence as a mode of interpellation is illuminating. My Chapter 4 addresses texts by women readers, historical subjects who "speak back" to Baudelaire's symbolic as well as textual legacy. Their own textual "counterviolence" can be read as negotiating between "hearing" and "deafness" to the interpellative force of Baudelaire's poetry.

28. Thélot astutely notes that Baudelaire's Parisian scenes often take place in marginal sites that illuminate the functioning of the centre or capital: "« La Femme sauvage et la petite-maîtresse » découvre le devenir de la capitale—comme régression à la barbarie sur laquelle elle repose—dans ses marges, ses « faubourgs », où en s'altérant elle se dévoile" (*Baudelaire,* 75).

29. For an analysis of the gendered underpinnings of Parnassianism, see Schultz, *Gendered Lyric,* 83–139, which interprets the rigid formalism of the Parnasse and its emphasis on objectivity, immobility, and rigor as "a rejection of Romanticism's perceived femininity and an attempt to reclaim poetry as a masculine domain" (84). Her analysis addresses the figures of "petrified femininity" in poets such as Gautier and Leconte de Lisle to argue that Baudelaire's manipulation of the legacies of romanticism and the Parnasse (and their affiliation with femi-

nine/soft attributes and masculine/hard ones), indeed, his manipulation of form itself, dislocates the traditional "gendering" of lyric poetry.

30. In an illuminating commentary on the significance of the word *sauvage* in Baudelaire's prose poems, Evans notes that "[t]hat which a culture rejects as 'barbarian' is also what helps to define that culture. In the prose poems, whenever *sauvagerie* is mentioned, whether it refers to individual behaviour which violates society's unwritten codes or whether it serves as a way of designating an exotic, alien culture, it *always* furthers the central project of interrogating the values of contemporary nineteenth-century Paris" (*Baudelaire and Intertextuality*, 111–12). For an excellent analysis of the Napoleonic code on marriage, and its reverberations in nineteenth-century literature, see Catherine Nesci.

31. For an alternate reading of this poem as a reflection on the poet's inescapable entrapment in literary imitation and counterfeit, see Thélot, *Baudelaire*, 137. For an illuminating analysis of the poem's intertextual references and the ambiguity of its irony, see Evans, *Baudelaire and Intertextuality*, 62–65. Regarding the punitive violence of Baudelaire's poem (and the association drawn between the poet and the husband), Evans astutely notes that "By 'having it both ways' the poem effectively interrogates underlying codes of masculinity and sententious didacticism whilst still situating itself as essentially masculine discourse. . . . By ironically undermining such discourse the prose poems call into question contemporary nineteenth-century assumptions about both *genre* and *gender* identity" (64).

32. Bartman's remains were transferred to South Africa in May 2002. Baudelaire's savage female is also reminiscent of Poe's deadly orangutan in the "Murders of the Rue Morgue" and echoes Poe's meditation on the fine line between man and beast in "Hop Frog" and the eight chained orangutans (see Chapter 2).

33. The remark about "that Hottentot Venus with a black cat" was made by Victor Fournel, cited in Bernheimer, *Figures of Ill Repute*, 120. For a reading of Manet's courtesan figure Olympia through the iconography of the Khoisanid, see Gilman, *Difference and Pathology*, 76–109. For a more extensive treatment of the figure of the "black Venus" in the French literary imagination, see Sharpley-Whiting, *Black Venus*. Ann McClintock discusses the mapping of race in progressive narrative of the "Family of Man" in *Imperial Leather*, 40–56.

34. Richon, *Jeanne Duval et Charles Baudelaire*, 32, 234. Emmanuel Richon gives a detailed portrait of Jeanne Duval's life and symbolic place in the imagination of Baudelaire's contemporaries and explains the complexity of the poet's treatment of "exotic femininity" in light of a hostile cultural context, noting that Gobineau's *De l'origine des inégalités des races* and its condemnation of miscegenation (associated with Western degeneration) had appeared in 1853. It is also worth noting that in 1834, the young Baudelaire asked his mother to send him a copy of *Voyage dans l'intérieur de l'Afrique par le cap de la Bonne-Espérance* (1790), the travel journal of the naturalist François Levaillant, his great uncle, which contains descriptions of Khoisanid women.

35. The most comprehensive and multifaceted examination of this phenomenon is found in *Zoos humains,* ed. Bancel et al.

36. As Paul Greenhalgh puts it, "The actual presence of peoples of empire at exhibitions went back to 1851, when representatives of most nations of the British Empire were constantly in attendance at the Crystal Palace. The first time people could properly be called part of the exhibit, though, was in 1867, at the Paris *Exposition Universelle,* when various North African exhibits were presented as *tableaux-vivants.* An Egyptian Bazaar contained craftspeople and vendors, a camel stable had real camels and Arabic attendants, an authentic Tunisian Barbershop was open for business" (Greenhalgh, *Ephemeral Vistas,* 85).

37. Raser, "Politics of Art Criticism," 338. Raser argues that Baudelaire's essay both shares and disavows the official ideology of the 1855 Exposition universelle, and by extension, the Second Empire's alleged principles—by valuing universality and tolerance of cultural difference, and by establishing an appreciation of art and tradition rather than simply fetishizing progress: "Baudelaire is thus developing and amplifying a position articulated by the Second Empire, while disavowing its origin" (342). Yet when read in light of the colonial dimension of the empire (one that forces us to reread the alleged universalism of the Exposition and its discourse of internationalist harmony), it appears that more is at stake in Baudelaire's essay than a relationship of unacknowledged debt to official ideology, a reiteration of its eclectic brand of universalism. Baudelaire illuminates a crucial, albeit repressed, dimension of the exhibition, namely, its symbolic legitimation of colonial expansion. And in this context, Baudelaire's remarks on the instability of France's position—or the French individual's psyche—seem quite distinct from the imperial ideology.

38. Raser, "Politics of Art Criticism," 344n5, rightly cautions us against seeing this internationalism in terms of current notions of multiculturalism: the European nations contributed the majority of the exhibits, although Argentina, Egypt, Brazil, Guatemala, Hawaii, and Mexico were also represented, along with Algeria and the other French colonies. See also Williams, *Dream Worlds.*

39. The first and third sections of Baudelaire's essay appeared in *Le Pays;* the second was refused because of its critique of Ingres.

40. *OC,* 2: 580. Baudelaire's allusion to Western decadence is a response to Maxim Du Camp's hymn to progress, *Les Chants modernes,* published in 1855, the year of the Exposition universelle.

41. See, e.g., his "Études sur Poe," where the critique of American-style materialism exposes the underlying savagery of civilization: "Brûler des nègres enchaînés, coupables d'avoir senti leur joue noire fourmiller du rouge de l'honneur, jouer du revolver dans un parterre de théâtre, établir la polygamie dans les paradis de l'Ouest, que les Sauvages (ce terme a l'air d'une injustice) n'avaient pas encore souillés de ces honteuses utopies, afficher sur les murs, sans doute pour consacrer le principe de la liberté illimitée, la *guérison des maladies de neuf mois,* tels sont

quelques-unes des traits saillants, quelques-unes des illustrations morales du noble pays de Franklin, l'inventeur de la morale de comptoir, le héros d'un siècle voué à la matière" (*OC*, 2: 327).

42. Baudelaire turns the self-affirmation of "progress" on its head. Like the proverbial scorpion that stings itself, human evolution is a regressive self-negation or suicide that will never yield the plenitude of satisfied needs: "Je laisse de côté la question de savoir si, délicatisant l'humanité en proportion des jouissances nouvelles qu'il lui apporte, le progrès indéfini ne serait pas sa plus ingénieuse et sa plus cruelle torture ; si, procédant par une opiniâtre négation de lui-même, il ne serait pas un mode de suicide incessamment renouvelé, et si, enfermé dans le cercle de feu de la logique divine, il ne ressemblerait pas au scorpion qui se perce lui-même avec sa terrible queue, cet éternel *desideratum* qui fait son éternel désespoir ?" (*OC*, 2: 581)

43. As Claude Pichois notes, the 1855 exhibit also housed a Chinese museum displaying a collection of art objects brought back by Montigni, an ex-consul at Shanghai and Ning-Po. It is worth noting that very few art critics showed Baudelaire's openness to cultural difference. Gautier, for instance, evoked the Greek *beau idéal* in contrast to the Chinese *laid idéal* represented in the Chinese museum.

44. The play on "conversion" is quite explicit in the passage, which ends with a reference to Sicambre, who once converted, burned what he once worshipped and worshipped what he once burned (*OC*, 2: 577).

45. Miller, *Nationalists and Nomads*, 165. My readings thus strive to nuance Miller's own positioning of Baudelaire as an architect of the French colonial imagination. In *Nationalists and Nomads*, 56–59, Miller proposes "Le Cygne" and "À une Malabaraise" as examples of Baudelaire's universalizing acceptance or outright rejection of the African subject. Baudelaire's poems are thus read as coordinates for a colonial imagination that either assimilates difference or excludes it. See Miller's earlier book *Blank Darkness* for a more extensive reading of Baudelaire's participation in the erasure of the African subject's specificity.

46. *OC*, 1: 1119. According to Claude Pichois, the prose version of "La Belle Dorothée" may very possibly have *preceded* its verse counterpart, since Baudelaire refers to the completion of the prose poem in 1861, whereas the lyric poem would not be published until 1864 (*OC*, 1: 1333).

47. "The black and the oriental are figments of an imaginary geography in Baudelaire's mind, into which one cannot read more precision than was written" (Miller, *Blank Darkness*, 120). Miller cites Baudelaire's use of the word *cafrine* as "typically Africanist in its arbitrary application of an inherited term to the totally unknown" (120), a statement that has led to a debate with Françoise Lionnet, who argues instead that the term *cafrine* is *not* an instance of derogatory Africanism, but rather, gives voice to the marginalized—if not silenced—Creole subject. See the end of my reading for a discussion of this last point.

48. Miller and Sharply-Whiting both argue that Dorothée's smile, directed at

metropolitan France, exemplifies the colonial subject's self-alienation as it is described in Fanon's *Peau noire, masques blancs.*

49. The allusion to Dorothée "being fanned" in her meager orientalist boudoir parodically rewrites "La Vie antérieure" and its final image of the slaves refreshing the languid poet's dolorous secret. For surely Dorothée has no slave at her disposal, although as we discover, she does have a secret, whose *douleur* remains unexpressed in the poem.

50. The sabotaging of such tropicalist stereotypes is significant given Baudelaire's deep appreciation elsewhere for the fertility of indolence (the *féconde paresse* of "La Chevelure," the languid rest at the feet of the *géante*). In the salon of 1859, Baudelaire pleasurably contemplates Eugène Fromentin's luminous and nostalgic African landscapes (*Bateurs nègres dans les tribus, Lisière d'oasis pendant le sirocco, Souvenirs de l'Algerie, Audience chez un Khalifat*) and especially *Une Rue à El Aghouat*, a painting that no doubt influenced the composition of "La Belle Dorothée," and that shows Algerian natives collapsed in the noontime heat, succumbing to a slumber that Baudelaire describes thus: "Il est présumable que je suis moi-même atteint quelque peu d'une nostalgie qui m'entraine vers le soleil ; car de ces toiles lumineuses s'élève pour moi une vapeur enivrante, qui se condense bientot en désirs et en regrets. Je me surprends à envier le sort de ces hommes étendus sous ces ombres bleues, et dont les yeux, qui ne sont ni eveillés ni endormis, n'expriment, si toutefois ils expriment quelque chose, que l'amour du repos et le sentiment du bonheur qu'inspire une immense lumière" (*OC,* 2: 650).

51. The disquieting force of this poem may have less to do with Dorothée's eventual exile in Paris in avatars such as the *négresse* in "Le Cygne" or "À une Malabaraise" than with the extent to which the native is already a state of exile and inhabits a phantasmagoria fashioned in the image of the European bourgeoisie. Explicitly presented as the African version of "La Beauté," "belle . . . comme un rêve de pierre" (Dorothée is "belle et froide comme le bronze"), her native habitat itself harbors uncanny resonances with the *métropole:* her charming little shack and the Sunday dances she attends are but cheap reflections of a well-appointed boudoir or a ball at the opera.

52. For different readings of Baudelaire as participating in an imperialist tropology, see Gayatri Spivak's "Imperialism and Sexual Difference" and Miller's *Blank Darkness,* 69–138.

53. Lionnet, "Reframing Baudelaire," 84. In *Blank Darkness,* Christopher Miller proposes that Baudelaire invented the word *cafrine* by adding the suffix *-ine* to the noun *cafre,* from the Arabic *kafir* (or "infidel"), thus overracializing and diminishing the black woman in a "double feminine" that "constitutes [Baudelaire's] most frankly Africanist scene" (122). In "Reframing Baudelaire," however, Françoise Lionnet takes issue with Miller's interpretation and argues that *cafrine* is a Creole neologism designating a woman of the black race. Baudelaire's inclusion

of local dialect in his poem "actually gives us the sound of the voice of the black woman herself" (72). For Lionnet, *cafrine* forges an encounter between French and Creole languages, colonial and local culture, male and female subject positions in a deconstructive gesture that prefigures francophone models of ontological and linguistic hybridity. Among the many issues at stake in this debate is the nature of the postcolonial archive. For example, where Miller consulted French dictionaries such as the *Littré*, Lionnet turns to *Le Léxique du parler créole de la Réunion*. Miller subsequently revisits the debate over *cafrine* and notes that Baudelaire may well have encountered the term long before his trip to the Mascarenes, in his great uncle François Levaillant's *Voyage dans l'intérieur de l'Afrique par le cap de Bonne Espérance*. Miller concludes that "the heteroglossia of this word thus *combines* the voice of the Creole and that of the avuncular French archive—it encompasses, to use Lionnet's terms, both the island female and the continental male. . . . To me this perfectly demonstrates in microcosm the necessity to recognize particularisms (including masters' voices) within in analysis of hybridity" (*Nationalists and Nomads*, 222).

54. "Je suis la pipe d'un auteur / On voit à contempler ma mine / D'Abyssinienne ou de Cafrine/Que mon maitre est un grand fumeur / Quand il est comblé de douleur / Je fume comme la chaumine / Où se prepare la cuisine / Pour le retour du laboureur" (*OC*, 1: 67).

55. Mallarmé, "Ballets," in *Oeuvres*, 229–30. See McCarren, *Dance Pathologies*, for a provocative analysis of Mallarmé's dislocation of gender in his writings on dance. McCarren argues that Loie Fuller's semiotic rendering of the dancer's body foils the masculine regime of scopic power and introduces a revolutionary mobility and indeterminacy in the conceptualization of gender.

56. This mediation of textuality and historicity has been brilliantly analyzed by Ross Chambers in terms of a "contextualizing self-figuration" characteristic of modernist writings. Chambers proposes that "self-figuration is always readable as an index of historicity and that its readability always functions as an invitation to interpret the textual enunciation (or "speech-act") in a historical manner, in relation to social positioning. The paradox of modernism is that by marking itself in this way in relation to its historical context, the modernist text also calls attention to its desire for autonomy and to its attempts to escape from history by showing the contextual reasons that underlie them" (*Writing of Melancholy*, 13). Whilst my approach to irony has been deeply informed by Chambers's important work on modernism and oppositionality, this project steers away from the modalities of melancholy and mourning and explores more self-conscious oppositional strategies. Rather than addressing Baudelaire's texts as melancholy or duplicitous sites of repressed violence, I have sought to foreground the theatrical, even exhibitionistic, displays of violence as forms counterviolence.

57. Teskey, *Allegory and Violence*, 19. Teskey is commenting on Spenser's *Faerie*

Queene and its depiction of Amoret's torture, as Busyrane the enchanter writes in her blood, as a moment in which the violence of the very process of allegorization is unveiled. As Teskey says of Dante and Spenser, however, certain poets reveal the resistance of allegory's totalizing capture: "The greatest allegorical poets do not simply transform life into meaning. They exacerbate the antipathy of the living to the significant by exposing the violence entailed in transforming the one to the other" (24).

58. The *Roman de la rose,* for example, sets up an allegory in which feminized matter—the rose—is conceptualized as both inviting and refusing its ravishment. In the next chapter, I show how Rachilde rewrites this particular scene and more generally, how her work may be read as an intervention that questions the sexual politics of allegory's separation of matter and form.

59. Ross Chambers's recent discussion of testimony as a flaunting of cultural hauntedness offers an illuminating lens for seeing how Baudelaire's spectacular violence "flaunts" the margins of a cultural formation by bringing to center stage its repressed, albeit constitutive, figures: "Flaunting is, par excellence, the gesture of visibility that requires reading, and the mediation therefore whereby the lacking object of representational or mimetic referentiality can be figuratively presenced as an interpretive, that is, recognizable object—an object that haunts. And if haunting is a mode of cultural infiltration, the vehicle by means of which it infiltrates is inevitably, to some degree and always relatively speaking, spectacular and confrontational, therefore, because it is necessarily the performance of a state of impertinence . . . of the lack of pertinence that characterizes the inexplicable as well as the supposedly irrelevant and makes it an untimely manifestation when, unexpectedly, it shows itself to be relevant" (*Untimely Interventions,* 230)

Part II: Unlikely Contestations

1. According to Richard Burton, the encounter between the philosopher-poet and the beggar in "Assommons les pauvres !" prefigures a totalitarian hierarchy of power, in which theory (and ideology) is transmitted through systematic brutality: "Beyond 'Assommons les pauvres !' duo of *bourreau* and *victime,* demagogue and lumpenproletariat, a still more fateful sado-masochistic pairing—Führer and Volk—comes dimly into view" (*Baudelaire and the Second Republic,* 363). For a recent intertextual allusion to Baudelaire's poem, see David Fincher's film *Fight Club* (1999), in which an underground homosocial club attempts to start an anarchistic rebellion on the streets by beating up strangers until these finally fight back.

2. Maclean, *Narrative as Performance,* 175. Maclean's powerful readings of Baudelaire's prose poems as allegories of reception were central to my initial encounter with Baudelaire and continue to inform my thinking about text, performance, and performativity.

Chapter 4: Matter's Revenge on Form

Epigraphs: Baudelaire, *Les Fleurs du mal,* "Projets de préface pour une édition nouvelle," in *OC,* 1: 182; Benjamin, *Arcades Project,* 332; Virginie Despentes in "Girls Just Want to End Oppression," interview with Nigel Andrews, *Financial Times,* April 11, 2002.

1. As Rita Felski has pointed out, citing Marshall Berman's influential account, modernity is persistently envisioned through masculine figures of quest such as the dandy, Faust, or the flâneur, which are opposed to the materiality and finitude of a feminized corporeality (Felski, *Gender of Modernity,* 1–10). Yet, as we saw in Chapter 3, such oppositions are dismantled in Baudelaire's mise-en-scène of the conditions that produce a body marked by gender and race. This critical genealogy of the body's production in aesthetic and urban modernity challenges dominant cultural assumptions about sexual difference. Its performative understanding of poetic and social discourse—as producing the bodies that they purport merely to designate—also, what is more important, offers a point of resistance to narratives of modernism as an essentially masculinist aesthetic movement predicated on the dissolution of reference and the erasure of the body. My discussions of Rachilde and Despentes—and their revisions of such masculine figures of quest—are offered in the hopes of opening this narrative up to alternate readings.

2. For a feminist counterviolent reading of Baudelaire by an English author, see Angela Carter's "Black Venus," a brilliant revisionist account of Charles Baudelaire's relationship with Jeanne Duval from the latter's perspective.

3. For a useful biography that situates Rachilde within the cultural current of her time, see Hawthorne, *Rachilde and French Women's Authorship,* which also has a detailed discussion of the circumstances of the publication of *Monsieur Vénus* (89–99).

4. See Barbara Spackman for an analysis of the rhetoric of sickness and of its ideological inflections in Baudelaire and the decadent imagination.

5. For a discussion of the "mise en discours" of sexuality in nineteenth-century history, see Foucault's *Histoire de la sexualité,* vol. 1, *La Volonté de savoir.*

6. There is a considerable body of criticism on the subject of hysteria in nineteenth-century France. For important interdisciplinary work on this topic, see Didi-Huberman, *Invention de l'hysterie,* Beizer, *Ventriloquized Bodies,* Matlock, *Scenes of Seduction,* and Ender, *Sexing the Mind.*

7. The role-playing Eliante's most compelling performance is, after all, the staging of her death. While juggling before her lover, she plunges one of the knives into her throat. The macabre final image of blood staining her throat like cosmetic paint may perhaps celebrate her embodiment of fusion between nature and artifice so cherished by the decadents. But her spectacular death suggests that if life is a stage, nevertheless, its scripts forbid such self-invention, masquerade, and play.

8. In *La Marquise de Sade,* for example, Mary Barbe awakens to the world's violence through the trauma of witnessing the slaughter of a bull whose blood will

be drunk by her mother. Raised in a militaristic, patriarchal family, Mary in turn witnesses her mother die in labor so that her son may live, just as her father—a colonel under Napoléon III—dies at the front during the Franco-Prussian war.

9. For an analysis of Barrès's preface as short-circuiting—or providing an antidote to—Rachilde's subversive text, see Rogers, *Fictions du scandale*, 239–62. See also Janet Beizer's astute reading of Barrès's preface as a strategy of hystericization that participates in a broader nineteenth-century preoccupation that Foucault termed as a "mise en discours" of sexuality: "Barrès's comments on Rachilde (on the novel as woman) constitute a virtual mapping of the power/knowledge apparatus Foucault calls the 'hystericization of the female body': a three-pronged strategy by which a woman's body is equated with sexuality, appropriated by pathology, and identified with the social body (which I take to mean language, among other things)" (232). In an analysis of Rachilde's subversive use of italics in *Monsieur Vénus,* Beizer goes on to show that Rachilde's novel prefigures and ironizes its own reception, thus defamiliarizing the horizon of expectations set up by Barrès's preface: "*Monsieur Vénus* is about the male colonization of female textuality and of woman *as* textuality: it is a novel that parodies its own reception, writes the intrusive reader into its text" (Beizer, *Ventriloquized Bodies*, 232).

10. See de Man's reading of Rousseau's reworking of *Le Roman de la rose* in "The Rhetoric of Temporality," 202. For an analysis of the sexual politics of the allegory of the rose, see Guynn, "Authorship and Sexual/Allegorical Violence."

11. For a discussion of Platonic and Neoplatonic idealism as a privileging of matter over form that is embedded in a metaphorics of gender, see Teskey, *Allegory and Violence*, 14–31.

12. When faced with Eliante's refusal to disrobe before him, Léon provokes her by claiming she must have leprosy. Yet, while Léon adopts Baudelairean lenses to read the authentic body behind the glaze of fashion and cosmetics, imagining it either in terms of the marmoreal perfection of Baudelaire's "La Beauté" or the leprous decay of "Une Charogne," Eliante herself retains her impenetrable aura of mystery until her death.

13. Rachilde, *L'Animale*, 34. Hereafter cited as *A,* followed by the page number, unless source is clear from the preceding text.

14. The exquisite, gastronomical excesses that accompany Laure's conception are described as poisoning the blood that courses through her veins: "À l'état latent, ils infuserent dans ces veines bleues, vertes à force d'être bleues, tous les poisons sensuels avec la science miraculeuse des caresses et avec l'appétit de tous les amours" (*A,* 33). See Baudelaire's "À celle qui est trop gaie" (one of the condemned pieces), which concludes on the image of the poet wounding his beloved in order to infuse her with his venom (*OC,* 1: 157).

15. See T. J Clark's discussion of the exchange between Baudelaire and Manet on the latter's *Olympia*: "*Olympia,* as Baudelaire described it in his letter, was a picture of a nude woman with a Negress and a cat. The poet pretended to doubt the

latter detail—'est-ce un chat, décidément ?'—which might suggest that it was added to the picture after he left for Brussels, or simply that he raised his eyebrows at the thought of such an overtly Baudelairean gesture" (*Painter of Modern Life,* 85).

16. Laure describes Lucien Séchard to the priest in terms that are steeped in imagery from Baudelaire's *charogne:* "Tenez, mon père, avez-vous rencontré quelque fois des chiens crevés sur votre chemin, le long d'un sentier, dans les champs ? J'en ai vu un, quand j'étais petite fille, près d'une ferme où je passais mes vacances, et ce chien mort avait les yeux bouffis, pleins d terre, garnis d'insectes grouillants, de brins d'herbe sèches. . . . Eh bien, mon père, le regard de mon amant est ainsi, je vous le jure, il a l'oeil du chien mort" (*A,* 93).

17. "La mécanique nous aura tellement américanisés, le progrès aura si bien atrophié en nous toute la partie spirituelle, que rien parmi les rêveries sanguinaires, sacrilèges, ou anti-naturelles des utopistes ne pourra être comparé à ses résultats positifs" (*OC,* 1: 665).

18. For a decadent iconography of lions and felines engaged in bestial relations with women, see Dijkstra, *Idols of Perversity,* chap. 9, "Gynanders and Genetics: Connoisseurs of Bestiality and Serpentine Delights: Leda, Circe, and the Cold Caresses of the Sphinx" (291–97). Rachilde is certainly not alone in exploring erotic connections between women and felines. See, e.g., José-Maria de Hérédia's sonnet "Ariane" in *Les Trophées* (1893), a graphic depiction of Ariadne's erotic ride on a tiger's back.

19. "Un Dandy ne fait rien. Vous figurez-vous un Dandy parlant au peuple, excepté pour le bafouer ?" (*OC,* 1: 684). The dandy's stance of resistance is not without its contradictions, since it was precisely as a consumer of goods (clothes, toiletries, knickknacks) that he purported to challenge a consumer-driven market. For an analysis of the dandy's relation to the marketplace, see Garelick, *Rising Star.*

20. Foucault argues that Baudelaire's ironic heroization of the present exemplifies a specifically post-Enlightenment scrutiny of one's historical mode of being. The dandy personifies this "modern" spirit of permanent critique, challenging the givenness of the self and the natural flow of history itself. Yet these modalities of resistance (to the vision of history as progress and of the humanist subject as an interiority to be discovered) are not political interventions with oppositional effects in the social domain. The literary text activates this spirit of permanent critique, but in modalities that resist transmission into the public sphere: "Cette héroïsation ironique du présent, ce jeu de la liberté avec le réel pour sa transfiguration, cette élaboration ascétique de soi, Baudelaire ne conçoit pas qu'ils puissent avoir lieu dans la société elle même ou dans le corps politique. Ils ne peuvent se produire que dans un lieu autre que Baudelaire appelle l'art" (Foucault, "Qu'est-ce que les Lumières ?" 571).

21. Several critics have offered compelling readings of *Monsieur Vénus* as an interrogation, if not a deconstruction, of established categories of gender. For Diana Holmes, Rachilde's treatment of gender as a "free floating artifice" in *Monsieur*

Vénus deals a subversive blow to the compulsory order of sex and gender, such that, "Anti-feminist as she was, Rachilde's work undermines contemporary orthodoxy on the gender divide" (165). Rita Felski reads this text as a "performance of the perverse" (*Gender of Modernity,* 193) and its theme of transvestism as a "governing metaphor for the formulaic, iterable, and hence transferable nature of gender identity" (200). Janet Beizer proposes that rather than merely inverting oppositions of gender and sexuality, Rachilde's irony disperses the conventions that undergird such oppositions. Teasing out the multiple interpretations generated by the text's citationality, its use of italics, and its framing by Barrès, Beizer illuminates the ambiguities of Rachilde's mimicry of established discourses on sexual difference, such as the hystericization of the female body. Her careful attention to the interpretive volatility of irony itself and the resistance that such a mode poses to ideological readings, is consonant with my approach to irony as a counterviolence open to heterogeneous readings. What I wish to stress is the novel's interrogation of the violence that inheres in decadent aestheticism (one worked out through Baudelairean intertexts, among other citational references). While my reading addresses the gender dislocations performed by this interrogation, it also seeks to recover an experience of shame and vulnerability embedded in the narrative's portrayal of the violated body.

22. For a discussion of class as a repressed—if not disavowed—category in Rachilde's text that problematizes her ludic play with other determinations of identity, see Felski, *Gender of Modernity,* 201–2.

23. For a detailed reading of the palimpsestic quality of Jacques's body, see Beizer, *Ventriloquized Bodies,* 254: "In and of himself neither poet nor poem, artist or painting, he is instead a periodically reinscribed tablet or canvas passed back and forth in an ongoing conversation between Raoule and Raittolbe."

24. Schor, *George Sand and Idealism,* 20, links Rachilde's automaton to Villiers's "L'Eve future."

25. As Sedgwick, *Touching Feeling,* 36, puts it, "Shame floods into being as a moment, a disruptive moment, in a circuit of identity-constituting identificatory communication." Shame thus marks a simultaneous moment of painful individuation *and* of uncontrolled relationality.

26. This may be why Giorgio Agamben views shame as subjectivity's most intimate tonality: "In shame," Agamben suggests, "the subject thus has no other content than its desubjectification; it becomes oblivious to its own disorder, its own oblivion as subject. This double movement, which is both subjectification and desubjectification, is shame" (*Remnants of Auschwitz,* 106).

27. Virginie Despentes quoted by Marie-France Etchegoin in "Quand les femmes disent tout," *Nouvel Observateur,* no. 1907 (May 29, 2001): 6.

28. See Alpozzo, "Roman rock," for a commentary that associates Despentes with writers such as Charles Bukowski, and, more recently, Philippe Djian (author of *37,2 le matin*) and Vincent Ravalec: "Force est de constater que dans ces livres la

musique est omniprésente, que les histoires se déroulent assez souvent dans des milieux rocks, hards ou punks, et à l'image des romans de l'auteur nippon Murakami Ryû, ou de la prose de l'américain Denis Johnson par exemple, la vision apocalyptique du monde moderne, la violence ahurissante qui est insufflée dans les descriptions comme dans l'écriture, traduisent bien cette réelle déconnexion, ce réel désaveu d'une littérature convenue, c'est-à-dire, bon chic bon genre. On admettra alors, malgré ses récentes déclarations (Technickart n°61) que Virginie Despentes a tout de l'écrivain rock, version trash. De *Baise-moi,* en passant par *Les chiennes savantes* et aujourd'hui *Teen spirit,* Virginie Despentes écrit selon des critères de l'école américaine : découpage cinématographique de l'action, un débraillé volontaire de la syntaxe et du vocabulaire."

29. Ironically, the so-called apolitical nihilism of this generation has been instrumental in resurrecting the question of "engagement" and literature in the public arena. See, e.g., the scandal around Michel Houellebecq's novel *Les Particules élémentaires.*

30. As Stéphane Spoiden has remarked about the film version of *Baise-moi:* "Pour Despentes, la revendication féministe fondamentale, sous quelque forme et sophistication qu'on lui ait donné, a peu changé la condition des femmes depuis les années 60. Dans le contexte culturel des ouvrages de Despentes, c'est-à-dire la zone et la culture banlieusarde de base, où le mot féministe est tout à fait étranger, cela se traduit par la permanence des attitudes dans la vie de ses personnages (féminins) qui sont souvent maltraités ou qui se prostituent depuis leur jeune âge. Dans *Baise-moi,* cette situation est représentée pour une des protagonistes par un viol insoutenable et pour l'autre, prostituée, par un ras-le-bol de se vendre à des hommes qu'elle trouve infâmes. . . . [O]n aura donc affaire dans ce film à une répétition désespérée, hard et destroy (selon les termes désormais utilisés en France pour caractériser ce genre d'oeuvres) de ce même message de revendication égalitaire" (Spoiden, "No Man's Land" 104).

31. "Trois femmes s'emparent du sexe."

32. For a cogent critique of how the film version of *Baise-moi* falls short of the ethical dilemmas raised in the novel, see Reynaud, "Baise-moi: An Angry yet Feminist Reaction."

33. That Manu incarnates the most disparaging attributes assigned to women by Baudelaire is suggested at several points in the narrative, where she must play the "savage" to the "bcbg" persona occasionally donned by Nadine. At one point, Nadine remarks that Manu is disheveled like a homeless person. Manu responds, "C'est ma vraie nature qui revient au galop," to which Nadine replies: "Ouais, soit t'as le naturel très fort, soit t'a pas fait d'effort pour le vernis" (Despentes, *Baise-moi,* 213). Hereafter cited as *BM,* followed by the page number, unless the source is clear from the text.

34. Karla's shrill demand that she justify her passivity, read here as an inconceivable lack of regard for her personhood, is itself shown to be suicidal. As their

assailants drive away, she waves her fist at them, and they turn around and run her down.

35. See Laura Brown, "Not Outside the Range," 100–112. See also Herman, *Trauma and Recovery,* chap. 1. While I find the category of insidious trauma immensely valuable in addressing the intersections between psychic, bodily, and less visible, structural, forms of violence, I am nevertheless cautious about the over-generalization of trauma as a model for thinking about violence. Katherine MacKinnon's work, for example, has been important in identifying the imbrication of sex and violence in law, culture, and everyday life. However, her emphasis on sexual violence as a ubiquitous trauma that defines gender itself risks positioning "women" exclusively in terms of their vulnerability to heterosexual violation, and consequently, through their victimization by sexual trauma: "Given the statistical realities [of rape], all women live all the time under the shadow of the threat of sexual abuse. . . . Given the statistical realities, much of women's sexual lives will occur under post-traumatic stress" (MacKinnon, *Towards a Feminist Theory of the State,* 149). My thanks to Colleen Pearl for pointing out this passage and for illuminating conversations both on this issue and in relation to *Baise-moi.*

36. As Susan J. Brison has shown in her powerful book *Aftermath,* rape is a trauma that dismantles traditional philosophical conceptions of personal identity, which rely on the continuity of one's memory of selfhood or of one's body as a constant over time. Survivors of rape have undergone such a violation of their psychic and bodily integrity that they frequently describe this breach as dividing them into separate beings. Brison underscores the importance of creating personal, social, and institutional spaces for the victim to narrate the events to a community of witnesses. Speech, narrative, and audience play a crucial role in the integration of traumatic experience and the restoration of a sense of psychic cohesion. One of the questions posed by Despentes's description of Manu's rape, then, is what happens when a subject has no prior sense of psychic integrity, when violation is constitutive of that person's emergence into social being? How are we to understand, or even feel compassion for an experience that takes us so far outside the range of normative views of psychic integrity and personal dignity?

37. In "Girls Just Want to End Oppression," an interview with Nigel Andrews in the *Financial Times,* April 11, 2002, Despentes discusses the censorship of her film in relation to the trials of Baudelaire and Flaubert: "Maybe we were naïve, but we didn't expect a fuss. Least of all in France which is supposed to be open-minded. We have a tradition of censorship—Flaubert, Baudelaire—but also of overcoming it."

38. As Walter Benjamin noted, "The figure of the lesbian woman belongs among Baudelaire's heroic exemplars." For Benjamin, Baudelaire's fascination with lesbians and their androgyny responds to a general cultural disquiet over women entering the workforce and challenging traditional conceptions of femininity: "The nineteenth century began openly and without reserve to include women in

the process of commodity production. The theoreticians were united in their opinion that her specific femininity was thereby endangered; masculine traits must necessarily manifest themselves in women after a while. Baudelaire affirms these traits. At the same time, however, he seeks to free them from the domination of the economy" (Benjamin, *Arcades Project*, 318).

39. Despentes's narrative may foreclose lesbianism, but it does represent incest. One of the characters, Fatima, has incestuous relations with both her father and, later, her brother, in a sexual configuration reminiscent of Baudelaire's *L'Invitation au voyage* and its address to "Mon enfant, ma soeur."

40. Despentes thus belongs to a new generation of feminists who refuse to condemn pornography and in fact redeem the pornographic medium as a space for the exploration of female desire. This is, of course, a striking departure from feminist condemnations such as that of MacKinnon, *Feminism Unmodified*, which argues for the inextricable links between pornography and sexual violence, between the representation and the enactment of violation. Despentes, however, questions this conflation of representation and practice and claims that the representation of violence through a medium such as cinema can serve as a critique of social life. For a series of interviews with female directors of films deemed "pornographic," such as Breillat and Despentes—among others—who argue for the need to reclaim the medium for woman-centered explorations of sexuality, see Marielle Nitoslawska's documentary *Bad Girl* (Cinema Guild, 2001).

41. Mazauric, "Culture populaire censurée," makes this point in the context of the film version: "Quand les bourgeois parlent de la misère, la compassion et l'humanitarisme sont consensuels. Quand les pauvres en parlent comme ils la vivent, la misère est choquante et la violence, crue, dérange. Cachez donc ce film que l'on ne saurait voir, parce qu'il ose montrer un quotidien dont on ne peut décemment faire une oeuvre : chômage, racisme, sexisme, viol, crime."

42. Again, Mazauric conveys the ideological stakes of Despentes's hypernaturalist representation of violence: "Film vengeur, enfin, sur la démesure fantasmatique et symbolique d'une réponse à la violence qui serait aussi violente que la violence elle-même. Dans une esthétique punk, en réponse à un univers sans éthique, la loi du talion qui règle notre monde peut provoquer cela, et nous pouvons nous préparer à cette extrémité : que reste-t-il des valeurs morales dont se targuent justement les censeurs de *Baise-moi* dans une société qui provoque et finalement admet cette misère-là" (ibid.).

Chapter 5: Broken Engagements

Epigraphs: Baudelaire, "Exposition universelle (1855)," *OC*, 2: 577; Camus, *Essais*, ed. Quillot and Faucon, 1427 (all further citations of Camus's nonfiction refer to this edition, abbreviated as *E*).

1. For Camus, the notion of "étrangeté," or disjuncture within and between

selves, forms the ontological and ethical basis for rebellion: "Le premier progrès d'un esprit saisi d'étrangeté est donc de reconnaitre qu'il partage cette étrangeté avec tous les hommes, et que la réalité humaine, dans sa totalité, souffre de cette distance par rapport à soi et au monde." *E,* 482.

2. By August 1945, Camus had declared that the purges were a complete failure: "il est certain désormais que l'épuration en France est non seulement manquée, mais encore déconsidérée. Le mot épuration était déjà assez pénible en lui-même. La chose est devenu odieuse. . . . L'echec en tous cas est complet." *E,* 289–90.

3. See Camus's essays on Algeria, gathered under the heading "Chroniques algériennes (1939–1958)," and in particular, "Algérie 1958" which dismisses the possibility of an independent Algeria, and proposes instead a federalist model that would give proportionate representations to Arab and French Algerians (*E,* 1011–18). Conor Cruise O'Brien's *Albert Camus of Europe and Africa* gives a damning critique of Camus's Eurocentric representation of Algeria, a critique taken one step further in Edward Said's "Camus and the French Imperial Experience." In an analysis that nuances Barthes's designation of the style of *L'Étranger* as "écriture blanche," Said argues that the neutrality of Camus's style glossed over the contradictions of French-occupied Algeria. Camus's literary output, for Said, is complicit with the imperialist, colonial project in Algeria: it "inflects, refers to, consolidates, and renders more precise the nature of the French enterprise there" (173). For a reevaluation of Camus's "colonialism" that delves into the complexity of his representations of Algeria, see David Carroll's forthcoming book, *Postcolonial Camus.* See also Carroll's article, "Camus's Algeria."

4. Hoederer: "Moi, j'ai les mains sales. Jusqu'aux coudes. Je les ai plongées dans la merde et dans le sang" (Sartre, *Mains sales,* 200).

5. See Judt, *Past Imperfect,* 101–16.

6. The rift between Sartre and Camus dated back to the publication of "Humanisme et terreur" in *Les Temps modernes,* which Camus read as an apology for the purges. See Todd, *Albert Camus,* 423.

7. *E,* 628. Camus's vision of dialectical materialism had been shaped by Kojève's presentation of Hegel and of historical progress as a terroristic battle for sovereignty. For the influence of Kojève's reading of Hegel on French intellectuals, see Descombes's *Le Même et l'autre.*

8. In his notes to the Pléiade edition, Roger Quillot recounts this discussion of Camus's *L'Étranger:* "Et le titre, dira-t-on ? J'avais, pour ma part, supposé que Camus l'avait emprunté à Baudelaire. S'il y avait eu emprunt, me répondit Camus, il était inconscient et de réminiscence" (Camus, *Théâtre, récits, nouvelles,* 1916). Subsequent references to Camus's fictional works are to this edition, cited as *T.*

9. The circumstances of this rupture are well known. Jeanson's negative review of Camus's essay had appeared in *Les Temps modernes,* leading to a defensive response by Camus, which was addressed not to Jeanson, but to Sartre, as the director of the journal, who in turn wrote a public letter harshly criticizing Camus's

prosecutorial methods in the letter itself (his refusal to address Jeanson was taxed as a form of rhetorical assassination). The ensuing exchange did not address the questions so urgently raised by *L'Homme révolté* but instead became a bitter *règlement de comptes* in which Camus was derided for his philosophical incompetence, historical naïveté, and ceremonious style. For a detailed examination of this breach, see Aronson, *Sartre and Camus.*

10. See Sartre, "Réponse à Albert Camus," *Les Temps modernes,* no. 82 (August 1952) 352. Sartre's "Réponse" is hereafter cited in the text and notes as *TM.*

11. *TM* 353. Sartre's diagnosis of Baudelaire as a fruitless rebel rather than a revolutionary is replicated five years later in his indictment of Camus as a mere "abstraction de révolté": "C'est au sein du monde établi que Baudelaire affirme sa singularité. . . . Mais précisément, il s'agit d'une révolte et non d'un acte révolutionnaire. Le révolutionnaire veut changer le monde, il le dépasse vers l'avenir, vers un order de valeurs qu'il invente ; le révolté a soin de maintenir intacts les abus dont il souffre pour pouvoir se révolter contre eux. Il y a toujours en lui les éléments d'une mauvaise conscience et commme un sentiment de culpabilité." (Sartre, *Baudelaire,* 49–50). Camus's Clamence will provide a spectacular illustration of this sterile rebellion steeped in bad faith and culpability. For a discussion of Sartre's essay on Baudelaire and of the debate it sparked (notably with Bataille) on the definition of poetry, see Blood, *Baudelaire and the Aesthetics of Bad Faith,* 57–93.

12. The character of Jean-Baptiste Clamence has often been read as an exercise in self-mortification, in which Camus crucifies the persona Sartre attributed to him. See Roger Quillot's commentary: "Puisqu'on le dénonçait, Camus allait clouer au pilori, non pas lui-même mais le personnage qu'on lui attribuait ; du même coup, l'injustice de ses contemporains éclaterait elle aussi" (*E,* 2011).

13. Sartre had already discussed Baudelaire's famous "dolorisme" in his psychobiography of the poet. An astute reader, he had also noted traces of Baudelaire in Camus's earlier works, traces that situated the former *résistant* within the tradition of French classicism and its hostility to history: "Bref vous restez dans notre grande tradition classique qui, depuis Descartes et si l'on excepte Pascal, est toute entière hostile à l'histoire. Mais vous faisiez enfin la synthèse entre la jouissance esthétique, le désir, le bonheur et l'héroïsme, entre la contemplation comblée et le devoir, *entre la plénitude gidienne et l'insatisfaction baudelairienne*" (Sartre, *TM,* 347; emphasis added).

14. See Gay-Crosier, *Albert Camus,* for a timely reassessment of *L'Homme révolté* that underscores the importance of irony in Camus's view of rebellion as a "négation affirmative."

15. "Il est certain que si l'on veut creuser cette situation, on trouvera au fond de la pensée du rieur un certain orgueil inconscient. C'est là le point de départ : *moi,* je ne tombe pas ; *moi,* mon pied est ferme et assuré. Ce n'est pas *moi* qui commetrais la sottise de ne pas voir un trottoir interrompu ou un pavé qui barre le chemin." Baudelaire, "De l'essence du rire" (*OC,* 2: 531).

16. *T,* 1515–16. "Ce n'est point l'homme qui tombe qui rit de sa propre chute, à moins qu'il ne soit un philosophe," declares the analyst of 'De l'essence du rire' (*OC,* 2: 532). This declaration is echoed in Clamence's portrait of laughter as the painful lucidity that only the contemplative mind can bear: "Voilà ce qu'aucun homme (sinon ceux qui ne vivent pas, je veux dire les *sages*) ne peut supporter" (*T,* 1516).

17. In his *Paradis artificiels,* Baudelaire describes the "victorieuse monomanie" engendered by hashish as a transformation of all phenomena into allegories of self-hood: "Expliquerai-je comment, sous l'empire du poison, mon homme se fait bientôt le centre de l'univers ? comment il devient l'expression vivante et outrée du proverbe qui dit que la passion rapporte tout à elle ? . . . Personne ne s'étonnera qu'une pensée finale, sûpreme, jaillisse du cerveau du rêveur : « *Je suis devenu Dieu* ! »" (*OC,* 1: 436–37).

18. *T,* 1547–48. Clamence is also a degraded version of Caligula, who transforms his empire into a specular reflection of his desire. This specularity is explicit in the use of the mirror in Camus's play: Caligula first erases all other figures in the mirror in a symbolic inauguration of his reign of terror, and at the play's conclusion, smashes its surface. Caligula and Clamence descend from a romantic lineage of self-deifying Baudelairean despots. They illustrate the dangerous intersection of an aesthetics of existence with a politics of terror. *Caligula* explicitly associates the intransigent idealism of lyricism and logic with murder, and indeed the whole play could be read as a meditation on Cherea's remark to Caesonia: "Nous discutons sur le point de savoir si la poésie doit être meurtrière ou non" (*T,* 43).

19. *T,* 1550. Anterior versions of *La Chute* emphasized the laughter of the interlocutor as a sign of resistance to Clamence's myth of penitence: "Ne riez pas ! Assez ! Vous riez trop." MS GO6 (10): 146 (Institut mémoires de l'édition contemporaine, Paris–Caen).

20. Shoshana Felman's influential reading of *La Chute* identifies Clamence's passivity before the drowning and his subsequent refusal to alert the authorities or to read the papers as recording the loss of a community of witnessing in wartime and postwar Europe. *La Chute* thus becomes a document of the erasure of history, as well as a testimony to the impossibility of representing history. Felman's broader analysis of the unspeakable nature of the Shoah and the silence it induces shifts from de Man to Camus/Clamence, to Primo Levi, thereby suggesting that their distinct predicaments in the face of the Holocaust are somehow analogous. This point is made through a series of rhetorical displacements reminiscent of Clamence's own erosion of such distinctions. See my Afterword for a more extensive discussion of the limitations of this approach. Dominick LaCapra has offered an alternative reading of *La Chute* that sees Algeria as its true hidden subtext in *History and Memory after Auschwitz,* 73–94. My own reading questions attempts to anchor *La Chute* in one particular historical framework, since the slippages between different contexts seem at the core of Camus's reflection on the complex re-

lations between allegory and history. I discuss this point in greater detail in the conclusion.

21. For an in-depth comparison of Camus's political thought with Arendt's, see Isaac, *Arendt, Camus, and Modern Rebellion.*

22. For a fascinating cultural analysis of hygiene as a postwar trope of domestic modernization that both represents and represses France's displaced relations to its colonies (specifically Algeria), see Ross, *Fast Cars, Clean Bodies,* chap. 2, "Hygiene and Modernization."

23. This vision of the modern bourgeois subject's blind consent to his own subjection echoes Baudelaire's condemnation of the popular consensus before the empire's authoritarianism and the forces of market production, as we saw in Chapters 2 and 3.

24. This anecdote appears both in the essay on rebellion and in *La Chute:* "Le cri pur de la maternité est lui-même tué, comme chez cette mère grecque qu'un officier força de choisir celui de ses trois fils qui serait fusillé" (*E,* 589). "Savez-vous que dans mon petit village, au cours d'une action de représailles, un officier allemand a courtoisement prié une vieille femme de bien vouloir choisir celui de ses deux fils qui serait fusillé comme otage ?" (*T,* 1481).

25. Camus's portrait of the intellectual as collaborator anticipates Primo Levi's analysis of the intellectual's defeatism before Nazism: "by his very nature, the intellectual . . . tends to become an accomplice of Power, and therefore approves of it. He tends to follow in Hegel's footsteps and deify the State, any State; the sole fact of its existing justifies its existence" (*Drowned and the Saved,* 143–44). Clamence's realism, or historicism (which legitimates a state of affairs because of its existence) was also central to Sartre's definition of the collaborator back in 1945: "Le collaborateur est atteint de cette maladie intellectuelle qu'on peut appeler l'historicisme. L'histoire nous apprend en effet qu'un grand événement collectif soulève, dés son apparition, des haines et des résistances, qui, pour être parfois fort belles, seront considérées plus tard comme inefficaces. . . . J'ai cent fois relevé chez les plus honnêtes professeurs d'histoires, dans les livres les plus objectifs, cette tendance à entériner l'événement accompli simplement parce-qu'il est accompli" (*Sit.,* 3: 52). Sartre argued that "[c]e choix de l'attitude historique et cette passéification continue du présent est typique de la collaboration" (ibid., 54–55). A decade after this analysis of collaboration, Sartre's own position on ends and means in relation to communism was itself an instance of "historicism," only not through a "making past" of the present but, rather, through its "making future." As Bernard-Henri Lévy notes in his critique of Sartre's later politics and its betrayal of earlier philosophical positions, "Qu'est-ce qu'un collaborateur" indicts the very position that Sartre was to endorse as a communist "compagnon de route." Lévy points out the irony in his reading of Sartre's essay: "Mais la description, comment ne pas le voir ? peut s'appliquer de la même manière, sans en changer un mot, à tous les collaborateurs de tous les totalitarismes, jusques et y compris, bien sûr, le totali-

tarisme soviétique. L'auteur de ces lignes se reniera, bien sûr ! Et la question sera de savoir par quel mystère il pourra—si vite ! Quelques mois plus tard, à peine !—oublier cette démonstration lumineuse pour, s'agissant, justement, de l'URSS, « se placer pour estimer ses actes dans le plus lointain avenir » et « masquer le caractère insoutenable » des camps en « sautant quelques siècles », en les « contemplant de loin » et en les « remplaçant dans l'Histoire » " (Lévy, *Siècle de Sartre,* 352).

26. See my discussion of *L'Homme révolté* and its critique of romanticism and terror as founded upon the plasticity of the human body.

27. This is particularly true by the time of the writing of *La Chute,* when Camus had been accused by Jeanson and Sartre of appropriating the voices of dead *résistants* for his argument in *L'Homme révolté.*

28. See LaCapra's reading of the Algerian subtext in *La Chute* in *History and Memory after Auschwitz* and Ungar's pages on Camus's novel in *Scandal and After-effect.* Both read the incident of the detention camp in North Africa as an allusion to French colonialism and argue for a historically differentiated reading of Camus's allegory, incorporating traumas other than that of the Holocaust.

29. For instance, Jeanine's ecstatic merging with the Algerian landscape in "La Femme adultère" provides an "embodied" solution to the otherwise unresolvable dilemmas of her position as an alien(ated) white, French-speaking woman on Algerian soil. For an excellent analysis of this tale and more generally of Camus's fictional Algeria, see Carroll, "Camus's Algeria."

30. Camus in 1951 had already evoked the massacre of the innocents in terms of the Holocaust, "La différence entre le massacre des Innocents et nos règlements de comptes est une différence d'échelle. . . . Voilà ce qu'est devenue la terre de l'humanisme que, malgré toutes les protestations, il faut continuer d'appeler l'ignoble Europe" (*E,* 726). Yet, as LaCapra has argued, it would be reductive to read *La Chute* primarily as an allegory of the concentration camps. The allusions to torture powerfully resonate with the reality of French measures in Algeria. By the time of the novel's writing, Camus was writing a series of articles on the unrest in Algeria for *L'Express* (between 1955 and 1956) and evoked the suffering of Arab Algerians in terms of cries that had fallen on deaf French ears: "Qui fermait ses oreilles aux cris de la misère arabe, qui a permis que la répression de 1945 se passe dans l'indifférence, sinon la presse française dans son immense majorité ?" ("La Bonne Conscience," *E,* 974).

31. See Alain Resnais's documentary *Nuit et brouillard* (1955) for images of such barracks in Auschwitz.

32. In 1956, when *La Chute* was published, Camus's indictment of complicity would have resonated with the French civilians' refusal to reckon with torture and repression in Algeria. Yet the treatment of the Algerian question in *La Chute* is more complicated than a mea culpa for the plight of Arab Algerians. It is likely that Clamence the *juge-pénitent* also represents intellectuals such as Sartre and Jeanson whose support for the FLN "sacrificed" the French Algerians in expiation

for France's colonial history: "Si certains Français considèrent que, par ses entreprises coloniales, la France (et elle seule, au milieu de nations saintes et pures) est en état de péché historique, ils n'ont pas à désigner les Français d'Algérie comme victimes expiatoires (« Crevez, nous l'avons bien mérité ! »), ils doivent s'offrir eux-mêmes à l'expiations. *En ce qui me concerne, il me paraît dégoûtant de battre sa coulpe comme nos juges-pénitents, sur la poitrine d'autrui,* vain de condamner plusieurs siècles d'expansion européenne, absurde de comprendre dans la même malediction Christophe Colomb et Lyautey. Le temps des colonialismes est fini, il faut le savoir seulement et en tirer les conséquences" (*E*, 897–98; emphasis added).

33. See, e.g., Sartre's preface to Frantz Fanon's *Les Damnés de la terre.* Sartre's theoretical reflections on violence are highly attuned to the systemic reification of human beings under capitalist, colonial, and neocolonial exploitation. His defense of counterviolent practices deployed to restore a dispossessed subject's humanity is worth considering seriously in an era of perpetual war against terror. For a close and thorough investigation of Sartre's shifting theory of violence that also compares his stance to that of Camus, see Santoni, *Sartre on Violence.*

34. Sartre, *Responsabilité de l'écrivain,* 54.

35. These brief remarks on violence are made in the hopes of dislodging Sartre and Camus from the oppositions they continue to represent, between the "philosopher of praxis" and the literary moralist, between *engagement* and *témoignage,* and most recently, between the apologist and the critic of terror and terrorism. For the latter reading (of Camus as terrorism's critic), see Paul Berman's application of *L'Homme révolté* and its definition of totalitarian terror to Islamic fundamentalist terrorism. Berman's slanted account of terrorism as a new form of totalitarianism makes no mention of Camus's explicit critique of the systemic and invisible forms of terror wielded by an expansionist empire—represented by the Soviet Union in the 1950s and all too resonant with American unilateralism today. It is unfortunate that discussions of Sartre and Camus should continue to pivot on how history "gives reason" to one or to the other, as we see in Claudie and Jacques Broyelle's *Les Illusions retrouvées : Sartre a toujours raison contre Camus* or Bernard-Henri Lévy's more recent discussion of "l'affaire Camus" titled "Pourquoi l'on a, tout de même, raison d'avoir tort avec Sartre plutôt que raison avec Camus" (*Siècle de Sartre,* 415). It is more useful to consider these intellectuals together, and to negotiate between the positions they have come to represent, that is to say, between a philosophical and political approach to the problem of violence and an ethical as well as literary inquiry into its representational logics and human costs.

Afterword

1. These slippages are readily discerned in Felman's reading of *La Chute,* which transforms *le fait concentrationnaire*—the fact of the concentration-camp universe—into a transhistorical and metaphorical wound whose trace is to be found

in the gaps and silences of testimonies by survivors, primary and secondary witnesses, and fictional characters alike. For a critique of Felman's approach and its relations to trauma theory's deployment in Holocaust studies, see Sanyal, "Soccer Match in Auschwitz."

2. On the inexpressibility of human pain, see Scarry, *Body in Pain*.

3. "En somme, devant l'histoire et devant le peuple français, la grande gloire de Napoléon III aura été de prouver que le premier venu peut, en s'emparant du télégraphe et de l'Imprimerie nationale, gouverner une grande nation. Imbéciles sont ceux qui croient que de pareilles choses peuvent s'accomplir sans la permission du peuple" (*OC*, 1: 692).

4. As Sartre put it in his indictment of Camus's rhetorical procedures, "la terreur est une violence abstraite" (*Temps modernes*, 353).

5. The relations between violence and its representation remain a primordial concern for thinkers invested in connecting theories of power to the lived reality of its operations across the globe. In a timely reflection, Judith Butler expresses several aspects of violence—as a dynamic, interpersonal, and fundamentally corporeal condition—that I have attempted to pursue throughout the literary readings in this book: "Violence is surely a touch of the worst order, a way a primary human vulnerability to other humans is exposed in its most terrifying way, a way in which we are given over, without control, to the will of another, a way in which life itself can be expunged by the willful action of another. To the extent that we commit violence, we are acting on another, putting the other at risk, causing the other damage, threatening to expunge the other. In a way, we all live with this particular vulnerability, a vulnerability to a sudden address from elsewhere that we cannot preempt. This vulnerability, however, becomes highly exacerbated under certain social and political conditions, especially those in which violence is a way of life and the means to secure self-defense are limited" (Butler, *Precarious Life* 29).

6. I am adapting Adorno's remarks on the critical power of autonomous art in the age of kitsch to a discussion of the critical power of ironic art in an age of terror: "Even in the most sublimated work of art there is a hidden 'it should be otherwise.' . . . As eminently constructed and produced objects, works of art, even literary ones, point to a practice from which they abstain: the creation of a just life. . . . Today every phenomenon of culture, even if a model of integrity, is liable to be suffocated in the cultivation of kitsch. *Yet paradoxically in the same epoch it is to works of art that has fallen the burden of wordlessly asserting what is barred to politics*" (Adorno, "Commitment," 317–18; emphasis added).

Works Cited

Adorno, Theodor. *The Adorno Reader*. Edited by B. O'Connor. Oxford: Blackwell, 2000.

———. "Commitment." In *The Essential Frankfurt School Reader*. Edited by A. Arato and E. Gebhardt. New York: Continuum, 1992.

———. *Minima Moralia: Reflections from Damaged Life*. Translated by E. F. N. Jephcott. London: New Left Books, 1974.

———. *Prisms*. Translated by Samuel Weber and Shierry Weber. Cambridge, Mass.: MIT Press, 1981.

Agamben, Giorgio. *Remnants of Auschwitz: The Witness and the Archive*. Translated by Daniel Heller-Roazen. New York: Zone Books, 1999.

Alpozzo, Marc. "Le Roman rock : Une Révolte des formes," December 23, 2004. www.bellaciao.org/fr/article.php3?id_article=11556 (accessed August 20, 2005).

Aronson, Ronald. *Sartre and Camus: The Story of a Friendship and the Quarrel That Ended It*. Chicago: University of Chicago Press, 2004.

Baer, Ulrich. *Remnants of Song: Trauma and the Experience of Modernity in Charles Baudelaire and Paul Celan*. Stanford, Calif.: Stanford University Press, 2000.

Balzac, Honoré de. *Histoire des Treize*. 1833–35. Paris: GF Flammarion, 1988.

Barrows, Susanna. *Distorted Mirrors*. New Haven, Conn.: Yale University Press, 1981.

Bataille, Georges. *La Littérature et le mal*. Paris: Gallimard, 1990.

Baudelaire, Charles. *Correspondance*. 2 vols. Edited by Claude Pichois. Paris: Gallimard, 1973.

———. *Oeuvres complètes*. 2 vols. Bibliothèque de la Pléiade. Edited by Claude Pichois. Paris: Gallimard, 1975–76. Cited as *OC*.

Behler, Ernst. *Irony and the Discourse of Modernity*. Seattle: University of Washington Press, 1990.

Beizer, Janet. *Ventriloquized Bodies: Narratives of Hysteria in Nineteenth-Century France*. Ithaca, N.Y.: Cornell University Press, 1993.

Benjamin, Walter. *The Arcades Project*. Translated by Howard Eiland and Kevin McLaughlin. Cambridge, Mass.: Harvard University Press, Belknap Press, 1999.

———. *Charles Baudelaire: A Lyric Poet in the Era of High Capitalism*. Translated by Harry Zohn. New York: Verso, 1973, 1997.

———. *Charles Baudelaire : Un Poète lyrique à l'apogée du capitalisme*. Translated by Jean Lacoste. Paris: Payot, 1979.

————. *Gesammelte Schriften* Vol. 1. Edited by R. Tiedemann and H. Schweppenhäuser. Frankfurt a/M: Suhrkamp, 1974.

————. "On Some Motifs in Baudelaire." In id., *Illuminations,* trans. Harry Zohn, ed. Hannah Arendt. New York: Schocken Books, 1968.

Berman, Marshall. *All That Is Solid Melts into Air.* New York: Penguin Books, 1982.

Bernheimer, Charles. *Figures of Ill Repute: Representing Prostitution in Nineteenth-Century France.* Cambridge, Mass.: Harvard University Press, 1989.

Bersani, Leo. *Baudelaire and Freud.* Berkeley: University of California Press, 1977.

————. *The Culture of Redemption.* Cambridge, Mass.: Harvard University Press, 1990.

Bishop, Lloyd. *Romantic Irony in French Literature from Diderot to Beckett.* Nashville, Tenn.: Vanderbilt University Press, 1989.

Blin, Georges. *Le Sadisme de Baudelaire.* Paris: Corti, 1948.

Blood, Susan. *Baudelaire and the Aesthetics of Bad Faith.* Stanford, Calif.: Stanford University Press, 1997.

————. "Modernity's Curse." In *Baudelaire and the Poetics of Modernity,* ed. Patricia Ward and James Patty, 147–56. Nashville, Tenn.: Vanderbilt University Press, 2001.

Bonnefoy, Yves. "'La Belle Dorothée' or Poetry and Painting." Translated by Jan Plug. In *Baudelaire and the Poetics of Modernity,* ed. Patricia A. Ward and James S. Patty, 85–100. Nashville, Tenn.: Vanderbilt University Press, 2001.

Booth, Wayne C. *A Rhetoric of Irony.* Chicago: University of Chicago Press, 1974.

Bourgeois, René. *L'Ironie romantique : Spectacle et jeu de Mme de Staël à Gérard de Nerval.* Grenoble: Presses universitaires de Grenoble, 1974.

Bowlby, Rachel. *Just Looking: Consumer Culture in Dreiser, Gissing and Zola.* New York: Methuen, 1985.

Breton, André. *Manifestes du surréalisme.* Paris: Gallimard, 1979.

Brison, Susan J. *Aftermath: Violence and the Remaking of a Self.* Princeton, N.J.: Princeton University Press, 2001.

Brooks, Peter. *Body Work: Objects of Desire in Modern Narrative.* Cambridge, Mass.: Harvard University Press, 1993.

Brown, Laura. "Not Outside the Range: One Feminist Perspective on Psychic Trauma." In *Trauma: Explorations in Memory,* ed. Cathy Caruth, 100–112. Baltimore: Johns Hopkins University Press, 1995.

Brown, Wendy. *States of Injury: Power and Freedom in Late-Modernity.* Princeton, N.J.: Princeton University Press, 1995.

Broyelle, Claudie, and Jacques Broyelle. *Les Illusions retrouvées : Sartre a toujours raison contre Camus.* Paris: Grasset, 1982.

Buck-Morss, Susan. *The Dialectics of Seeing: Benjamin and the Arcades Project.* Cambridge, Mass.: MIT Press, 1989.

Burt, E. S. *Poetry's Appeal: Nineteenth-Century French Lyric and the Political Space.* Stanford, Calif.: Stanford University Press, 1999.

Burton, Richard. *Baudelaire and the Second Republic: Writing and Revolution.* Oxford: Clarendon Press; New York: Oxford University Press, 1991.

Butler, Judith. *Bodies That Matter: On the Discursive Limits of "Sex."* New York: Routledge, 1993.

———. *Excitable Speech: A Politics of the Performative.* New York: Routledge, 1997.

———. *Precarious Life: The Powers of Mourning and Violence.* New York: Verso, 2004.

Calinescu, Matei. *The Five Faces of Modernity.* Durham, N.C.: Duke University Press, 1987.

Camus, Albert. *Essais.* Edited by Roger Quillot and Louis Faucon. Bibliothèque de la Pléiade. Paris: Gallimard, 1965. Cited as *E.*

———. *Théâtre, récits, nouvelles d'Abert Camus.* Edited by Roger Quillot. Bibliothèque de la Pléiade. Paris: Gallimard, 1962. Cited as *T.*

Carroll, David. "Camus's Algeria: Birthrights, Colonial Injustice, and the Fiction of a French-Algerian People." *Modern Language Notes* 112, 4 (1997): 517–49.

———. *Postcolonial Camus: Literature, Terrorism, Justice.* Forthcoming.

Carter, Angela. "Black Venus." In *Burning Your Boats: The Collected Short Stories,* 230–44. New York: Holt, 1996.

Caruth, Cathy. *Unclaimed Experience: Trauma, Narrative, and History.* Baltimore: Johns Hopkins University Press, 1995.

Chambers, Ross. "Baudelaire's Dedicatory Practice." *SubStance* 56 (1988): 5–17.

———. *Untimely Interventions: AIDS Writing, Testimonial, and the Rhetoric of Haunting.* Ann Arbor: University of Michigan Press, 2004.

———. *The Writing of Melancholy: Modes of Opposition in Early French Modernism.* Translated by Mary Seidman Trouille. Chicago: University of Chicago Press, 1993.

Clark, T. J. *The Absolute Bourgeois: Artists and Politics in France, 1848–1851.* Berkeley: University of California Press, 1973.

———. *The Painting of Modern Life: Paris in the Art of Manet and His Followers.* Princeton, N.J.: Princeton University Press, 1984.

Cohen, Margaret. *Profane Illumination: Benjamin and the Paris of Surrealist Revolution.* Berkeley: University of California Press, 1993.

Compagnon, Antoine. *Cinq paradoxes de la modernité.* Paris: Seuil, 1990.

Corbin, Alain. *Les Filles de noce : Misère sexuelle et prostitution.* Paris: Flammarion, 1982.

Crow, Thomas. *Emulation: Making Artists for Revolutionary France.* New Haven, Conn.: Yale University Press, 1995.

Cvetkovitch, Ann. *An Archive of Feeling: Trauma, Sexuality, and Lesbian Public Cultures.* Durham, N.C.: Duke University Press, 2003.

Dane, Joseph. *The Critical Mythology of Irony.* Athens: University of Georgia Press, 1991.

David, Marcel. *Fraternité et Révolution française, 1789–1799.* Paris: Aubier, 1987.

de Lauretis, Teresa. "The Violence of Rhetoric." In *The Violence of Representation: Literature and the History of Violence,* ed. Leonard Tennenhouse and Nancy Armstrong, 239–58. New York: Routledge, 1989.

de Man, Paul. *Allegories of Reading: Figural Language in Rousseau, Nietzsche, Rilke and Proust.* New Haven, Conn.: Yale University Press, 1979.

———. "Allegory and Irony in Baudelaire." In *Romanticism and Contemporary Criticism: The Gauss Seminars and Other Papers,* ed. E. S. Burt, K. Newmark, and A. Warminski, 101–19. Baltimore: Johns Hopkins University Press, 1993.

———. "Anthropomorphism and Trope in Lyric." In id., *The Rhetoric of Romanticism,* 239–62. New York: Columbia University Press, 1984.

———. "Literary History and Literary Modernity." In id., *Blindness and Insight: Essays in the Rhetoric of Contemporary Criticism,* 142–65. Minneapolis: Minnesota University Press, 1977.

———. "Lyric and Modernity." In id., *Blindness and Insight: Essays in the Rhetoric of Contemporary Criticism,* 166–86. Minneapolis: Minnesota University Press, 1977.

———. "The Rhetoric of Temporality." In id., *Blindness and Insight: Essays in the Rhetoric of Contemporary Criticism,* 187–228. Minneapolis: Minnesota University Press, 1977.

Deleuze, Gilles. *Sacher-Masoch: An Interpretation.* London: Faber & Faber, 1971.

Descombes, Vincent. *Le Même et l'autre : Quarante-cinq ans de philosophie française (1933–1978).* Paris: Minuit, 1978.

Despentes, Virginie. *Baise-moi.* Paris: J'ai lu, 1994.

Didi-Huberman, Georges. *L'Invention de l'hysterie : Charcot et l'iconographie photographique de la Salpêtrière.* Paris: Macula, 1982.

Dijkstra, Bram. *Idols of Perversity: Fantasies of Feminine Evil in the Turn of the Century.* New York: Oxford University Press, 1986.

Du Camp, Maxim. *Les Chants modernes.* Paris: Michel Lémy frères, 1855.

Dumas, Alexandre, père. *Georges.* Paris: Michel Lévy, 1848.

Ender, Evelyne. *Sexing the Mind: Nineteenth-Century Fictions of Hysteria.* Ithaca, N.Y.: Cornell University Press, 1994.

Evans, Margery. *Baudelaire and Intertextuality: Poetry at Crossroads.* Cambridge: Cambridge University Press, 1993.

Fanon, Frantz. *Les Damnés de la terre.* Paris: Gallimard, 1991.

———. *Peau noire, masques blancs.* Paris: Seuil, 1995.

Felman, Shoshana, and Laub, Dori. *Testimony: Crises of Witnessing in Literature, Psychonanalysis, and History.* New York: Routledge, 1992.

Felski, Rita. *The Gender of Modernity.* Cambridge, Mass.: Harvard University Press, 1995.

Flaubert, Gustave. *Le Dictionnaire des idées reçues.* Edited by E. L. Ferrère. Paris: L. Conard, 1913.

Foucault, Michel. *L'Histoire de la sexualité.* Vol. 1. Paris: Gallimard, 1976.

———. "Qu'est-ce que les Lumières ?" 1984. In *Dits et écrits*, vol. 4: *1954–1988*, ed. Daniel Défert and François Ewald. Paris: Gallimard NRF, 1994.

———. *Surveiller et punir : Naissance de la prison*. Paris: Gallimard, 1975. Translated by Alan Sheridan as *Discipline and Punish: The Birth of the Prison* (New York: Pantheon Books, 1977).

Les Français peints par eux-mêmes. 1841–42. Reprint. 2 vols. in 1. Paris: N.-J. Philippart, 1861.

Freud, Sigmund. "The Aetiology of Hysteria." 1896. In *The Standard Edition of the Complete Psychological Works of Sigmund Freud*, vol. 3, ed. and trans. James Strachey et al. London: Hogarth Press and Institute of Psycho-Analysis, 1962.

———. *Beyond the Pleasure Principle*. Translated and edited by James Strachey. New York: Norton, 1961.

Friedrich, Hugo. *La Structure de la poésie moderne*. Translated by Michel-François Demet. Paris: Denoël, 1976.

Furst, L. R. *Fictions of Romantic Irony*. Cambridge, Mass.: Harvard University Press, 1984.

Garelick, Rhonda K. *Rising Star: Dandyism, Gender and Performance in the Fin de Siècle*. Princeton, N.J.: Princeton University Press, 1998.

Gasarian, Gérard. *De loin tendrement : Étude sur Baudelaire*. Paris: H. Champion, 1996.

Gay-Crosier, Raymond. *Albert Camus : Paradigmes de l'ironie : Révolte et négation affirmative*. Toronto: Éditions Paratexte, 2000.

Gilman, Sander. *Difference and Pathology: Stereotypes of Sexuality, Race and Madness*. Ithaca, N.Y.: Cornell University Press, 1985.

Greenhalgh, Paul. *Ephemeral Vistas: The Expositions Universelles, Great Exhibitions, and World's Fairs, 1851–1939*. Manchester: Manchester University Press, 1998.

Guerlac, Suzanne. *The Impersonal Sublime: Hugo, Baudelaire, Lautréamont*. Stanford, Calif.: Stanford University Press, 1990.

———. *Literary Polemics: Bataille, Sartre, Valéry, Breton*. Stanford, Calif.: Stanford University Press, 1997.

Guynn, Noah D. "Authorship and Sexual/Allegorical Violence in Jean de Meun's *Roman de la rose*." *Speculum* 79 (2004): 628–59.

Habermas, Jürgen. *The Philosophical Discourse of Modernity: Twelve Lectures*. Cambridge, Mass.: MIT Press, 1987.

Handwerke, Gary. *Irony and Ethics in Narrative: From Schlegel to Lacan*. New Haven, Conn.: Yale University Press, 1985.

Hannoosh, Michele. "The Allegorical Artist and the Crises of History: Benjamin, Grandville, Baudelaire." *Word and Image* 10, 1 (1994): 38–54.

———. *Baudelaire and Caricature: From the Comic to an Art of Modernity*. University Park: Penn State University, 1992.

Hanssen, Beatrice. *Critique of Violence: Between Poststructuralism and Critical Theory*. New York: Routledge, 2000.

Harter, Deborah A. "Divided Selves, Ironic Counterparts: Intertextual Doubling in Baudelaire's 'L'héautontimoroumenos' and Poe's 'The Haunted Palace.'" *Comparative Literature Studies* 26, 1 (1989): 28–38.

Hartman, Geoffrey. *The Longest Shadow: In the Aftermath of the Holocaust*. Bloomington: Indiana University Press, 1996.

Hawthorne, Melanie C. *Rachilde and French Women's Authorship: From Decadence to Modernism*. Lincoln: University of Nebraska Press, 2001.

Hegel, G. W. F. *Aesthetics: Lectures on Fine Art*. Translated by T. M. Knox. Oxford: Clarendon Press, 1975.

Herman, Judith L. *Trauma and Recovery: The Aftermath of Violence—from Domestic Abuse to Political Terror*. New York: Basic Books, 1997.

Hiddleston, J. A. *Baudelaire and "Le Spleen de Paris."* Oxford: Oxford University Press, 1987.

Holland, Eugene. *Baudelaire and Schizoanalysis: The Sociopoetics of Modernism*. Cambridge: Cambridge University Press, 1993.

Holmes, Diana. *Rachilde: Decadence, Gender and the Woman Writer*. New York: Berg, 2001.

Hunt, Lynn. *The Family Romance of the French Revolution*. Berkeley: University of California Press, 1992.

Hutcheon, Linda. *Irony's Edge: The Theory and Politics of Irony*. London: Routledge, 1995.

Isaac, Jeffrey. *Arendt, Camus, and Modern Rebellion*. New Haven, Conn.: Yale University Press, 1994.

Jameson, Fredric. "Baudelaire as Modernist and Postmodernist: The Dissolution of the Referent and the Artificial Sublime." In id., *Lyric Poetry: Beyond New Criticism*. Ithaca, N.Y.: Cornell University Press, 1985.

———. "The Dialectics of Disaster." In *Dissent from the Homeland: Essays after September 11*, ed. S. Hauerwas and F. Lentricchia, 297–304. Durham, N.C.: Duke University Press, 2003.

———. *Postmodernism and the Cultural Logic of Late-Capitalism*. Durham, N.C.: Duke University Press, 1991.

———. *A Singular Modernity: Essay on the Ontology of the Present*. New York: Verso, 2002.

Jankélévitch, Vladimir. *L'Ironie*. Paris: Flammarion, 1964.

Johnson, Barbara. *Défigurations du langage poétique : La Seconde Révolution baudelairienne*. Paris: Flammarion, 1979.

Judt, Tony. *Past Imperfect: French Intellectuals, 1944–1956*. Berkeley: University of California Press, 1992.

Kaplan, Edward K. *Baudelaire's Prose Poems: The Esthetic, the Ethical, and the Religious in the Parisian Prowler*. Athens: University of Georgia Press, 1990.

Kierkegaard, Søren. *The Concept of Irony with Continual Reference to Socrates*.

Translated by Howard and Edna Hong. Princeton, N.J.: Princeton University Press, 1989.

Klein, Kerwin Lee. "On the Emergence of *Memory* in Historical Discourse." *Representations* 69 (Winter 2000): 127–50.

Knox, Norman. *The Word Irony and Its Context, 1500–1775.* Durham, N.C.: Duke University Press, 1961.

LaCapra, Dominick. *History and Memory after Auschwitz.* Ithaca, N.Y.: Cornell University Press, 1998.

———. *Soundings in Critical Theory.* Ithaca, N.Y.: Cornell University Press, 1989.

———. *Writing History, Writing Trauma.* Baltimore: Johns Hopkins University Press, 2001.

Leconte de Lisle, Charles-Marie. *Poèmes barbares.* 1862. Librairie Alphonse Lemerre, n.d.

Levaillant, Francois. *Voyage dans l'intérieur de l'Afrique par le cap de la Bonne-Espérance.* Paris: Imprimerie de Crapelet, 1803.

Levi, Primo. *The Drowned and the Saved.* New York: Vintage Books, 1989.

Lévy, Bernard-Henri. *Le Siècle de Sartre.* Paris: Grasset, 2000.

Leys, Ruth. *Trauma: A Genealogy.* Chicago: University of Chicago Press, 2000.

Lionnet, Françoise. "Reframing Baudelaire: Literary History, Biography, Post-colonial Theory, and Vernacular Languages." *Diacritics* 28, 3 (1998): 63–85.

Lucey, Michael. *The Misfit of the Family: Balzac and the Social Forms of Sexuality.* Durham, N.C.: Duke University Press, 1993.

MacInnes, John. *The Comic as Textual Practice in "Les Fleurs du mal."* Gainesville: University of Florida Press, 1988.

MacKinnon, Katherine. *Feminism Unmodified: Discourses on Life and Law.* Cambridge, Mass.: Harvard University Press, 1987.

———. *Towards a Feminist Theory of the State.* Cambridge, Mass.: Harvard University Press, 1989.

Maclean, Marie. *Narrative as Performance: The Baudelairean Experiment.* New York: Routledge, 1988.

Mallarmé, Stéphane. *Oeuvres.* Paris: Bordas, 1992.

Marcus, Sharon. *Apartment Stories: City and Home in Nineteenth-Century Paris and London.* Berkeley: University of California Press, 1999.

Marder, Elissa. *Dead Time: Temporal Disorders in the Wake of Modernity (Baudelaire and Flaubert).* Stanford, Calif.: Stanford University Press, 2001.

Marsan, Eugène. *Les Cannes de M. Paul Bourget : et Le Bon Choix de Philinte : Petit manuel de l'homme élégant.* Paris: Le Divan, 1923.

Marx, Karl, and Friedrich Engels. *The Marx-Engels Reader.* 2d ed. Edited by Robert C. Tucker. New York: Norton, 1978.

Matlock, Jann. *Scenes of Seduction: Prostitution, Hysteria and Reading Difference in Nineteenth-Century France.* New York: Columbia University Press, 1994.

Mazauric, Marion. "La Culture populaire censurée." *Libération,* July 5, 2000.

McCarren, Felicia. *Dance Pathologies: Performance, Poetics, Medicine.* Stanford, Calif.: Stanford University Press, 1998.

McClintock, Ann. *Imperial Leather: Race, Gender and Sexuality in the Colonial Contest.* New York: Routledge, 1995.

Mehlman, Jeffrey. "Baudelaire with Freud: Theory and Pain." *Diacritics* 4, 1 (1974): 7–13.

Mercier, Louis-Sébastien. *Le Nouveau Paris.* 6 vols. Paris: Fuchs, 1798 [?].

Miller, Christopher. *Blank Darkness: Africanist Discourse in French.* Chicago: University of Chicago Press, 1985.

———. *Nationalists and Nomads: Essays on Francophone African Literature and Culture.* Chicago: University of Chicago Press, 1998.

Muecke, D. C. *The Compass of Irony.* London: Methuen, 1969.

Murphy, Steve. "Inquest and Inquisition in 'La Corde.'" *Dalhousie French Studies* 30 (1995): 65–91.

———. "La Scène parisienne : Lecture d'Une mort héroïque de Baudelaire." In *Le Champ litteraire, 1860–1900,* ed. K. Cameron and J. Kearns, 49–61. Amsterdam: Rodopi, 1996.

Nesci, Catherine. *La Femme mode d'emploi : Balzac, de la Physiologie du mariage à La Comédie humaine.* Nicholasville, Ky.: French Forum Publishers, 1982.

Newmark, Kevin. *Beyond Symbolism: Textual History and the Future of Reading.* Ithaca, N.Y.: Cornell University Press, 1991.

———. "Off the Charts: Walter Benjamin's Depiction of Baudelaire." In *Baudelaire and the Poetics of Modernity,* ed. Patricia Ward and James Patty, 72–84. Nashville: Vanderbilt University Press, 2001.

———. "Traumatic Poetry: Charles Baudelaire and the Shock of Laughter." In *Trauma: Explorations in Memory,* ed. Cathy Caruth, 236–55. Baltimore: Johns Hopkins University Press, 1995.

Newton, Adam Zachary. *Narrative Ethics.* Cambridge, Mass.: Harvard University Press, 1995.

O'Brien, Conor Cruise. *Albert Camus of Europe and Africa.* New York: Viking Press, 1970.

Oehler, Dolf. *Le Spleen contre l'oubli, Juin 1848 : Baudelaire, Flaubert, Heine, Herzen.* Translated by Guy Petitdemange. Paris: Payot & Rivages, 1996.

Orr, Linda. *Headless History: Nineteenth-Century French Historiography of the Revolution.* Ithaca, N.Y.: Cornell University Press, 1990.

Pachet, Pierre. *Le Premier venu : Essai sur la politique baudelairienne.* Paris: Denoël, 1976.

Parent-Duchâtelet, Alexandre. *La Prostitution à Paris au XIXe siècle.* Edited by Alain Corbin. Paris: Seuil, 1981.

Perec, Georges. *W, ou, Le Souvenir d'enfance.* Paris: Denoël, 1975.

Pichois, Claude, and Jean Ziegler. *Baudelaire.* Paris: Julliard, 1987.

Poe, Edgar Allan. *Contes, essais, poèmes.* Translated by Charles Baudelaire and Stéphane Mallarmé. Paris: Laffont, 1989.

———. "The Fall of the House of Usher." In *The Complete Tales and Poems of Edgar Allan Poe.* New York: Barnes & Noble, 1992.

———. *Nouvelles Histoires extraordinaires.* Translated by Charles Baudelaire. Paris: GF Flammarion, 1965.

Poggenberg, Raymond. *Baudelaire : Une Micro-Histoire.* Paris: Corti, 1987.

Prendergast, Christopher. *Paris and the Nineteenth-Century.* Oxford: Blackwell, 1992.

Rachilde [Marguerite Vallette-Eymery]. *L'Animale.* 1893. Paris: Mercure de France, 1993.

———. *La Jongleuse. 1900.* Paris: Des Femmes, 1982.

———. *Madame Adonis.* Paris: Edited by Monnier, 1888.

———. *La Marquise de Sade.* 1887. Paris: Mercure de France, 1981.

———. *Monsieur Vénus.* 1884. Paris: Flammarion, 1977.

———. *La Tour d'Amour.* 1899. Paris: Mercure de France, 1994.

Ramazani, Vaheed. "Writing in Pain: Baudelaire, Benjamin, Haussman." *Boundary 2* 23, 2 (1996): 199–224.

Rancière, Jacques. *Malaise dans l'esthétique.* Paris: Galilée, 2004.

Raser, Timothy. "The Politics of Art Criticism: Baudelaire's *Exposition Universelle.*" *Nineteenth-Century French Studies* 26, 3 and 26, 4 (1998): 336–45.

Reynaud, Bérénice. "Baise-moi: An Angry yet Feminist Reaction." www .sensesofcinema.com/contents/02/22/baise-moi.html (accessed August 20, 2005).

Richon, Emmanuel. *Jeanne Duval et Charles Baudelaire : Belle d'abandon.* Paris: L'Harmattan, 1998.

Rogers, Nathalie Buchot. *Fictions du scandale : Corps féminin et réalisme romanesque au dix-neuvième siècle.* West Lafayette, Ind.: Purdue University Press, 1998.

Rony, Fatimah Tobing. *The Third Eye: Race, Cinema, and Ethnographic Spectacle.* Durham, N.C.: Duke University Press, 1996.

Rorty, Richard. *Contingency, Irony and Solidarity.* Cambridge: Cambridge University Press, 1989.

Ross, Kristin. *Fast Cars, Clean Bodies: Decolonization and the Reordering of French Culture.* Cambridge, Mass.: MIT Press, 1995.

Rousseau, Jean-Jacques. *Les Confessions. Vol. 1.* Paris: GF Flammarion, 1968.

Said, Edward. *Culture and Imperialism.* New York: Knopf, 1993.

Santoni, Ronald E. *Sartre on Violence: Curiously Ambivalent.* University Park: Pennsylvania State University Press, 2003.

Sanyal, Debarati. "A Soccer Match in Auschwitz: Passing Culpability in Holocaust Criticism." *Representations* 79 (Summer 2002): 1–27.

Sartre, Jean-Paul. *Baudelaire.* Paris, Galllimard, 1947.

———. *Les Mains sales.* Paris: Gallimard (Folio), 1972.

———. *Qu'est-ce que la littérature ?* Paris: Gallimard (Folio), 1985.

———. "Réponse à Albert Camus." *Les Temps modernes,* no. 82 (August 1952): 334–53. Cited as *TM.*

———. *La Responsabilité de l'écrivain.* Paris: Verdier, 1998.

———. *Situations.* Vols. 3–5. Paris: Gallimard, 1945–64. Cited as *Sit.*

Scarry, Elaine. *The Body in Pain: The Making and Unmaking of the World.* New York: Oxford University Press, 1985.

Schor, Naomi. *Breaking the Chain: Women, Theory, and French Realist Fiction.* New York: Columbia University Press, 1985.

———. *George Sand and Idealism.* New York: Columbia University Press, 1993.

Schultz, Gretchen. *The Gendered Lyric: Subjectivity and Difference in Nineteenth-century French Poetry.* West Lafayette, Ind.: Purdue University Press, 1999.

Schwartz, Vanessa. *Spectacular Realities: Early Mass Culture in Fin-de-Siècle Paris.* Berkeley: University of California Press, 1998.

Sedgwick, Eve Kosofsky. *Touching Feeling: Affect, Pedagogy, Performativity.* Durham, N.C.: Duke University Press, 2003.

Seltzer, Mark. *Serial Killers: Death and Life in America's Wound Culture.* New York: Routledge, 1998.

Sharpley-Whiting, T. Denean. *Black Venus: Sexualized Savages, Primal Fears and Primitive Narratives in French.* Durham, N.C.: Duke University Press, 1999.

Spackman, Barbara. *Decadent Genealogies: The Rhetoric of Sickness from Baudelaire to d'Annunzio.* Ithaca, N.Y.: Cornell University Press, 1989.

Spivak, Gayatri. "Imperialism and Sexual Difference." *Oxford Literary Review* 8, 1–2 (1986): 225–40.

Spoiden, Stéphane. "No Man's Land : Genres en question dans *Sitcom, Romance,* et *Baise-moi.*" *L'Esprit Créateur* 42, 1 (2002): 96–106.

Staël, Madame de (Anne-Louise-Germaine). *De l'Allemagne.* 1813. Paris: Garnier-Flammarion, 1968.

Stark, Jared Louis. "Beyond Words: Suicide and Modern Narrative." Ph.D. diss., Yale University, 1998.

Stephens, Sonya. *Baudelaire's Prose Poems: The Practice and Politics of Irony.* Oxford: Oxford University Press, 1999.

Swain, Virginia E. *Grotesque Figures: Baudelaire, Rousseau, and the Aesthetics of Modernity.* Baltimore: Johns Hopkins University Press, 2004.

———. "The Legitimation Crisis: Event and Meaning in 'Le Vieux Saltimbanque' and 'Une Mort héroïque.'" *Romanic Review* 73, 4 (1982): 452–62.

Terdiman, Richard. *Discourse/Counter-discourse: The Theory and Practice of Symbolic Resistance in Nineteenth-Century France.* Ithaca, N.Y.: Cornell University Press, 1985.

———. *Present Past: Modernity and the Memory Crisis.* Ithaca, N.Y.: Cornell University Press, 1993.

Teskey, Gordon. *Allegory and Violence.* Ithaca, N.Y.: Cornell University Press, 1999.

Thélot, Jérome. *Baudelaire : Violence et poésie.* Paris: Gallimard, 1993.

Tocqueville, Alexis de. *De la démocratie en Amérique.* 1835–39. Edited by Eduardo Nolla. 2 vols. Paris: J. Vrin, 1990.

Todd, Olivier. *Albert Camus : Une Vie.* Paris: Gallimard, 1996.

Todorov, Tzvetan. *Facing the Extreme.* New York: Metropolitan Press, 1996.

Trezise, Thomas. "Unspeakable." *Yale Journal of Criticism* 14, 1 (Spring 2001): 39–66.

"Trois femmes s'emparent du sexe : Catherine Breillat (« Une vraie jeune fille ») dialogue avec Virginie Despentes et Coralie Trinh Thi (« Baise-moi »)." Interview by François Armanet and Béatrice Vallaeys. *Liberation,* June 13, 2000. www.liberation.fr/cinema/archives/tendances/20000613sexe.html (accessed July 4, 2005).

Ungar, Steven. *Scandal and Aftereffect: Blanchot and France since 1930.* Minneapolis: University of Minnesota Press, 1995.

Valéry, Paul. *L'Âme et la danse.* Paris: Gallimard, 1945.

———. *Degas, danse et dessin.* Paris: Gallimard, 1938.

Vouga, Daniel. *Baudelaire et Joseph de Maistre.* Paris: Corti, 1957.

Williams, Raymond. *Marxism and Literature.* New York: Oxford University Press, 1977.

Williams, Rosalind. *Dream Worlds: Mass Consumption in Late Nineteenth-Century France.* Berkeley: University of California Press, 1982.

Willson, A. Leslie, ed. *German Romantic Criticism.* Translated by Ernst Behler and Roman Struc. New York: Continuum, 1982.

Wing, Nathaniel. *The Limits of Narrative: Essays on Baudelaire, Flaubert, Rimbaud, and Mallarmé.* New York: Cambridge University Press, 1986.

———. "Poets, Mimes and Counterfeit Coins: On Power and Discourse in Baudelaire's Prose Poetry." *Paragraph* 13, 1 (March 1990): 1–18.

Zoos humains : De la Vénus hottentote aux reality shows. Edited by Nicolas Bancel, Pascal Blanchard, Gilles Boëtsch et al. Paris: La Découverte, 2002.

Index

Adorno, Theodor, 8–10, 200, 204, 208n15, 209n20, 258n56; Sartre and, 9–10

Agamben, Giorgio, 214n19, 248n26

agency, individual, 1, 2, 10–11, 33, 36, 37, 43, 50, 67, 74, 76–77, 120, 148, 149, 152, 162, 175, 189, 196–98, 237n20; art and, 4, 6, 8–11, 21, 27–28, 64, 76–77, 107, 165, 202, 206n7, 213n15; body and, 141, 148–49, 159, 171

Algeria, 173–74, 195–96, 252n3, 256nn29–30, 256–57n31

allegory, 7, 27, 64, 97, 140; Baudelaire and, 41–42, 47, 64, 84, 87–89, 91, 94, 102, 104–7, 110–11, 116, 124, 133, 134, 178, 203, 223n1, 224n2, 226–27n13, 228n17, 228–29n21, 232–33n44, 254n17; Benjamin and, 106, 238n25; the body and, 133–34; in Camus, 174, 179, 185–87, 192, 194, 200, 216n25, 256n28, 256n30; de Man and, 219n37; irony and, 37, 39, 41, 42, 221n48; in Rachilde, 143–44, 149; Teskey on, 133, 243–44n57; violence and, 84–85, 91–92, 97, 111–12, 133–34, 143–44, 149, 178, 185–86, 203–4, 213n15, 243–44n57

L'Animale, 144–48

l'art pour l'art or *art pur*, 3, 5–6, 57, 59, 71–72, 104, 139, 140; "Assommons les pauvres !" 66, 81–82, 136–37, 170–71, 185, 187, 244n1

bad faith, 31, 183, 184, 195, 209n20, 213–14n17, 223n1, 253n11

Baer, Ulrich, 25–26, 120n2, 213n17

Baise-moi, 154–72, 194, 248–49n28, 249n30, 250n37, 251n40

Balzac, 235nn9–10; *La Fille aux yeux d'or*, 98–101, 104, 105, 235n9

Bara, Joseph, 88, 89, 231n36

Barrès, Maurice, 142, 246n9

Bartman, Saartjie, 118, 239n32

Baudelaire, Charles: canonization as poet of trauma, 1–4, 19–26, 136–37, 170, 171, 244n1; legacy, 135–38; modernism and, 12–14, 53–56, 96–99, 104–5; revolution and, 58–59, 79–82, 89–92

Baudelaire's works: "À une passante," 23, 106, 143–44; "La Belle Dorothée," 123–29, 241–42n48, 242n49–51; "Les Bijoux," 165; "La Corde," 83–94, 97, 231nn36–37, 232–33n44, 233n47; "Le Cygne," 64, 226–27n13, 241n45; "De l'essence du rire," 38, 39–52, 184, 217–18n30, 219–20n42, 220n44, 221–22n52, 254n16; Exposition universelle de 1855, 117–23; "Femmes damnées," 163, 164; "Les Fenêtres," 186; "Les Foules," 84, 102–3, 104, 108, 236n15; "Le Gâteau," 90, 92, 227n15, 230n29, 232n42; "L'Héautonti-morouménos," 31–36, 37, 54, 59, 69–70, 214–15n21, 217n27; "L'Invita-tion au voyage," 65, 145, 251n39; "Une Martyre," 105–12, 235n11, 237n18; "Une Mort héroïque," 65–79, 227n15, 227–28n16, 228n20, 229–30n24, 231–32n39; *Le Peintre de la vie moderne*, 19, 98, 148; "Salon de 1846," 157–58, 176; "Les Sept Vieillards," 206n7; "La Solitude," 231n35; *Le Spleen de Paris*, 53–94, 112–29; "Les Yeux des pauvres," 80–81

decadence, 140–44, 156, 169, 192;
Le Décadent, 140
deconstruction, 3, 7, 12, 20–21, 25,
36–40, 50
Delacroix, 100, 237n18
"De l'essence du rire," 39–52
Delphine and Hippolyte, 163, 164
de Maistre, Joseph, 232n43
de Man, Paul, 20–21, 25, 26, 38, 44–46,
47–48, 207n10, 210n2, 219n37,
220n47, 221n49, 221n51, 222n56; "The
Rhetoric of Temporality," 44–46,
47–48, 210n2, 219n37, 220n47, 221n49,
221n51, 222n56
de Saint-Pierre, Bernardin and Virginie,
40–43
Despentes, Virginie, 5, 13–14, 138, 139–40;
Baise-moi, 154–72, 194, 248–49n28,
249n30, 250n37, 251n40
"Les Dons des fées," 227n14
Duval, Jeanne, 118–19, 239–40n34

engagement. *See* commitment
English pantomime, 51–52, 223n58
"L'Étranger," 173, 251–52n1
Evans, Margery, 158, 238n28
exoticism, 46–47, 117–23, 239n30
Exposition universelle de 1855, 117–23,
240n36, 240n38, 241n43
Eymery, Marguerite. *See* Rachilde

Felman, Shoshana, 199–200, 254–55n20,
257–58n1
Felski, Rita, 245n1
"La Femme sauvage et la petite-
maîtresse," 112–17
"Femmes damnées: Delphine et
Hippolyte," 163
"Les Fenêtres," 186
fetishism, 98–102, 107, 139, 237n22
La Fille aux yeux d'or, 98–101, 104
Flaubert, 61, 80, 101, 163, 211–12n10
form: commitment and, 5–6; experimen-
tation with, 8; ideology and, 53–69;
prose poem and, 59–65; violence and,
93, 149, 167, 178–80

Foucault, Michel, 29, 148–49, 180, 205n3,
214n20, 215n22, 247n20, 256n9
"Les Foules," 84, 102–3, 104, 108, 236n15
Freud, Sigmund, 23, 211n8, 212nn11–12
Friedrich, Hugo, 223–24n2

Gasarian, Gérard, 226–27n13, 238n27
"Le Gâteau," 90, 92, 227n15, 230n29,
232n42
Gautier, Théophile, 5, 53, 92, 210–11n6
Guerlac, Suzanne, 208n13, 217n29
guilt, 186, 195–96; politics of, 187–91
Guys, Constantin, 102, 213n15

Habermas, Jürgen, 54
Hannoosh, Michèle, 220n44, 220–21n48,
228n19, 238n25
Hanssen, Beatrice, 28, 214n20
héautontimorouménos, 31–36, 37, 54, 59,
69–70, 214–15n21, 217n27
Hiddleston, James, 230n29
Hoffmann, E. T. A., 48
Holocaust, 9, 25–27, 195–96, 199–201,
214nn18–19, 254n20, 257–58n1;
Auschwitz, 199–200, 208n17
L'Homme révolté, 175–82
"Hop Frog," 70–71
Horace, 74–75, 229n22
Hugo, Victor, 19
hysteria, 245n6, 246n9

identification in art, 11, 15, 35, 64, 103,
107–8, 110–11, 172
imperialism, 117, 119–24, 173; logic of,
177–79
intellectual defeatism, 255–56n25
"L'Invitation au voyage," 65, 145, 251n39
irony, 4–6, 11, 13, 15, 136, 184–85, 193, 199,
216n25, 217n28, 218n33, 219n37; Ca-
mus and, 184–86, 189–90, 192–93; as
counterviolence, 29–30, 49–52, 182,
189, 198; "De l'essence du rire," and,
39–52; "L'Héautontirouménos,"
and, 31–36; history of relations to cri-
tique, 36–39; *surnaturalisme* and,
56–59; as trauma, 44–48